GOD ONLY KNOWS

GOD DOESN'T KNOW?

GOD ONLY KNOWS

The Story of Brian Wilson,
The Beach Boys and the California Myth

DAVID LEAF

OMNIBUS PRESS

London / New York / Paris / Sydney / Copenhagen / Berlin / Madrid / Tokyo

Acknowledgment is made for permission to reprint material from the following sources:

'Break Away' by Brian Wilson and Reggie Dunbar copyright © 1969 by Bri-Mur Publishing Company/BMI, administered by Wixen Music Publishing. All rights reserved.

''Til I Die,' 'It's Over Now' and 'Still I Dream of It,' Words and music by Brian Wilson. Copyright © by Brother Publishing Company (BMI), administered by Wixen Music Publishing. All rights reserved.

"Goodbye Surfing, Hello God!" by Jules Siegel, copyright © 1972 by Jules Siegel. By permission of the author.

By permission of Straight Arrow Publishers: editorial by Jann Wenner; "Frank Words from Brian Wilson" by Jack Rieley and "Monterey Pop's Closing Show" by Jann Wenner; "The Beach Boys: A California Saga—Parts One and Two" by Tom Nolan (with additional material by David Felton) and "Correspondence, Love Letters and Advice" by Loren Schwartz; "The Healing of Brother Brian" by David Felton, copyright © 1967, 1970, 1971, 1976 by Straight Arrow Publishers.

'Beatrice from Baltimore' and 'Teeter-Totter Love,' by permission of New Executive Music.

"A Child Is Father to the Band—The Return of Brian Wilson, Parts One and Two" by Timothy White; "Little Deuce Coup: Two Beach Boys Sail Solo" by Timothy White, copyright © 1976 by the Crawdaddy Publishing Company; editorial by Peter Knobler, copyright © 1977 by the Crawdaddy Publishing Company.

Endless Summer Quarterly magazine interviews with Seymour Stein, Russ Titelman and Lenny Waronker © 2018 by David Beard, used by permission of the author.

DISCLAIMER

What you are about to read is based on personal experience, decades of research, interviews conducted by the author and conversations with Brian Wilson, his late mother Audree, his brothers Dennis and Carl, Brian's friends (from high school to today), musicians, engineers, journalists, publicists, lawyers, concert promoters and record company executives. Whether they spoke for attribution or anonymously, care has been taken to quote them accurately. As for the body of the text, the statements made and conclusions drawn are presented only as the opinion of the author.

David Leaf
June 2022

CONTENTS

An Overture from Sir Paul McCartney   1

A Note from Melinda Wilson   3

"Words" by Sir Barry Gibb   5

Welcome   7

My California Myth Begins and Is Renewed   12

The Stall Dog   19

"All I Know": An Introduction from Jimmy Webb   25

THE CALIFORNIA MYTH   29

INTRODUCTION TO THE 1978 EDITION   37

1. RHAPSODY IN BLUE   41

2. FIVE FRESHMEN   60

3. LET'S GO SURFIN'   67

4. IF EVERYBODY HAD AN OCEAN   80

5. DON'T WORRY BABY   93

6. PLEASE LET ME WONDER   104

The Beach Boys' Sound   114

7. PET SOUNDS   120

8. GOOD VIBRATIONS AND SMILE   138

9. HEROES, VILLAINS AND NO SMILES   158

10. BEACHED   177

Charles Manson   196

11. SURF'S UP   200

Murry Wilson   219

12. ENDLESS SUMMER   228

13. BRIAN IS BACK   237

Epilogue, 1978   264

14. CODETTA, 1977–1985   271

Requiem for the Beach Boy   290

15. RETROSPECTIVE, 1985   293

Shades of Grey   300

The Legacy   313

AUTHOR'S NOTE TO THE 2022 EDITION   317

16. 'TIL I DIE: *The Battle for Brian Wilson*   328

17. MELT AWAY: *Brian Wilson's Personal Renaissance Begins*   356

18. BRIAN HITS THE ROAD!?   379

19. THE TRIBUTE AND THE QUEEN   388

20. BEAUTIFUL DREAMS AND BEAUTIFUL DREAMER   407

21. THAT LUCKY OLD SUN   422

AN EPILOGUE: *With Love and Mercy*   434

MYTHS AND LEGENDS 452

ACKNOWLEDGMENTS: 1978, 1985, 2022   464

AN OVERTURE FROM SIR PAUL MCCARTNEY

I've been asked so many times over the years what my favourite song is. One song I always come back to is 'God Only Knows.' When I played it, it made me cry and I don't quite know why. There are only certain pieces of music that can do that to me. There is just something so deep in it. It reaches right down in me, these little vibrations reaching your heart. It has this powerful effect, it's brilliantly done. And that's the genius of Brian Wilson.

Paul McCartney,
London, January 2022

Brian and Paul, in September 2003, at the recording session
for their first ever duet, 'A Friend Like You.'
Credit: Melinda Wilson

Clockwise from upper left: Brian, Melinda, Daria, Dylan, and Delanie. Melinda is holding
baby Dash. Daria: "This is the day in 2009 we finalized his adoption."
Courtesy of BriMel Archives

A NOTE FROM
MELINDA WILSON

When I met David Leaf and his (late) wife Eva on June 1, 1989, I'd been dating Brian for three years. I loved the sensitive but strong soul behind the music legend but was concerned about his well-being. And that's what brought the three of us together.

At the time, I didn't even know David had written a biography about Brian that, as I came to learn, was considered something of a bible on the subject.

When I read it, I quickly understood why. From the very first page, it was clear that he deeply loved Brian and his music and, even more importantly, cared about him as a friend. As did Eva. I felt like I had met two of Brian's guardian angels.

Through the years, as the four of us bonded and became closer, we shared a lot of memorable moments, both personal and professional. Eva was a bridesmaid and David an usher when Brian and I were married in 1995. And we were blessed when they said yes to being godparents to our oldest child, Daria Rose.

In terms of Brian's career, David was and is a tireless champion. I watched as they worked on the award-winning, groundbreaking *Good Vibrations* and *Pet Sounds* box sets. We watched and cheered as Brian returned to the spotlight, like when he inducted the Bee Gees into the Rock and Roll Hall of Fame, and Brian's first 1999 solo tour, one of the most thrilling and nerve-wracking weeks ever. Of course, the first *Pet Sounds* tour was another massive milestone.

"Unforgettable" is the only word for the tribute to Brian that David and Chip Rachlin conceived. Phil Ramone, and so many generous and legendary artists, along with a gigantic production team, brought their dream to life at Radio City Music Hall in March of 2001. The following year, we celebrated Brian's participation at the Queen's Jubilee concert at Buckingham Palace.

We shared many powerful moments, and you'll learn about them and much more in the new chapters of this book. But perhaps the most remarkable turning point came in 2004. Looking back, it now seems miraculous.

When I first met Brian, I had never heard of *SMiLE*. By the time we reached London in February of 2004, as the world premiere of *Brian Wilson Presents SMiLE* approached, I had been riding an emotional roller coaster with Brian, as you can see in *Beautiful Dreamer*, David's masterful documentary on *SMiLE*.

Finally finishing *SMiLE* seemed to clear away so much of the baggage of Brian's past, and it set him on a new course of making lots of great *new* music. What a blessing for his fans and those who love him as an artist.

As our family grew and David's career as a filmmaker bloomed, the bonds between us never faded. So as Brian's eightieth birthday approached, David thought a new edition of this book would be the perfect gift to honor Brian and everything he's done in the years since we all first met.

Unbelievably, that's now over thirty years ago. Just as amazing is this new edition of the book, in which David brings back to life the thrilling events we experienced along our journey.

David's always been a fascinating storyteller, and Brian is his favorite subject, as you'll read in the original text from his book. And I share the joy he brings to the telling of all that's happened since his book was last published in 1985.

We can all read about the behind-the-scenes moments that helped Brian, in the twenty-first century, reclaim his place as one of the greatest artists of the twentieth century.

Thank you again, David. Your writing about my husband always hits me right in the heart.

Melinda Wilson
Beverly Hills, Spring 2022

"WORDS"
BY SIR BARRY GIBB

I have never been as close to Brian Wilson as I would have liked to have been.

A distant admirer? Certainly! Someone I feel I have grown up with? Definitely!

My life growing up in Australia with its white beaches and huge surf was always in front of me. Saturated in Beach Boys and Brian Wilson's magical falsetto.

The first time I ever heard his music was when I was walking down a street in Glebe, Sydney, and I heard for the first time a song called 'I Get Around,' which made me feel for the first time in my life, insignificant!

I thought to myself, maybe I can get better as a songwriter but I was hearing something that I don't think anyone could have beaten.

Brian Wilson's music was the backdrop to my life in Australia. So many songs to hear, so many creative ideas to explore. He opened so many doors and countless windows with regard to the song that over the years thousands of artists have imitated that sound and those songs, myself included.

The first time I met Brian was during the first recording sessions for *Children of the World* when he and the rest of the group came to visit us in our rented house in L.A. It was a wonderful moment and far too short. I had so many questions but there was no time for him to answer.

The next time we met was at the Rock and Roll Hall of Fame where Brian was gracious enough to induct us. All of those years in Australia listening to Brian, digging deeper and deeper into the wonders of songwriting gave me so much inspiration and curiosity as to what a great song could really be.

There are many great songs that became lost because they were not recorded properly. Brian was the master at recording a great song the right way. I love all of his inspirations. I love all of his songs. As long as I live, there will be one song that stays in my heart. The song is called 'In My Room.' I love this song with every fiber of my being. I identify with this because, in my family, I never had a room, but Brian Wilson's voice became my pillow and Brian Wilson's music found a home in my soul.

I love you, Brian.

Barry Gibb
Miami, January 2022

WELCOME

HELLO . . . AND WELCOME TO THE NEW AND UPDATED EDITION OF
The Beach Boys and the California Myth, over forty years since it was first
published in the fall of 1978. A special salute to those of you who've read
it before: thank you for returning.

So much has happened since 1978—to Brian Wilson, to the Beach
Boys, to me, and to my work with and for Brian. The first edition of this
book turned me from a fan into a friend. While I'm almost certain Brian
has never read the book, I think he began to have confidence in me
because those he trusted assured him the book had treated him fairly.

What follows is designed to both recount what's happened since 1985
and to be a celebration of my friend's life and career as, in 2022, he
approaches two astonishing milestones: his eightieth birthday and the
sixtieth anniversary of the Beach Boys signing with Capitol Records.

Given what Brian's been through, his mere *survival* is something of a
miracle. And in the past thirty years, he has shown an enormous determination not just to endure but to conquer his fears and cast out his
demons. Perhaps the spiritual power with which he infused his most
beloved music is what's given him the strength to make it through what
could be fairly described as endless (cliché alert) "trials and tribulations."

Sadly, neither of his younger brothers, Dennis and Carl—the very heart
and soul of the Beach Boys and their harmony blend—are here to celebrate. In 1975 or 1982 or 1990, it would have seemed very unlikely that
Brian would be the last of the Wilson brothers still standing.

Perhaps equally as surprising is that Brian has toured almost every year
since 1999. As I write this, Brian is preparing for a (COVID-19-permitting)
2022 co-headlining tour with the rock band Chicago.

Most astoundingly, on many of Brian's solo tours, he and his truly talented, versatile and dedicated band have triumphantly performed the Beach Boys' most legendary albums, *Pet Sounds* and *Brian Wilson Presents SMiLE*. *From start to finish.*

In 2007, Brian even premiered a new rock opera, *That Lucky Old Sun*, live in London. And Ray Lawlor, a close friend of mine and Brian's, was in downtown New York City a dozen years ago on the memorable night when Brian played his entire *Gershwin* album live.

All told, since this book was last updated in 1985, Brian has released more than a dozen (studio, live and soundtrack) solo LPs. None of this would have seemed possible back then. But all of it is true. Check Wikipedia. Or brianwilson.com.

Now, over sixty years since he first entered a recording studio, over forty years since the first edition of this book, Brian's achievements as a composer, arranger and producer are not just part of the cultural conversation. His stature as an artist is transcendent.

His 1960s peers recognized it at the time. But back when I wrote *The Beach Boys and the California Myth*, you couldn't just Google Brian's name and see what people were saying about him. Now, all these years later, waves of praise can be found everywhere: in articles and documentaries and from interviews I've done. What they say confirms what we fans already believed; more significantly, it makes it clear that Brian's work was special even to the greatest creators of his time.

Bob Dylan: "Jesus, that ear. He should donate it to the Smithsonian."

Burt Bacharach: "Brian is one of the greatest innovators of my decade or any decade."

David Crosby: "The most highly regarded pop musician in America."

Graham Nash: "He was way advanced of what anybody was doing at that point. And I think the Beatles recognized that. And I think every harmony group in the world recognized there was something different going on . . . something very sophisticated."

Neil Young: "He's like Mozart or Chopin or Beethoven. This music will live forever."

Pete Townshend: "I think he's a truly, truly, truly great genius."

Roger Daltrey: "Brian deserves his place in the history books . . . I hold him in such awe."

WELCOME

Stevie Wonder: "What he did was incredible."
Paul Simon: "I love his music."
Art Garfunkel: "Our Mozart of rock 'n' roll."
Jimmy Page: "The man's a genius."
Randy Newman: "One of the greatest creative artists in the history
of popular music."

The list is endless, but it's important to understand the effect he's had on generations of musicians from every genre. Here are three comments from the Don Was film, *I Just Wasn't Made for These Times*. John Cale of the Velvet Underground, who wrote a song about Brian called 'Mr. Wilson,' said: "What Brian came to mean was an ideal of *naïveté* and innocence . . . *Pet Sounds* was adult and childlike at the same time." In that same documentary, Tom Petty claimed: "I think I would put him up there with any composer. I don't think you would be out of line comparing him to Beethoven . . . You really have to admire him as an artist for having that kind of vision." Linda Ronstadt, referring to the previous half-century, unequivocally stated: "I don't think there's anyone his equal in popular music."

Billy Joel demonstrated his fandom with a marvelous version of 'Don't Worry Baby' at 2001's *All-Star Tribute to Brian Wilson* at Radio City Music Hall. Elvis Costello expressed his admiration of Brian in my film, *Beautiful Dreamer: Brian Wilson and the Story of SMiLE*. It's also musically evidenced in two reverent covers of *Pet Sounds* songs on *For the Stars*, his album with Anne Sofie von Otter. Elvis Costello: "*Pet Sounds* is like classical music . . . wonderful compositions."

Elton John, another headliner at the Radio City event, made it clear in a 2007 *Washington Post* interview that to him, Brian "is to pop music what Aaron Copland is to classical music. He's an American genius. I mean, he's a genius wherever he is; but he's really an American treasure. His music, his imagination, his way of writing songs, it's just so unique. And he really influenced me—the way he arranged songs, the structure, the chord changes."

In *Long Promised Road*, Brent Wilson's intimate 2021 documentary about Brian, Elton explained: "Brian just threw away the rule book. Took you to another place . . . When I hear his music, it makes me smile . . . And I have that love of him that will never, ever die." In that same film, Bruce

Springsteen declared: "There's no greater world created in rock and roll than the Beach Boys, the level of musicianship, I don't think anybody's touched it yet."

Lindsey Buckingham of Fleetwood Mac, Ann and Nancy Wilson of Heart and so many artists who came of age in the 1970s revere him. Musicians are staggered by what he's created, and the power of the music crosses generations from "war babies" to "baby boomers" all the way to "Gen Z." Peter Buck of R.E.M., Steven Page of the Barenaked Ladies (he wrote "Brian Wilson"), Roland Orzabal of Tears For Fears (he wrote "Brian Wilson Said"), Robin Pecknold of Fleet Foxes, and Henry Rollins are serious devotees; all marvel at how his music touches them, at what Brian's accomplished.

Nate Reuss (formerly of Fun) puts "Brian Wilson in my Mt. Rushmore of artists." Sean Lennon said, "Brian Wilson is my Bach." Janelle Monae and Kacey Musgraves loved collaborating with him, and Kesha did too. She called Brian "one of her musical heroes." Questlove calls Brian, "A modern-day Stravinsky."

You can read even more at Brian's official website, www.brianwilson.com.

John Lennon, never easy to impress, was a fan. In conversations I have had with both Sir Paul McCartney and Sir George Martin, their admiration for Brian is boundless.

Perhaps nothing is more impressive than what Sir George said to me. When he stated it all those years ago, I was stunned, and in retrospect it now seems even more extraordinary. George Martin: "His genius seemingly encompassed everything . . . Nobody made a bigger impact on the Beatles than Brian . . . the musician who challenged them most of all . . . Without *Pet Sounds*, *Sgt. Pepper* wouldn't have happened. *Pepper* was an *attempt* to equal *Pet Sounds* . . . If there is one person that I have to select as a living genius of pop music, I would choose Brian Wilson."

Even in the classical world, Brian's music has its fans. Philip Glass described *Pet Sounds* as an "instant classic." Gustavo Dudamel—the Musical Director of the Simón Bolívar Symphony Orchestra, the Los Angeles Philharmonic, and the Opéra national de Paris—made his feelings known in *Long Promised Road*. "*Pet Sounds* is for me like a group of songs by Mahler. A group of songs by Schubert. I would put it on that level . . . 'God Only Knows'—that song touched me profoundly at the time I discovered it. It filled my soul."

WELCOME

Perhaps the last place I expected to see Brian's name pop up was in a December 2021 review of Steven Spielberg's *West Side Story*. Owen Gleiberman wrote in *Variety*: "It has what may be the greatest set of songs in any American musical, composed by Leonard Bernstein as if he were the magic link between Richard Rodgers and Brian Wilson." That's exalted company. And it's most deserved.

I believe that Brian's life story is in his music: the melodies and the harmonies, the chords and chord changes, his brilliant vocal and instrumental arrangements, and his production. In a lot of the song titles and self-penned lyrics too. That's where we can always find Brian Wilson.

I'm not a musician. While I love to sing, especially the high parts, I do that just for fun. Brian calls it "casual singing," and I've done a bit of that with him too, memorably, karaoke style, at a party in the courtyard of my old apartment building in Santa Monica. We sang 'A Teenager in Love'; Brian took Dion's lead and my older brother Bob and I were the Belmonts.

There was the time in 2005 at Baldoria, one of our favorite Italian restaurants in New York, when Brian, Ray Lawlor, Jerry Weiss (another close friend) and I serenaded Barry Mann and Cynthia Weil with a verse from their classic, 'You've Lost That Lovin' Feelin'.' Carole King, also at their table, joyfully watched. The moment defies belief. But it happened.

Special times like that are treasured. This new edition of what I'll refer to as *The Myth* is my gift, my way of expressing my gratitude for everything Brian and the Beach Boys have given me, given the world.

Those of you who have read the original book might be wondering, "What's changed since it first came out in 1978?"

Well, everything and nothing. The text of the original book is essentially the same. What's changed is *me*. I've gone from a fan on "the outside looking in" to a friend *on the inside*. I've been involved in so many things that have happened with, to and for Brian. It's quite a complicated story. Believe me, being a fan is much easier. More straightforward fun too.

Yet despite all of the ups and downs, my appreciation of Brian as a friend and for his music hasn't diminished. He still makes me *feel* deeply. As you read the original book and this update, I hope you will feel the same way too.

David Leaf
Los Angeles, 2022

MY CALIFORNIA MYTH BEGINS
AND IS RENEWED

This was impossible. Even in my wildest dreams, I wouldn't have conjured up this moment. But, like a scene from a movie, it surely was unfolding right in front of me, in reel and real time.

I had only been in California for thirty-six hours. I had just left the dreary office of California's Employment Development Department, having transferred my jobless claim from New York to my new home state. I would be getting unemployment insurance of $95 a week. Enough, back in the fall of 1975, to just about pay the bills in L.A.

As I crossed Broadway, heading north on 5th Street in Santa Monica, there *he* was. Walking towards me. I recognized him in a flash. It was Dennis Wilson—Brian Wilson's younger brother. The teenager who as a surfer had started it all with the suggestion that his musically gifted sibling write a song about surfing.

Nobody has ever accused me of a lack of (over)confidence, so without hesitation, I went right up to him and introduced myself. "Hi Dennis. My name is David Leaf, and I just moved to California to write a book about your brother Brian." I can still hear his booming laugh. And the two-word response he offered. "Good luck." He then walked into a low, anonymous, brick building which I would later learn was Brother Studio. The Wilson brothers' studio.

The journey toward the first edition of *The Myth* suddenly, momentarily at least, seemed real. Or at least less impossible. Incredibly, almost exactly three years to the day from that chance meeting, *The Beach Boys and the California Myth* was in stores from coast to coast. And I, a student who had avoided college courses that required a term paper, was now an author.

What I hadn't told Dennis was the main reason I was inspired to write a book about Brian. In 1971, when I first heard the song 'Surf's Up,' I had endlessly listened to it and, in discussing Brian with my college roommate, eventually defined my purpose: "I'm going to move to California, write a book about Brian, become his friend, and help him finish *SMiLE*."

It was, in part, because I believed Brian could do it, but more than that, I *needed* him to finish *SMiLE*. It would be thirty-three years before it happened. The original edition of this book is where that insane dream began to genuinely take shape.

Flash forward. A little more than six months after I met Dennis. June 1976. I was shooting baskets at the West Los Angeles YMCA with my good friend from college, Barry Bernstein. A couple of guys walked onto the court and asked if we wanted to play "two on two." The taller of the pair was Stan Love (father of NBA superstar Kevin Love and brother of Beach Boys co-founder Mike Love). Stan had recently retired from the NBA. With him was his cousin, Brian. Brian Wilson.

Of all the unlikely places to meet Brian, this seemed close to the top of the list. A man who, according to legend, was overweight, hiding out in his bedroom. And here he was. In gym shorts. I don't remember how long the game lasted. But when I told friends about meeting Brian on a basketball court, my quick summary was that Brian was a shooter, not a passer, and he didn't care to play any defense. "All offense. No 'D'."

Ironically, given what was to come, neither Dennis nor Brian was the first Beach Boy I'd come upon. That "Close Encounter of the First Kind" took place on November 7, 1971. It was after a Beach Boys concert, outside Georgetown University's McDonough Gym. The concert was amazing, and unlike the first time I'd seen them, they played well over two hours, including *seven* songs from the just-released *Surf's Up* album.

According to the published set list, the group *opened* with 'Good Vibrations.' That's how incredible they were; they could *start* with their best record. I also remember an endless standing ovation after the final encore. The primarily college-aged crowd would not stop calling for more. Finally, Jack Rieley, the group's manager, came out to thank the audience. But "The guys," he said, had given it their all. While I would see them over a dozen times in the next fifteen years, it would remain the greatest Beach Boys concert I ever saw. And afterwards came the providential meeting.

I was on crutches (surgery was just weeks away), standing with Bob Brown, the Resident Assistant in my dorm who had loaned me his collection of Beach Boys albums. We were waiting for a ride back to campus, George Washington University. Suddenly, Bob said, "Look." I didn't know what he meant, but he pointed again and said, more forcefully, "Look." I turned the other way, and there he was. Standing right next to me. The Beach Boys' lead singer. Brian's co-writer on many of the group's biggest hits and best songs.

I had just read the first half of the landmark Tom Nolan/David Felton two-part article in *Rolling Stone*, bought the *Surf's Up* album, and, thanks to the one-two-three punch of the article, a brand-new song ("Til I Die') and the title song of the LP, had instantly become fascinated by Brian Wilson's story and the legend of *SMiLE*.

I had a million questions. And here, right in front of me, was somebody who could answer them. So, like any crazy fan, I began firing away. I only got to ask a few of my fevered queries before he politely said something like, "I'll answer all your questions in my book." I'm pretty certain he has no memory of that event.

About four and a half years after our first "meeting," in June 1976, I was at that same Beach Boy's stunning seaside estate in Santa Barbara, interviewing him for a local newspaper article about the group's upcoming concert at Anaheim Stadium. In the middle of the conversation, he stood up, took off his small terrycloth cover and climbed into the hot tub. Given the countless interviews he's done in his career, I doubt he recalls that afternoon either.

Forty years later, in 2016, his informative autobiography, *Good Vibrations: My Life as a Beach Boy*, was published. But now, I wasn't a fan buying the book. I was *in* the book. And it seemed, at least as I read it, that the author didn't like what I'd written. His name is Mike Love. I'd bet he does remember what he and his co-author wrote about me.

What I do know for sure is that between that first fan encounter in 1971, my interview with Mr. Love in 1976 and the publication of *his* revealing memoir, I wrote *The Beach Boys and the California Myth*.

In the summer of 2021, in year two of the COVID-19 pandemic, I wasn't planning on writing an update for a new edition of *The Myth*. In fact, I really wasn't planning on *ever* writing it. But the confluence of events and anniversaries was such that I decided it was the right time. What else could I give Brian Wilson to celebrate his eightieth birthday?

As the creative force behind the Beach Boys' iconic sound, he's beloved all over the world. For those of us who revere the group's best records, their work has been an aural feast we've returned to for as long as we can remember. To give you an idea of how I once thought, I used to believe that when Brian reached thirty-two, the last age that's vocally tolled on the fade of 'When I Grow Up (To Be a Man),' Brian's problems would be in the past. That would have meant 1974. As you already know—or you'll read—that didn't happen.

The first edition of *The Myth* sold close to 10,000 copies, hardly a bestseller; but it was the realization of "Phase One" of my *SMiLE* dream and the beginning of "Phase Two." And despite the review in *Rolling Stone* that crucified it (they called it "almost a non-book"), *The Myth* had and has several fans worth mentioning.

Nineteen ninety-two was the first year of my decade-long stretch as the scriptwriter of *The Billboard Music Awards* show. Having just helped George Harrison rewrite his acceptance speech, I was backstage next to him and Tom Petty, when, much to my surprise, Tom leaned over to me and whispered, "Great book, man."

In the chapter titled "Melt Away," I'll recall an amazing moment with Lindsey Buckingham, who might be thought of as "the Brian Wilson of Fleetwood Mac."

When I updated my website in 2021, I included testimonials from industry friends and colleagues.

Elliot Easton, the lead guitar player for the Cars and a Rock and Roll Hall of Famer, emailed this: "I credit David Leaf with much of the resurgence of interest in Brian Wilson and the Beach Boys, among other things. His book from forty years ago, *The Beach Boys and the California Myth*, was the first and best explanation and analysis of exactly what happened to Brian, the myth of *SMiLE* and all the other 'inside' information the fans take for granted today. They have David Leaf to thank for most of it."

In his inimitable style, Van Dyke Parks dispatched: "*SMiLE*, in its most evolved form, would not have been an album reality were it not for the pivotal gifts of impresario David Leaf to ignite the multimedia campaign. It took diplomacy, tireless vision, and the ability to bring others together in reframing my constitution—with the success of sincerity and conviction. Hat's off, David. Crows will always cry over cornfields . . . and I now have nothing to cry about." When I read that, *I* teared up.

Through the years, I've been contacted by authors and journalists who've written major pieces on Brian and the Beach Boys. I would try and help them untangle the story.

Peter Carlin, who wrote *Catch a Wave*, one of the best biographies of Brian, told me that my writing had inspired him: "It is not an exaggeration to say that David Leaf's book, *The Beach Boys and the California Myth*, is one of the most influential popular culture books ever written. Deeply reported and composed with the power of a cultural document, Leaf's first book, published when he was in his mid-twenties, was more than riveting. It transformed Wilson's reputation from sunny surfer boy to an overlooked musical genius and served as a call to action for a new generation of writers and musicians, some of whom would become a part of Wilson's personal and creative resurgence.

"Indeed," Carlin continued, "when I worked on my own book about Wilson, I learned that the one thing I had in common with key band members Darian Sahanaja, Probyn Gregory and others was that we had all read *The Beach Boys and the California Myth* as teenagers. Such is the power of David Leaf's writing. Clear-eyed, probing and compassionate, his words enrapture and inspire. I can't think of many other writers who have even come close."

I met Jason Fine, the former editor-in-chief of *Rolling Stone*, well over a decade ago when he was writing a major feature about Brian. Jason and Brian became good friends, and he co-starred with Brian in the illuminating 2021 documentary *Long Promised Road*. Reflecting on what *The Myth* meant, Jason sent me this note: "David's thoughtful, free-ranging, joyous book mapped the idea that Brian Wilson was a separate entity from the Beach Boys, his own man—a pioneer who transformed the beautiful complexity of what he heard in his mind into some of the most crystalized, perfect pop music of all time. Sometimes he did that with the full support of 'the boys,' and sometimes he did it in a lonely place all his own, even pitted against them."

Jason pointed out that "The book made the case for Brian's singular artistry in a way we all recognize now but wasn't as well known then. It's a powerful artifact of time and place, written in a period when the myths and dreams of the previous decade were unraveling, essential reading for anybody who cares about Brian Wilson and the Beach Boys and the evolution of rock 'n' roll."

So what I've finally come to accept is that, while the audience for the book wasn't gigantic, many of those who read it were truly moved. In retrospect, I can now rejoice in the meaningful impact *The Myth* had on others.

In that regard, perhaps nothing was more rewarding for me than this: in the early 1990s, two young musicians came to my apartment in Santa

Monica to listen to my collection of tapes from the original *SMiLE* sessions. The twosome, Darian Sahanaja and Nick Walusko (R.I.P.), had formed a brilliant melody and harmony-filled "progressive pop" band called the Wondermints. They were big Brian Wilson devotees, and in those pre-web days, it was great fun to listen to unreleased music with fellow fanatics.

On that day, I came to viscerally understand the power of the written word. Darian—who would become a key member of Brian Wilson's band and was (no pun intended) instrumental in helping put *Brian Wilson Presents SMiLE* together—told me he'd read *The Myth* in high school. And reading it, he told me, had changed his life.

The wheel had turned. To Darian, my book had almost the same effect on him that the 1971 *Rolling Stone* article had on me.

Darian's calm presence hides an unwavering determination to make sure that Brian's music is performed live as it was originally conceived: not only the right chords and melodies and sounds but with the right *feeling*, with note-perfect soul. To do otherwise would be disrespectful. He's now spent over twenty years helping make sure that Brian Wilson concerts are incredible musical experiences. Darian's work with Brian, on-stage and in the studio, has always been of the highest order, as close to perfection as anything can be.

Can I say that about *The Myth*? Not exactly. While my heart was always in telling Brian's story as best as I could, I begin this new edition with a personal admission. Even though I have written hundreds of thousands of words about Brian and the Beach Boys . . . despite having interviewed and worked with his beloved studio musicians, his best friends, his greatest peers . . . even though I co-created, wrote and produced a tribute to Brian at Radio City Music Hall in 2001 and wrote/directed/produced 2004's *Beautiful Dreamer: Brian Wilson and the Story of SMiLE* . . . even having spent innumerable hours with Brian just "hanging out" or on tour or in the studio, I don't know it all. Not even close. Nobody does.

My goal in this edition of *The Myth* is to provide you with some new and true behind-the-scenes stories from *my* personal experiences that will enhance your understanding and appreciation of Brian's life and career. So that I didn't forget anything essential, I spoke with those who have been part of my journey; they shared a few special reminiscences of their own, reminded me of important moments I've incorporated in the update, jogged my memory.

I learned important new lessons in how memory works when I went back to school a dozen years ago. Since 2010, I've been a professor at the UCLA Herb Alpert School of Music; one of my courses is called "The Reel Beatles." Every week, onstage or via Zoom, I interview at least one person who worked closely with the Beatles or with one of the Fabs during their solo careers.

As part of the first week's lecture, I explain to the students that what they'll learn is that each person in the Beatles story remembers it in their own way. And nobody remembers it all perfectly. And that even includes one of my greatest musical heroes, Sir Paul McCartney, who in recent years has become a self-described "Biggest Beatles fan."

For the Beatles course, my students watch every Beatles film and over a dozen documentaries. And in *The Beatles Anthology*, they see the Beatles themselves recall certain moments (like meeting Elvis) differently.

My class also sees Zoom interviews I've done with the deservedly revered Beatles historian, Britain's Mark Lewisohn. Mark's currently finishing volume two of his exhaustive, what will be untouchable, three-volume Beatles history. He is the best. Yet, as diligently as Mark works, as dedicated as he is, as scrupulous as his research is, there will undoubtedly be a thing or two missing from the books that someone else thinks is important. Or maybe he'll relate something that somebody who was there doesn't think is quite right.

Our mind's camera just isn't a perfect instrument.

As with Michael Lindsay-Hogg's 1970 film *Let It Be* and Peter Jackson's 2021 *Get Back* docu-series, what my students also discover in the course is that what the creator chooses to leave out can be as significant as what is included. Whether in my documentaries or in my prose, I learned that lesson long ago.

In the Beach Boys story, everybody sees the events of the past sixty years from their point of view, through their own eyes. Has their own recollections. While that would lead to disagreements regarding what *anybody* writes, one of my favorite memories, one of the funniest moments in my work, came shortly after the 1978 publication of *The Beach Boys and the California Myth*. Dennis Wilson called me at three in the morning. He was reading the book and wanted to know who had told me one certain fact. But it was an anonymous quote. "Dennis," I softly replied, "Normally, I wouldn't reveal a source, but in this case, I'll make an exception. It was your mother." Dennis exclaimed, "*Why did you listen to her?*" And then we both burst into laughter.

That's the way it is with all myths and *The Myth*.

THE STALL DOG

I never imagined this. In 1999, when Brian Wilson began touring as a solo artist, I was by his side. At his request.

For a nervous performer embarking on one of the boldest adventures of his life, I was there as a friend. I would later describe my position as that of a "stall dog." I had been told by an old boss that in thoroughbred racing, a stall dog is a puppy they put in horse stalls to keep the ponies calm before a big race.

In our Wikipedia world, I found no definition or attribution for the phrase, but it's a good description of what had become part of my role in Brian's life. I was a comforting presence. We could go to the movies. To dinner. Or take a walk. Just *be* together. There was no pressure on him to be "Brian Wilson of the Beach Boys." To write a song or make a record.

His first mini-tour, in March of '99, had been a triumph, kind of like an out-of-town try-out for a Broadway play. And now here we were in June of 1999, actually on Broadway, uptown at the Beacon Theater. Brian was about to play New York "solo" for the first time, in a venue filled with devoted fans, eager to see their legendary hero onstage.

Before concerts, especially in New York, I liked to spend a little time in the lobby. I would get to see old friends. I was also curious to hear what people were talking about. Why they were there. If somebody told me a particularly meaningful story, I would give them a backstage pass to meet Brian after the show. In that pre-web Wilson world, I was still mostly anonymous.

And that's when it happened. A young man, who couldn't have been much older than twenty-one, came over to me, very excited. "Mr. Leaf," he exclaimed. "I just bought a copy of your book for $500!" He was thrilled. I was horrified. Without thinking, the words that popped out of my mouth were, "Oh, I'm so sorry." And from that point on, I knew I had to get this book back into the world. Nobody should have to pay what to me was an insane price for it. That fan who paid $500 on eBay was always on my mind when somebody asked me for a copy. Copies I didn't have.

You see, I know what it means to be so devoted to an artist that no matter the cost, there were, to use Jason Fine's description, certain "artifacts" I had to have. In my twenties, I prowled collectors' stores. Went to swap meets. Taped the concerts I went to, recorded shows off the radio and TV. Traded collectors' tapes. Robbie Leff, my first best friend in L.A., and I were more than a bit Beatles and Beach Boys obsessive. We had to hear every outtake, every interview.

It had once been so much simpler. You listened to the radio. Played songs on a jukebox. Bought a few records. I was a Beach Boys fan. Loved most of their hits. Even had a few of their singles. The first Beach Boys concert, the first rock concert I ever went to, was in November 1967 at the Westchester County Center. I was fifteen. My friends from the bowling team and I went to the box office that night without tickets. The ticket seller was apologetic. The only seats available were for the more expensive floor seats. In my memory, they were $2. That's not a typo.

In their sets, the opening acts—the Soul Survivors ('Expressway to Your Heart') and the Strawberry Alarm Clock ('Incense and Peppermints')—each ended with their big hit; it was then that I first felt and understood the excitement of hearing a current hit record in person. It was like a positive mass hysteria.

Then the Beach Boys came out and ran through a bunch of their latest and greatest. The crowd loved every minute. The group played for less than a half-hour. When my friends got up, I stayed in my seat. I had been to a few Broadway shows; I figured this was intermission. I thought they were going for refreshments. When I said I didn't want anything, they laughed. Told me the concert was over.

The Beach Boys were really terrific. I had no idea who was on the stage; Brian wasn't. Unlike the Beatles, whose names I knew from the back cover of *Meet the Beatles*, I never thought of them as anything other than "The Beach Boys." I'd never even *heard* the name Brian Wilson. Four years later, in 1971, as my roommate and I constantly played the rescued-from-the-archives *SMiLE* song 'Surf's Up' and his new ballad, ''Til I Die,' I became an overnight proselytizer for the genius of Brian Wilson.

20

THE STALL DOG

Up until that very moment in November 1971, I had been a sports-writer. When I was sixteen, I was making $32.50 a week (big money back in 1968) writing for *The Standard Star*, the local newspaper. Now, I was driven to express my thoughts and feelings about music. Within a couple of weeks, I had penned a rave review of the *Surf's Up* album for *The Hatchet*, the college newspaper. I called "Til I Die' a "high class 'In My Room.'" That was my way of saying the song had moved me. Years later, I would describe it as something of a suicide note. Neither was right; it was just a beautiful song with haunting, heartbreaking lyrics.

In the half-century since that first music article, I have made friends all over the world writing and talking about Brian Wilson and the Beach Boys. Because of Brian, I met my late wife, Eva. Come to think of it, I'm sure I bored some of my friends too, with my endless chatter about how great Brian was, how important his work was and how he could still be great. If he would just finish *SMiLE*. Sometimes, I would then have to explain that it was this legendary lost album from 1966/1967.

Our group of "Beachnuts" were like Egyptologists, reading and listening for any clue that Brian might come back. "He's writing," the press would be told. He's coming back. "Brian is Back!" No. Despite the hype, he isn't back. But he still *might* come back. There was always hope.

How did our group of fans meet? In 1973, before I moved to L.A., when I was still relatively new to the *SMiLE* story, I went to the House of Oldies, a collectors' record store that back in '73 was on Bleecker Street in Greenwich Village. As I navigated the narrow aisle to the counter, I squeezed past another customer on the right side who was thumbing through albums. At the counter, I asked the clerk, "Do you have a record called *SMiLE*?"

That other customer instantly wheeled towards me, almost accusingly. "What do *you* know about *SMiLE*?" And that's how I became friends with Ed Mandlebaum. A few years later, one of Ed's best Beach Boys friends was going out to L.A. Ed told him, "You've got to call this guy David Leaf." That's how I met Ray Lawlor, and Ray and I instantly bonded forever . . . over Brian, New York sports (especially the Yankees), politics, and New York pizza. And *SMiLE*.

By 1977, our East Coast group had connected with an L.A. contingent, headed by Debbie Keil and Eva Easton. In 1969, as a teenager, Debbie had worked for the Beach Boys at the group's Hollywood office. Had begun seeing Brian outside of work. I met Debbie in 1977 because she had gotten the first edition of my *Pet Sounds* fanzine. She and her roommate, Eva, befriended me when I was writing *The Myth*.

Peter Reum, who wrote a collector's column for the *Pet Sounds* fanzine, lived in Colorado, but we had endless phone conversations. And he was there for key moments. Later additions to our trusted team included the very sweet soul Lauri Klobas (R.I.P.), who I met through another big Brian fan, my very good friend Wayne Johnson of Rockaway Records.

The last person to join our "team" was the irrepressible Jerry Weiss, who I accidentally "recruited." I met Jerry in the fall of 1988 because of a "Letter to the Editor" he'd written to *People* magazine. He was upset about a less-than-stellar review of Brian's first solo album. I cold-called him to say "Thank you," we connected, and within a few years, he and his wife Lois had become part of our small band of Brian believers.

Of all of us, Ray, to this day, is the most sensible. Perhaps it's the fatalism ingrained in his Irish blood. Perhaps it's because he's a real New Yorker and sees everything with clear eyes. An example of what I mean: as Ray once said, referring to the psychologist who had taken over Brian's life, "Scumbags and charlatans like Landy, you can see through so easily. And they're very predictable."

Through the Cyclone roller coaster ride of the decades, filled with endless promise and disappointment, those who truly loved Brian, not because he was their meal ticket but just as he was, never gave up on him. I'm thinking of his few real friends like Danny Hutton, best known as one of the founders and lead singers of Three Dog Night.

In 1977/1978, while I was researching and writing the first edition of *The Beach Boys and the California Myth*, thanks to Debbie and Eva, I got to spend time with Brian. I didn't interview him. When he was at their apartment on Montana Avenue in Brentwood, they would invite me over and I got to "hang out" with him, have dinner with him. It was a chance to meet the man I was writing a book about. The real person behind the legend, behind *The Myth*. "Introverted and shy" would be the words I would use to describe Brian. He didn't know me yet.

In my first-year college journalism course, I had been inspired by *Prime Time*, Alexander Kendrick's biography of the legendary CBS News reporter Edward R. Murrow. I instantly came to believe that it was a journalist's job to shine a light on a story and create a critical mass that would cause positive change. Murrow had done it magnificently, most famously exposing the Communist witch hunter Joe McCarthy and in *Harvest of Shame*, a television program on the plight of migrant farm workers.

It was "fixing" Brian's life I chose as my mission impossible. In February 1977, I published the first issue of *Pet Sounds*. Through a series of cascading circumstances, that little fanzine—circulation peaked at around 900—dedicated to Brian and the Beach Boys led to my getting a contract to write *The Beach Boys and the California Myth*.

I wrote the original edition of *The Myth* with the intensity and certainty of youth, with a kind of compulsive confidence that everybody needed to pay attention to Brian and his musical genius. *Needed* to know his story. It was as if I was trying to grab the world by the collar and convince everybody that Brian was a modern-day Mozart. Given the fact that my knowledge of Mozart doesn't extend too far beyond the film *Amadeus*, it's a bold comparison. But one I would repeatedly make in promoting Brian. Actually, his scowl is more like Beethoven's, and Brian has said he thinks of himself as more like Bach. Has even demonstrated how he was influenced by Bach.

I genuinely believed *The Myth* was necessary, was important, would inform people's understanding of Brian. Through the years, as I went from fan to true believer to author to friend . . . from outsider to insider . . . the one thing that never wavered was my unshakable belief in Brian's significance as one of the greatest composers of the twentieth century. To me, he was a man whose music, in his words, "helped and healed."

It had and has done that for me, and I remained driven for decades to show that to the world. It took a long while, but my grand passion has been realized. England, thanks in large part to what the Beatles said and Derek Taylor's "Brian Wilson is a genius" campaign back in 1966, always knew it. It took some time for America to catch up. In 2022, Brian Wilson is now an honored musical legend throughout the Western world.

As George Eastman, the founder of Eastman Kodak, wrote in his suicide note, "My work is done."

However, in the fall of 2021, when David Barraclough at Omnibus Books told me they wanted to reprint *The Myth* with an update, I was like an old fire horse when the alarm bell rings: eager to get to the laptop keyboard, fingers flying, to once again happily write about the man whose life had given *my* life so much meaning. I now think of the original edition of *The Myth* as my Old Testament in my writings about Brian. Given everything that's happened since 1985, I've written this extensive update from a different perspective—my "bird's-eye view" as Brian's friend and sometime collaborator.

But fear not. This "stall dog" hasn't had a change of heart or mind. The new chapters were composed from the same point of view as *The Myth*, long after it took its place in the once small but now very extensive library of Brian Wilson and Beach Boys books. The big difference, however, is that in 2022, I'm looking back at what happened to Brian *and* me.

I can't speak for anybody else, but for so many years, what I wished for was for Brian, in the lyrics of his beautiful ballad 'Still I Dream of It,' to find his world. All I wanted was for Brian to *SMiLE*. I believed it would heal his broken spirit. And bring new music from his heart. We got both.

"ALL I KNOW":
AN INTRODUCTION
FROM JIMMY WEBB

BACK IN 1977, DAVID LEAF DROVE OUT TO THE SAN FERNANDO VALLEY to interview me at my home, a place I memorialized in my song 'Campo de Encino.' He was writing a book about Brian Wilson, *this* book, and he wanted to know what Brian's music meant to me. As you are about to read, my quotes from that interview are sprinkled throughout the *California Myth* section that opens David's book. I was happy to talk about how revolutionary Brian's music and productions were. And still are.

In fact, I could probably write a book about what *Pet Sounds* meant to those of us who were in the music industry when it came out. As important as the Beatles were, as many great songs as they recorded, I don't think they . . . or anybody . . . ever voiced their emotions and poured their heart onto vinyl the way Brian did on that album. As Dylan gave us the freedom to speak our mind, Brian's work on *Pet Sounds* told us it was OK to write about our innermost insecurities. And he did it in such a way that *Pet Sounds* is as important today as it was nearly sixty years ago.

It's now more than forty years since we first met, and David and I are both still here, still doing what we love the most, he writing books and making films about legendary artists, me writing songs and performing. We've worked together quite a few times on various projects during the years, on the Songwriters Hall of Fame show, in his film about Brian Wilson, in the standout documentary he produced about my dear friend, Harry Nilsson. Once I spent an entire afternoon as a guest in David's very cool songwriting class at UCLA. It was a thrill interacting with the next gen of songwriters.

25

But one event that David wrote and produced stands out as an epic evening. Truth is, perhaps nothing was more amazing than the group of artists he and Chip Rachlin and Phil Ramone gathered for a tribute concert to Brian at Radio City Music Hall in 2001.

That night, I found myself in two brand new trios, first with Carly Simon and David Crosby. We sang three-part harmony on one of Brian's earliest heartbreaking hits, 'In My Room.' That was easy compared to my other song that night: 'Surf's Up.' I still can't figure out how Brian and Van Dyke Parks came up with that one. And I had to learn to play and sing it with my partners in the trio, David Crosby and Vince Gill.

If you've never seen Vince Gill sing 'Surf's Up,' you're in for a treat. You can find it on YouTube. Sitting there, playing the beautiful chords and chord changes that Brian came up with . . . listening to Vince's magnificent voice . . . well, that's one for the ages.

I was so happy to be there that night, so proud to be on the same stage with so many musical greats, including my friend Billy Joel and Paul Simon and Elton John. Not easy to get busy songwriters together all in one place. But that's how highly each of us regards Brian. You will revel in the stories David tells in this updated edition of the book about that night at Radio City Music Hall.

What I never expected was that Brian would return the favor a few years later. Linda Ronstadt, who may be my favorite person to record my songs, was doing a version of 'Adios.' And Brian Wilson was recording the background vocals for it. Oh my God, and I don't use that phrase lightly, what an amazing sound Brian created. It gives me goosebumps just to think about how beautiful it is.

So when David's publisher asked me to write an introduction for this updated edition of the book, it was an easy "yes." I love reading what David writes about Brian . . . almost as much as I love listening to Brian's music.

Because when you make a list of the all-time great composer, arranger and producers of my generation . . . or any century actually . . . he's always #1, or close to it.

Jimmy L. Webb
March 2022

THE BEACH BOYS AND THE CALIFORNIA MYTH

1978 Edition

THE CALIFORNIA MYTH

"I don't think that the California Myth, the dream that a few of us touched, would have happened without Brian, and I don't think Brian would have happened without the dream. They're inseparable."
—*Jimmy Webb, noted composer of such pop classics as 'Up, Up and Away,' 'MacArthur Park,' and 'Wichita Lineman'*

THIS IS THE STORY OF BRIAN WILSON, AN UNPRETENTIOUS KID WHO FOOLED around at the piano, captured the teenage soul and became an artist. As a young man, Brian created a California myth through his music. Ultimately, he became one of the myth's most tragic victims.

It wasn't Brian's main intention that the rest of the world would embrace his dream. Brian Wilson's California was his personal musical fantasy, a reflection off the back wall of his mind of what he felt. This shy teenager never "hung-ten" on a surfboard, but despite his hang-ups about the ocean, he created a body of music that had everyone wishing they were surfin' and draggin' and having 'Fun, Fun, Fun.'

Unfortunately for Brian, the success and the pressure for more success was more than he could handle. It drove him to search for an "answer," and along the way, he tried all the occult parasciences as well as many of the chemical solutions. LSD provided Brian with one answer, but it produced too many new questions. Brian found his escape in drugs, but it was a peace with a false bottom. In his own words, drugs for Brian became "heaven and hell."

Brian's search wasn't unusual. Most artists and great thinkers are experimenters, people who consistently test the limits. Often, as in Brian's case, it's the result of a beautifully innocent, childlike curiosity that produces a fascination with all things new. For Brian, that meant new sounds, but his experimentation wasn't a simple or sole preoccupation.

When Brian's music turned from the carefree California sound to *Pet Sounds*, a serious examination of his emotional life, there was resistance. Simply, Capitol Records wanted more hits, and the band wasn't always in synch with his progress, his new directions. Perhaps the group was afraid that he might move so far ahead that he would leave them behind. The family band relied on Brian to create more myth-music for them; he retreated into an eccentric character called "Brian Wilson," seemingly a prisoner of his own talent. Eventually, art would take a back seat to paying the bills. The Brian Wilson mystique was at the core of the Beach Boys' machine; unfortunately, the game consumed Brian.

As 1978 begins, it appears that Brian has become bored with all the posing and playing and suffering and may be about to step out of the long shadow cast by his past triumphs.

There was a time when it was much simpler, much happier. Brian's personal life has always been difficult, but the music was once easy and perfect. Artistically, Brian Wilson was an instinctive genius. He took his emotions and, with songwriting partners such as Mike Love, Gary Usher and Roger Christian, put them on wax. The catharsis of his personal life, by a pleasant coincidence, happened to be perfect medicine for those schooltime and summertime blues. Kids in Kansas City and Toledo could hardly go surfing. Instead, they had the car radio and the Beach Boys telling them about this magical place where life revolved around the beach, and that short step from your woodie to the sand would attract Amazonian blondes. Sexist? Yes. But eternally seductive.

Brian Wilson's special magic in the early and mid-1960s was that he was at one with his audience. Most often, he was collaborating with cousin Mike, but regardless of which lyricist he was working with, there was no "writing down" to the listeners. Brian had a teenage heart, until it was broken. Before that happened, Brian used the Beach Boys music to "invent" California.

California has always occupied an exalted position in popular American culture, whether it was the Gold Rush days or the heyday of Hollywood. Brian Wilson's particular California myth is a product of the 1960s, and it is important to remember that to teenagers in 1961, California was just a state, not yet a state of mind.

California in the late fifties and early sixties was a peaceful place, the repository of the middle-class American dream, but it was the dream of the adults. Their children hadn't taken over; that came later.

When the Beach Boys started out, surfing was just a sports fad with little chance of spreading to the rest of the country for the simple reason that most of America is landlocked. Because of their geographical predicament, America's children turned to the Beach Boys for their surfing. Surfing, in this musical idiom, stood for freedom, the ocean, the sun, and the cruising fun that the Beach Boys supposedly enjoyed "out there" in coastal California.

That teenage lifestyle was immensely appealing to the rest of the country and eventually to much of the world. Writer Nik Cohn described California as a teen heaven, "a hugely enlarged reality [that] verges on complete fantasy . . . it is the joob-joob land far beyond the sea where age is suspended at twenty-five, school is outlawed, Coke flows free from public fountains and the perfect cosmic wave unfurls endlessly at Malibu." For kids whose oceans and beaches were made by intersecting asphalt and fire hydrants, whose winters were filled with long, cold, snowy nights, California had to be the end of the rainbow.

As rock writer and native Californian Ken Barnes admitted, "If locals knew 'Surf City' was an idealized phantom on the order of the 'cities-paved-with-gold' hype which attracted the Spanish explorers to the state in the first place, they never let on to outsiders. Compared to anywhere else, the general in-state attitude held, California was close enough to paradise anyway."

This also meant that the Beach Boys' appeal was greatest in places where making waves in the bathtub was the closest anyone got to the surf. The Beach Boys' initial big successes were in California towns that were located inland. San Bernardino, one of the first hotbeds of Beach Boys fever, is over sixty miles from the ocean. It might as well have been a thousand, because San Bernardino's teenagers mostly just dreamed of the surfing life, a dream that was lived out through the Beach Boys.

That vicarious lifestyle was particularly appropriate since Dennis Wilson was the only Beach Boy who was really a surfer. In the vernacular of the time, the Beach Boys were "gremmies," that is, they did not surf. Many of the genuine surfers came to resent the Beach Boys for the false image the group's name created. The natives didn't need rock 'n' roll fantasies; they were at the beach every day, living them.

Singer/songwriter Jimmy Webb was living in Oklahoma in 1963 and recalls that "the first time I heard a surfing record, I was riding a tractor.

I had my radio taped to the tractor, and I was driving out through the corn patch dragging a big plow and I had my shirt off. I heard this group singing about 'Surf City.' And I thought, 'What the hell is a surf city?' It meant nothing to me in Oklahoma; I'd never seen the damn ocean. But the sound was infectious . . . it was young, and it was obvious that they were talking about something that I would like to find out about."

A year later, Jimmy Webb was a teenager living in San Bernardino. He remembers his first California summer as "one of those endless summers with the orange blossoms, and you could smell the orange groves just hanging in the air, and it was kind of a magic time. We weren't completely up to our necks in the war; there weren't any economic crises threatening the country. For two or three years, those summers were very idyllic. There were no responsibilities. We were young; the girls really were, no matter how chauvinistic it may sound, soft and feminine and lived their own version of the myth."

To a newcomer visiting the West Coast, the California that existed in Brian Wilson's music is infinitely more appealing than the reality of the place itself—because the California dream doesn't exist anymore. It couldn't exist. I've certainly looked for it.

My search began a few years ago on my first visit to Los Angeles. More accurately, it began when I first heard the music of the Beach Boys and Jan and Dean. What normal (or abnormal) drooling adolescent could resist the call to 'Surf City' where it was "two girls for every boy"? For me as a teenager living in New Rochelle, New York, the California fantasy has always been powerful, strong enough to lure me—and millions like me—to California. Back in the sixties, though, California seemed distant and unreachable, and my personal California dream was relegated to the back burners of my mind. Still, its glow was always tantalizing.

As my idealism turned into protective cynicism, California represented a last outpost of innocence and optimism. Because I lived in the East, the Beach Boys' music became my refuge, my California. By the time I made my pilgrimage to California in 1974, almost everyone's American dream had been shattered. I knew deep down that there wasn't a "better way of life" but . . . it was still exciting to step into the Pacific Ocean for the first time. California has always held out the hand of romance. And while it sometimes appears to be an elaborate tease, California is an incredible and unique place.

My initial view of Los Angeles was from an American Airlines 747. As I stared past my reflection in the tiny double window, I was immediately struck by the suburban blandness. Could this be Chuck Berry's 'Promised Land'? Hardly. Still, there is and always will be one key to Southern California's appeal—the omnipresent sun and the boundless ocean. After all, hadn't the Beach Boys promised that all my problems could be solved by 'The Warmth of the Sun'?

My first visit to the West was more of a quick inspection than anything else. I do remember driving north on the Pacific Coast Highway listening to a song called 'Beach Baby,' and how that song was a perfect soundtrack for an outsider touring California—"Beach baby, beach baby, give me your hand, from July to the end of September / Surfin' is fun, we'll be out in the sun every day."

When I moved to Los Angeles in 1975, I realized immediately that the standard clichés were mostly inoperative. California is basically a benign place, much like any other locale. By virtue of its vastness, Los Angeles does offer more opportunity than most parts of the country. The one drawback to its size is that it gobbles up people and lets them get lost in themselves. If you want to hide from the world, this is the perfect place. At the same time, Southern California is really just a gigantic small town trying to become a cosmopolitan city. One observer called it "Iowa by the Beach." The people are a curious blend of city sophisticate and country farmer, but in 1978 a provincial mentality prevails. The weather is always a chief topic of discussion. As Jack Smith, author and chronicler of *The Big Orange* noted, "Our spirits rise with our reservoirs."

The California clichés really haven't been changed or challenged since Brian Wilson and the Beach Boys created them fifteen years ago. For teenagers, they remain incredibly powerful fantasies, so powerful that in 1978 they have become institutionalized clichés. The media men and women of Madison Avenue are partially at fault. They use California as a giant soundstage for their product pitches. Almost everyone, thanks to those millions of advertisements, aspires to the good life that supposedly exists for all in California. If Madison Avenue has helped create a culture that idolizes beautiful, unblemished, everlasting youth, then California is home for the victims of that false god.

Skeptical? Turn on the tube, listen to the radio anytime. Those jingles are Beach Boys' melodies, the pictures are Beach Boys' fantasies. As Hal

Blaine, a world-famous session drummer, notes, "The king of commercials in L.A. is the Beach Boys' sound." The advertising community shouldn't take all the blame. After all, they took their cue from one of the great salesmen of all time, Brian Wilson. If, in 1978, they sell shampoo with his music, remember that Brian first used those tunes in 1963 to sell California.

The myth was at its most potent in the early sixties before my generation came of age and decided that what Los Angeles had to offer wasn't worthwhile. When Southern California did epitomize the ideal of youth, when the drive-in movie screens were showing films like *The Girls on the Beach* or *Beach Blanket Bingo*, the Beach Boys represented that way of life to the world. Behind that facade, the group always had internal and personal difficulties. Those problems made their image a false one, but that wasn't unusual for show business. The Beach Boys became a commodity, a very attractive one, and they became California's ambassadors to the world, selling good times that no longer existed.

The Beach Boys were so tied to Southern California that their decline in popularity can be directly traced to the emerging psychedelic era centered in San Francisco. As the media focus shifted briefly from Los Angeles to San Francisco, the Beach Boys became the "Bleach Boys" and "The California Hypes." By late 1967, Los Angeles had lost its position as the hippest town around.

Certainly, Southern California is a plastic place, but so is much of America. As a major media city, Los Angeles may have over-commercialized its product, but its contribution to youth culture shouldn't have been trivialized. The Sunset Strip curfew riots were one of the first "calls to arms" for the sixties generation. Los Angeles gave birth to folk rock (through the Byrds) and allowed an expression of outrage through protest music. It was slick—sure—but it was effective. But by 1967, there was no objectivity. Los Angeles was bankrupt and that was that.

The Beach Boys were simply lumped in with all the "hipper-than-thou" put-downs of Los Angeles. Few people were willing to admit that Brian Wilson was at the forefront of the musical revolution. Unfortunately for Brian and the Beach Boys, few were willing to look past the striped shirts and short hair. It was easier to condemn the Beach Boys for what they once were than to try and understand what they were becoming. The Beach Boys' failure to play the Monterey Pop Festival in 1967 more than damaged their own career. It was a signal that Los Angeles was no longer at the center of the action. The media picked up on that and crowned San Francisco as the new home of hippiedom. By the time it was on the cover of *Life* magazine, the Summer of Love was almost over.

The latter half of the sixties was filled with youthful idealism tinged with the selfishness of middle-class white youth who didn't want to go into the armed forces. Vietnam was an immoral war, but few of us questioned the morality of student deferments. It was more convenient for us to fight our war in the streets of Berkeley, California, and Washington, D.C. If we suffered from the guilt of undeserved wealth, the least we could do was to demonstrate for peace and equality. "Ho, Ho, Ho Chi Minh, NLF is gonna win." Indeed.

Through all of this, California was always in the vanguard, be it the Free Speech Movement or the use of psychedelic drugs. Los Angeles's Sunset Strip and San Francisco's Haight-Ashbury influenced a generation of young people and brought about a westward migration. A hip teenager just had to be where "it was happening."

California was once looked on by America as its final frontier. Today, it's more like a last chance on its last legs. The Beach Boys are in a similar position, but nobody wants to accept that fact. Even though they are balding and paunchy, they are all we have left to remind us of our own golden summers. The Beach Boys, like Southern California, are a fading jewel.

The 1970s are one long, nostalgic look at a better time. That means movies like *American Graffiti*, TV programs like *Happy Days*, and rock groups like the Beach Boys. While the first two are idealized and cleansed versions of what it was like in the late fifties and early sixties, the Beach Boys are still the original. They may be in their thirties, with divorce, drugs, and personal disaster behind them, but they are still the same guys churning out a music that struck a basic chord in white middle-class American society. The Beach Boys' music created a myth that didn't work, for them or anyone else, and when nothing else worked, a disillusioned America returned to that myth.

The music, however, has transcended their personalities and the ravages of time. Brian Wilson's music is for the ages, and the Beach Boys' concerts have become celebrations of a long-lost, imaginary past that seventies youth can only truly experience through the Beach Boys.

I came to California to test the myth, to meet the Beach Boys, looking for symbols. What I found was an incredibly complex human situation. I kept peeling away at the surface, and the more I dug, the harder it got. It wasn't long before my journey went too far. My journalistic investigations and excavations discovered more human suffering than I really wanted to know.

Art and suffering are always found together, but in this case, the hardship has overwhelmed the artistry. And this is the story of an artist—Brian Wilson—growing up, growing out, growing away from his family. It's the story of his creative development. It's also about the snuffing-out of his visionary spark just as he neared the peak.

Because Brian Wilson has a unique sense of humor, this book has funny moments. Because of what happened to Brian, this is a tragic story. It is never easy to examine one's heroes, but this is what I found when I came to California in search of the Beach Boys.

David Leaf
Los Angeles, 1978

INTRODUCTION TO THE 1978 EDITION

"Music is Brian Wilson's best friend, lover, everything. On a one-to-one basis, it's the only thing that has never wronged him. It's when people and gossip and record companies came into play that things went askew. The music never betrayed him. And given Brian's vulnerable, exclusive nature, it's only natural that it's the central fact and concern in his life. He may forget a name or a contract, but he never forgets the music. It's a consequence of devotional thinking, and geniuses are prone to it."

—Van Dyke Parks, one of Brian Wilson's closest friends (Crawdaddy, *June 1976*)

ALL AROUND HIM, HIS MUSIC SWIRLED—'CALIFORNIA GIRLS,' 'I GET AROUND,' 'Surfin' U.S.A.' Most everybody in the audience was getting off on those timeless songs, feeling fine as the harmonies washed over them. Everybody, that is, except Brian Wilson.

For Brian, the concert—any concert—is an ordeal. This particular show was at the Los Angeles Forum on a rainy December evening in 1977, and while the "oldies" succeeded in getting the crowd on their feet, nobody in the audience could look at Brian Wilson and enjoy the music.

Stoically, he sat at his grand piano, sometimes playing, sometimes singing. Mostly, though, his face was a mask, and while his voice revealed no emotion, his onstage behavior was a spectacle of nervousness. Dennis Wilson, aware of his older brother's discomfort, went to Brian's side, hugged him, offered encouragement and attempted to get Brian to sing along . . . "Gotta keep those lovin' good vibrations a-happenin' with you." Brian

37

opened his mouth once and nothing came out; another time and he emitted an atonal squeal. He turned to Dennis with a look that said, "I'm too scared."

It's a sad, strange and touching scene that has been played out in concert halls all over the United States for the past few years, a picture straight out of the sadist's textbook. Why is this troubled man part of a rock 'n' roll show? Why is he being put on display?

Those questions have one very simple answer and dozens of more complex ones. At the heart of the situation, though, is the fact that Brian Wilson is the goose that laid the golden egg, and if it's been a while since he's turned out any fourteen-karat songs, at least he attracts a crowd. People are always interested in looking at someone who once did something important.

Brian Wilson is the man behind the Beach Boys, America's longest surviving rock band, and, by now, a legitimate institution. And, like the place they're from and have mythologized in their songs, the group has become a lie, a well-polished fun house mirror that serves as nostalgic entertainment for America's youth. As one associate of the group remarked of the Beach Boys' last five years, "The only place there was ever any harmony in the group was when they sang onstage." That has been true of most of their lives.

Regardless of that false image of harmony, I love the Beach Boys, or rather, I love the music that Brian Wilson created and transmitted to the world through the group. What I love and cherish about the Beach Boys is the feeling in their music. No matter what, that can never be taken away. The music is for all times.

The people who are the Beach Boys have been the objects of love for many years. It is they who are the tangible link between ourselves and our youth. More than that, the Beach Boys are the messengers that, once upon a time, Brian Wilson sent out into the world to spread his gospel. Long ago, tired of rehashing the same thing night after night, Brian left the road to explore his creativity. Eventually, the Beach Boys became a traveling revival show living off Brian Wilson's gift. Brian hasn't been part of the Beach Boys for a long time.

That's why it's so strange to see him onstage again. Brian Wilson is a private person; he doesn't belong in a huge arena with over fifteen thousand pairs of eyes bearing down on him. He is a sensitive, shy, introverted man who often feels uneasy when there is one stranger in the room. Brian never could handle the gaze of the public eye; that was one of the key reasons for his retreat. Yet his family has put him into a situation where there are quite a few strangers. It gets complicated. There is the family's love of Brian. And then there is the family's love of fame and fortune.

In 1966, Brian Wilson wanted the freedom to make the music that was in his head and didn't want to be restricted solely to the Beach Boys. The group and his family fought him over that desire, and he eventually withdrew from the Beach Boys. Brian Wilson wasn't a Beach Boy for many years, but his name has been used to keep the family business going. To this day, Brian isn't free to make music outside of the family situation.

This book is written for one man, Brian Wilson. It is written with the hope that he will one day soon be treated with all the care and respect due to each of us. As a man who has made millions happy, he has certainly more than earned it. Even though his musical development was arrested before he fully articulated his revolutionary concepts, what Brian has created has influenced every popular composer. All of our lives have been enriched by Brian Wilson's art.

CHAPTER 1

RHAPSODY IN BLUE

MUSIC. ALWAYS, THERE WAS MUSIC IN THE WILSON HOME. FROM THE VERY beginning, Brian, Dennis, and Carl Wilson enjoyed the sounds of their parents playing duets at the piano and organ. It was this early and constant exposure that created a love of and devotion to music that would dominate their adult lives.

Lots of children are hit over the head with music lessons and never learn much more than 'Chopsticks.' What made the Wilson kids different is what they all refer to as "Brian's God-given talent." Wherever it came from, Brian Wilson was in the music and the music was in Brian very early on. Outside of the house, he was a fun-loving jock; inside, he was an avid musician.

As father Murry Wilson once noted, "All they ever heard was music in their house. And, on occasion, family arguments."

Those "family arguments" were the other constant in the core of the Beach Boys, and the punishments meted out by Murry included severe physical beating as well as verbal degradation. Some people loved Murry, others insist he was a "sick man," but few will deny that he physically and verbally abused his children. There is no way to precisely measure the effect of such an upbringing, but it can be safely said that the troubled adulthood of the Wilson brothers can be attributed partially to their difficult childhood.

The love/hate relationship that Brian and his brothers had with their father cannot be ignored. It has had a great effect throughout their careers and in their personal lives.

★　　★　　★　　★

As Holden Caulfield once said, "If you really want to hear about it, the first thing you'll probably want to know is where I was born and what my lousy childhood was like."

As Dennis Wilson often admits, "Our father beat the shit out of us. His punishments were outrageous."

Brother Brian Wilson puts it more diplomatically: "I don't have really great memories as far as [being] a family member. It wasn't all that super; we had a tough enough time of it . . . it was sort of a lower middle-class family for a while. We struggled."

Brian wasn't just talking about a financial struggle; he was also referring to the emotional struggle of growing up in a home dominated by Murry Wilson.

Father Murry was a self-made businessman who mortgaged his modest home to start his own heavy machinery business. A man driven to succeed, he was a failed and frustrated songwriter, and he was always trying to get his tunes recorded. Once, Lawrence Welk (an accordionist, a popular albeit old-fashioned TV host and bandleader) played a song of Murry's called 'Two-Step, Side-Step.' There was even a little dance to go with it, but it hardly replaced the Lindy or the cha-cha-cha. Despite his lack of substantial musical success, Murry made his presence known to a few people in the industry, and these contacts would pave the way for the Beach Boys' easy, early rise. That, however, is getting way ahead of the story.

Brian Wilson, circa 1944.
Credit: BriMel Archives

It began in the Midwest, as do so many California stories. Murry Gage Wilson was born in Hutchinson, Kansas, and his family moved to California when he was nine years old. Audree Neve Korthof's family was from Minneapolis, Minnesota, and they traveled westward when Audree was ten. Murry and Audree met at Washington High School in Los Angeles and were married in 1938 when they were both twenty. Their first home was a small rented house at 8012 South Harvard Boulevard in the South Bay section of Los Angeles. Brian Douglas (born June 20, 1942) and Dennis Carl (born December 4, 1944) both came along before the Wilsons moved to Hawthorne, California, in early 1943.

Hawthorne at that time was a mostly white, lower middle-class town. It is located only five miles inland from the Pacific Ocean. Carl Dean (born December 21, 1946) completed the family that would fill the small five-room house at 3701 West 119th Street. For years, the three Wilson brothers shared a bedroom, until the garage was remodeled into a music room that saw double duty as Brian's bedroom.

Murry Wilson was an ambitious and generous man who wanted to provide his family with the best things in life. After a number of years at the Goodyear Tire and Rubber Company (where he lost an eye in an industrial accident), Murry started his own modest company. ABLE (Always Better Lasting Equipment) Machinery's chief source of income was renting out building equipment such as cranes. Murry operated ABLE through the early sixties until his work with the Beach Boys demanded his full-time attention. Eventually, he made a fortune as the group's publisher.

When Murry Wilson died on June 4, 1973, a Warner Brothers Records obituary read, in part: "Murry Wilson was a hard, oyster shell of a man, aggressively masking a pushover softness which revealed itself at the sound of a beautiful chord . . . " The music moved Murry. Unfortunately, it appears that little else the Wilson brothers did satisfied their "old man." In 1976, Dennis recalled, "We had a shitty childhood . . . my dad was a tyrant. He used to whale on us, physically beat the crap out of us. I don't know kids who got it like we did. His big number was, 'Don't ever lie, I'll beat the shit out of you!' . . . I thought it was insane." In another interview, Dennis further explained that, despite the risk, "I used to lie to him when I was very young. I learned at an early age to be very protective of myself; I played a great mind game."

Brian didn't play mind games. He was always trying to please his father.

"Sometimes," Brian remembered, "I would almost *have* to do something, to do what he'd like . . . I found myself getting As and Bs in school and saying, 'Hey look, Dad,' and him saying, 'Very good, son.'" Brian said he was always "wanting to accomplish something for him." In his youth, Brian was a fine athlete, a varsity performer in a number of sports. Still, Murry found fault in his performance on the field. Brian recalled, "I had him come to my football games and I'd say, 'What did you think of me?' and he'd say, 'You sloughed off, you're lazy.'" It wasn't an occasional occurrence, remembers Brian: "I used to catch it from him all the time over that stuff. It bothered me because it made me feel like I was goofing up, that I was inferior, it made me feel worthless and a number of emotions like that."

Apparently nothing, not even worldwide fame and the sale of millions of records, could please Murry. As children, they found it almost impossible to do the "right thing." Because of that, they often came in for a lot of punishment. Besides the frequent private beatings, Dennis remembered that Murry "burned my hands for playing with matches and beat me up in front of my friends."

A 1977 *New West* magazine article claimed that Murry Wilson "took out his rage on his three sons. Audree sobbed quietly and helplessly in the background, she says, while Murry unleashed an arsenal of sadistic punishments on the boys." These punishments, according to that article, included "forcing a preteen Brian to defecate on a newspaper to humiliate him," and another of Murry's favorite forms of retribution was making the boys "stare in the empty socket of his missing eye." In private, many people confirm that the Wilson brothers had it very hard.

Yet they were still boys, and despite the abuse, they had a lot of spunk, particularly Dennis. According to one tale, Murry had two glass eyes, one for everyday use and a special bloodshot model for hangovers. One night, Murry drank quite a bit and Dennis stole the bloodshot model and took it to school. Dennis was punished for this trespass.

One of the more amazing aspects of Brian Wilson's success as a composer and record producer is that he is almost entirely deaf in his right ear. Audree Wilson explains that Brian suffers from "nerve deafness. They [the doctors] say it might be congenital or it may have been caused by an injury." In preparing his epic 1971 *Rolling Stone* article, writer Tom Nolan confronted Murry with the rumor that Brian's deafness had been caused by a childhood blow on the ear from his father. That article (which used additional material by David Felton) also first presented the story that as a childhood (revenge?) prank, Brian had defecated on a plate and set it in front of Murry at the dinner table.

Murry, of course, vehemently denied both stories. Thinking that Brian was probably the source of the "rumors," Murry telephoned Brian and angrily demanded that he retract the stories. Brian reportedly laughingly told his dad, "I'll tell you what. Let's tell them that I shit in your ear, and you hit me in the head with a plate." Still, there is no firm evidence as to what caused Brian's deafness. It could have been from a birth defect or an infection, or the consequence of a fight with a neighbor. It could have been the result of Murry's hitting Brian in the head.

Regardless of the origin of the deafness, treatment and an operation in the sixties never restored Brian's hearing, and to this day, he's never heard stereo. As Brian told Mike Douglas in 1976, "It was sort of like being robbed of something, some pleasure of life. Stereo, when it came in in the fifties, everyone was so flipped, and here I was, Brian Wilson didn't hear stereo." For the man who created some of the greatest sound experiences of the sixties, it is a cruel irony that he could never fully comprehend sound. Possibly Brian's hearing problem contributed to his record-making skills. Because he could only hear mono sound, he may have been more attuned to what made a record sound good on the radio. "I still miss it," Brian remarked. "I think it's a little like being born blind . . . I'm not complaining, but it's a little bit of a setback not to hear stereo."

Murry Wilson was a harsh parent, but there was no overt malice involved in his actions. Murry was bringing his boys up to make them men the best way he knew how. If this included physical violence and tongue-lashings, Murry still had his boys' interests in mind. That makes his actions more understandable but no more excusable. Audree Wilson, who was a very devoted and loving wife, was also at times a victim of Murry's abuse.

One person who knows the Wilson brothers as adults and who observed Murry Wilson's interactions with them thinks that, in many ways, the brothers are all part of Murry, the result of Murry's images of what his children should be.

Dennis, for instance, has Murry's incredible physical energy. He is very much a loner, driven by this incredible power that gives everything he does, including his music, an emotional intensity that is not often present in contemporary popular music. Generous to a fault, Dennis's emotions are always exposed, like a raw nerve that is constantly being jolted. As a child, Dennis was also a fighter, the only one of the three Wilson brothers to reflect their father's penchant for fighting. That may be because, as Audree Wilson remembers, "Dennis had it the hardest; he got some very hard spankings. [Murry] was tough; I used to think he was too tough." Audree also feels that Dennis is the most like Murry, "the temper, sort of bombastic at times. It's just like Murry revisited. They were certainly the most alike."

Carl, who has always been the silent buddha of the Beach Boys, didn't get beaten nearly as much as Dennis. As Audree recalls, "Carl had very little of it. He was always sitting, watching the parade go by, very calm." In that respect, Carl didn't change very much except that he asserted his leadership onstage, and when Brian retreated from his musical responsibilities, Carl picked up the reins and formed new music in his older brother's style. Carl, underneath the beard, also seems to resemble Murry the most physically, and the equanimity of his personality (helped along by TM and est, an intensive group therapy training popular in California in the 1970s) became crucial in keeping the Beach Boys together as a functioning band.

The family that sings together stays together, circa 1955. Back L–R: Brian, mother Audree, father Murry. Front L–R: Carl and Dennis.
Credit: BriMel Archives

The brothers are all quite dissimilar, and Audree thinks that Brian isn't really like Murry, "but there are times when he just reminds me of him.

I can't put my finger on what characteristic . . . Brian's really a gentle soul." Brian, more than his two brothers, reflects Murry's eccentric behavior, which may be, in part, a reaction to the pressure to excel that an oldest son feels. Like Murry, Brian's energies were directed toward achievement. Brian claims that "the Beach Boys' success hinges on the fact that Murry Wilson was like a spark plug personality behind the group." It was Murry's drive, transferred to Brian, that would help create the Beach Boys.

All of that was far away. Before there could be Beach Boys, there had to be music. Audree Wilson remembers Brian's first musical moments. "When Brian was two he was singing nursery rhymes . . . When Brian was seven, he had a beautiful voice, and would often sing with the church choir. He was a soloist. He was asked to sing at school functions, and he was already playing the piano . . . By the time he was eight years old, he had a truly beautiful boy soprano voice, and he wasn't bashful about it. One time, a lady heard him sing and asked if he could sing with the choir at her church for Christmas . . . he was just a little guy, and it was really a thrill to see Brian with this chorus behind him. They did 'We Three Kings of Orient Are,' and he did a solo . . . an incredibly talented young guy."

In 1977, Brian recalled his first musical memory: "The very first song I was exposed to was *Rhapsody in Blue*. There's no better way to come into this world . . . than to hear a song like that being played . . . I'm certain every time I hear it that I'm going back to age two. Actually, when I was two weeks old, they used to play *Rhapsody in Blue* at my grand-mother's house, where my mother used to go visit a lot." Brian said that the song "has become one of the songs of my life. It sort of became a general life theme." One friend of Brian's notes that the first song Brian ever sang in front of his family was 'When You Wish Upon a Star.'

Murry loved music, and Brian remembered that "he would sing to me. My mother would play the organ, and my dad would sing. They'd do duets, organ and piano. So as far back as I can remember, there's been music in my life." According to Brian, "The three brothers used to harmo-nize in bed. We'd all sleep in the same room. We used to sing this song, 'Come Down, Come Down from the Ivory Tower'; that was our special one we'd sing. We developed a little blend which aided us when we started to get into the Beach Boys stuff."

Even then, the music could cause Brian pain. Dennis recalls that "in the sixth grade, he used to sing so beautiful . . . Brian sang in school, and he sang very high, and all his buddies that he'd hang out with laughed at him. And he ran home from school, and I chased after him, and it broke my heart to see him emotionally involved in the music at such an early age and have his friends laugh at him, call him a girl or something. But every time that he's ever stuck it [his music] out, put it out for people to see, to share it with people, a lot of times he's been hurt."

Besides the Wilson brothers' developing musical blend, there was more than a little comedy. Brian's outrageous sense of humor has become part of the Beach Boys' legend, and their early singing nights provided Brian the opportunity to create hysteria. Audree recalls that they "were all in the same room, they would just howl. They would make up crazy stories. [Brian] was really just so full of fun," making funny faces or telling funny stories. Carl remembered that "after we went to bed, Brian would sit there trying to make us laugh. So we'd be trying not to laugh, covering our mouths, hiding under the sheets and Brian would keep cracking us up." These typical childhood nighttime frivolities did not go unnoticed or unpunished. Again, Carl: "First, my mother would come in and warn us. If our father came in, then it was curtains."

Despite his often overbearing, strict nature, Murry was also a generous man. He filled the Wilson home with as much music as their limited budget could afford. When Brian was very young, he took lessons on a toy accordion for six weeks. Audree recalls that "the object of that game was after six weeks, you buy the big accordion." Brian "just excelled, he flew through the lessons; but we couldn't afford to buy the accordion." Otherwise, Brian might have become the first rock 'n' roll accordionist. Brian did spend many hours at the family's piano and organ, basically teaching himself how to play. As Carl Wilson once noted, "There were many years of [Brian's] life where he did nothing but play the piano. Months at a time. Days on end. Four Freshmen records. Just all music."

Carl's first musical interest was in stringed instruments. Audree fondly recalls that when Carl was three, he used to watch a children's show that featured cowboy Spade Cooley playing the fiddle. "Carl would stand with his foot up on a stool, pretending he was playing the violin." Carl began to show more serious interest almost ten years later. "Carl was twelve, and he decided he wanted to play guitar. So we bought him an inexpensive one, and he took lessons from a neighbor. One day, he came home, and he was playing an old standard and one chord was way off. Brian said, 'How can you let him take lessons when he's learning the wrong chords?' That didn't last long, and Carl began playing on his own." Somewhere along the line, Carl also took lessons from John Maus, who later gained fame as one of the Walker Brothers.

"Dennis," Audree says, "was the last one to really participate. He started playing the piano when he was fourteen . . . and all of a sudden, he was playing boogie-woogie." The last to learn an instrument, Dennis never took part in the family music. Audree remembers that Dennis, before he could walk, would just sit by the front door and stare at the outside world. When he got his land legs, Dennis quickly became an outdoor person; he was (and occasionally still is) a surfer, the only true Beach Boy in the group. Besides being an outdoor type, Dennis considered himself an outsider and felt he didn't fit in with the rest of his family.

The Wilsons had a Hammond organ, and Brian remembers the days when "my brother Carl, my mother, myself, and my father used to harmonize . . . used to imitate the Four Freshmen songs." Brian's early musical influences included the Four Freshmen and the Hi-Los. Brian claims that he "was sort of patterning my life or my music around the Freshmen style. Carl was into Chuck Berry and Little Richard and things like that before I was . . . Carl was into rock 'n' roll radio before I was . . . So, in a sense, he got just as much [rock 'n' roll] education as I did. He's had as many years' education in that field."

Besides listening and learning, Brian was working on his own skills. By the hour, he would sing along with the Four Freshmen records, stretching his vocal range so that he developed a unique voice—he could sing high without resorting to falsetto. At the same time, he developed a beautiful, effortless falsetto that would eventually be the soaring sound of the Beach Boys' records.

Murry Wilson's musical ambitions gave the young Wilson children a chance very early on to develop musical skills, and Murry welcomed their participation in his music. Once Murry's sister Emily (Mike Love's mother) gave a concert in Murry's honor. This private recital, the music equivalent of the vanity press, featured Murry's songs. They were performed by a trio that Emily hired to play at the concert, which was attended by school friends of Mrs. Love. Mike had written a song called 'The Old Soldier' about a soldier who had been killed in the war. As Murry recalled, "He was only nine and a half when he wrote it. I thought it was just darling."

Ever the egotistic tinkerer, Murry went home and composed new lyrics to the song because he felt that he heard the song as a hymn. His revised version of Mike's tune was now retitled 'By His Side,' subtitled 'When Jesus Calls His Soldiers.' Murry taught Brian both sets of lyrics and bought his eight-year-old son his first suit with long pants. Brian sang both versions of Mike's song at the concert, and according to Murry, "he brought the house down." Later, when Brian and Mike began to write songs together, it would make the Beach Boys stars and earn the group millions of dollars.

Recalling Brian's youth, Murry felt that Brian was full of early promise. Murry admitted that he was "one of those young, frightened fathers . . . but I just fell in love with him, and in three weeks, he cooed back at me and responded." According to Murry, at the age of eleven and a half months, Brian could hum the entire Marine Corps Hymn.

Brian's musical skills developed quickly. Constant practice and exposure to music created a very pleasant obsession that found perfect release at the piano. There were always ideal family opportunities to display his growing talent.

"Mike and Brian became close at family gatherings," Audree remembers, and they loved to sing together. "When they were real little, we [the Wilsons and the Loves] were real close and we saw them a lot. [Emily Love] always had a big Christmas party, and we'd go caroling around the neighborhood." Audree laughs, "Brian always had his solos." As the families began to grow, they also began to spend less time together. It should be noted here that Mike Love was also experiencing a difficult childhood.

Meanwhile, Brian's musical development continued unabated, aided by the radio. "In junior high school," Audree recalls, "he'd eat dinner, and he'd go into his room, and that radio would be on constantly. I remember once Murry saying to me, 'Do you think we should worry about him?' I said, 'No. He's just loving the music.' Played it constantly." Away from the radio, Brian and Audree used to listen to records together, everything from Henry Mancini to Rosemary Clooney to the Hi-Los and, of course, the Four Freshmen.

Behind Murry Wilson's bluster was a man who could at times be incredibly thoughtful. "Brian was fourteen years old," Audree recounts, "and the Four Freshmen were at the Crescendo. Murry found out they were there, and he knew Brian loved them so much. We couldn't afford, actually, for more than two of us to go at that time, so Murry took Brian and it was really a thrill."

Even when Murry did something good, he managed to upset Brian's sometimes fragile tendencies. As excited as Brian was at seeing the Freshmen perform, Murry felt that meeting them in person would be an extra treat—as it was. Audree recalls, Brian "was so thrilled" but he was also "scared to death." Somehow Murry bluffed his way backstage "and got into the dressing room and introduced Brian to them." Audree corrects herself. "Introduced *them* to Brian. And I'm sure that was a highlight" of Brian's youth.

"Before the Beach Boys were born," Audree remembers, "Brian used to write four-part arrangements in the style of the Four Freshmen. We had given him, for his sixteenth birthday, a tape recorder, and he and I used to sing two parts into the tape recorder," and then play back the tape and sing the other two parts along with it "so we'd have four parts." When the whole family would gather around, Brian would "teach Murry the bass line and I could read well enough to read my line, and then he would teach Carl. Dennis would never have any part of that in those days . . . Brian would teach himself to write those parts, absolutely. He will say today that he can't write music, but that's not so. He used to make incredible arrangements, not only vocal. I have seen him do arrangements for a track with professional musicians, just incredible. And he did teach himself." Supposedly, Brian learned how to arrange instruments from one listening to a do-it-yourself record, *The Instruments of the Orchestra*, which taught the sounds of the individual instruments. Brian learned quickly in those days; he just gobbled up information, particularly when it came to music.

Brian's first public musical appearances took place toward the end of his high school days. The exact chronology is impossible to pin down, but there were two particular events that stood out in the reminiscences of the Wilson family and their friends. Rich Sloan, a high school friend and classmate of Brian's, remembers that during their senior year "Brian had written a little song for one of the girls who was running for class president, Carol Hess, whom Brian was very fond of. It was to the tune of 'Hully, Gully' . . . 'Vote for Carol, Carol Hess.' He and several underclassmen sang it at the assembly, and it went over real big."

The seminal Beach Boys group also made their performing debut around this time. Brian, Mike, Carl and a friend of Brian's formed a quartet. According to Audree Wilson, "They were asked to perform for some evening program at school. Carl said, 'No, I won't do it.' And I remember coming down kind of hard on Carl. And Brian called the group 'Carl and the Passions.' Everybody's memory is fuzzy on that last point. If you ask Carl, he'll say, 'No, there never was a Carl and the Passions, that was just Brian putting somebody on.' That sort of contradiction is fairly typical of the whole history of the group. In 1972, when the Beach Boys were searching for an album title, they decided to name their new release *Carl and the Passions— 'So Tough.'"*

Regardless of the name of the group, Brian was spending a lot of time singing. Mike Love, looking back at the early days, recalled the many nights he and Brian "used to sing together. We'd go to Wednesday Night Youth Night at Angeles Mesa Presbyterian Church . . . after singing church songs, we'd walk home with my sister Maureen singing three-part harmony, Everly Brothers' songs." Mike and Brian also spent quite a few late nights singing with the radio. Brian would "get in his old car, it was a Nash Rambler; he would come by my place, and we would listen to the radio, play the piano, carry on and then, about eleven o'clock, my father would yell at us, 'If you're going to play that music and make a racket, get outside.' We'd go outside and stay in the car and listen to the radio and sing . . . Sometimes we'd spend the night in the car."

Looking back, those nights may have been just plain fun for Mike, but Brian's memories make those times sound intense. "My favorite was KFWB in Hollywood," Brian recalled. "I used to love radio anyway. Every record had something you would listen to. Every record had some kind of twist in it that gave you that feelin' you'd say, 'Oh, man.' You'd go to the piano and say, 'Now, how did they do that.' You'd start learning about it. It's an education. Anybody with a good ear is gonna pick up on those records."

AM radio was kind of an underground music school that influenced all the young rock musicians in their formative years. Those countless hours spent listening to the hits would be invaluable when it came time for Brian to make his records. As Brian noted, "It was a great education to hear the radio." For Brian, it was more valuable than any classroom could ever have been.

While music was certainly important in Brian's early years, his youth was hardly all music and no play. Although Brian looks back on those times with negative emotions (particularly when it comes to his home life), a close friend of Brian's from those teenage years recalls that there was a lot of plain, uncomplicated fun. Rich Sloan is now sales manager for a Los Angeles computer company. Back in the late fifties, he and Brian spent many hours together.

Rich remembers, "Brian and I met playing Little League baseball. He played for the Seven-Up team, a bunch of losers. I don't think they ever won anything. I played for the Airport Octos, and *we* always had a very good team. Brian was a good baseball player, and he played left field. Brian's dad always used to be really interested in Brian's athletic ability; he used to stand on the left field sideline and tell Brian where to play. Murry would yell instructions like 'Play more to the left, come up, go back,' that type of thing." According to Rich, "Murry was always very helpful."

Brian Wilson, circa 1959.
Credit: Courtesy of Rich Sloan

As a football player, Brian was sometimes ineffective because of his dislike of physical contact, a dislike that may have been a reaction to the childhood violence of his upbringing. Rich Sloan describes Brian's style: "Not being real aggressive, Brian didn't like to run into people, didn't really like people running into him when they would tackle him." His varsity football career wasn't a huge success, but his days on the varsity baseball team were quite impressive. "Brian could hit the ball a long way, didn't have a high batting average, but was a strong hitter. Brian played first-string varsity our senior year."

That year, Brian also ended his gridiron (i.e., football) career and ran cross-country instead. "Brian had good endurance and was the type who could run all day; he had good muscle tone," Rich Sloan comments. "A lot of people today don't think of Brian as being athletic, but he was athletic by desire and by build." It has often been claimed that Brian could have been a professional baseball player. What Rich Sloan thinks is that Brian wasn't "serious enough to be totally dedicated to anything but his music."

Off the field, Brian and Rich Sloan were part of a group of friends that was developing into a close-knit pack. Rich claims that "we weren't a clique; we were just the baseball and football players and really nice girls." At a middle-class school in the fifties, the chief form of socializing was parties. "Brian was part of our group," remembers Rich. "We'd play records at the parties. Brian didn't sing or play any instrument at those get-togethers."

What Brian would do is make everybody laugh. Just like the nights with his brothers, Rich recalls that "Brian would do anything to get a laugh, even if it meant punishment to himself . . . He got enjoyment out of seeing other people have fun. Brian liked to be part of what was happening." Brian also "liked practical jokes. But he was always a little bit shy, a little reserved even though he wanted to be more outgoing. However, once he was introduced into the group, Brian would become Brian." That last phrase crops up again and again when people try to describe what Brian Wilson was or is like. At a loss for words, people fall back on that non-explanation. What is strange is that it does make sense; it just doesn't mean anything unless you know Brian. And when you try to describe what he's like, well, Brian very often is Brian.

What is also evident is that the teenage Brian liked to be around people.

With all the success of the Beach Boys, Brian still loved people, needed people, needed human contact. Even when he was isolated from most of the world, those who did see Brian say that he loved to talk . . . sometimes seriously, sometimes putting people on. Later Brian partially withdrew from people because they treated him as something special. Audree Wilson remarked that "one thing Brian says [is] that he wishes people would just treat him like any other guy, just down to earth . . . He's really a very simple person." Before the mass success, Brian was liked for himself. "Everybody who knew Brian," says Rich Sloan, "whether it was a brother or a sister or your parents, they really took him in as one of the family. Brian liked to be liked by parents, liked to be liked by anybody . . . The [senior] girls accepted Brian as a brother rather than a boyfriend. Robin Hood [one of Brian's best friends] and Brian both dated juniors."

Brian's affable personality often got him into trouble, particularly when he became the butt of a practical joke. Rich Sloan remembers "one time when we were in the showers. There were about five or six showers in a big stall area, and then there'd be a wall and five more showers. After baseball practice one day, these guys were throwing wet gym towels over the wall. They were pretty heavy, and they could hurt a guy 'cause they were tied up in knots. So Brian said, 'Next time they throw one over, I'll hit my hand against the wall and lie down on the floor and you tell everybody that I was knocked out.' . . . Sure enough, here comes a towel, Brian bangs the wall and lies down in the middle of the floor with all the water running all over him.

"So I hollered, 'Hey, Brian's hurt! You guys come here quick.' So every-body comes running over, Brian's the center of attention. Brian's down there with all the water spraying all over him, and everyone's looking at him. So I thought, 'What would really make this funny would be if I urinated on him.' And everyone's laughing. Brian thinks everyone's laughing at him. When he found out the truth, he wasn't too pleased but that was a joke, and he got over it because he was the center of attention. Brian never was one to carry a grudge."

Rich Sloan was a great instigator. He tells the story of "another time [when] we were out on the Wilsons' front lawn. Brian, Dennis, myself, and maybe Carl were out there, and Brian's dad asked Dennis to get his pipe. By the time he brought the pipe out of the house, Brian's dad had gone into the garage. I told Dennis, 'Hey, give me the pipe.' We took it and filled it with grass [from the lawn], and we put the tobacco on top of it. We gave it to Murry, and he was puffing on it, and he broke it apart and pulled the filter out and put the filter back in and started puffing again. Nothing. All the time, we're there snickering. That was the kind of humor Brian liked."

Rich Sloan recalls one trick the guys would pull on Brian. "Brian drove a '51 Mercury, and we used to come up to stop lights and we'd holler out to the car next to us, 'Hey, you son of a bitch,' and we'd all duck down. So this guy would look over and see Brian by himself, and Brian would panic."

When Brian was with Rich Sloan, he consistently ended up with the short end of the stick. "One time, Brian and I went to St. Vincent's Hospital to visit his cousin. We couldn't find her room, and we were just looking around the hospital. I forget how it came up, but it was decided that I would wrap up Brian's head in toilet paper, making him look like a patient, and walk him down the corridors of the hospital. We got on the elevator, and Brian could see just a little bit out of one eye. There was a doctor in there, and Brian didn't know what to do. Obviously, a doctor could look at a guy's head and know it was wrapped in toilet paper, so we got off at the next floor."

Brian seems to have had a special talent for being in the wrong place at the wrong time. Rich Sloan remembers one trip home after a baseball game in Culver City. "We would always drive our cars to the baseball game; mine was the lead car. We had this thing called a Chinese Fire Drill. When we would stop at a red light, everybody would get out of the car, run around it, the light would turn green and everybody would pile back into the car. So we pulled up to this red light (and we were in our baseball uniforms), and we started running around the car. Steve Anderson's car was next in line, and they started running around the car. Brian's car was next in line, and I'll never forget this, I go to get in my car, and I look up and see Brian had jumped up on the hood of Steve's car and was jumping up and down. Brian's dancing on the top of this car, and our coach pulls up right alongside. Brian looked over and saw the coach and slid down the windshield of Steve's car and went back into his car, and we all took off. Needless to say, the coach wasn't happy at all. He said, 'My wife thought it was pretty funny until I told her you all had on Hawthorne High uniforms.' From then on, we took buses to the games."

On occasion, Brian would get back at Rich. "The first time I met Mrs. Wilson, Brian and I were in their family room. Audree [then] was a fairly good-sized woman; she might have been forty or fifty pounds overweight. So she appeared, and Brian said, 'Oh, Mom, I'd like you to meet Rich.' And she said, 'Hi, Rich,' and Brian said, 'Oh, yeah, Mom, Rich thinks you're overweight and ought to go to Vic Tanny's [a health spa].' And I said, 'Wait a minute!' but Mrs. Wilson interrupted and said, 'That's OK, Rich, I know my son.'" Those times when Rich was the victim were rare.

According to Rich, "Brian's whole life-being was very casual and fun-loving . . . nothing really serious was Brian's way of doing things. Brian's nature was just to be honest, play fair, play hard, and enjoy it for what it's worth." Because Brian was so easygoing, he "used to allow people to take advantage of him. If there were four people and Brian wanted to go to the beach and someone else wanted to play miniature golf, Brian would always go along with the other guy's wishes. He wanted to be a part of it." Brian, it seems, could be convinced to do most anything. Rich recalls that whether "it was running a mile or having a party at Brian's house, he would go along with whatever you wanted. But everybody wanted Brian around. He was always a lot of fun."

Brian was a true innocent, and he was often pretty gullible, but despite everything, his basic sweetness came through. Because of his good nature, his friends often took advantage of him. Some guy would say, "Hey Brian, why don't you sit out in the car while we go in and have a Coke or something and make sure the engine doesn't stop." Rich notes that Brian wasn't taken in—not always anyway. "Sometimes, he would do this just to pacify whoever he was with. In that respect, he hasn't changed very much."

In Brian's senior year, he took a music class that required each student to write a sonata for the final project. Brian's sonata, according to Audree, was definitely *not* 'Surfin'.' Whatever it was has been lost in time, but Brian did share some unusual music with Rich Sloan, such as that better-left-unknown tune 'Larry, Larry Dingleberry.' In the Sloan's family room there was a piano, and as Rich recounts, "Brian would come over and play his boogie-woogie. I enjoyed it very much, and if you enjoyed hearing it, Brian would play it as long as he could, and at such a fierce pace and for such a long duration that his forearm muscles would get hard as rocks. He would just bang on the piano and play a couple of songs, nothing serious, but he liked to play the piano, not so people would say, 'Look how great he is.' He just wanted people to recognize what he could do and enjoy what he was doing, share with other people what he could do." In April 1959, Rich recorded Brian at the piano. It is a unique tape in that it is the only recorded evidence of Brian's boogie-woogie piano playing. It is fascinating to hear Brian playing the piano in a style that never became an obvious part of his Beach Boys work.

At a Hawthorne High school assembly, circa 1960.
L–R: Bob Barrows, Brian, Keith Lent and Bruce Griffin.
Credit: Courtesy of Rich Sloan

On that same tape, Rich Sloan's ancient recorder also captured a teenage Brian that is often lost with all the talk of musical genius, mental problems and drug abuse. Rich and Brian's conversation reminds us how typical Brian was. The discussion, as you might expect, centered around girls. Brian and Rich talk about whom they planned to take to the prom and other personal matters that can only be important to a teenage heart. There's the usual assortment of four-letter words and game-playing, but what the tape shows above all is that Brian was a pretty normal kid—whatever that means.

Still, Brian's childhood was filled with enough trauma that when he was placed in the role of a father he virtually abdicated all responsibility. As Marilyn Wilson (Brian's wife) recalled, Brian demanded that Marilyn discipline the kids because he was afraid he would do it wrong. Marilyn felt that this was "because he had it really rough, he didn't want to do the same things to his kids, therefore he backed out of it totally . . . He didn't have an easy childhood."

Murry Wilson was the dominant personality in the lives of his sons, and they never emerged from the shadow of his control. Murry made his presence felt throughout their career, and if he wasn't always by their side physically, his spirit was always a part of their personalities.

As Brian rounded the corner into adulthood, emotional problems began to stalk his path. As a youth, Brian had friends who fondly remember him as a "regular guy." At home, banging at the piano, listening to records or the radio, singing with his mother—music had become Brian's best friend.

There was still no indication that Brian would devote his life to music. At that point, music was just his favorite escape. In time, it would be his only refuge.

CHAPTER 2

FIVE FRESHMEN

THE WAY BRIAN WILSON REMEMBERS IT, THE CREATION OF HIS "CALIFORNIA Sound" was as quick as it was easy. "One day, my brother Dennis came home from the beach and said, 'Hey, surfing's getting really big. You guys ought to write a song about it.'" So Brian and cousin Mike Love composed a primitive tune called, not surprisingly, 'Surfin',' and it became an instant hit in Los Angeles.

Was it that simple? Yes and no. Success came painlessly to the Beach Boys; there was no "dues-paying" period while they honed their craft before taking it to the general public. The Beach Boys came into being before the guys could really play their instruments. Maybe it's appropriate that the world's most famous vocal group made it with amateur instrumentation.

Nineteen sixty-one was the year of the birth of the Beach Boys. As might be expected, the early history of a group as renowned as the Beach Boys has taken on mythic proportions. Each Beach Boy, their families and associates have told the story many times. However, nobody tells it exactly the same way. Fortunately, the actual details aren't as significant as the verifiable facts. That is, the Wilson brothers, Mike Love, and friend Al Jardine recorded a song called 'Surfin',' the group was named the Beach Boys, and it was the beginning of the most successful career ever enjoyed by an American group. For the Beach Boys, though, 1961 was mostly a year of false starts, of groups with names like "Kenny and the Cadets" and "The Pendletones" . . . of kids on a lark, forming a band, making a record. The year ended with the first live performance of a group that was called "The Beach Boys."

★　　★　　★　　★

Until the 1960s, California was never very important to the pop music world. New York was the center, whether it was Tin Pan Alley or its obvious successor, the Brill Building. In 1961, all the hits seemed to emerge from this one Manhattan locale. This centralized source of songs joined forces with the powerful network television exposure of Dick Clark's *American Bandstand* to dominate the teen sounds.

It should be remembered that the beginning of that decade was easily the nadir for memorable rock 'n' roll. Elvis had gone Hollywood. Buddy Holly had been killed in a plane crash. Others, like Chuck Berry, had made their statements. Good-looking kids like Frankie Avalon had been propelled into stardom by the aforementioned axis of musical power. Chubby Checker made the only noticeable sociological impact that year. His recording of Hank Ballard's 'The Twist' launched America's teenagers on a chain of dance crazes that wasn't finally broken until the arrival of the Beatles.

Back in California, the not-yet Beach Boys didn't really care for many of the 1960s East Coast records; what was happening on *American Bandstand* wasn't vital, wasn't important. The influences on the Beach Boys, from Chuck Berry to the Four Freshmen, were pretty much set. An occasional newcomer like Dion or Dylan would become meaningful, but mostly the Beach Boys were children of the fifties' rock 'n' roll explosion. The fact that the current music was so dismal may have been one reason for starting a group. More likely, the Beach Boys happened because Brian Wilson wanted and needed a vehicle for his emerging songwriting and performing skills.

Before the Beach Boys hit, Brian took two minor potshots at record making, two discs that are now only footnotes to his musical history. One was 'Barbie,' performed by Kenny and the Cadets. Brian was Kenny; Audree and a friend of Brian's were the Cadets. The other record was 'The Surfer Moon' by Bob and Sheri. Bob was Bob Norberg, Brian's first roommate outside of the Wilson house. Sheri was Bob's girlfriend.

While neither record was memorable, both played valuable roles in the Beach Boys' history. The Kenny and the Cadets record is crucial because it brought Brian in close, professional contact with Hite and Dorinda Morgan. Hite Morgan's Guild Music was the publisher of a few of Murry Wilson's songs, and Hite was the Beach Boys' first producer and publisher. The significance of 'The Surfer Moon' lies in another area. The record was the first to bear the credit "Produced by Brian Wilson." In the years to come, Brian's credit on a Beach Boys single or album was a sign of excellence. More than that, when Brian's credit disappeared from the Beach Boys records, they stopped having Top Ten hits.

In examining the pre-Beach Boys days, the most striking element is the total ordinariness of the situation. There was really no reason to believe that something of consequence was about to happen.

Brian, for instance, was going to El Camino Junior College and taking a lot of psychology courses. Most of the great pop composers of the sixties and seventies had little formal musical education, and Brian was no exception. Oddly enough, it may have been a music course that helped drive Brian out of school. "In college, I took a music appreciation course," Brian told an interviewer in 1964. "The teachers were one hundred percent against anything except operas, symphonies, cantatas, chamber and classical stuff. Well, I wasn't going to sit there and let any guy tell me that pop music is bad. I love both. After a year and a half, I became a college dropout and I'm not sorry. My hunger for knowledge is very strong, but I can learn more through self-study."

The other almost-Beach Boys were also experiencing difficulties. Al Jardine was a college classmate of Brian's, but the rest of the guys had very little classroom learning. Carl eventually graduated from Hollywood's Professional High School (after being kicked out of Hawthorne High for various disciplinary infractions). Dennis consistently resisted the textbooks. As for Mike, a graduate of nearby Dorsey High, PhDs weren't exactly in his future. The oldest Beach Boy, Mike was already part of the adult world. "Before the group," Mike joked, "I was in the oil business. 'Gas and oil, check the tires.' I was a sheet-metal apprentice at my father's factory, too. I was married [the first of three marriages for Mike]. I married a cheerleader when I was twenty and she was eighteen . . . we 'had to' get married." Looking back on an obviously hard time, Mike is full of wisdom. A shotgun marriage, according to Mike, "is in the Great American Way. That's where we glean our experience." Maybe, but being married meant two jobs for Mike, two jobs to quit when the Beach Boys became a reality.

Because Mike Love was the oldest and the first of the Beach Boys to accept adult responsibilities, it is understandable that he would be the first to grasp the importance of money. More than anybody in the group, Mike was concerned with commerce in the early years of the Beach Boys. In later years, his stress on what might be called "formula" success would strain his creative relationship with Brian. In 1961, though, it was OK to want money.

Still, there was no indication of impending success and wealth. Brian remembers "we never fantasized" about there being a group. "That developed very quickly, over a period of weeks, when I was about nineteen years old . . . We kind of developed into a group sort of through the wishes of Dennis. He said that . . . the kids at school knew I was musical because I had done some singing for assemblies and so on. And he said, 'Why don't you write a song about surfing?' because surfing was becoming a big fad. So, it happened that we got together and Mike Love came up with 'bop-bop-dit-dit,' you know, that Jan and Dean-type riff. And I came up with some of the background music, and we just flowed right into a career from nowhere. It was just an amazing start."

One problem that had plagued the Wilson/Love singing group was the constant search for a fifth voice. Al Jardine, the only original Beach Boy who wasn't family, was a student at El Camino when Brian was there. One day they ran into each other on campus and decided to do some singing. "The next day," Al recalled, "in the nurses' room of the college . . . we got together [with] a football player, some deep bass singer who couldn't carry a tune, one of my friends from early high school days . . . We all sang anything we could think of. Well, that group didn't cut it too well. So Brian said, 'Hey, my little brother Carl can really sing, he's really good.' And I said, 'Him? Are you kidding?' . . . He says, 'My cousins Mike and Maureen, they can sing too. And there's Dennis . . . ' So we went over to Brian's the day after that and met Mike and Dennis and Carl." Brian had written "a couple of songs about a girl that he was going out with." One was 'Judy' and the other was 'Surfer Girl.' Both songs were written for Judy Bowles, Brian's first serious girlfriend, who eventually broke his heart.

Mike Love remembers that Al Jardine's arrival on the scene was the final solution to their search for a fifth voice. Al's voice fitted in perfectly. The players were now all set. Murry Wilson remembered that it was in "early 1961 when Mike Love and Al Jardine were coming over to the house and Brian was teaching them songs, with Carl. They sang Four Freshmen songs almost like the Four Freshmen, except they had a sweeter, younger sound." Interestingly, Dennis was not part of the singing.

In either late summer or early fall, the Beach Boys became, if not a reality, at least a possibility. Audree Wilson begins the story. "We had guests from England. We took them to Mexico City for a three-day trip, and left the refrigerator stocked. We left them adequate money if they chose to eat out." Carl Wilson remembers that amount to be $800, a rather unlikely figure, but he tells what happened after their parents went on their vacation. "The day after they left, we all went down to a music store and got instruments with our food money . . . I was gonna play guitar, Alan could play stand-up bass, Brian could play keyboards already . . . Dennis just chose the drums. And then Brian said, 'I'm gonna play bass and you play guitar and then it'll be a rock sound, be rock 'n' roll.' Michael didn't play anything, but he got a saxophone, he thought he'd play sax, but Mike never practiced." Carl noted, "The group really learned how to play after we made records." It's Audree Wilson's turn again. "We barely got in the door, and they said, 'We've got something to play for you.' Well, we saw all this stuff . . . and they had an act . . . and that's when 'Surfin'' was born, that's when they sang it and put it together . . . It was a lot of fun, but they were serious about it. They were having fun, but yet they wanted to do something with it. They were just very excited."

Nothing more might have happened except that Al's interest in folk music brought the guys into the studio. Audree recalls that one day "Alan came over, and he had a folk song he wanted to record. He asked Murry what to do, and he [Murry] said, 'Go see Hite.'" Gary Winfrey, a lifelong friend of Al's, remembers that he and Al "invited Brian to help sing the song, because we couldn't play and sing at the same time." Brian brought a friend of his, Keith Lent, and the four of them went to Hite Morgan's studio and recorded a song about the Rio Grande. Sometime after that, as Audree Wilson remembers, Brian, Mike, Carl and Al were at the Morgans' studio recording a demo when they said, "We want to play this for you." Dorinda Morgan was willing to listen, and what she heard really excited her, Audree recalls. "Immediately, she said, 'Drop everything. We want to record that!' He [Hite] wasn't so much in favor of it, but she heard something she thought would click."

The song was 'Surfin',' and the recording featured a Mike Love vocal, Carl on guitar, Al on stand-up bass, and Brian playing drums on either a garbage pail cover or a pie tin. This first-ever group effort did not include

Dennis because he was not part of the group. It was Audree who made the guys accept Dennis as part of what was happening. After all, it was only fair. Dennis had suggested they write the song about surfing in the first place.

Of course, having cut a tune for a publisher didn't mean it would automatically be released as a record, but Hite Morgan had connections with Candix Records, and the group was signed to Candix. One small detail remained. What was to be the name of the group? The guys opted for "The Pendletones" in honor of their favorite Pendleton shirts. The people at Candix didn't like that. Fortunately, their choice, "The Surfers," was short-lived. How it became the Beach Boys was a beautiful accident that may have saved the group from the junk pile of fads and one-hit wonders. If they had been named the Surfers, they would have been restricted to only surfing records. At least a more generic name like "The Beach Boys" allowed them the flexibility to record songs about an entire lifestyle and not just the surfing aspect of beach life.

Russ Regan, now a major figure in the recording industry, was just starting out in late 1961. His career as a recording artist had been fairly dismal, and he was working for Buckeye Record Distributors, which distributed Candix. Regan remembered that the "A&R [artists and reper-toire] man over there was a friend of mine named Joe Saraceno. He called me to play a record over the telephone. So I listened, and I thought, 'Wow, it sounds like a Jan and Dean record." [It is interesting that the Beach Boys began by borrowing from Jan and Dean. Jan and Dean would return the favor many times in the future.]

"So," Russ continued, "I said, 'Who is it?' And he said, 'It's a new group we're signing over here at Candix; they're called the Surfers.' And I said, 'Joe, you can't call them the Surfers. There's a group over on Hi-Fi Records called the Surfers. They're from Hawaii.' And he said, 'You know something, you're right. I forgot about that. We're gonna have to come up with a name.' So I laughingly said, 'Why don't you call them the Lifeguards or the Beach Bums, the Woodies, anything to do with the beach.' So finally I said, 'I got it, why don't you name them the Beach Boys!'"

Although the group reportedly didn't like the name at first, they accepted it. The name was really a perfect fit for the music, an ideal reflection of the lifestyle. When the music eventually changed, the name became an albatross. Released on December 8, 1961, 'Surfin'', according to Russ

Regan, "actually exploded here in the city of Los Angeles. Their record was a big record here. It was just a natural Southern California record."

For Dennis Wilson, nothing has equaled "the first time we ever heard our record played [on the radio]. We [Carl, Dennis, Brian, and David Marks] were all on Hawthorne Boulevard in Brian's 1957 Ford . . . they said, 'Here's a group from Hawthorne, California, the Beach Boys, with their song, 'Surfin'.' It was a contest; they played three songs and the one that got the most requests over the phone was the one they would add to the playlist. We were screamin' in the street, and knockin' on everybody's door, '*We* got a record on the radio!' . . . That was the biggest high ever. Nothing will ever top the expression on Brian's face. Ever. THAT is the all-time moment."

Their recording and radio careers underway, the Beach Boys were ready for their first public performance. On New Year's Eve, 1961, the Beach Boys played three tunes at the Long Beach Municipal Auditorium. Mike Love recalled that "we got three hundred dollars to play a Richie Valens Memorial dance. I can still remember it because we got paid for something besides working, which was really a trip. We got paid for playing music."

CHAPTER 3

LET'S GO SURFIN'

AS 1962 BEGAN, THE BEACH BOYS HAD A NAME AND A HIT, BUT THEY WERE soon to be without a record label. Record companies weren't exactly breaking down the door at the Wilson residence. The industry attitude was that surfing was just a fad, and one wonders if the group would ever have gotten a recording contract without the persistence of Murry Wilson.

Years later, Brian would take note of his dad's push and recognize its importance. As a father, Murry may not have been ideal, but as a manager of a rock group, he had unrelenting drive and ambition. He hadn't made it as a songwriter; no matter, his boys would make up for his failure. He'd see to that—and he did.

This second year of the Beach Boys' existence would enable them to prove that the success of 'Surfin'' wasn't just a fluke. The history of popular music is littered with groups and solo artists who have one or two hits and forever disappear. What separated the Beach Boys from that scrap heap were two very disparate elements—Murry Wilson's perseverance and Brian Wilson's musical talent. It was this strange brew of ego and ability combined with events that brought the Wilson family to the threshold of major success in the record business.

For the Beach Boys, 1962 was filled with growing pains, but it was also full of success—hit singles, club dates, recording contracts and personnel changes . . . the Beach Boys were in their youth.

★   ★   ★   ★

The Beach Boys' first hit, 'Surfin',' made it into the Top Three in the L.A. radio hit charts and peaked in *Billboard* magazine's national charts at number 75. The record sold somewhere between ten and fifty thousand copies, and the group received a check for less than a thousand dollars. Murry Wilson generously added a few dollars from his own pocket to make the total an even thousand, so that each Beach Boy got two hundred dollars.

One of the earliest Beach Boys concerts took place in the early spring of 1962. William F. Williams, one of the disc jockeys at KMEN in San Bernardino, recalls that time. "We at KMEN were one of the first stations to play the Beach Boys records, and San Bernardino was a big Beach Boys town. Harris department store had a 'Deb-Teens' department and the girls at the area high schools who bought their clothes there became members of a 'club.' Harris had a fashion show/concert each year for the girls who were members. KMEN was in charge of putting together the talent for Harris's concert, and I remember Murry Wilson came to us and literally begged us to let the Beach Boys be the opening act. As I recall, they barely knew which end of the guitar case was up. They looked very badly, played very badly, and sang very badly."

Candix Records was having financial trouble, and it folded sometime before the summer of 1962. Russ Regan remembers that "Candix sold their masters to ERA Records. Because of that, Murry had the right to terminate. They had a clause in their contract that the Beach Boys couldn't be sold to another record company." Without a label, Brian was concerned over the future of the group. Audree remembers that Brian asked his father for help. "We're really serious; we want to make more records . . . Would you please help us?" Actually, Murry had already assumed the reins. Although he never liked 'Surfin'' (he called it "rude" and "crude"), he took charge from the very moment he smelled success. Brian recalled Murry's reaction to 'Surfin',' a record with no overdubs or hint of sophisticated recording techniques. "We did it all live. Our mix wasn't as good [as today's mix], it wasn't as balanced. You couldn't hear the guitar playing . . . you didn't hear the bass notes as well . . . some of the vocals were a little buried. It wasn't mixed and balanced very well. And my father was critical of the first thing we did, he said, 'Well, look, you don't hear the guitar, you don't hear this, what is going on here? Listen, I'm going to have to take over as producer,' which he did. He took over as producer." Offering help and encouragement, Murry honed in on the action. Without Murry's presence, there might never have been even one record. With Murry, there was at least one adult who believed in the Beach Boys.

Hite Morgan was still the group's publisher, so he and Murry began a search for a new recording deal. The group also went into Western Studios and cut a number of songs (probably 'Surfer Girl,' 'Judy,' 'The Surfer Moon,' 'Surfin' Safari' and '409'), which Hite and Murry used to help sell the group.

Russ Regan, who had become Murry's confidant in the record business, recalls that Murry didn't want to sign with another company as small as Candix: "He wanted to be with a big company." So Regan sent the demo of 'Surfin' Safari' to Wink Martindale, who was then an A&R man at Dot Records. According to Regan, Wink "heard the record, loved the record and played it for his boss. His boss turned it down because he felt that surfing music was just a flash in the pan."

Audree Wilson remembers that Murry and Hite "cooled their heels at Dot and Decca and Liberty." Murry recalled in 1971 what had come next. "Finally, I asked Mr. Morgan what we should do. He says, 'I don't know, Murry, you're their dad and manager, *rots of ruck* to you.' And he says goodbye." Nine years after the fact, Murry would still gloat: "That cost him two million, seven hundred thousand dollars, that statement. It cost him," Murry repeated, "two million, seven hundred thousand dollars." Murry, of course, was referring to the income that Morgan would have made as the publisher of Brian Wilson's songs.

At the same time that the Beach Boys were searching for a record deal, they were undergoing their first lineup change. Al Jardine felt that the financial future of being a Beach Boy wasn't all that promising, and he quit the group and returned to college with the intention of eventually going to dental school.

Taking Al's place was a neighbor of the Wilsons, fifteen-year-old David Marks, a youngster who fitted well into the group. Audree Wilson, however, claims that "David played at guitar." According to Audree, "Brian would not allow him to sing on record because he couldn't sing . . . David was a pain in the neck, he really was. He would drive everyone crazy." There are also reports that David's mother, Joanne, was bent on making David a star, and that she and the Wilsons clashed frequently. Nik Venet, who supervised production on the Beach Boys' early Capitol albums, recalls that Marks was as musically competent as all of the other Beach Boys (except Brian).

For the moment, nevertheless, Marks was a full-fledged Beach Boy. And when the group finally signed a contract with Capitol Records, it was

David Marks, not Al Jardine, who was the fifth Beach Boy. By late '63, Al Jardine had replaced Marks on a permanent basis, and David Marks was relegated to the land of trivia contests.

The signing of the Beach Boys to Capitol Records in mid-1962 was a key element of the success story. Without a major label, these five potential rock stars probably wouldn't have made it. Brian might have had success as a composer, but it is unlikely that the others would have had musical careers. But that is all idle speculation because the group did sign with Capitol.

Russ Regan: "I had written and done some songs with Nik Venet, so I told Murry, 'Look, go over to see Nik Venet at Capitol because I think this is something Nik'll really go for.' . . . The rest is history."

Nik Venet was a twenty-one-year-old staff producer at Capitol Records in 1962 and was one of the few men in the record business who seemed to understand the importance of "teen" music. As a producer, he had already achieved some success at Capitol, but in those days, the record producer wasn't very involved. Sometimes, the producer's most important role was just deciding which songs the artist should record. These "producers" were sometimes called "A&R" men.

It was into this world that Murry Wilson brought a demonstration record. That same day, he emerged from the Capitol Tower with a recording contract for the Beach Boys. Nik Venet was the man responsible for signing the Beach Boys to Capitol. Nik, however, is not a man who the Wilson family remembers fondly. Because Venet has been outspoken about his dealings with Murry Wilson and his role in the early Beach Boys' records, he is disliked by the Wilsons.

The relationship got off to a shaky start. Murry had called for an appointment, and Nik asked Mr. Wilson to wait for two weeks because he was on his way to Nashville on business. Nik believes that Murry was insulted by the delay. They finally got together at the Capitol Tower and Murry played the demonstration record. As Venet remembered, "Every once in a while as a producer . . . before the second eight bars have spun around, you know that the record is a #1 record." Venet was talking about 'Surfin' Safari.' He recalled that there was something special about it. "I wasn't one for hiding my feelings. I mean, if I wanted to drive a bargain, I should have just sat there mum, but I got all excited, and I started jumpin' around, and I said, 'We have to make the deal.'"

Murry Wilson remembered it quite differently: "Nik acted real cool. He said, 'You come back in an hour, and we'll let you know if we want you to become Capitol artists.' He didn't act like he was too excited."

This historical contradiction is the first in a series of disagreements that have occurred in print between Venet and the Wilson family. Audree Wilson thinks "the main problem was that he didn't tell the truth." Carl Wilson was more blunt. He said that Venet was "full of shit" when it came to the Beach Boys.

Venet told writer Tom Nolan that Murry Wilson's visits to his office were to be dreaded. He had the receptionist warn him of Murry's impending arrival and he would hide under his desk. One day, Murry burst past Venet's secretary, not believing her claim that Venet wasn't in, and spent the entire day using Venet's phone while Venet crouched under his desk. Audree Wilson counters that recollection by noting that Venet "really used to tell some copped-up stories . . . Murry never used to go see Nik Venet after the first time, never. He had no reason to . . . [Venet] said, for instance, that he'd see Murry coming and he'd hide under his desk . . . Venet made Murry out to be some kind of monster. He lied, he really did."

Murry was abrasive in his dealing with Capitol, but he was fighting for his sons. What Venet really objected to were Murry's musical ideas. Venet noted that Murry felt that Brian could be the next Elvis Presley. Venet also recalled that Murry "wanted to elevate the boys by putting them into 'pretty music.'" According to Venet, Murry Wilson's music was from another time, the schmaltz of the early and mid-twentieth century, and Murry didn't really know "where his sons were at . . . I think Murry really fucked up the group for a couple of years."

The feud reveals a lot about the worst side of both camps, and their intermittent battles made the early years of the group's Capitol stay very unpleasant. But regardless of the bad feelings between Venet and the Wilsons that immediately developed, Venet did persuade Capitol Vice President Voyle Gilmore to purchase the Beach Boys' demos for three hundred dollars. The signing also included a five percent royalty, and although it wasn't a generous deal, it was fairly typical for the times. For the Beach Boys, it was an exciting opportunity to make more records.

L–R: Mike, Brian, Carl, Dennis, and David Marks, at one of their first
recording sessions at Capitol Records, late summer 1962.
Credit: Michael Ochs Archives/Getty

The group's first Capitol release was 'Surfin' Safari' on one side and
'409' on the other. The co-author of '409' was Gary Usher, the newest
member of the Beach Boys family. Usher's uncle, Benny Jones, lived near
the Wilsons in Hawthorne. Uncle Benny suggested that Gary go over and
meet the Wilsons as Gary also had a record out, and they would have
something in common. Finally, one Sunday, as Usher recalls, "I went over
and talked to them, they were practicing, you could hear them all over
the neighborhood.

"I seemed to hit it off with Brian right away; I seemed to have a soul
affinity with him. We could touch each other on inner levels, even though
neither of us knew anything about it at the time or how to do it." This
meeting took place in January 1962, and Usher remembers that "the first
day I went over there, we wrote together. I played a little rhythm guitar
and a little bass, not much, and Brian played interesting piano. He knew
all the progressive progressions. He knew all about the Four Freshmen,
but he needed someone to help him break it down into contemporary
forms and make that vast knowledge apply to rock 'n' roll. In some respects,
I was a channel for that . . . In the beginning stages, it was vital."

Gary Usher's role in Brian's development was important, but as Gary notes, "Sometimes, after your usefulness has been used up, the creative spirit moves along. And that's good. It should happen that way, if it's honest." Brian has stated that it was Gary Usher who "showed me how to write songs; showed me the spirit of competition." The first song they wrote together was 'The Lonely Sea,' which, as Gary recalls, only took about twenty minutes to write. Besides working together, Brian and Gary also became very close friends.

One of the early songs they wrote together was '409,' a paean to a hot rod that Usher hoped he might someday own. That song was part of the package sold to Capitol. 'Surfin' Safari' was a big overnight hit in cities like Phoenix, Arizona. '409' was also a hit, giving the group its first two-sided success. Most rock groups had a few hits and disappeared, but it was beginning to look like the Beach Boys might be around for a while.

Between that second hit and the release of their first album, the Beach Boys garnered some valuable recording and performing experiences, which would greatly influence the careers of a Southern California duo who were "between hits."

Dean Torrence, of Jan and Dean, first heard the Beach Boys "on the radio, driving down Pacific Coast Highway." Dean remembers thinking, "'My God, that sounds like our stuff,' and being flattered that somebody thought it was good enough to copy . . . I don't remember ever feeling threatened. I was kind of interested."

Jan and Dean finally met the Beach Boys at a concert. In those days they were called hops, and the two groups were doing their first show together. "Since we weren't a self-contained band, [the Beach Boys] were going to back us up. So we met a couple of hours early in a house trailer and practiced . . . they learned our four songs and they had their six or seven."

The scene of the hop was near Hawthorne, the Beach Boys' home turf, and although Jan and Dean were the headliners, Dean recalls that "the audience was very pro-Beach Boy." After all, they were "local town heroes."

Live performances by rock groups were short in those days, and Dean noted that "it went by pretty quickly. After they did their songs, we did our songs . . . We didn't talk very much . . . The total concert was maybe a thirty-minute job." But the audience wanted an encore. The two groups hadn't rehearsed anything else, so Jan and Dean decided to perform two Beach Boys songs, 'Surfin'' and 'Surfin' Safari.'

Dean remembers, "They kind of looked at us as if to say, 'You'd do our songs with us *and* let us stand up front?' They thought they had to stand in the back . . . they were really amazed. We had a lot of fun doing it."

Jan and Dean realized that the trend in surfing music was a bandwagon they wanted to jump on, and they decided to record a couple of surf tunes on their next album, which they titled *Jan and Dean Take Linda Surfin'*.

At that time, Brian Wilson was writing the only vocal songs about surfing, so Jan and Dean called the Beach Boys and said, "We had so much fun at that concert, why don't you guys get together and we'll put your two songs on the album . . . and you can come and help us [record it]. They were thrilled. It was the first time their songs had been on an album." Jan and Dean were the first to recognize the potential of the surfing trend. When Brian Wilson and the Beach Boys ignited new fads, like hot-rod songs, Jan and Dean were there. Aided by Brian's songwriting, they had a long run on the charts milking the fads that the Beach Boys popularized and quickly deserted. Besides the records, which were Jan Berry's province, Jan and Dean were great performers. As native Californians, their tanned, sun-bleached looks epitomized California to the world. To some, the Beach Boys and Jan and Dean were one and the same. It was all California music and all full of fun.

The arrival of the Beach Boys presaged a new trend in popular music—the self-contained band: a group that wrote, produced and performed their own material. Nik Venet offers an interesting perspective on what effect they had on the record business. "It was a shot in the arm for the entire industry . . . It was a new form of . . . teenage music. It had nothing to do with your girlfriend, breaking up or driving off a cliff. It was a pure California phenomenon. The Beach Boys just represented California to the rest of the country . . . some sort of fantasy that was out there that just got triggered by the Beach Boys records."

Taking care of the business angle, Nik notes that their sales were overwhelming. Without the sales, the California fantasy would have been stillborn in Brian Wilson's head. Part of Brian Wilson's struggle as an artist was the resistance that he received from the record industry. Nik Venet was part of that resistance; still, he has come to understand what Brian was trying to do. Venet believes that Brian was five years ahead of the industry and that he has suffered for it. Brian and the Beach Boys were one of the first acts to break out of what Venet termed "the major label syndrome." Up until that time, all groups recorded in the studios provided by the label, used the engineers and producers and musicians that the label told them to use. Brian (with help from Murry) forced Capitol to let the group record outside Capitol's studios and to produce themselves, a first for the business. By forcing that policy change, Brian helped free California for young up-and-coming producers and musicians. Venet noted that, until then, New York had been the center for recording. Brian used young unknown musicians, and, along with Phil Spector, made people like Glen Campbell and Leon Russell studio stars long before they were successful on their own.

Roger Christian, a disc jockey and songwriter who co-authored a number of great tunes with both Brian and Jan Berry, felt that "the Beach Boys were not accorded the respect [by Capitol] because they were kids . . . and half the time, they'd come in, they wouldn't be wearing shoes, because that's the way it was. It was a hard thing to get the older people at Capitol to accept [the fact] that the Beach Boys were keeping them alive at the record company. Everything the Beach Boys did at Capitol, they had to fight for." Christian recalls the battle over where the Beach Boys were going to record and notes that part of the Capitol contract was that you had to record in their studio. Roger believes that the Beach Boys wanted to get out of Capitol because the studios were too large for the kind of music the group was doing.

Chuck Britz, who engineered almost all the Beach Boys' hits at Western Studios, thinks the group didn't feel comfortable at Capitol, and that Western was isolated from the business and therefore "they felt more free to do what they wanted to do." Britz notes that in any in-house studio, "It's easy for people to walk in and out and destroy the process that gets you going. If you're in a groove, there's nothing worse than somebody coming in and asking a political or a financial question."

Venet admits that the record companies in those days didn't care about the artists. "If you had a hit record and wanted to spend all your money, fine, because the law of averages was that you weren't going to have one tomorrow." The record industry at that time was filled with a lot of "old men" who had no vision, no understanding that the music that was happening was going to revolutionize their business. "The First Tycoon of Teen," Phil Spector (recognized as one of the greatest record producers ever), had already fought his battles and had established his own company so that he would have artistic freedom. Brian was the first artist to battle the executives successfully.

Brian and Phil were loved for what they were doing. Hal Blaine, considered the leading session drummer in the world, worked with both Spector and Brian Wilson and notes that "we, as the 'older musicians,' appreciated Brian 'cause at the time, I did sessions with guys who were into big band stuff, no pop music. They used to say things like, 'Now, I don't want you to tune up because we gotta play rock 'n' roll.' That's why so many [of those] people are not in the business today; they felt that rock 'n' roll was so *beneath* them . . . Everyone said, 'That's garbage, that's junk, it's crap. Why should we be subjected to play that kind of fourteen-year-old high school music?' No one knew that music was taking over the world, that it was what the world needed."

The musicians dug Brian, but Capitol Records never really tried to understand him; they never cared about him as a person. Capitol's disregard for Brian as an artist would severely damage Brian and the group's career when they started to grow musically away from the surfer image. As Dean Torrence recalls, "The whole idea with the record companies is to use you up as fast as they can, and once they do, they move on."

The move away from Capitol was an important step in Brian's development as a producer. Roger Christian notes that Nik Venet "had a definite idea of what a record would sound like, and Brian had his idea. Brian could take it from start to finish. He'd create the idea, produce it, and perform on it. Brian can handle it all. He knew what he could get out of his brothers, and how to work with them because they'd been doing it at home for years, and they didn't really feel they needed Nik . . . So those early records Brian produced, and Nik executive-produced."

Murry recalled that Brian came home one day and was almost crying and asked his dad for help: "Will you go down and tell Capitol we don't want [Venet] anymore, he's changing our sound." Murry then told Capitol's Voyle Gilmore, "You folks don't know how to produce a rock 'n' roll hit in your studios downstairs . . . Leave us alone," Murry demanded, "and we'll make hits for you." Murry and the group won two major battles. They were given the right to record outside of Capitol, and they quickly pushed Nik Venet totally out of the picture.

The first two Beach Boys albums bear the credit "Produced by Nik

Venet." Audree Wilson remembers that "Venet had his name on as producer, which was totally inaccurate. He had nothing to do with producing." Venet explains what he did as the Beach Boys' producer. "I would help Brian choose which songs to record from the dozens he had written. Also, I was an objective viewpoint. I would say to Brian, 'I don't think you need to do the record over.' The difficulty was, everybody was trying to write and arrange with him. As a producer, my job was to let him arrange and write, keep his theories alive. His ideas were always better than anyone's."

Whatever Venet's contribution, there can be no doubt that Brian was responsible for the development of the Beach Boys sound. Nobody, except Murry Wilson, would dispute that: "See, the whole world trade has given Brian credit for everything. Truthfully—I'm not beating myself on the back, but knowing them as their father, I knew their voices, right? And I'm musical, my wife is, we knew how to sing on key and when they were flat and sharp, and how they could sound good in a song." Murry's claim that he put on the echo and surged on the power "to make them sound like gods" isn't exactly accurate.

As engineer Chuck Britz remembers it, "That was his favorite line. Surge. He always said that. Surge here, surge there. I wouldn't do it because you can only surge so much." What Britz would do was to raise the volume of the control room monitor so that Murry would think that Britz was doing what Murry told him to do. On the actual recording, though, Britz wouldn't "surge." Britz notes that "basically, his ideas were right, like the dynamic power he wanted in a record, but you can only do so much. He was great; I really liked Murry." When it came to musical decisions, Britz recalls, it was almost always Brian. "Brian is the Beach Boys as far as I'm concerned. Brian was the only guy who could put all the parts together. The other guys helped a little, you'd see names, co-writer [etc.] . . . but you're talking about a guy getting credit that maybe just came up with a couple of changes, line-wise. The basic principle and the basic song were his . . . [A co-writer's credit] doesn't mean you actually have much to do with the song. There's a lot of people who give credit to other people. I still think the heaviest burden of it all was on Brian's shoulders, and he knew it."

In regard to the songwriting, Nik Venet has a similar opinion to Chuck Britz's. Concerning the insanity of the record business, Venet points out that "they pressured him into doing an album every twenty-four hours. They [the records] were incredible, but I think they also were burning him up and making him crazy."

Britz engineered every Beach Boys hit from 'Surfer Girl' to 'Good Vibrations,' but wasn't involved in the recording of the Beach Boys' first flop single, a rather lame 'Ten Little Indians,' the children's chant given the Beach Boys vocal treatment. Even though it wasn't a hit, the Beach Boys had a strong enough following by the fall of '62 that the record made it into the Top Fifty in the *Billboard* charts, peaking at number 49. But it only remained in the charts eight weeks, compared to seventeen weeks for 'Surfin' Safari.'

The Beach Boys' success as recording artists, momentarily slowed by the relative failure of 'Ten Little Indians,' picked up with the release of their first album, *Surfin' Safari*. Its success firmly established the Beach Boys as the nation's number-one surfing group and, combined with the hit singles, made them a lot of money.

For Brian, that "overnight success, overnight wealth . . . hit me the hardest." Brian welcomed his new lifestyle: "Just think, I don't have to get up and go to work and make my money. The money's rolling in from sales of records; I was just really set. It gave me a lot of confidence." But sudden fame "was frightening to me . . . there were a lot of challenges to overcome . . . I just felt it was a challenge at first, to handle it, to handle the success that had come."

The chief focus for Brian in those days was making hit records; as Brian once noted, "I don't need money, I could care less about money as far as having to spend it. I really could care less about how rich I get." As Audree Wilson recalls, "Brian was interested in the music. If it was a hit, great, but he did not think about money."

Mike Love recalled that it was "just unbelievable, the swift rise to a relatively secure position in music. People ask, 'Wasn't it a struggle? How long did it take before you were recognized?' And I say, 'About two weeks.'" That joking, hyperbolic boast aside, Mike continued, "The first song we did became a hit. The second song we did was a bigger hit."

While the Beach Boys' recording career was beginning to earn them considerable money, the Beach Boys as a live act was not a particularly impressive money-making machine in 1962.

By Murry's own admission, he held them back from major concerts because he didn't think they were ready for the "big time." He booked them at record store openings and local dances. Audree remembers that they used to drive to San Bernardino and other cities to play free shows. "It was a smart move, actually," Audree points out. "The DJs were all putting on their own dances at that time. They'd call, and we'd go." What no one will admit "on the record" is that, although the guys were never paid for what Murry called the "forty freebies," the Beach Boys did receive compensation in the form of valuable airplay. Because payola or plugola is illegal, nobody will acknowledge being involved, although it appears to have been a standard practice in the small towns for DJs to play the records of the groups who played "for free" at their dances. On the surface, it's not a very sinister practice, and it was a very good way for a group to build a following. Today, payola has been refined and is practiced as a very subtle and sophisticated art. Rock writers and DJs receive free records and concert tickets and press junkets (and drugs?), and there is the implied promise of advertising for your magazine or radio station if you give exposure to one of the company's artists. Airplay is strictly controlled today, and it is hard to purchase it overtly.

Besides the free shows, the steadily improving Beach Boys did play many gigs for pay, both as a featured attraction and as a backup band. Roger Christian remembers that he "used to do record hops, and the Beach Boys or the Surfaris were my backup group. I used to pay them about a hundred dollars a night, twenty dollars a man." Bob Eubanks, best known for hosting TV's *The Newlywed Game*, was a Los Angeles DJ in 1962. He recalls, "When I was a DJ at KRLA, I would hire the Beach Boys. I would pay them a hundred and fifty dollars to come out on Friday night and play Rainbow Gardens." Bob "had a good relationship with the guys, they were very nice . . . It was obvious that the father was the true boss of what was going on . . . I always thought Murry was a bit of a bullshitter, but he was in there plugging for his boys. For that, I admired him." Eubanks also tried "to get them to change their name because I felt that their name was so regional that they wouldn't have much success out of a coastal area."

Their records were *already* making the Beach Boys a well-known group *inland*, but, as performers, they hadn't strayed too far from L.A. The Beach Boys were still basically a regional act as 1962 came to a close. Nineteen sixty-three would be the year they'd become national stars.

CHAPTER 4

IF EVERYBODY
HAD AN OCEAN

THE THIRD YEAR OF THE BEACH BOYS' EXISTENCE, 1963, WAS THE YEAR THEY made their first mark on the burgeoning youth culture. In fact, the Beach Boys' impact was an important step toward creating a "sixties youth" that was different from the "Happy Days" of the fifties. The Beach Boys were singing about surfing and hot-rodding and surfer girls, but the song content was really more a metaphor for a sense of freedom. The group's music didn't have anything to do with adults, and that message came through quite clearly.

For teenagers in 1963, the Beach Boys were one of the first groups that was singing directly to them. The Beach Boys weren't singing about dissent and drugs—that wasn't what was happening at that time. The music functioned as a bridge between generations. It was the Beach Boys who blasted the teen idols into chart oblivion. After all, who needed them (they could only carry a tune) when there was a group of good-looking guys who not only could really sing but were writing their own songs and playing their own instruments?

Only a few of the group's fans rushed out and bought surfboards. Many of them, however, did buy the image of the ocean, the sun, and all the guys and girls who "were either out surfin' or they've got a party going." That's from 'Surf City,' an irresistible idyllic fantasy that appealed to millions. Actually, it was only part of a two-pronged musical attack masterminded by Brian Wilson that first cemented the allure of California firmly in the hearts of America's youth.

First, there was the Beach Boys' own 'Surfin' U.S.A.' Brian took an old Chuck Berry hit, 'Sweet Little Sixteen,' and transformed it into a surf anthem. *Surfin' Safari*, the Beach Boys' first album, had extolled the virtues of the surf life, but hadn't quite made it on sociological (let alone musical) terms. This time out, Brian struck a truly responsive chord. His universal surfer hit home in even the most landlocked locales, and 'Surfin' U.S.A.' reached #3. Brian had conquered the airwaves; next he would control the fantasies.

With superlative ease, Brian conceived 'Surf City,' a place where there were "two girls for every boy." In those blissfully chauvinistic days, what red-blooded male could willfully resist this picture of two tall, blonde California girls hanging on his arms while he braved the waves? Curiously, it wasn't the Beach Boys who got to sing about 'Surf City.' Friends and cohorts Jan and Dean had the #1 smash with the song, a sore point between Brian and the family, especially when they realized that Brian was singing on the record. It really didn't matter to the kids who was singing. The one-two punch of 'Surfin' U.S.A.' and 'Surf City' brought the "California Sound" and lifestyle attention on a national level.

With this magnificent myth in their back pockets, the Beach Boys finally broke out of the Southern California club scene and began playing dates all over the country, and, almost as importantly, began to make considerable money. The group's success on the road, however, wasn't the result of careful planning between Capitol Records and the William Morris Agency. Those agencies often signed talent without knowing what to do with it. That was the case with the Beach Boys. Their touring success was due to the foresight of a nineteen-year-old promoter named Fred Vail, who lived in the decidedly non-surfing city of Sacramento, California.

★　　★　　★　　★

El Camino High School in Sacramento had a problem. They had to raise money for the senior grad night party. Car washes and candy sales were all right as fundraisers, but not good enough to make the kind of money that was needed. So the high school kids went to one of their near peers, Fred Vail, who had just graduated the year before but who was known around town as a go-getter. From his early teen years on, Fred had worked at local radio stations and had been involved in concert promotion.

Fred knew that the Beach Boys' records were popular in Sacramento and thought they would be a good group for a concert. Doing a little investigative work, he found out that the boys were stuck in a rut in L.A., playing the local clubs for just a few hundred a night. Bob Eubanks remembers booking them into his chain of Cinnamon Cinder clubs in early '63. "We always did capacities when they played." Capacity, however, meant only four hundred people.

So the group was readily available for local shows, but they still hadn't headlined any real concerts.

Vail found out from Capitol Records that the Beach Boys were represented by the William Morris Agency. When he called the Morris Agency, Fred found out that "they weren't aware of the Beach Boys, didn't even know that one of their agents had signed the Beach Boys, didn't know who the Beach Boys were."

The young agent who had signed the group was Marshall Berle (nephew of comedian Uncle Miltie) who remembers that he first approached the Beach Boys when he saw them as one of the supporting acts at a Dick and Dee Dee show. Fred Vail picks up the story again: "Marshall had signed the Boys [they are always 'the Boys' to Fred] and we got together for negotiations. We agreed on five hundred dollars for one night's performance. So he went to Murry and Audree and presented the offer, and it was acceptable to them. Then, they realized that that kind of money wouldn't really take care of travel, so they came back to me and said, 'OK, we'll do it for five hundred dollars plus six round-trip air fares, or we'll do it for seven hundred and fifty dollars guaranteed.'" Unfortunately for the Beach Boys, Fred Vail's arithmetic was better than the Wilsons', so they ended up with the seven-fifty. Round-trip air fare at that time was about sixty dollars per person. Although this wasn't multimillion-dollar mismanagement, it was indicative of the Wilson parents' being in over their heads. Their hearts were in the right place; their financial skills weren't.

The deal was made, and Fred notes that "on the day before the show we made the deposit. You used to have to send fifty percent, and they'd send you a copy of the contract . . . Audree had signed the contract, and it was for Carl Wilson and four musicians." It is interesting that as early as 1963, a not yet seventeen-year-old Carl Wilson was the acknowledged onstage leader of the group.

Concert promoter Vail went to work, printing posters and tickets. The show was set for the Sacramento Auditorium, a hall that to that point had been used primarily for concert stars like Johnny Mathis and orchestras and traveling ballets. Most concerts in those days featured a half-dozen or more acts playing their current hit or two with a headliner. There weren't many rock concerts per se in 1963.

The tickets, which were only one dollar and seventy-five cents, were selling at a brisk pace. Vail used his radio contacts "to convince them that since we were doing it to raise money for El Camino High School's graduating class, they should give us public service announcements." With that clever claim, Vail got free radio advertising.

The afternoon of the concert, Vail got in his old station wagon and went to the airport to meet the Beach Boys. When the plane arrived, Murry and the Beach Boys got off. Significantly, that lineup included Al, Mike, Carl, Dennis, and David Marks. Brian, never a happy traveler, had stayed home.

Vail continued, "Now, you gotta remember that we're all kids . . . We're loading the equipment into the wagon and Carl says, 'Who's the promoter?' I said, 'I am,' and Carl says, 'You can't be, you're just a kid.' So I said, 'Well, you guys are young. I've been around.' And Carl said, 'Fine. Well, who's on the show tonight? Who's the opening act?' I said, 'Well, you guys.' And he said, 'Well, who else? Who's carrying the show?' And I said, 'You guys are the headliners.'"

Fred remembers that the boys all shared looks of astonishment "and said, 'We're not headliners.' And I'll never forget, Carl then said, 'You're going to take a beating tonight, aren't you?' And I said, 'No, I don't think so.'" Advance sales were over a thousand, so all the expenses had been covered; but it remained to be seen how many people would show up the night of the show. Fred was confident and reassured the guys, "'Just worry about the show, and let's get down to the auditorium and set up.' So we went to the auditorium, and we all got along great because we were all kids. It was my first big auditorium presentation, and it was their first shot as a featured act at an out-of-town show. We weren't a beach city, we were inland, and they didn't even know their popularity stretched that far."

As Vail recalls, "I was the kid with the radio voice; I emceed it. I went out there and introduced the boys as 'America's number-one surfing band.' They came out and did a forty-minute set, and the kids went crazy. Then there was a ten-minute intermission and then another forty-minute show. The Boys didn't know that much material, so primarily they just repeated what had gone over well for the first set and did a couple of other things . . . a lot of Chuck Berry, Dion. Al sang 'Runaway.'

"We had a super gate that night; we ended up with about three thousand kids, which was a tremendous crowd for just the Beach Boys back then." Indeed, the Beach Boys were used to playing small clubs for a few hundred people. A crowd of three thousand was an incredible rush, and it was an extra big surprise to them because they had expected to be only a supporting act.

Still unaware of how big an attraction they were rapidly becoming, the Beach Boys and Fred Vail went back to the hotel. The block-and-a-half walk took forty-five minutes because "the kids were trailing us . . . girls, guys asking for autographs, talking to us." When they got to the hotel, they sat at a long table to go over the financial results of the night. "Murry was counting the money," Vail remembers, "and they were all excited about it because it was their first time out of Southern California. Murry says, 'Hey, fellows, guess what? I just figured out how much we made tonight, and after the Morris commission and our expenses and stuff, we made fifty-two dollars apiece.' And the guys are all exclaiming 'Great! Super!' They'd spent it all already. And they said, 'Fred, how'd you do tonight, how'd you come out?' And I said, 'Oh, we made about four thousand dollars.' There was silence at the table; you probably could have heard a pin drop. They had to pick themselves off the floor . . . They were all astounded, and I said, 'Well, don't you guys make money like this normally?' I was really naive. I said, 'Hey, you guys did all the work, I just put the show together. The Morris office is really underselling you if you're only getting five hundred dollars a night. They're cleaning house on you guys.'"

Fred then made what he called a "naive, stupid blunder," but it has to rank as one of those showbiz legends that can't possibly be true. It was like Mickey Rooney saying, "I've got a great idea; why don't we put on the show ourselves!" Fred said, "'Why don't you guys just do your own shows?', not thinking about the ramifications of that statement. So Murry said, 'What do you mean?' And I said, 'You're popular in other cities besides Sacramento. Why don't you go into cities where you're popular, rent a hall, buy radio time, print tickets and do your own show?' And Murry said, 'Well, I can't because I have ABLE machinery company. I'm just doing this part-time, and the boys aren't generating that much money where I can give up my livelihood and support my family off this.' And I said, 'Well, I'll tell you what. I'd love to set up shows for you. We could work out something where I'd get paid out of the receipts or something.' And that was the beginning of what became American Productions, just one of those off-the-wall things whereby I made a naive statement that I thought was a natural idea." That "naive statement and natural idea" that was the birth of the Beach Boys' own company resulted in the growth of the activity that would provide the Beach Boys with a major portion of their income for years to come. Eventually the group's tours of the United States and the rest of the world would help make them one of the premier live "acts" in musical history. The tours would also be the only source of income after the hits stopped in 1968.

The growth of the Beach Boys as a concert attraction wasn't just important monetarily. The live shows were crucial in building the group's soon-to-be massive following. When a young fan buys records, it's for one set of reasons. Put that same fan in a concert hall with the group that made those hit records, and you've created a fanatic, a loyal follower who will buy your every record, come to see your concerts and join your fan club. Fred Vail may have stumbled onto the Beach Boys accidentally, but his contribution, which has usually been overlooked, was definitely an important part of the Beach Boys' success story.

One other interesting aspect of the Fred Vail/Murry Wilson discussion was Murry's contention that the Beach Boys weren't generating enough income to merit his full-time attention. Murry's failure to see the group's potential is odd. He pushed his sons so they could be the best, yet he didn't think they could make enough money to warrant his total attention. Nik Venet, the Wilsons' nemesis, claims that Murry thought so little of the group's future that Murry took Beach Boys income, and instead of buying much-needed new sound equipment and instruments, he leased a crane for his heavy machinery business. That doesn't sound like a man who was devoted to developing his sons' careers at any cost.

With their careers as live performers on the upswing, thanks to Fred Vail, the Beach Boys' recorded efforts were also showing significant improvement. Brian told the group's first interviewer, the writer/publicist/ photographer Earl Leaf (no relation to the author), that on 'Surfin' U.S.A.' "we developed a stylish sound, the high sound became our sound. It was the first time we had ever sung our voices twice on one record. It strengthens the sound. Sing it once, then sing it again over that, so both sounds are perfectly synchronized. This makes it much brighter and gives it a rather shrill and magical sound without using echo chambers. It makes it sound spectacular, so much power." To the listener, the type of vocal that Brian described was an important part of the appeal of their records and was an early use of vocal double-tracking in rock 'n' roll.

The sound was improving and so were the sales. Not only was 'Surfin' U.S.A.' a Top Ten hit, but the flip side, 'Shut Down,' was the group's first big car hit. Just as they launched the surfing fad in '62, the Beach Boys in 1963 reflected the teenage interest in cars. Although the Beach Boys have been typecast as musical faddists who cashed in on the latest teen crazes, it is important to realize that the Beach Boys, musically and lyrically, didn't stay in one area long enough to go stale or allow the public to get bored. Brian Wilson said, "When a new fad comes along, we'll be the first to ride it."

Brian, however, was quite aware of the fleeting quality of fads. He told Earl Leaf in 1964, "We can't become too dedicated to fads because our name could be too closely associated to them. Starting a fad is easier than ending it gracefully, like a love affair, and it's too dangerous to base a format on a temporary fad." Significantly, 'Surfer Girl,' released in the summer of '63, would be their *last* surfing hit. Within two years, the Beach Boys had started two major trends. Rather than continuing to exploit these fads, Brian Wilson left the spoils for groups like Jan and Dean. The Beach Boys' music remained in the teen genre only for the next two years. By the summer of '64, Brian was already examining broader themes. To Brian's and the group's detriment, the image of the Beach Boys never caught up with Brian.

Back in '63, though, Brian and the Beach Boys were the kings of surf, thanks to their hit with 'Surfin' U.S.A.' Brian explained the story behind that song. "I was going [out] with a girl named Judy Bowles at the time. And her brother Jimmy was a surfer, and he knew all the spots . . . I started humming the melody to the song 'Sweet Little Sixteen.' And what happened was I got fascinated with the fact of doing it. And I thought to myself, 'God, what about trying to put surf lyrics to the "Sweet Little Sixteen" melody!' . . . The concept was about 'they're doing this in this city, they're doing that in that city,' the Chubby Checker concept. So I thought of calling it 'Surfin' U.S.A.' (much like Checker's 'Twistin' U.S.A.'). I talked to Jimmy. I said, 'Jimmy, I want to do a song mentioning all the surf spots.' So he made a list and, by God, he didn't leave one out."

What the Beach Boys did leave out was a label credit for Chuck Berry. The early pressings of the record credited the song solely to Brian Wilson [Mike Love's name was left off too]. There was no mention of Berry's having written the melody, or of the Beach Boys' receiving permission to change Berry's original lyrics. That omission resulted in all future records crediting Chuck Berry as the author of 'Surfin' U.S.A.' It's noteworthy that with all the great compositions Brian was to write, the tune that established the Beach Boys as big recording artists was not an original melody. But Brian immediately made up for that with one of his own tunes, his first hit outside the Beach Boys.

"One day," Dean Torrence remembers, "Brian sat down at the piano and said, 'Do you want to hear our new single?' . . . and he does 'Surfin' U.S.A.' We [Jan and Dean] said, 'Hey, why don't you give that to us? We can make that a bigger hit than you.' Brian said, 'Nah, we're really looking forward to doing it . . . Well, I've got more, what about this?' . . . and he played 'Surf City,' which hadn't been completed but Brian had worked out the opening, a verse, and the chorus." Jan Berry finished the song with Brian, and Jan and Dean had a #1 hit, the first #1 song to emerge from the new "California Sound."

Besides co-writing 'Surf City,' Brian also sang on the record. Reportedly, Murry was heartbroken and furious at Brian's participation on a record by another surf group. Murry called Jan Berry a pirate for taking the song away from the Beach Boys. One day, knowing that the Beach Boys' family was at Western Studios, Jan arrived on the scene in full pirate's costume, complete with a patch over one eye. Most everybody thought it was funny.

Murry wasn't the only person upset over Brian's participation on 'Surf City.' The record caused quite a stir at Capitol Records when the field promotion men called Hollywood to find out why the new Beach Boys record had been released without their knowledge. Brian was contracted to Capitol, so his presence on the Jan and Dean record wasn't legal. Not much ever happened even though the cross-pollination between Jan and Dean and the Beach Boys continued for a number of years. Dean smugly recalls, "They were always threatening to sue and hold up royalties, but they could never figure out whose voice was whose because everybody sounded so much alike, especially on the background vocals."

There never were any lawsuits over Brian's "extracurricular" singing, but the Beach Boys were continually having problems with Capitol. When the Beach Boys had their first big two-sided hit, 'Surfin' U.S.A.'/'Shut Down,' the group released an album named after the surf hit. Capitol and Nik Venet exploited the Beach Boys by releasing an album called *Shut Down* which included only two Beach Boys songs, both already released; the rest of the album was hot-rod music that the Beach Boys had nothing to do with. Capitol was trading on the Beach Boys' success without even mentioning their plans to the group. The Beach Boys did learn their lesson, and when 'Surfer Girl' and 'Little Deuce Coupe' were both hits, the Beach Boys made sure *they* had the albums named after the hits. Although the three 1963 Beach Boys albums contained some of the same songs, it didn't seem to matter to the fans, who bought them all, particularly *Little Deuce Coupe*. That album, filled with car tunes, was the Beach Boys' first theme LP.

The sun, the surf and the cars were the images most closely associated with the Beach Boys' big sellers, but the band wasn't a fad. Kids learn to separate the novelty groups from those they want to keep around for a while. Brian Wilson's music had gotten very good, very quickly. For instance, there was 'Surfer Girl,' a song with one of the prettiest introductions Brian's ever done. It was also one of the first songs that Brian ever wrote, and it has remained special to the fans and to Brian for an important reason. The song was written about Judy Bowles, and as Gary Usher recalls, "Brian's girlfriend when I met him was Judy. Bonnie, my first wife, and I used to double-date with Brian and Judy and go out and drink beer, make love. They went through some incredible trips, those two. Brian was sensitive at that age, and she left her fingerprints on him for life. I think she was the one who broke off the relationship." Usher notes that they were close to getting formally engaged, but then the affair ended. "The going together and the breaking up and the ons and offs and the pressures and the problems and the hurtings were all a trauma for Brian. Sometimes he couldn't write for weeks at a time. This was in 1962 and '63. Aside from the times with Judy, his highs were high and his lows were low, like most creative people. In that respect, Brian was quite a ways out on a limb, even in those days." As Usher recalls, "Judy was the first girl he really fell in love with, and she definitely left her mark on him."

Usher also remembers the more personal times he spent with Brian, when they "would talk about deep, philosophical subjects as well as we were capable of at the time. Brian and I were close, though. We shared a lot of viewpoints." Often the two friends had great fun because, as Usher recalls, "Brian had a great sense of humor. We would sit and laugh like a bunch of goons. It was a good release for him. We used to sit and laugh and go crazy. We liked to tease Murry, and this would of course infuriate Murry. I would say to Brian, 'Look what he did, I can't believe he did that; we should get even with him for that.' That's one of the ways I was a bad influence. Brian couldn't do too much, because he has to live with the guy, he's a son, but I didn't have that over my head. I would always be loose with him because I wasn't his son, and that looseness influenced the guys."

One time they decided to play a trick on Murry. "There was this myna bird whistle that reminded us of Murry. So one night, at about three in the morning, we snuck up to his window. He always slept right by the window, wanted to keep an eye on the neighborhood. So we took the tape of this bird call and hooked it up under his window, got inside Brian's car and turned it on. A couple of minutes later, we heard, 'I know you're out there! I know it's you, you better step forward now. Brian, is that you? I know it's Usher!' Of course, it's a tape recording so he can't find anybody, and we're out in the car. I couldn't hold it in any longer, and I let out a shriek, and then Brian let out a shriek. And here's this car with no visible occupants, but all this incredible laughter coming out of the car because the windows were down. He could tell our laughter and that did it. I was always on his blacklist from that day."

With Brian at the piano, (L-R) Al, Mike, Carl and (in the foreground) Dennis gather to hear and learn a new song.
Credit: Michael Ochs Archives/Getty

'Surfer Girl' was the Beach Boys' first ballad hit, reaching #7 in the summer of '63, and it established the group's versatility. Whether it was an up-tempo or a slow number, the harmonies were special. According to Brian, "I incorporated some Freshmen harmony in 'Surfer Girl'; we retained a certain amount of the influence of the Freshmen in our group sound."

The harmonic appeal as well as the quality of innocence in songs like 'Surfer Girl' make the music as current in 1978 as it was in 1963. That kind of longevity is rare in pop music and it's not an achievement to be ignored in an age of disposable everything, including music.

Brian was creating beautiful and timeless music by 1963, but there were already musical indications that everything was not right in his world. Each album included at least one melancholy tune, like 'The Lonely Sea' or 'In My Room.' Gary Usher remembers the latter as one of the last songs he wrote with Brian, and that to him and Brian your room is just like your world, "and Brian and I had just gone through that, having your world be your room. We were just trying to write anything that would relate to kids. It was probably the most sensitive song up to that time."

Usher remembers that it was written in the Wilsons' old rehearsal room, and that "Brian was playing the organ and I was playing the bass. We would just sit and ideas would fly out fast and furious. We edited each other." The writings were in the vein of trying to relate "to kids like us or kids younger." Brian remembers that "I had a room and I thought of it as my kingdom. And I wrote that song, very definitely, that you're not afraid when you're in your room . . . It's absolutely true." What is eerie is that Brian musically predicted the place he would pick to retreat to when the world became more than he could bear. During his so-called "reclusive period," the answer to the question "Where's Brian?" was often answered, "He's in his room."

Besides the already increasing demands on his creativity, Brian was also expected to perform at all the group's personal appearances. As Fred Vail recalled, "Brian never really got off on performing and as early as May 1963 he was missing concerts." As demanding as they were on his time, Brian did get a certain amount of pleasure from the live singing. He once remarked, "It was the most amazing thing I could think of." In 1964, Brian told Earl Leaf that "we've been hearing screams [from the audience] for three years straight and we've grown dependent on that sound. So much fun. Believe me, nothing better for the ego—maybe it's too good for the ego." As Roger Christian notes, "Brian did and didn't like to play live, it's hard to explain." What he didn't like was the time away from his work, the stage fright, and the increasing sound volume that was beginning to bother his one good ear. Those reasons never changed, and it is curious that Brian returned to touring in the latter half of the 1970s.

In addition to his dislike of live performing, Brian was also having difficulties in other areas. He was having trouble dealing with the group's rapid rise and the increased pressures that success brought. Brian was not a stay-at-home as a teenager; he was an athlete, an active person. Less than two years into the Beach Boys' existence, Brian was already partially in retreat, although in 1963, the highs and lows were relatively balanced and Brian was a "happy" person.

As a hitmaker, Brian was having no problems at all. He was incredibly prolific; the melodies seemed to spill from his head onto the records and resulted in an incredible string of seven straight Top Ten singles. As Chuck Britz remembers, Brian was so fruitful that "he could write a song on the spot that would be a hit" and he might not use it because "he'd come up with something better and he'd use it" instead.

The music world loved Brian's work, yet Murry could still find fault with Brian's ideas. Audree Wilson insists that Brian and Murry "didn't fight a lot about the music," but she relates one disturbing incident that may exemplify the kind of arguments that occurred between father and son. "When Brian wrote 'Surfin' U.S.A.,'" Audree recalls, "I was down in the music room with him and Murry was up in the bedroom watching TV. Murry came rushing down, and he criticized his [Brian's] rhythm. Brian was furious, just furious. He said, 'Fuck you!' It was just horrible. And I said, 'Brian!' And Carl was sitting down there, too, and he said, 'Brian!' Murry never got over that . . . he used to bring that up to me. I was supposed to go over there and hit Brian with a board, or clobber him or some horrible thing because he said that. I didn't approve of it [the profanity], but I didn't think it called for that."

There were two other noteworthy events that took place in 1963. Brian broke up with Judy Bowles, and Gary Usher helped his lovelorn pal by introducing him to Marilyn Rovell, a cousin of a girl he was dating, Ginger Blake (whose real name is Sandra Glantz). Marilyn eventually became Mrs. Brian Wilson.

The other big happening was the return of Al Jardine to full-time status as a Beach Boy. With Al back in "the family," the Beach Boys' lineup appeared to be set; however, 1964 would be the last year Brian Wilson would be a full-time Beach Boy.

It was also the year that the decade called "the sixties" finally began in California. The years from 1960 to 1963 had been an extension of the fifties' easygoing complacency. The assassination of President John Kennedy may have ended the fifties for California. If it hadn't, the Vietnam War certainly would have. Still, as 1963 ended, California was mostly preoccupied with itself. It took the arrival of the Beatles to shake that sunny state out of its blissful provincialism.

The Beach Boys on *The Ed Sullivan Show*, September 1964.
Courtesy of SOFA entertainment.

CHAPTER 5

DON'T WORRY BABY

FOR THE BEACH BOYS, 1963'S "TEEN TITANS" OF POP MUSIC, 1964'S BRITISH invasion was as welcome as the war of 1812. The Boys didn't have much choice, however, and they watched morosely as the Beatles took control of the charts. The Beatles were all that mattered in the world of popular music in 1964. They would often have more than one song in the Top Ten (once, the Top Five singles), and it was virtually impossible to turn on the radio or the TV or read the newspaper or a magazine without the Beatles jumping out and hitting you over the head.

While many American groups fell by the wayside, the Beach Boys rose to the challenge of fresh competition and continued their string of hits that was only rivaled by the Beatles' own success. Brian's self-proclaimed war with the Beatles was just one of the competitive struggles that he placed himself in. His other major foe was Phil Spector. As a producer, Spector was an early idol, occasionally a co-worker, and the ultimate influence for Brian in production technique. In 1964, Brian's battle for production superiority only stimulated his creative juices. The Beatles' fame was unbeatable, so Brian fought the group on record. At the time, the Beach Boys couldn't match their sociological significance, but he could and did make records that were better produced, incorporated more sophisticated harmonics, and, in their own way, were the first real concept albums. *Shut Down, Vol. 2* and *All Summer Long* stand today as the peak of Brian and the group's "simpler" period, when he had begun to master the studio. His compositions were tight, and the spare, teenage lyrics, collaborations with Mike or with others, were a perfect reflection of what a Beach Boy was supposed to do and be. Brian's harmonies and arrangements, on songs like 'Hushabye' and 'Girls on the Beach,' were incredibly full and lush. It would be unfair to compare the Beatles' earliest productions to Brian's 1964 work.

93

The arrival of the English bands also began to change the Beach Boys' listening audience. In '62 and '63, the group's fans included more guys than girls. The "tough" British groups like the Rolling Stones and the Animals attracted many of the Beach Boys' male fans. They had originally liked the group's masculine surfer image, but they left the Beach Boys for the new, "cooler" groups. The girl fans, though, stuck by the group. This imbalance in fan appeal would eventually contribute to the group's downfall. The girls would be stolen away by groups like Herman's Hermits and the Monkees, and the more socially aware, older fans would be turned off by the group's non-political stance. (Despite the fact that Carl Wilson would be indicted for refusing induction into the army as a religious conscientious objector against the war in Vietnam.) All that was in the future, but these first stirrings of healthy competition may have been one of the factors contributing to Brian's imminent nervous breakdown.

There were certainly enough hints in some of the more melancholy songs like 'In My Room,' 'The Warmth of the Sun' and 'We'll Run Away'; those tunes, however, were reflecting emotions that hadn't yet become overwhelming. By the end of 1964, the pressures were to prove too much for this still youthful man. Shortly after marrying sixteen-year-old Marilyn Rovell, Brian Wilson suffered a nervous breakdown. Before the break, Brian and the Beach Boys were to travel the world and enjoy fan acclaim second only to the Beatles. Troubled times were ahead, but first there was a peak.

★   ★   ★   ★

Brian Wilson: "The Beatles' invasion shook me up an awfully lot . . . They eclipsed a lot [of what] we'd worked for . . . eclipsed the whole music world. Michael and I got together and had a meeting and we talked it over. We were very threatened by the whole thing."

To Mike Love, the Beach Boys really held their own: "Even with the Beatles being enormously successful, we still had 'I Get Around'" as a #1 record at the height of Beatlemania. That song, backed by 'Don't Worry Baby,' is one of the best single records ever released, and it became the group's first #1 hit. Mike also felt that the Beatles "further challenged Brian musically in his creativity."

Brian was definitely up to the challenge. He and Mike began the year by consolidating all their ideas on cars and girls and hamburger stands into a huge hit, 'Fun, Fun, Fun.' It was one of their last hits to present a simplistic, trouble-free world.

Brian's world was growing increasingly difficult. Part of the problem was that Capitol Records still treated Brian as some kid who made a lot of hit records, and they never realized he was a sensitive young man. Incidents like the following story demonstrated Capitol's disregard for Brian as a person, and probably helped push him into a protective shell.

Roger Christian recalls that late in 1963, "Capitol was throwing a big reception at the Beverly Wilshire [Hotel] for Kyu Sakamoto, who had a big record called 'Sukiyaki.' The Beach Boys had had a couple of big records for Capitol, but they didn't have a party. So I was going and I asked Brian to come with me . . . we were writing together. We got there, and Brian was talking to somebody, and he came over kind of discouraged. [The Capitol executive] Voyle Gilmore had told him that he had no business being there, he was upstaging Kyu. And I said, 'Just a minute, you're here as my guest, and we're writing some songs that are eventually going to make this goddam company some money. What is this little game?' This is just one example of the typical things Capitol would do."

Roger Christian was a DJ at KFWB in Hollywood, and Gary Usher took Brian up to the station one night after Roger got off the air at midnight. They began writing songs together and Brian later noted that Roger "was like a guiding light to me." Brian and Roger spent many late nights eating hot fudge sundaes at Aldo's coffee shop and talking and writing songs. Christian, very much a macho personality, is another admirer of Murry Wilson and he remembers how Murry had to fight the people at Capitol all the time. "It was only through Mr. Wilson's persistence that the Beach Boys did get a fair shake, because Capitol was bugged because they didn't record at the [Capitol] Tower; [also,] they weren't crazy about the surf image."

Christian was intimately involved in the creative process with Brian in 1963 and early 1964. One song they co-authored, 'Don't Worry Baby,' became the first pop standard created by Brian Wilson. Although its sometimes indecipherable lyric was love-oriented, not everyone realized that Brian was singing about a drag race. Regardless of the lyrical content, the melody is so good that many singers and groups have recorded the song, usually rewriting the lyrics. As recently as the summer of 1977, the song was a major hit for B.J. Thomas, an indication of the staying power of the music.

Christian was witness to many of the battles that the Beach Boys had with Capitol and remembers that to "the people at Capitol . . . the Beach Boys had always been a thorn in their side, Mr. Wilson especially, because he wasn't going to put up with anything that wasn't fair and square." Capitol was always trying to assign overhead costs to the Beach Boys, like shifting to their account a "five-thousand-dollar expense for Studio A at Capitol" when the Beach Boys weren't even using the studio. Murry would have to fight the accountants. "So every time Murry would come to the [Capitol] Tower, Karl Engemann would get a few more grey hairs because he knew he'd have to referee a battle between Voyle and Murry." (As a brief aside, Karl Engemann is one of the few Capitol executives that the Beach Boys remember fondly, Audree Wilson noting that Engemann would often have dinner at the Wilson house. He was a gracious businessman.)

Christian claims that, "if it weren't for Murry in those early days, pushing, the royalties wouldn't have been what they were . . . Murry fought hard to get things straight." As hard as Murry fought, it took a lawsuit and years of out-of-court wrangling in the late sixties before the Beach Boys got either a proper accounting of sales or the money that was due Brian for producer's royalties. The Beach Boys were taken advantage of by their record company, but that wasn't rare. None of the early rock talent, with few exceptions, ever saw the money they really earned from their records.

Back on the Beatlemania front, the Beach Boys embarked (in November) on a twenty-four-day trip to England and the continent that included radio and television appearances, promotional stops, and a few concerts. The tour was one of Brian's last until 1976, and Roger Christian offers additional insight into how Brian felt about live performing: "Brian liked it for a while . . . but it was tiring on him . . . Brian was a private person; he wanted to be left alone so he could create. The guys would come back from the tour all exhausted" and they would rest and relax. But "the record company would say to Brian, 'OK, where's the single? Where's the album?' So he'd have to sit down and write it, arrange it, polish it all up, and go into the studio, perform it, and then get out of the studio and mix it and master it and *then* go back on the road again. He couldn't do it, there was no way he could do it."

Circa, Fall 1965, "the boys" gather at Capitol in front of a wall of their gold records.
(L-R) Mike, Al, Dennis, Carl and Brian.
Credit: Michael Ochs Archives/Getty

The pressure from the record company was just one of the forces at work on Brian. As the music got more sophisticated, Brian relied more and more on studio musicians to get the sound he wanted. Christian remembers Brian saying, "'I don't know how to tell Dennis that the drumming on "Little Deuce Coupe" isn't his.' Brian didn't want to hurt his brother's feelings." Christian reminded Brian that "in the past when you haven't felt something was right, and let it go, you've lived to regret it. Dennis will understand. He won't be very happy about it, but . . . everyone in the group really respects you and your opinions." It was never easy for Brian to hurt anyone; often he would take the hurt himself. All Brian wanted to do was make music, but the politics got to him.

Brian's confidence could also be easily shattered. Brian was planning to release 'Little Honda' as a single, but as Chuck Britz recalls, "All you had to do was have somebody give him some doubts and it would make him start thinking negatively. And it would hurt. It could be a perfect stranger. [This happened] mainly because he wanted to please everyone." Brian decided not to release the song and the Hondells had a huge hit with the disc, produced by Gary Usher, who copied Brian's harmony lines note for note.

Brian's efforts to create the best records were inhibited not only by outsiders, but from within himself. Roger Christian recalls that, "as confident as he was, or as he should have been because he was a master, he still needed someone to encourage him and give him confidence . . . Brian was the most talented creator I'd ever worked with. Brian could do it all, he could write the words, write the music, teach the guys the harmony, produce the record." In explaining why Brian often worked with a collaborator, Christian saw "that sometimes somebody just needs a sounding board, almost like a competition thing . . . Two creative people get together and they bring out the best in each other. [But] he did a lot of things by himself."

November 1964, it's a bit of "BeachBoymania" on the group's first trip to England.
Credit: RB / Getty Images

For Brian, songwriting was a solitary pursuit. In a conversation with Earl Leaf in 1964, Brian described the drives and inspirations involved in songwriting. "I usually get down to writing songs late at night . . . I'm very inspired—mostly when I'm feeling inferior. Probably my greatest motive for writing songs is an inferiority feeling, or I'm lacking in something. I have to feel right on top. I just have that competition feeling. I hear something that is really good and all of a sudden, I feel like an ant. I must create something to bring me up on top. Perhaps some write because they think of money. Money is not my motive. I've never written a note because I think the song will make money." Brian's sense of inferiority and lack of self-worth would become increasingly troublesome. The financial security the songwriting gave Brian was important at first, but as the years wore on, money didn't mean a lot to him except that he could indulge a few special whims, like putting his piano in a sandbox.

Even in those fabulously successful days, "Brian was up and down," according to Christian. "One day he knew he had it made, and the world was digging what he did, and the next day, one little thing would happen and put him on a downer. When he was happy, he produced great stuff. It was easy for me to see that and encourage him." As an example of the kind of negative things that could happen, Christian relates the story of what happened when the Beach Boys recorded 'The Lord's Prayer.' Capitol "sort of went, 'I don't know,' and that crushed Brian because that was a work of art. No matter how great his accomplishments were, he'd pick up the negative vibes and retreat."

Brian was well aware of what the pressure was doing to him. He told Earl Leaf that he just wanted "to adjust to the music industry as much as possible." Brian must have also been uncertain about the future in September '64 because he told Earl that "I only like to plan not more than a month ahead of time." Lyrically, was Brian (with Mike's wordplay) expressing the first signs of his dissatisfaction with the group's career direction in 'I Get Around' . . . serving notice that he was looking for new horizons? "I'm getting bugged driving up and down the same old strip / I gotta find a new place where the kids are hip."

In 'When I Grow Up (To Be a Man),' he and Mike would express anxieties over the changes everybody would experience as an adult. "Will I dig the same things that turned me on as a kid? / Will I look back and say that I wish I hadn't done what I did? . . . What will I be? When I grow up to be a man." Brian: "I think I took a chance, made it a little too modern and harmonic. I'm kind of worried about it."

The song featured one of Brian's most inventive arrangements to date, and the background vocals ominously tolled the years as they quickly passed by: "Twenty-two, twenty-three / Won't last forever." Brian's almost prescient awareness of his future is frightening in retrospect. There is no question about it. Brian, in 1964, was a man who knew that his life would soon be taking new directions, and he was concerned as to how he would cope with adulthood complicated by massive success.

One other song played a role in an ironic misprint. The last song on side two of the group's final original studio LP in 1964 was called 'Don't Back Down.' On early copies, the song was titled 'Don't Break Down' on the album covers. This rather prophetic mistake aside, this Wilson/Love song contains an interesting lyric sung from a parental point of view. 'Don't Back Down (Not My Boys).' Brian was singing to the surfers when he sang, "You gotta be a little nuts / But show 'em now who's got guts." As Brian sang it, "They grit their teeth / They don't back down." Was Brian singing the song to himself? This excerpt from a 1977 interview indicates that it was at least a possibility: "There was a compulsion involved [in pouring out singles]. We did it out of a compulsive drive. You see so many pressures happening at once, and you grit your teeth, and you more or less flip out. There were a lot of pressures and a lot of scenes going down that I couldn't handle, that I couldn't quite understand, that I couldn't fathom." Before the pressure forced a cave-in. Brian thinks it put him "in a state of creative panic, where you begin to use your creativity to give to people. Something was lacking. I felt the creativity, but something was lacking; something was wrong somewhere."

As the pressures mounted, the group began to reflect the tension and, after an Australian tour, they fired Murry as their manager. As Audree recalls, "There was a lot of strife and problems in Australia." Dennis says that the guys just got tired of "hundred-dollar fines for swearing," but it was more than that. As Brian explained, "We changed from our father to outside management basically because of the emotional strain we were under. We didn't feel that we were driving for the things we should have been since we are in a golden position to progress and become possibly more successful. We felt that even though my father had his heart behind it and had good intentions, because of the situation between father and son, you just seem to go nowhere. It's an emotional struggle, and that's more or less a crippled situation, so we eliminated it. It was done more or less maturely. Finally, we decided he is better as a father than a manager."

The firing left Murry "just devastated," Audree notes. "It really crushed him. And he went to bed for about five weeks, totally just stayed in bed." That was an interesting precedent for behavior that would soon get Brian labeled "crazy."

On December 7, 1964, Brian married sixteen-year-old Marilyn Rovell. Audree Wilson remembers that, although "Brian had known her for quite a while, my husband was scared. Oh God! He would have had them stay unmarried for a long time had he had his own way. I don't suppose he ever thought there was anyone good enough for his boys; he was one of those kind of fathers."

Looking worn down on tour, circa 1964. Brian and Dennis up front,
Al is over Dennis's left shoulder.
Credit: Michael Ochs Archives/Getty

Shortly after the wedding, Brian and the Beach Boys left for a short tour of the Southwest. At the airport, Brian thought he saw Marilyn and Mike Love exchange romantic glances. Brian, in a 1966 interview with Earl Leaf, described what happened that night. "We were on tour December twenty-third. I said goodbye to Marilyn. We weren't getting along too good. The plane had been in the air only five minutes. I told Al Jardine that I was going to crack up any minute. He told me to cool it. Then I started crying. I put a pillow over my face and began screaming and yelling. Then I started telling people I'm not getting off the plane . . . started to get far out, coming undone, having a breakdown, and I just let myself go completely. I dumped myself out of the seat and all over the plane, I let myself go emotionally. They took care of me well. They were as understanding as they could be. They knew what was happening, and I was coming apart. The rubber band had stretched as far as it would go.

"That night, I cooled off, and I played that show. Next morning, I woke up with the biggest knot in my stomach, and I felt like I was going out of my mind. In other words, it was a breakdown period. I must have cried about fifteen times the next day. Every half hour I'd start crying. Carl came to my hotel room, I saw him and I just slammed the door in his face. I didn't want to see him or anybody, because I was flipping out. Nobody knew what was going on. I wouldn't talk. I just put my head down and wouldn't even look at anybody. That night, the road manager took me back to L.A., and I didn't want to see anybody except my mother. She was at the airport to meet me. As soon as I saw her, I started crying again. I just needed to hear her talk to me; it's a kind of security to be able to talk to your mother as I can talk to Audree. We went over to the house and we had a three-hour talk there. I told her things I'd never told anyone in my life, and she sort of straightened me out. Generally, I dumped out a lifelong hang-up."

Remembering that night, Audree Wilson describes what happened. "We received a phone call . . . saying that Brian was coming home and that he had been crying and breaking down and couldn't carry on. He [Dick Cummings—an accountant and a road manager] made it very clear that only I was to meet Brian, not his father . . . Once again, my husband was just crushed, and oh, just furious with me." Instead of being totally concerned with what was happening to Brian, Murry had found a reason to get angry and be hurt. As Brian said, looking back on the whole experience, "My dad always had a problem of understanding people and their feelings."

Audree Wilson resumes the story: "I met Brian at the airport, and we got in the car" and went to the house in Hawthorne, which the Wilsons still owned even though they were living in Whittier. At the house, Brian was "really in a bad state, he was crying and then he would stop crying, and he'd talk about . . ." At that point, Audree refused to reveal any more. The "lifelong hang-up" Brian unloaded that night is a secret that Brian and Audree still share. The fact that Brian didn't want Murry at the airport indicates that Murry was part of the problem. The precise cause of Brian's first breakdown, or the two that followed in the next seventeen months, will never be known for sure, but some of the serious problems certainly centered on the pressures from the record company, his family, and the group.

As 1964 ended, Brian Wilson noted that "there were four Beach Boys on the road . . . they finished that tour without me. When they came back, I didn't want to talk to them or anybody. I just wanted to sit and think and rest, pull myself together, check my life out, and once again evaluate what I am, what I'm doing, and what I should be doing." The Beach Boys' troubled leader was at home, making a fateful decision.

CHAPTER 6

PLEASE LET ME WONDER

BY MID-1965, THERE WERE TWO SEPARATE AND VERY DISTINCT "GROUPS." On the road, the Beach Boys were five guys singing the hits night after night, Brian Wilson's musical messengers to the world. Back home in Los Angeles, Brian Wilson was composing songs, producing backing tracks that awaited the return of the touring Beach Boys for their vocals. Brian was almost a self-contained band himself; he could play most every instrument and sing all the parts. When the group was in town, they were Brian's vocal musical instrument.

In popular music, the year was one of considerable upheaval. The Byrds broke through with Bob Dylan's 'Mr. Tambourine Man.' The Beatles' *Rubber Soul* album was more complex lyrically than their earlier work, reflecting Dylan's influence as well as their use of an exotic "new" herb. The effect Dylan was having on rock music didn't go unnoticed anywhere, even in the hedonistic sounds of the Beach Boys.

Because Brian Wilson was always progressing musically, the new lyrical slant of pop music didn't catch him by surprise. In songs like 'When I Grow Up' and 'Please Let Me Wonder,' Beach Boys records were already focusing on more adult themes. It was a very short step for Brian to create the introspective *Pet Sounds* that brought him both critical acclaim and business problems. The Beach Boys themselves, underneath the striped shirts, were also growing and changing. Two more of them were now married. There was a definite disparity between the group's image in the fan magazines of the time and the reality of their non–Beach Boys existence.

★　　★　　★　　★

For Brian Wilson, 1965 was the last year that he bowed to commercial pressures. The record company (as did the fans) wanted tunes like 'California

Girls' and 'Help Me, Rhonda'; Brian, in a sense, was marking time until he was ready to spring his concept on the music world. That surprise was a year away, and Brian Wilson in 1965 wasn't the troubled, brooding introvert so much as he was a single-minded artist in pursuit of an ultimate sound and a man in search of himself.

Brian's retirement from the road didn't really hurt the group's reception at their concerts and personal appearances. The Beach Boys sounded and looked the same as always, and their fans sensed nothing amiss. At that stage of the group's career, there weren't that many fans who knew the individuals in the band except for the girls screaming for Dennis. The Beach Boys have always been a sound and a feeling; they've been a perpetual good-time music machine. In 1965, the faces were slightly different, but the music hadn't really changed.

Brian stayed at home and made new music; the Beach Boys went on the road and recreated the older sounds. What isn't so well known is that, in 1965, Brian took his first step toward self-discovery with LSD. Drugs, quitting the road, experimental sounds—three years into their existence and the Beach Boys' leader was undergoing significant personal changes. Problems soon arose, as Brian moved ahead of the rest of the group. As one writer put it, "Brian wanted to drop a tab [of acid], while the other guys wanted to keep hanging out at the hamburger stand." Those growing differences would be reflected in the music, and the dichotomy of their personalities would eventually create conflict within the group, particularly, by most accounts, between Mike and Brian. That was still a year away, but its beginnings were rooted in Brian's experimental 1965.

It's been said that Brian Wilson, despite all the pressures of the business, rarely did anything important that he didn't want to do. By the end of 1964 Brian no longer wanted to tour; he was into making records and wanted to devote his time to studio music. His breakdown provided him with the excuse he needed to get off the road, and he rapidly reached his decision to retire from live performing. Now, he had to tell the Beach Boys. It was during the recording of *The Beach Boys Today* album that Brian dropped his bombshell.

"One night, I told the guys I wasn't going to perform onstage anymore, that I can't travel. I told them I foresee a beautiful future for the Beach Boys group, but the only way we could achieve it was if they did their job and I did mine. That night, when I gave them the news of my decision, they all broke down. I'd already gone through my breakdown, and now it was their turn. When I told them, they were shaken. Mike had a couple of tears in his eyes, he couldn't take the reality that their big brother wasn't ever going to be onstage with them again. It was a blow to their sense of security, of course."

Brian, in his interview with Earl Leaf in 1966, remembered how the guys reacted to his announcement: "Mike lost his cool and felt like there was no reason to go on. Dennis picked up a big ashtray and told some people to get out of there or he'd hit them on the head with it. He kind of blew it, y'know . . . Al Jardine broke out in tears and broke out in stomach cramps. He was all goofed up and my mother, who was there, had to take care of him." One of the Beach Boys did handle it well. "Good old Carl was the only guy who never got into a bad emotional scene. He just sat there and didn't get uptight about it. He always kept a cool head. If it weren't for Carl, it's hard to say where we'd be. He's the greatest stabilizing influence in the group. He's been like that ever since he was a kid, and he's like that now together with a lot of experience and brains. Carl has mastered his emotions. He cooled Dennis, Mike and Al down."

Earl Leaf: "Carl's a serious type of guy; he used to take the responsibility that everything would go smoothly . . . he held it all together at times. And he worried a lot, but he never complained." As Audree Wilson notes, "Carl was born thirty."

Nervous breakdowns are often regarded as escape valves, the only way out of an untenable situation. Life on the road was unacceptable for Brian Wilson, and he had to get off the road. He knew he couldn't quit without a good excuse, and the breakdown, as real as it was, provided Brian with that excuse.

Brian's guilt over quitting was inappropriate, but that retrospective comment doesn't help him. What it does is point out that there was a basic battle raging within Brian that centered around a very crucial area. Would Brian do what was best for Brian, or would he do his "manly duty" and what was best for everyone else? It is a classic artistic dilemma. An artist must put aside obligations to family and friends; he must put his art and himself first. For a while, Brian was able to do that to a remarkable degree, but the clashing emotions of artistic integrity versus family responsibilities would eventually be resolved in favor of the family. When

Brian was hurt, even though his family caused much of that pain, he retreated to the safety of the family situation. The family's way of life may not have been what Brian wanted, but it was a secure existence. Artists rarely have secure or safe lives. Brian ventured out into the artistic world, and wounds inflicted upon him by that world, combined with the effects of LSD, drove him into retreat. It was and still is a tragedy that Brian, who really only wants to make music, has to deal with so much "static." The static eventually overwhelmed Brian.

That, however, was all in the future. Back in '65, Brian stood up for his artistic beliefs and remembered saying, "If you want me to be able to be creative like I really want to, I'm going to have to stay at home." As Brian recalled, "Sure enough, I got my way." Indeed, for a short time, Brian did get his way. Yet that first breakdown became part of a pattern that would repeat itself with increasing and alarming regularity. Brian would eventually deal with his problems only by retreating and/or having a nervous breakdown, and it would become a familiar role, a comfortable role, and most definitely a very dangerous game.

Because of his upbringing, Brian felt that quitting the road wasn't a manly thing to do—"A winner never quits and a quitter never wins"—and he knew in advance that his decision to stop touring would bring him much grief from his family and the group. Brian also knew that it was the right thing to do, for his own personal survival as well as for his musical development. There really was no alternative. In that '66 interview with Earl Leaf, Brian fully explained his reasons: "I felt I had no choice. I was run down mentally and emotionally because I was running around, jumping on jets, one-night stands, also producing, writing, arranging, singing, planning, teaching." According to Brian, it was "to the point where I had no peace of mind, no chance to actually sit down and think or even rest. I was so mixed up and so overworked." Brian summed up his problems in making the break. "What it amounted to was a guilt feeling. I knew I should have stopped going on tours much earlier to do justice to our recordings and business operations. I was also under pressure from my old man [Murry] who figured I'd be a traitor if I didn't travel on one-nighters with the other guys . . . I had a lot of static from everyone outside the group as well as the members. The only way I could do it was breaking down as I did."

In the Earl Leaf interview, Brian had noted, "I used to be Mr. Everything."

Quitting the road was Brian's first step away from the responsibilities of pop stardom. It would hardly be the last.

The Beach Boys were now faced with the task of replacing Brian on tour. Glen Campbell was the first substitute, and although he fitted in musically, Glen wasn't comfortable as a Beach Boy. Audree Wilson recalls that "Glen is tall and his hair is lighter than Brian's, but a lot of kids in the audience would think he was Brian. They'd yell, 'Brian! Brian!'" Although the Beach Boys asked Glen to join permanently, he refused. Glen: "If the Beach Boys did something, then I did it. And I didn't like that at all . . . I'm probably too much of an individual."

The next man to fill in for Brian in concert stayed for seven years. In 1965, Bruce Johnston was a staff producer at Columbia Records. He also was one-half of the musical duo of Bruce and Terry (Melcher) who made Beach Boys-soundalike records, most notably 'Summer Means Fun.' Bruce and Terry were also the studio voices of the Ripchords, who had a Top Five hit with another Beach Boys imitation record, 'Hey Little Cobra.' Terry (Doris Day's son) becomes a part of the story later on as one of Brian's few trusted friends.

When Bruce received that fateful phone call, he was a perfect fit for the Beach Boys' situation. As Bruce recalls, Mike Love called him in early 1965 wondering if Bruce knew of anybody who could fill in for Glen Campbell, who couldn't make part of a tour. Bruce couldn't find anybody (his search included current touring bass player Ed Carter) and offered his own services. Bruce flew to New Orleans, rehearsed a couple of songs and became a Beach Boy in one night. After a few shows, Glen rejoined the touring band, and Bruce became an observer and a student as Carl taught Bruce the songs on the bass. On April 9, at a Wilmington, Delaware concert, Bruce became a full-fledged bass-playing member of the band, and Campbell didn't do any tours after that.

Bruce claims he "didn't want to join permanently . . . After that two-week tour, we came home and I thought, 'OK, now Brian'll bounce back, or Glen will bounce back or they'll get someone.'" Instead, Bruce went to his first Beach Boys sessions as a singer. "Brian just said, 'Here, sing a part,' and I sang a part and it worked." That became part of 'California Girls' and Bruce has been on virtually every album since; even after he parted company with the Beach Boys, he always seemed to be called in to do some singing.

Bruce really fitted perfectly. His falsetto voice sounded a lot like Brian's; he was young and handsome and looked like a surfing Californian. In those first days, Bruce was known as the "Phantom" Beach Boy, but his talents as a musician, arranger and songwriter helped fill the creative void left by Brian's eventual withdrawal from the Beach Boys records.

The Beach Boys road unit was again complete, but Brian Wilson's world was starting to take a direction toward the frontier of the 1960s—inner space. In 1966, Brian told writer Tom Nolan: "About a year ago, I had what I consider a very religious experience. I took LSD, a full dose of LSD, and later, another time, I took a smaller dose. And I learned a lot of things, like patience, understanding. I can't teach you or tell you what I learned from taking it, but I consider it a very religious experience." In 1977, Brian noted: "I had one retreat before *Pet Sounds*, which was LSD, and then about a year's worth of paranoia. In that year, I did 'California Girls' and 'Help Me, Rhonda' and stuff like that." What those somewhat contradictory statements indicate is Brian's changed perspective on those times. Appearing on *The Mike Douglas Show* in 1976, Brian claimed that LSD "shattered my mind." It is impossible to measure the effects of acid on Brian, particularly when you consider that his first acid forays were followed by *Pet Sounds* and 'Good Vibrations.' Some people who know Brian posit that his alleged late '66/ early '67 acid activities are what sent him into his retreat.

Back in '65, Brian's experimenting with drugs, particularly LSD, was way ahead of the rest of the world—and that included the music world. The Beatles and acid didn't really meet until later, when they helped popularize "tripping" as part of the psychedelic lifestyle. LSD in those "pre-acid" days was a beautiful experience for Brian. He told a number of people that LSD helped him to see himself for the first time. At the time, it was a spiritual awakening for Brian. With a new perspective on himself, Brian's music took a radical shift. Rather than a reflection of the world around him, Brian's music became, in his own words, "the deepest expression of my soul." Brian looked at his music as a way to reach people. Withdrawn from the daily interaction of on-the-road life, somewhat secluded in his own home or the recording studio, Brian used his songs to talk to his millions of "friends." Brian, in 1965, didn't "think there could be a more beautiful way of communication."

Besides Brian's need to "speak" to people through his music, songwriting was a way to prove his worth, to himself and to Murry, who was still pushing Brian to have more hits. Except now it was from a different angle. Murry had formed a Beach Boys imitation group (the Sunrays), and father and son were now in direct competition.

Although many of the Beach Boys lyrics remained within the "fun in the sun" vein, Brian's personal changes were quickly absorbed within the music, which was coming together in an astounding fashion.

The first album of 1965, *The Beach Boys Today*, perfectly reflected the new Beach Boys set-up and also showcased Brian's personal writing. Side one, the fast side, consisted mostly of hits that had been written and recorded in 1964. Side two, the slow side, had the melodies that were very special to Brian—songs like 'In the Back of My Mind,' 'Please Let Me Wonder,' and 'She Knows Me Too Well.' The back of the *Today* album graphically showed the growing creative division that Brian was working around. The headline reads, "A Program of Big Beach Boy Favorites . . . Plus Some Great New Brian Wilson Songs." Those side two songs were and are great. Collaborating with Mike, Brian was musically voicing exactly what was on his mind. Like little pools of emotion, these songs unabashedly and sometimes melodramatically expressed Brian's post-adolescent anxiety, a mode of communication that would see full flower on *Pet Sounds*. The poignant words and music meshed perfectly. Sometimes melancholy, sometimes searching, it all came out in the music; Brian's production enhanced these songs with the first serious stirrings of orchestration.

How did Brian put his emotions into music? He described the lengthy process of putting together the ideal creative atmosphere with the right frame of mind in a fan magazine article titled "Brian Wilson: Why I Stay Home": "Six months ago, I bought a new house up in Beverly Hills . . . I arranged the house so I had a big room full of music and atmosphere, and I started to plan the new direction of the group . . . I wanted to move ahead in sounds and melodies and moods. For months, I plotted and planned.

"For a month or two, I sat either at a huge Spanish table looking out over the hills, just thinking, or at the piano playing 'feels.'" "'Feels,'" Brian explained, "are musical ideas, riffs, bridges, fragments of themes. A phrase here and there." This method of songwriting had ambitious aims. "I wanted to write a song containing more than one level. Eventually, I would like to see longer singles . . . so that the song can be more meaningful . . . A song can, for instance, have movements, in the same way as a classical concerto, only capsulized." Long before 'Good Vibrations' was recorded, the ideas that would shape that song were already swirling in his head.

Brian's vision was usually exciting to the group, although he noted that "we're often into different things." Unfortunately, Capitol felt that Brian was moving in a direction that wouldn't be as successful commercially. Audree Wilson remembers that, after quitting touring, "Brian threw himself into [making records] with everything he had and seemed to be very happy doing that. He really handled the record company's requests very well; he just plugged away and did it." Capitol wanted Brian to keep churning out those sprightly melodies and good-time lyrics. It is ironic that during a troubled period in his life, Brian and Mike wrote a song called 'California Girls,' a song that epitomized to the world what the Beach Boys were, and the fantasy they represented. In this ultimate salute to his home state, Brian may have created a greater fantasy world because he needed a more powerful escape. Brian once said that "I can't listen to the vocal," because he feels that Mike Love rushed the singing. The song itself has a stirring introduction that majestically unfolds into one of Brian's most sophisticated and intriguing productions to that point. The lyric created an image that has become part of the Beach Boys, and it is unlikely that they have since given a concert without performing it.

In mid-'65, Brian stepped outside the group to produce a Glen Campbell record, 'Guess I'm Dumb.' Written with Russ Titelman, it was Brian's most ambitious outside production effort, and one of the first records that consolidated all his ideas into a coherent sound. The instrumental sophistication, the intricate voices, the forlorn lyrics—this song and production were an obvious foreshadowing of *Pet Sounds*. It was a commercial bomb. (Brian's non-Beach Boys productions met with little success; but Brian did have hits as a composer and singer with Jan and Dean. Besides the Honeys and Spring (Marilyn's groups), Brian produced unsuccessful records for Sharon Marie, Paul Petersen, Gary Usher, Rachel and the Revolvers, and Ron Wilson. Brian also produced a record in 1964 called 'Pamela Jean' by the Survivors, using friends and studio players. This attempt to use the Beach Boys sound without the name worked musically but not commercially.)

The Beach Boys' records in 1965 were central to the growing experimentation that Brian was pursuing. Although the *Summer Days (and Summer Nights!!)* album was, for the most part, not as emotionally revealing as

Today, Brian's musical growth was continuing at a rapid pace. Brian was approaching the Phil Spector sound he yearned for, but for the first time, it was apparent that Brian had the potential to outdo Spector. The airy, spacey vocals, the inspired arrangements, the full orchestration of rock rhythms and horns and strings, the unique melodies . . . Brian was stretching out his musical skills. On 'Guess I'm Dumb' or a *Summer Days* song like 'Let Him Run Wild,' Brian exhibited many of the textures that would characterize 1966's masterpiece, *Pet Sounds*. That progress, however, was causing commercial difficulties.

In the fall of 1965, the Beach Boys released 'The Little Girl I Once Knew' as a single. It was not an instant hit, even though it was the follow-up to smashes like 'Help Me, Rhonda' and 'California Girls.' Radio programmers, notoriously conservative, didn't know what to make of this avant-garde record, and with good reason. Full of complete stops (dead air) and tempo changes, it was jarring to Top Forty sensibilities. When it stalled at "only" #20, it became the group's first "flop" single since 'Ten Little Indians.' The record's quality didn't prevent its relative failure with the record-buying public.

In the midst of all of Brian's growth and musical experimentation, Capitol Records was pushing the Beach Boys for more "product." Capitol wanted another album, and Brian, in the beginning stages of *Pet Sounds*, wasn't about to rush out another package. He'd already done one "quickie" that year (*Summer Days*). So the Beach Boys decided to do another "live" album, except that instead of Sacramento (where they had recorded their first live album in 1964), this one was to be recorded in the studio at a simulated *Beach Boys' Party!* in Studio 3 at Western Recorders. The record itself is a charming period piece and contains more of the self-parody that the Beach Boys had explored on earlier studio snippets like 'Cassius Love vs. Sonny Wilson,' 'Our Favorite Recording Sessions' and 'Bull Session with "Big Daddy."' The Beach Boys' humor was corny and high school locker-roomish, but they could poke fun at themselves and others in a very unselfconscious way that translated into a lot of fun for the fans.

At the same time, one wonders why the group would do such a light album when Brian's music was becoming so involved. Carl Wilson explains that "it was really just to give us time. We just did that so we'd have time to do *Pet Sounds*. It only took a few days, and that was it. I thought it was a pretty odd record at the time. But then, we were having pressures from Capitol Records to give us another one of these [fun records], give us another record. So we got caught up" in the business part of it. "We really did."

The Beach Boys' Party! album was a quick way to get "product" out. It became (not including hits repackages) the biggest seller in their history. It included a fun cover of 'Barbara Ann,' a song that featured the lead singing duo of Brian and Dean (Torrence). It reached #3 in the U.S.; the song was also the first major hit for the group in England and opened up that important country for them.

The release of 'Barbara Ann,' however, sealed the doom of 'The Little Girl I Once Knew' and was an unexpected and unwanted shift in style for the group. The Beach Boys hadn't been told that it was to be released as a single. Not that they were displeased at its huge success, but at a time when the group's music was progressing, it didn't help the audience adjust to that shift when the record company "snuck out" a record that further cemented their fun-loving image.

The headliners at sound check, July 1965 at the Hollywood Bowl. *The Beach Boys Summer Spectacular* featured the Byrds, the Kinks, the Righteous Brothers, Sonny & Cher and Dino, Desi & Billy.
Credit: Michael Ochs Archives/Getty

The release of 'Barbara Ann' and the *Party* album was the turning point. It was the peak of the Beach Boys' popularity with the American record-buying public, and with the exception of 'Good Vibrations,' the Beach Boys' days as major hitmakers and million-sellers were just about over. Simultaneously, Brian Wilson was in the midst of a musical maturation that would influence virtually every rock musician and change the course of pop music.

The Beach Boys ended 1965 with a gold record and a big hit single, but it was the last time that the teenage public and the Beach Boys were on the same wavelength. For Brian Wilson, *Party* was a meaningless record because he wasn't emotionally involved with it, or, for that matter, with the Beach Boys. Brian was at work, hard at work, on his "solo" album. It was to be called *Pet Sounds.*

THE BEACH BOYS' SOUND

"The first time we went into a studio," Brian Wilson recalled, "we were like five green idiots. All I know is that we had a song and we'd rehearsed it. It wasn't like we knew what we were doing." The recording experience that Brian referred to resulted in the first of the group's hits. It was only a short time before Brian developed into one of the best record producers in the history of popular music—if not *the* best.

One of the things that made Brian unique is that he heard sounds and tried sound combinations that nobody else ever attempted. Maybe it was his deafness in one ear. It's possible that Brian heard different sounds because he heard differently than a "normal" person. His hearing impairment meant he couldn't grasp stereo, and all the albums Brian produced in the 1960s were made in monophonic sound. Like Phil Spector's legendary "Wall of Sound," Brian's records were so full that they didn't need the extra sound dimension. *Pet Sounds*, for example, was cut in mono. Nevertheless, it stands as an unparalleled sound achievement.

Even though he is almost totally deaf in one ear, Brian has near perfect pitch and remarkable hearing. Marilyn Wilson remembered, "Brian sat down and hummed each note of the piano to the [piano tuner]. Each note! It was Brian's tuning; he didn't want regular pitch, he wanted it tuned to his ears. He wanted the notes to ring a certain way—I could never explain it. But it was the greatest tuning job you ever heard." The first component of his musical skills was a superhuman hearing that allowed Brian to detect the slightest deviation from a note, a talent that eventually made the Beach Boys' harmonies a standard for other recording acts to try and match.

Jimmy Webb explains that "one of the secrets of how their voices blend is that they use very little vibrato, which is really old-style church singing of five or six hundred years ago. The way the voices fitted together was very complex, yet parts of it were very simple. They sang very straight tones. The voices all lie down beside each other very easily; there's no bumping between the voices because the pitch is very precise. Everybody knows the pitch, and they would sing it and do it until they got it right. That was especially obvious on *Pet Sounds.*" One aspect of their vocal blend that can't be taught is the influence of genes. With three brothers and a first cousin, the Beach Boys began with a certain natural blend.

Nik Venet notes that Brian was the perfectionist, the "first guy to do it until it was right. He damned everyone until it was right, and then he gave them the record . . . a lot of us would say, after about four hours, 'We'd better get off that tune.' Brian would hang in there for nine hours, no matter what the cost. I used to think he was crazy, but he was right. Brian was tough to work with. Brian really demanded . . . If I had him under contract, he could take four years between records. As long as he was happy with the record, that's all."

The recording studio, like any musical instrument, requires a lot of practice before an artist can master it. There is a tremendous difference between performing a song live and capturing the emotion of the song on a record. Listening to the Beach Boys' records in chronological order, it is evident that their studio technique improved very quickly. In the beginning, like all new groups, the Beach Boys' recorded efforts sounded primitive. 'Surfin'' and the *Surfin' Safari* album were raw, barely professional. That untrained vocal approach worked to the group's advantage because the singing had an energy that was so obviously youthful. That quality was part of the group's basic appeal.

After the first album, the Beach Boys records had a sound and feel that was unmistakable. The sound was easily copied, as Jan and Dean and many others proved, but the emotion of the Beach Boys' records was inimitable.

115

Chuck Britz engineered almost all the Beach Boys' vocal sessions during the hitmaking years. He describes the group's recording process. "When I worked with him [Brian], we did everything live. After we did the instrumental tracks, I just set three mics out there, and I'd put Carl, Dennis, and Al on one and I'd put Brian on one. And Brian would either sing into the lead mic when it was his lead or into the background mic when Mike sang lead. Mike was always on a separate mic. Brian always doubled the lead; there were times he would sing it so right on that it was hard to figure out whether there was a delay or not. And, of course, I'd use pretty good echo . . . they could sing a cappella and make tears come to your eyes."

When Brian would finish a new song, the group would gather around the piano to hear it and work out their vocal parts. Brian relied on Carl for feedback. Brian: "If Carl doesn't dig it, I'll do something he and I both like. I like Carl's ear."

In those early days the record making was a more collaborative process, but by 1964, when the group fired Murry, the Beach Boys' records were the sole province of Brian Wilson. Others could make suggestions, but Brian was in charge.

As Brian began experimenting with new sound textures, he found that the instrumental skills of the Beach Boys were inadequate. While the voices were always those of the band, from 1963 through 1966 Brian used studio musicians on the instrumental tracks. Chuck Britz engineered many of those sessions and remembered that "mostly everybody was playing to some degree, but basically . . . ninety-five percent of it was studio musicians." This didn't bother the Beach Boys. "Everybody seemed happy that they didn't have to be here for all that hard work."

Drummer Hal Blaine remembers that "Brian used to come in and sing us a song. We would individually take it over ourselves, the way we felt it. That's the way we made records. Brian would basically give us a chord chart, and we built our sections." Chuck Britz explains that Brian "knew basically every instrument he wanted to hear, and how he wanted to hear it and the different formations that go into making a helluva good record. He had a form in his mind where he had a sound that he wanted to hear. What he would do is, we would call in all the musicians at one time (which was very costly), but still, that's the way he would do it. We'd start out maybe with a bass or maybe a marimba or something." And Brian would work with that instrument until it had the sound he wanted. There are stories that Brian would sometimes spend hours trying to get a bell to ring a certain way. This may sound eccentric, but Brian's devotion to sound was crucial. Tied in to that single-minded approach was Brian's openness to new sounds. Jimmy Webb pictures Brian "like a child, making those early records, just experimenting, so involved with the process."

The process often took hours, as Brian and each musician worked out the parts. Chuck Britz recalls that "usually the horns were the last thing we'd work on. There'd be a guy in the horn section [most often, Steve Douglas] who would take Brian's idea and transpose it for the other horn players." Ray Pohlman did the same thing for the guitar players.

The recording sessions were long affairs because Brian spent so much time working out the individual sounds. But once each player had his part and the arrangement was complete, they might need only one or two takes to get the song down on tape. As the recordings were being made, Brian directed the mixing, all of which was done in mono. After he had a satisfactory mix of instruments and vocals, they would listen to the recording on a small speaker. The purpose of this was to hear how the record would sound on a car radio.

Brian was famous for his ability to keep everything in his mind. He knew where he was going to use strings, horns, voices, etc. Steve Douglas recalls that it was Brian's ability to hear the whole record that was one of his more astounding attributes as a producer. "We had a pretty large rhythm section over at Western 3, and Brian was trying to get the guitar to play a certain thing. And I remember Tommy Tedesco [a well-known session guitar player] saying, 'Hey man, it won't work; it just won't work.' And Brian said, 'Play it.' And it sounded like it didn't make sense until he overdubbed the strings and it all fell together. It was just amazing. He heard that in his head. That's what has always blown me out about him—that he could hear these complex orchestrations."

Because Brian is easily bored, his songs are full of unusual chord changes and tempo shifts. Brian's boredom translates into constant surprise for the listener. To create those unique sounds, Brian worked with a group of studio musicians. The regulars included: Hal Blaine (drums); Steve Douglas, Jay Migliori, Roy Caton, Lou Blackburn (horns); Ray Pohlman, Glen Campbell, Tommy Tedesco, Jerry Cole, Barney Kessel (guitar); Carol Kaye, Lyle Ritz, Julius Wechter (bass); Tommy Morgan (harmonica); Carl Fortina, Frank Marocco (accordion); Leon Russell, Al De Lory, Don Randi (piano).

The ability to hear the entire record that so amazed the musicians was something Brian said that he picked up from Phil Spector. Brian reportedly would listen to Spector records like 'Be My Baby' for hours on end, analyzing exactly what Spector was doing. From that intense listening, Brian learned "how to conceive of a framework of a song, to think in terms of production, rather than just songwriting . . . I was unable to really think as a producer up until the time where I really got familiar with Phil Spector's work . . . Then I started to see the point of making records. You're in the business to create a record. So you design the experience to be a record rather than just a song. It's good to take a good song and work with it. But it's that record that counts. It's the record that people listen to. It's the overall sound, what they're going to hear and experience in two and a half minutes that counts."

Brian and Phil Spector did some sessions together and Brian recalled that "I was able to perceive very much more than he thought I could. I was a little more alert . . . I basically knew all that was to be known about that [Wall of Sound] simply by listening, using my ears." Brian explained that Spector's technique of combining certain instruments achieved a new sound, "Rather than just say, 'That's a piano, that's a bass.' Now, we have what you call a piano-guitar. Which you're going to call something else. It sounds like something else. Although it may be two or three instruments combined playing the same notes, it now sounds different." Daryl Dragon (a musician who played with the Beach Boys before becoming the "Captain" of the Captain and Tennille) notes that Brian has "said he tried to copy what Phil Spector did, but Brian had a unique approach."

Brian's use of vocals was one of the most important happenings in popular music in the 1960s. When he combined those voices with his studio technique, the results were astounding. Hal Blaine thinks that "Brian started using voices in rock 'n' roll. That's what made most of us [the studio musicians] really perk up. It was a really beautiful blending. It set a trend." Mike Love was amazed that Brian "could, first of all, have in mind four different parts. It's hard enough to get one down and hold onto it while you're singing, hearing three other parts. But he'd have four- and five-part chords in his mind and dish them out to all of us and then take the top which is the melody. It never ceased to blow my mind that he could know those notes and retain them."

Most of the Beach Boys' hits were recorded on three tracks; because of this, the instruments were all recorded together. Daryl Dragon notes that Brian is "master of production when everything is happening at once. I think what screwed Brian up a little was when they brought in eight-track and sixteen-track, because there's too many choices. You can't work with timbres of sound. You have to say, 'Well, I hope this works when we overdub.'

"I think Brian Wilson should go back to the way they recorded when they made all the hits, back to the three tracks. Have all the musicians come in there and do it. Stay away from the sixteen tracks, stay away from the twenty-four. He's the kind of guy that when the flow is right, he gets the job done."

Brian Wilson is one of the most important composers and producers in popular music. Not because he had a lot of hits. More, because he created a kind of music that was brand new, sounds that nobody had heard before. Daryl Dragon says, "I went to high school and college and majored in music, and I have yet to take a course that had what Brian Wilson has in his head. There aren't any courses. It's like, he makes the laws. I believe the things he does will be analyzed in fifty years and that they will fit into the music history of what's going on today. He's going to make music history someday; they're going to have to name something after him. I think he's much more inventive than the Beatles were. They never really got me like what Brian did."

CHAPTER 7

PET SOUNDS

PET SOUNDS AND 'GOOD VIBRATIONS,' AN ALBUM AND A SINGLE RELEASED by the Beach Boys in 1966, established the group as the leaders of a new type of pop music: art rock.

First came *Pet Sounds*, an album fraught with emotional, personal and introspective songs, an album that was a significant departure from almost all that had gone before and the first album by the group that was a commercial disappointment to the record company. At the same time, *Pet Sounds'* release gave rise to the belief within the "hip" artistic and critical community that Brian Wilson was a genius.

While the American public had some trouble relating to Brian's new direction, he was also experiencing resistance within the group. While he disputes this characterization, from those I interviewed who were at the sessions, Mike Love has been singled out as the Beach Boy who was most worried by the subject matter of the lyrics. Murry Wilson also voiced his concern. In general, there was a sense that Brian was moving too fast, was getting too experimental, was advancing ahead of his audience, and maybe even using *Pet Sounds* as a stepping stone to a solo career.

'Good Vibrations' is probably the one record most readily identified as a Beach Boys song, and it too was a battleground for Brian's artistic impulses and commercial interests. This one last time, Brian and the public clicked.

Despite the success of this single, the Beach Boys in 1966 found themselves falling out of favor on the home front, while they were concurrently enjoying worldwide acclaim. The Beach Boys juggernaut traveled from Japan to Europe to England. Everywhere, acceptance and love of the Beach Boys and their music were at an all-time high. Everywhere except the United States.

Within the Beach Boys, there was growing turmoil. Without, they were experiencing their first drop in popularity. Despite the artistic achievement of *Pet Sounds* and the million-selling success of 'Good Vibrations,' 1966 was the beginning of the end of the Beach Boys as Brian Wilson's group, and the start of the most frustrating era in Beach Boys history.

★ ★ ★ ★

"Marilyn, I'm gonna make the greatest album, the greatest rock album ever made." That's what Brian Wilson told his wife just before he began the creation of *Pet Sounds*. In his self-imposed, escalating battle with the Beatles, Brian had shifted his focus from creating great single records to creating an entire album, partly because he was so impressed with the Beatles' *Rubber Soul* ("It was a whole album with all good stuff"). Brian felt it was time for him to make a complete statement instead of just a collection of singles and other songs composed to fill out the sides. Not that Beach Boys records had a lot of "filler." There was just a need to go further, to create something new and exciting, an entire album experience.

Brian's creative growth had been frequently interrupted in the latter half of 1965. Already into the planning and recording of what was to become *Pet Sounds*, he had to take time out to make the *Party* album, a record that was a 180-degree turnabout from his last '65 studio production, 'The Little Girl I Once Knew.' As '65 ended, the Beach Boys took to the road for a major tour of Japan, and Brian was free to work on his music. Working alone, however, wasn't the solution for Brian. He was having problems articulating the thoughts in his head and felt the need for a collaborator . . . somebody to bounce ideas off and help him with lyrics.

Tony Asher was working as a jingle writer in an advertising agency in late 1965 when he received an unexpected phone call from Brian Wilson. Asher and Brian were casual acquaintances because Asher used to hang around recording studios. "In those days," he recalls, "everybody would play their songs at the piano. For some reason, I played a couple of tunes for Brian . . . I was thinking, 'Wouldn't it be great if he said, "Fabulous! I'll record that on my next album."' The point is that I did apparently demonstrate to him some ability to write; I wasn't trying to say to him, 'Let's write some tunes together.' I was just trying to impress him that I was also a player and a writer.

Tony Asher

"About a year and a half went by from the time I'd played for him, and I got a call. I must say it was a shock when somebody said, 'Brian Wilson's on the phone.' I said, 'Yeah, sure.' I thought it was somebody in the office fooling around." According to Asher, Brian said something like, "'I've got this album that's way overdue at Capitol. We were supposed to have it out months ago, and I haven't even started it. I've only done one or two tunes on it, and I hate them, and it's really driving me crazy. How would you like to write some tunes for me?' Well, that was like saying, 'How'd you like twenty-five thousand dollars?' Aside from the prestige, aside from the fact that the guy was just one of my idols . . . you could take all that away. But it was a guaranteed certain number of record sales."

Asher got a leave of absence from his job and went to work at Brian's Beverly Hills home. "I'd go over there in the morning, and by the time we got him out of bed and rolling, got everything going, had something to eat, farted around . . . it would be four o'clock in the afternoon before we got to the piano." It was the hanging around, the socializing, that Tony Asher didn't like. With the exception of their creating together, Tony Asher didn't enjoy his association with Brian Wilson. Asher has expressed his dislike for Brian's taste in everything, from art to his absorption in an ever-changing array of philosophies. Brian's fascination with spiritualism, what Asher called the "marshmallow mystics," was not a common ground between the two men and made Asher uncomfortable in the non-working hours. Asher was once quoted as saying that Brian was a genius musician but an amateur human being. He denied that quote but indicated that he didn't think it was too far from the truth. The one aspect of Brian's personality that Asher couldn't comprehend was Brian's irresponsibility toward anything except the music. As Terry Melcher once noted, "To be that much involved in just one thing, you can't be on your guard . . . choosing not to have to be aware of certain things. He chooses not to bother." Or, as Van Dyke Parks (Brian's next lyricist) noted in 1971, "It's cute when he ignores someone else's needs, because he can always plead insanity."

Tony Asher observed that Brian "was a bit eccentric" but his "immaturity or irresponsibility was more like a kid who forgets his glove at school" and there was no malice involved. Brian just wasn't interested in the business aspects of his career by 1966, and Tony Asher remembers how hard it was to deal with Brian. "I got calls from B.M.I. [Broadcast Music Incorporated—a firm that collects performance royalties for songwriters] and from attorneys and executives and all kinds of people who'd say, 'You're seeing Brian. Can you please help us? He's got this contract that he's GOT to sign . . . hundreds of thousands of dollars are involved, and we've sent him fourteen copies and hand-delivered them and had goons go up and stand around with nightsticks! We can't get him to sign, [or] he signs it and can't find it, that kind of stuff!'" As Asher recalls, there were frequent "pleas from people . . . 'Can you *please*, somehow, get him, it's to his advantage, all we want to do is send him some money.'"

When Brian and Tony Asher first started working together, Brian played Asher 'Sloop John B,' which had already been completed. According to Asher, Brian "had a big studio-size tape recorder in his house and a couple of monitor speakers. He said, 'That's all I've got.' Then, he played one other tune that had a lyric that he didn't like. He didn't even like the melody. It was a completed track called 'In My Childhood.' We wiped off those vocals and that melody and rewrote it . . . The [chord] changes were the only thing that stayed the same." The song became 'You Still Believe in Me.' "The bicycle bell part—that was all kept . . . not because anybody thought it was a good idea to keep it. It was kept because it was mixed down into a track. You didn't have twenty-four tracks in those days, and you mixed some tracks that would lock in."

Beginning with *Pet Sounds*, Brian's recording methods changed considerably from his past work. Rather than going into the studio with a completed song, Brian was writing music in the manner of an impressionistic painter. Brian, according to Asher, "used to go in and record [instrumental] tracks. We didn't know what they were going to be. They didn't even have melodies. They would just be a series of chord changes that Brian liked, with some weird or not-so-weird instruments . . . Then, we would bring these back [to the house] and play them and kind of write a melody to them and then write some lyrics. [It was] a terrific way to write songs . . . it's a luxurious way to write. But it's great because you get a good feeling."

Next, Asher recalls, Brian would "just be banging out at the piano. He or I would sing dummy lyrics . . . whatever popped into your head. By the time you had spent two or three hours, you had kind of written the song. We didn't say, 'Wouldn't it be great to write a song called 'God Only Knows' . . . It wasn't that kind of thing.

"When we got through at the end of the day, maybe it was three or four hours working on that one song, he'd have a pretty complete melody, partial lyrics, and a kind of bridge and some other stuff. But not a complete song. I'd go home at night and work on the lyrics a little bit, then go back, and he might say, 'Hey, that's terrific' or 'I don't like those lines.' He did a lot of editing on them."

Like any joint creative endeavor, it's very hard to say who wrote what, but Asher recalls that although "it was a little different on each tune, there's no doubt that I did much more lyrics and Brian did much more melody. On almost every tune, he certainly wrote some words. I would submit things to Brian, and he would make comments and suggested changes. When he wrote lyrics or music, it was less likely for me to make comments about what he was doing."

Pet Sounds is considered Brian's masterwork, and it was critically acclaimed at the time even though its sales were a relative failure by Beach Boys standards. The combination of Brian's music and Tony Asher's lyrics was an important ingredient, but it was the production that Brian has always been most proud of. "Well, I felt that the production was a masterpiece. *Pet Sounds* is an offshoot of the Phil Spector production technique. My contribution was adding the harmonies, learning to incorporate harmonies and certain vocal techniques to that Spector production concept.

[It was a] production achievement. It was the fact that everything on that album was interesting, everything flowed."

Brian acknowledges the conceptual nature of the production, but the common lyrical thread was not anything more than a reflection of what was going on in Brian's mind. And it wasn't a premeditated concept. Tony Asher insists that "we never wrote a song with a certain kind of lyric because it fit into a predetermined concept for the album. I continually hear people talking about that, but I confess I just didn't know what they were talking about." Asher's insistence is convincing, but an examination of the lyrics and the song order makes for a strong argument, because if one looks, it is possible to find a story on *Pet Sounds*. It's a story about a man's search for love and acceptance. It begins with hope, 'Wouldn't It Be Nice,' and ends with a final loss of innocence, 'Caroline, No.' It's not really stretching the content of the album at all to make that point, and if it was unintentional, then it was a very happy accident.

It has been suggested that much of the record is about the marital difficulties that Brian and Marilyn were experiencing, including a much talked-about crush that Brian once had on Marilyn's older sister Diane. As Tony Asher notes, 'Caroline, No' was written about "sweet innocent little girls . . . and his wife's sister, well you probably heard tales about that. So, writing about girls with long hair" was autobiographical. "It was evolving into a nice song, [but it became a sad one] because he was saddened to see how sweet little girls turned out to be kind of bitchy, hardened adults." Taken in that context, the record is more than just a reflection of what was on Brian's mind; it stands as a startlingly honest look at this human being.

Another especially personal song was 'I Just Wasn't Made for These Times.' In the lyric, Brian expresses the realization that he doesn't fit into society. Brian: "[It's] about a guy who was crying because he thought he was too advanced, and that he'd eventually have to leave people behind. All my friends thought I was crazy to do *Pet Sounds*." In the midst of this work of art, Brian was already coming to an awareness that if he wanted to pursue his creative muse, there were going to be major changes in his life. What these changes would have been won't ever be known, because Brian ultimately abandoned his art rather than break from the security of his life as it was.

From a production standpoint, a number of the songs had unusual stories connected with them. 'Wouldn't It Be Nice,' according to Brian, "has a very special and subtle background . . . one of the features of this record is that Dennis sings a special way, cupping his hands. I had thought for hours of the best way to achieve the sound, and Dennis dug the idea because he knew it would work." On 'You Still Believe in Me,' Tony Asher remembers that "the strange opening is Brian and I on the piano. One of us had to get inside the piano and pluck the strings, while the other guy had to be at the keyboard pushing the notes so that they would ring."

In a 1967 interview, Brian stated that 'Let's Go Away for Awhile' was "the most satisfying piece of music I've ever made. I applied a certain set of dynamics through the arrangement and the mixing and got a full musical extension of what I'd planned during the earliest stages of the theme. I think the chord changes are very special. I used a lot of musicians on the track—twelve violins, piano, four saxes, oboe, vibes, a guitar with a Coke bottle on the strings for a semi-steel guitar effect. Also, I used two basses and percussion." Brian's use of sounds was virtually unheard of for the rock world, but the resulting music was more than just a virtuoso production in the Phil Spector mold; it was emotional music. As Brian noted, "The total effect is 'Let's Go Away for Awhile,' which is something everyone in the world must have said at some time or other . . . nice thought. Most of us don't go away, but it's still a nice thought." It was a thought that must have become increasingly attractive to Brian, because only months after that interview, he went away for a long while. There is one additional noteworthy fact about 'Let's Go Away for Awhile.' Brian said that he intended for the released version "to be the backing track for a vocal, but I decided to leave it alone." Tony Asher adds the note that he did write lyrics for the song.

On each track of the album, Brian used studio musicians to create unusual instrumental combinations that were the backdrop for the vocals. The album's title, *Pet Sounds*, had multiple meanings, from Brian's use of his two dogs, Banana and Louie, on the end of 'Caroline, No' to Brian's contention that the music itself was his own "Pet Sounds." Brian's arranging skills combined the sophisticated instrumentation with the layered vocals to construct the textured sounds that make the album so special. Whether it was his use of voices or horns or a banjo or a theremin, the instruments became integral parts of the record. Nothing was too exotic. On 'Caroline, No,' the soft hollow percussion effect is Hal Blaine playing the bottom of a Sparklett's water jug. The bicycle bell on 'You Still Believe in Me,' as Tony Asher indicated, was unintentional, but it fit. On 'Here Today,' you can hear Brian's voice directing the musicians. His voice too becomes an instrument. It's not sloppy recording; it's part of the music.

Considering the relatively unsophisticated recording equipment that was at Brian's disposal in 1966, Brian's accomplishments are even more impressive. Also, there wasn't very much overdubbing in those days, so Brian had to hear the mix in his head, and then get the musicians to play it live. *Pet Sounds* was and remains an unparalleled achievement in popular music. It predated the Beatles' *Sgt. Pepper's Lonely Hearts Club Band* album by a full year, and that album, upon its release, was considered the ultimate in production. Both have worn well, but *Pet Sounds'* emotional content has stood up through the years while the glow of the Beatles' production advancement is now taken for granted.

Because the creative process was all-consuming in Brian Wilson's 1966 existence, Tony Asher's first-hand reminiscences are particularly interesting when they focus on Brian's business decisions. Tony Asher might not have been into drugs or spiritual pursuits, but he and Brian did have many conversations about the record-buying public and what would and wouldn't sell. For example, 'God Only Knows' became a topic of discussion because of the word "God" in the title. Asher remembers that "from a purely commercial aspect, Brian said, 'You're not going to get any airplay on this song.' He had a good point. At the time, there was a song with the word hell or damn in it, and it was banned [from the radio]. There were songs that weren't being played, particularly in the South, because of those words. We both recognized that it was a real pretty song and had a good chance of being a single . . . I had to really fight with him to retain that title." Asher thinks that Brian decided to keep "God" in the title because some people told Brian that it was "an opportunity to be really far out [because] it would cause some controversy, which he didn't mind." The album was Brian's first bid for acceptance by the hip community and a battle with the establishment would increase his credibility as a "now" artist.

Within this very serious project, there were some fun moments. There had to be, if Brian Wilson was involved, because even in his most troubled days, he loved to laugh. Brian's reputation for outrageous behavior and his noted ability for a "put-on" were partly an outgrowth of his infatuation with humor. Tony Asher describes one of the more lighthearted moments he spent with Brian: "There was an album out called *How to Speak Hip* . . . a lampooning of the language instruction albums. I played it for Brian, and it destroyed him, killed him . . . The funny thing was, there are a lot of references to dope smoking, which must have meant virtually nothing to the public in 1957 when they put out this album. There must have been maybe twenty guys in the whole country sitting and rolling a joint and falling down laughing . . . Brian picked up on a couple of references on the album . . . He started saying phrases that were on the album, the way people did with Vaughn Meader or Bill Cosby. One of them, this hip character, said if everyone were 'laid back and cool, then we'd have world peace.' So Brian started going around saying, 'Hey, would somebody get me a candy bar and then we'll have world peace.'" According to Asher, Brian "even made an acetate disc with a label on it with the title . . . He talked about calling 'Let's Go Away for Awhile,' 'And Then We'll Have World Peace.'"

Having 'Fun, Fun, Fun', Brian "helps" Mike see the view at a photo session, Pacific Ocean Park, on the pier at the Santa Monica/Venice border, March 1966.
Credit: Michael Ochs Archives/Getty

The music was taking a very satisfying direction for Brian, and he awaited the return of the Beach Boys so that they could add their vocals to his new songs. Sometimes, as on 'Caroline, No,' he sang a solo vocal. On other songs, Brian did all the singing himself. It was painstaking work, but Brian could do it. He could sing all the parts. Tony Asher remembers that sometimes after a session with the guys, Brian would "completely wipe off everything they'd done and do the rest of it himself." The fact that Brian Wilson no longer needed any of the band to make "Beach Boys" records must have been a scary concept. What had been a perfect set-up—the Beach Boys tour and Brian records—was starting to show signs of strain. Afraid that their mentor might be getting ready to step out on his own, the Beach Boys were experiencing their first serious conflicts with Brian—conflicts that both Murry and the record company joined.

The problems with the record company were straightforward enough; they wanted more "fun" hits and Brian refused to deliver them. That battle Brian could handle. The war within his family was another, much more serious problem. Tony Asher recalls that Murry would ask him, "What's the problem with Brian and why doesn't he get along with the other guys?" At the same time, according to Loren Schwartz (a friend of Brian's), Murry was stabbing Brian in the back. "I remember Brian leaving the booth to confer in the studio with the veteran musicians who idolized him, and Murry waiting for the door to close before he would say things like, 'Brian doesn't know what he's doing—no talent. I'm his father, and I know. He can't hear a thing—deaf in one ear. I taught him everything. He'd be nobody if it weren't for me. I made him. He needs me. I'm really the great songwriter—Brian writes terrible songs.'" Schwartz added, "Poor Murry."

Some of the Beach Boys didn't like the new direction that Brian's music was taking, and they were voicing their concerns. Tony Asher remembers that Al Jardine told him that "'I really like some of the stuff; I'm not sure how people are gonna react to this album.' I think he was really trying to find a nice way to say, 'I like the tunes, but I'm not sure they're what we ought to be doing.'" Dennis reportedly didn't have anything but love for the music, and Bruce Johnston, who idolized Brian, was happy to be part of it. Brian and Carl were very close during the recording of *Pet Sounds*. Brian: "Carl and I were into prayer. We'd pray a lot together, and we prayed for light and guidance through the album. We kind of made it a religious ceremony." In another interview, Brian noted that "Carl and I have a strong affinity for each other. He's so reasonable and practical. He keeps me in check in case I get too far out. I tend to get deep into what I'm doing, not exactly obsessed, but too intense for the people around me."

According to close observers, that intensity did not meet with Mike Love's approval. As it was explained to me, Mike said something like "sure doesn't sound like the old stuff to me." If that's indeed what he said, he was right. And that was the point of the new music. Mike was Brian's most successful wordsmith; his lyrical stories were often in the Chuck Berry style. But Mike had watched as a parade of people periodically became Brian's songwriting partner, and there may have been some professional jealousy on his part. Also, there are reports that Mike felt very strongly that Brian's music had become too avant-garde, and that it wouldn't sell records. Again, at the time, he was right, although with Capitol's lack of support, it may have become something of a self-fulfilling prophecy.

Mike Love is now publicly very proud to have been involved in the creation of *Pet Sounds*, and he has belatedly recognized its artistic importance. In 1966, however, Brian's "commercial daredevilism" and progressive ideas were meeting with resistance from the record company, from Murry, and from within the group. The vocal recording sessions of *Pet Sounds* sometimes were contentious.

Tony Asher recalls that, as a producer, Brian was "very single-minded. He knew what he wanted . . . He was a slave driver with the guys, but they needed it. Their tendency was to fuck around and he'd say, 'Guys, goddam it, let's do it again!' He'd scream and yell, and they'd go 'Ah—,' but they'd do it, and it ended up great." Because Brian could have done all the vocal parts himself, he had little tolerance for the foul-ups. "He knew exactly how he wanted it," Asher recalls, "and if it wasn't done that way, he'd do it until he got it that way. It wasn't because he was patient . . . he was very impatient. By just being unreasonable, [particularly] when the guys would make a mistake on only the second time they'd done something that was very difficult—he'd just go crazy." Brian, however, "was clearly in control and got strong when he had to . . . He'd do it over and over again . . . not patient . . . almost a fanaticism . . . He had a patience about it coming out right," and Brian made sure that every note on the record was perfect, even if it meant hours of singing by himself.

It was the lyrics that the guys most objected to, because they were aware that the music was great. Tony Asher remembers that when they would hear certain lyrics, "Someone would say, 'Weird.' I can remember someone saying, 'Boy, they're going nuts over Tony Asher.'" Tony also recalls that Brian said to him once that "people are sure going to know that's a

Tony Asher lyric" as opposed to a Brian Wilson lyric: "It was a compli-ment." Asher also notes that the family's dislike of the lyrics was beginning to bother Brian a lot and that he had "these nagging fears because he was aware that the music was really different." Brian was concerned that it might not be accepted, but he knew it was the right thing to do, even if he wasn't getting total support from his family.

Brian recalls that "at first, the group thought it was a little too artistic . . . After they heard it for a while, they realized I was right, and they under-stood the validity of art records." Brian didn't indicate how long it took them to come to that realization (it may have taken a few years), and in the meantime there were fights. One incident that stands out centered on a song called 'Hang On to Your Ego.' At least one of the guys reportedly refused to record that song, and Brian gave in and rewrote it, and it became 'I Know There's an Answer.' The new lyrics included the line: "I know there's an answer . . . But I have to find it by myself."

Despite the issues over the lyrics, Brian really had been given virtually total creative freedom for this album. Tony Asher remembers that they had "five or six tunes totally finished, words and music, and the guys hadn't heard a note." There were only a few compromises in the final product, most notably the forced (and out of place) inclusion of 'Sloop John B' for commercial reasons. And that song worked production-wise, even if it had nothing to do with the rest of the album lyrically.

'Sloop John B' was released in March of '66. At the same time, Brian released his first and only solo record. Steve Douglas, a session musician who was working at Capitol Records, remembers pushing Brian to make a solo record. "I was really instigating him to put it out under his own name, and he did." That record was 'Caroline, No,' and according to Douglas, its release "caused problems, man, I just can't tell you."

The Beach Boys, who relied on Brian for all their music, were begin-ning to wonder if their leader was planning to desert them. Brian, in 1976, recalled the fighting during *Pet Sounds*: "I think they thought it was just for Brian Wilson only. I think the problem was that they knew that Brian Wilson was gonna be a separate entity, something that was a force of his own." Brian felt that his artistic control was part of the reason for the intra-group struggle. How did they resolve this conflict? Brian explained that the group "figured, 'Well, sure it's a showcase for Brian Wilson, but it's still the Beach Boys.' In other words," here he flashes a cagey smile, "they gave in. They gave in to the fact that I had a little to say myself, so they let me have my stint . . . I told them it was only a temporary rift where I had something to say, and I wanted to step out of the group a little bit, that's all. And sure enough, I was able to."

(Agent) Marshall Berle: "I saw Brian one day in '66 in a cassette duplicating place about to go to Capitol to a big meeting. The Beach Boys loved to have meetings . . . they'd fight and scream and yell. Brian had eight loop tape cassettes made. One said, 'No comment.' Another said, 'I like that idea.' So every time during the meeting it came time for him to say something, he'd just put the right tape on; he wouldn't say a word. He had seven or eight tapes that said different things."

The complex political maneuvering that went on behind the scenes is hidden in the memories of the participants, and the ultimate result of their resistance to Brian's ideas is hard to measure. With the exception of 'Hang On to Your Ego,' Brian did express himself without any interference. *Pet Sounds*, despite the group's vocal participation, was really a Brian Wilson solo album in that the songs expressed the innermost feelings of its creator. *Pet Sounds* was the record of a singer/songwriter years before that kind of expression came into rock vogue. The exploration of his mind and emotions gave *Pet Sounds* a coherence that was totally new in rock music.

The songs on the album are a perfect insight into Brian Wilson in early 1966, and, in many ways, are still appropriate today. Particularly in songs like 'I Just Wasn't Made for These Times,' 'That's Not Me,' and 'Caroline, No,' Brian Wilson had given the world a window into his soul. It was and is a most troubling self-portrait, a portrait of a man foundering in his emotional ocean and unsure of the new course he's chosen.

The album concludes with 'Caroline, No,' a heartbreaking song of lost innocence that Brian today thinks of as a song that "represents the sweetness, the child in me, the gentle side."

Bruce Johnston has an interesting theory as to what that song meant to Brian: "I always thought that when he wrote 'Caroline, No,' he was writing it about himself. I think that Brian realized that it was going to be over soon, that special door that opened for him, where he'd do special things naturally . . . 'Caroline, No' was how he felt about himself."

Even on a song that was so obviously important to Brian, Brian and Murry clashed on the sound of Brian's vocal, and Murry, according to

Bruce Johnston, took the completed record and sped up the master from the key of G to the key of A so that Brian would sound younger.

Finally, in May 1966, *Pet Sounds* was released. Everyone had his or her opinion as to why it wouldn't be commercial, and all were able to say, "I told you so," when the album was not as big a success as a typical Beach Boys album and became the first record of new material to begin a downward spiral of sales and acceptance of the group's music. In retrospect, it is hard to comprehend the record's sales problems. It contained a Top Five hit in 'Sloop John B' and a double-sided Top Ten hit in 'Wouldn't It Be Nice'/'God Only Knows.' Even 'Caroline, No' made it into the Top Forty on the national charts.

It is important to remember, though, that record-buying habits in 1966 still centered around singles. The Beach Boys did have hits on *Pet Sounds*, but to the average listener, the album was inaccessible at first. It took many listenings for a fan finally to appreciate and absorb what Brian had accomplished.

Capitol didn't really do anything to help combat the "image" problem, and rather than deal with the problems of a maturing artist, they hastily assembled a *Best of the Beach Boys* package. Instead of promoting *Pet Sounds*, Capitol concentrated their efforts on the *Best of* album, which quickly went gold. What many critics consider to be one of the best and most important albums in rock history was never embraced by American record buyers, and it never sold enough to become a gold record.

There were many critics, like Richard Goldstein and Paul Williams, who perfectly understood and related to what Brian was saying in *Pet Sounds*. One tribute to the record comes from an unexpected source, the man who created "The Fonz," actor Henry Winkler: "In 1966, one of the great albums in rock 'n' roll history was made, *Pet Sounds*, by the Beach Boys. Ahead of its time. Even today, it holds up. I would sit there and listen to it and moan, sit on my bed encircled in a knee-high pile of paper and write poetry."

That kind of comment could be found in scattered reviews of the album in America, but over in England, it was a totally different story. Through the efforts of the unlikely trio of Bruce Johnston, publicist Derek Taylor and record producer Kim Fowley, the album became a huge record in England and Europe and opened up a whole new audience for the Beach Boys. Without the prejudices of the American fans as to what the

Beach Boys were and what kind of records they should make, the English were able to express their love of the album and were not overly concerned with the group's relative "cool."

British rock newspapers were hailing *Pet Sounds* as the most progressive pop album ever. There were a few who thought that the album was at times boring and not nearly as good as earlier Beach Boys records. For the most part, the music community agreed that it was indeed revolutionary. Andrew Oldham, the Rolling Stones' manager (and the Beach Boys' publisher in England) felt that it was the pop equivalent of Rimsky-Korsakov's *Scheherazade*. Eric Clapton (then with Cream) said that "all of us, Ginger [Baker], Jack [Bruce], and I consider it to be one of the greatest pop LPs to ever be released. It encompasses everything that's ever knocked me out and rolled it all into one. We're all gassed by it. Brian Wilson is, without a doubt, a pop genius."

Elton John: "That was one of the first albums by a group who were known for pop singles that really started to make people sit up and listen. The *Pet Sounds* album was a turning point."

In 1966, Bruce Johnston was entertaining England's pop royalty in a hotel suite when the Who's Keith Moon brought over the kings, John Lennon and Paul McCartney. They listened to and were duly impressed by the LP. According to one of Kim Fowley's colorful tales, John and Paul went into an immediate songwriting huddle and emerged with 'Here, There and Everywhere.' Fowley exclaims, "Do you realize what that means? The two Beatles were able to gauge the whole essence of the album in one listening." That claim is somewhat overstated, although 'Here, There and Everywhere' is an impressive harmony production.

The acclaim of his peers was what Brian had sought with the creation of *Pet Sounds*, but the fact that the kids didn't buy it in (the typical) huge numbers, that they didn't snap it up on instinct, was more than slightly disturbing to Brian. As Audree Wilson remembers, *Pet Sounds'* rejection "hurt Brian a lot because he was very proud of it. He felt that he had accomplished something good and he was very hurt." Marilyn Wilson recalls that, one night, Brian came home with the finished, dubbed-down acetate disc of *Pet Sounds*. "He prepared a moment . . . we went in the bedroom . . . and he said, 'OK, are you ready?' But he was really serious. This was his soul in there . . . We just lay there alone all night . . . and just listened and cried . . . It was really, really heavy. But *Pet Sounds* was not a big hit. That really hurt him badly, he couldn't understand it. It's like, why put your heart and soul into something? I think that had a lot to do with slowing him down."

David Anderle, who was just coming into Brian's life at that point, remembers that Brian "cared a lot 'cause he knew it was good. We talked about it. I thought it was a crime. He didn't take it [the sales figures] quite that seriously."

Pet Sounds was the first major musical change for the Beach Boys, as, for the first time, the music reflected a mostly adult perspective. At the same time, the Beach Boys' media image was undergoing swift and appropriate changes through the tireless efforts and skills of publicist Derek Taylor. Taylor, an Englishman who once had worked for and with the Beatles (and would again), was now located in Los Angeles and was the chief pipeline to the fan magazines like *Flip* and *Teen*, which were then the only oracles of rock happenings. He had been publicist for the Byrds and the now defunct duo of Bruce and Terry, so it only took a clever move by Beach Boy Bruce Johnston to set up a meeting for Derek with Brian.

Brian was smitten with Taylor, partly because of the Beatles association. Derek remembers: "He was fascinated by my then semi-alcoholic existence. Southern Californians don't drink a lot." Derek and the Beach Boys began an off-and-on working relationship that would last until 1968. It was Taylor who was architect of the campaign "Brian Wilson is a genius," and it was Taylor who helped the Beach Boys update their image. At long last, the group's marriages were made public, and they started to shed the striped shirt, short hair, surfer look. As David Anderle notes, "Derek, because of his Beatles situation, obviously had tremendous power and influence as a critic or a soothsayer or a seer of pop . . . He really did a number with the English press, made them [the Beach Boys] accessible to the press and the critics. He did a huge amount of work for the Beach Boys. More than I think they to this day know."

With Taylor hyping Brian as a pop genius upon the release of *Pet Sounds*, the public's perception of the Beach Boys was beginning to change. One album like *Pet Sounds* doesn't make a new image, and the Beach Boys themselves hadn't significantly changed, even though their hair was beginning to creep over their ears and an occasional marijuana cigarette found its way to their lips.

It was Brian who was forging ahead, wildly experimenting with everything imaginable. With a new circle of friends attracted by the new music, Brian's mind expansion, begun with LSD, continued as he consumed different religions and philosophies such as Subud, I Ching, astrology and numerology. As Brian said in May of 1966, "I've been through a zillion bags, more bags in the last year than you can believe. Each little adventure taught me something about myself and people and life. I've been through so many changes. And I went on pills because I was curious, not so much for kicks as for exploration. Some pills won't hurt you but stimulate your mind. Including the psychedelics."

Brian felt that "it all starts with religion . . . I believe in God—in one God, some higher being who is better than we are. But I'm not formally religious. I simply believe in the power of the spirit and in the manifestation of this in the goodness of people. I seek out the best elements in people. People are part of my music. A lot of the songs are the results of emotional experiences, sadness and pain. Or joy, exultation and so on . . . like 'California Girls,' a hymn to youth." In 1976, Brian felt that the same song was "an example of ego—I love girls; they're so young and innocent." Those are qualities that Brian no longer possesses.

Brian's songwriting, especially in 1965 and 1966, was part of a vicarious lifestyle. "I can write through understanding others. The surf songs are a simple example of that—I have never surfed, but I was able to feel it through Dennis." Personal pain was also an important source of inspiration for Brian. "I find it possible to spill melodies, beautiful melodies in moments of great despair. This is one of the wonderful things about this art form—it can draw out so much emotion, and it can channel it into notes of music in cadence. Good, emotional music is never embarrassing . . . music is genuine and healthy and the stimulation I get from molding it and from adding dynamics is like nothing else on earth." Already riding his emotional rollercoaster, Brian found salvation only in his music. His other searches, be it with drugs or religion or psychic fads, weren't nearly as successful.

Brian's artistic battles in the first half of 1966 resulted mostly in victory for his ideas, but he still had to watch as *Pet Sounds* failed to achieve the success he had hoped for. Yet, Brian wasn't disillusioned with the record business or the Beach Boys. In fact, he seemed to have reached an intellectual understanding of the group, and had come to grips with their relationship. "You learn so much about people's motives, especially when you're in a position to bring out greed and such in people. But understanding the weakness of other people helps you to see your own weaknesses as well as strengths, and so it's been helpful to us all . . . The fellows are just growing up and adjusting to the position in life which we are in. I think that being actually originally a teenage group that made that much money and success in such a short time was a little bit hard to handle for obvious reasons. It's been almost five years since we started, and it's taken just about that long to adjust and reach present maturity." Satisfied with his present artistic status, Brian looked at the future and noted that he didn't "think there'll ever be a dull moment in my career as I'm too dedicated to some kind of a scene. I don't want to be static; I must keep functioning . . . No, I'm not a genius. I'm just a hardworking guy."

Brian's self-appraisal was quite honest, and he seemed to understand the need for growth as an artist. *Pet Sounds* was his first big step as an artist, and it had brought him the critical praise he had hoped for. Still, Brian was a troubled man. As he noted in 1976, "When 'God Only Knows' came out, Paul [McCartney] called it the greatest song ever written. If that's so, what was there left for me to do?" Brian's confidence and drive in 1966 were beginning to reflect his growing unease, and his thought processes were starting to work in most unusual ways.

Brian, however, was still in the midst of a creative snowball, and even though it lasted only a short while, he had unlocked a door and had entered a room where nobody had been before or has gone since. Brian's musical searching would manifest itself on his next record, a rhythm and blues-based song with the title 'Good Vibrations.' Having produced the best album up to that point in pop music, Brian set out to create a single that would make the world pay attention.

CHAPTER 8

GOOD VIBRATIONS
AND SMILE

THE SONG 'GOOD VIBRATIONS' HAD BEEN COMPOSED DURING THE CREATION of *Pet Sounds*, and Tony Asher had written a set of lyrics for the formative melody. At one point, the song was even considered for inclusion on the *Pet Sounds* album. The original lyrics didn't satisfy Brian, and he scrapped them and concentrated on the production of the record. At a cost of approximately $50,000 (and maybe more), Brian Wilson's work on what he called a "pocket symphony" stretched out over six months, ninety hours of recording tape, and eleven complete versions as he experimented with sounds and musical ideas.

Engineer Chuck Britz: "We went to at least ten of the studios around town, but I preferred Western. It seemed to have the best echo chamber for what we were doing vocally."

Although there were many sessions for 'Good Vibrations,' Chuck Britz recalls that the ultimate record was "the first session we did in [Western] Studio Three, with the exception of a few bars from Gold Star and a few bars from RCA." To Britz, "That song was his whole life's performance in one song. He wanted it right . . . Basically, it was a hit song the minute he cut it. But at that period of time, he was striving to do something that was totally different than what he'd done before." Brian accomplished that, but it took a great deal of studio time trying out various sound combinations.

In the recording of *Pet Sounds*, resistance to Brian's experimentation had cropped up for the first time, and with the continued search for sound evidenced in the number of sessions necessary to produce 'Good Vibrations,' Brian began to run into more resistance, as he recalled in 1976. "There was a lot of 'Oh, you can't do this, that's too modern' or 'That's going to be too long a record.' I said, 'No, it's not going to be too long a record; it's going to be just right.'" Brian didn't name the opposition, just saying that "it was people in the group, but I can't tell ya who. We just had resisting ideas. They didn't quite understand what this jumping from studio to studio was all about. And they couldn't conceive of the record as I did. I saw the record as a totality piece."

According to Jimmy Webb, "'Good Vibrations' was an important record because it crossed over 'the boundaries' of the three-minute record . . . it definitely pointed the way, said, 'Hey, the drums don't have to play all the way through the record. You can have a slow part; you can have a choir part.'"

Those who heard the original track to 'Good Vibrations' remember it as a very funky rhythm and blues track. In fact, Brian once intended to sell the song to Warner Brothers for use by an R&B act. Wilson Pickett's name has been mentioned over the years as being the type of singer that the song would have been perfect for. Whatever happened to that idea, the song evolved so that, as Brian put it, it "had a taste of modern, avant-garde R&B to it." In a capsule description of the production, Brian noted that within the "three minutes and thirty-five seconds . . . it had a lot of riff changes. It had a lot of movements . . . changes, changes, changes. Building harmonies here, drop this voice out, this comes in, bring the echo chamber in, do this, put the theremin here, bring the cello up a little louder here. I mean it was a real production. The biggest production of our life."

Although Brian had used the theremin before, its use on 'Good Vibrations' was a first for a rock single. Chuck Britz remembers when Brian "brought this thing in, and I went out and looked at it 'cause it had nothing but two little arcs sticking up with a vibrator going in between. And he played it for me. I couldn't believe that he would use it because it was strictly a thing that had been used years before. He was into sound; he was definitely into sounds. So we just started doing it, and it worked out beautifully. I really couldn't believe it would work like that."

The other major instrumental innovation on 'Good Vibrations' was the use of cellos as a rhythm instrument, an idea that Van Dyke Parks is credited with suggesting, but it was Brian's openness to new ways that brought that sound to the record.

Brian is extremely proud of the "series of intricate harmonies and of the mood changes." Those swift changes of mood can almost be considered a reflection of Brian at that time. His up-and-down emotions were beginning to take alarming swings, and his use of drugs, particularly uppers, was concerning his family. During the period that 'Good Vibrations' was coming together, Brian was beginning to hang out with a "faster" crowd, and drugs were just part of the accepted lifestyle. This new group of people had come to watch this magical music person in action, and Brian was, in turn, taking up their ways.

Pet Sounds and 'Good Vibrations' were art records and their appeal to the emerging hip generation was real. Brian had been striving for the approval of the trendy tastemakers and had won many of them over with *Pet Sounds*. As word of Brian's continued musical growth and experimentation spread, all those who considered themselves the "in-crowd" had to see what was going on. For Brian, this influx of new people was both stimulating and scary. It was what Brian wanted, but it was all so new. These people were very different from the Hawthorne crowd that had always surrounded Brian, be it his brothers or cousins or his nice, mostly average, "square" friends.

Tony Asher was one of the first outsiders from a different, more sophisticated upbringing. Another was Loren Schwartz, purportedly the man who turned Brian on to LSD. Loathed by Brian's family, this ever-widening circle turned Brian's head. It was both their use of drugs and the new ideas they constantly introduced into Brian's consciousness that the family didn't understand or approve of. These people exhibited an openness of thought, and Brian, who loved to talk, found an audience for his ideas. Because he was unworldly, their ideas fascinated Brian. They were also new companions for his experiments because those who came around most definitely rode on Brian's trip. He loved the power he had over them, and they loved the ride. Brian's education had been interrupted by the success of the Beach Boys; this new group was feeding Brian new information, and he absorbed it all with an incredible hunger. A voracious reader, Brian sought out new philosophies and religions, searching for the kernels of wisdom in each that he could adopt for his ever-changing personal philosophy. Yet this massive sensory input was ultimately too much. The contradicting thoughts were impossible to understand fully without deeper study. Brian grasped many things intuitively, but in the end, his naive wonder at the magnificence of the arts, particularly painting, gave way to a fascination with the less scientific, more spiritual, studies such as numerology and astrology.

Within this new circle of friends, there were two key people who, for a brief while, were at the core of Brian's new creativity. Both hopped on the bus during the making of 'Good Vibrations,' and both were gone by the following summer. Van Dyke Parks and David Anderle were the two men most influential in Brian's new direction. Both soared with Brian as he created music out of the cosmos. Both were brokenhearted when their association with Brian ended before their work reached fruition.

Van Dyke Parks in 1966 was a hotshot young composer/lyricist/musician who had played on a number of Beach Boys sessions. His clever if sometimes obscure lyrics would soon be married to Brian's new music and those who witnessed the emerging combination described it in words so glowing that it sounded as if Brian and Van Dyke were reinventing pop music. When songs like 'Surf's Up' were finally released to the public, those claims seemed quite valid.

Brian: "Van Dyke Parks is [a] music man who is just amazing. He got involved with me quite heavily and steered me in some directions and turned on some light."

David Anderle, described as "impossibly cunning," was considered to be one of the hippest people in L.A. One writer even dubbed him "The Mayor of Hipness," and Brian in '66 was very much in pursuit of hipness. As a fledgling record industry figure, Anderle was credited with masterminding a record/TV/movie deal at MGM that briefly lured Bob Dylan away from Columbia Records. He was, in '66, manager of Van Dyke Parks and another man who became one of Brian's closest friends, Danny Hutton. Brian and Anderle hit it off immediately. Anderle loved Brian's creative methods and his unique thought processes, and Brian liked Anderle for his reputation, for his mind, and eventually for his friendship and support. Brian saw in Anderle a link to all he wanted to achieve as an artist.

This mutual admiration society encircling Brian in mid-1966 watched with awe and respect as Brian's music entered a more experimental phase with the production of 'Good Vibrations.' In the approximately fifteen sessions (at four different studios) that Brian held for the song, he tried many instrumental combinations including a heavy fuzz bass, clarinets and a Spectoresque wall-of-sound section including the obligatory dense rhythms and layered percussion. As Chuck Britz explains, all these musical ventures were because Brian "wanted it better and better . . . [but] the emotional aspects of a song can be done the first time the best you're ever going to do . . . Let's face it, you can only do something so well." There are reports of many completed versions of 'Good Vibrations' (one was even played on a radio documentary in 1976), and there's no telling how long Brian would have continued working on the song. There are numerous tales that he decided to shelve it.

Circa 1966, in a 'Good Vibrations' era photo, Brian reflects his messengers.
(L-R) Mike, Al, Carl, Bruce and Dennis.
Credit: Michael Ochs Archives

Finally, one night, it was finished. Brian recalled "the time we had it. It was at Columbia. I remember I had it right in the sack. I could just feel it when I dubbed it down, made the final mix down to mono. It was a feeling of power; it was a rush. A feeling of exaltation. Artistic beauty. It was everything . . . I remember saying, 'Oh my God, sit back and listen to this!'"

David Anderle, who was fast becoming a major influence in Brian's life, thinks that Brian just needed a little shove of confidence concerning the record. "I remember the night I heard that real well. I heard it, and

I thought, that's got to get out . . . I think he just had to be told [to release it]. It's one of those things, as with so much on your own, you lose perspective. And once in a while, somebody has to come in and say, 'Hey, man, that's really good.' That's all we did with that. Say, 'That's it, Brian, let's get it out.' I had a feeling that if we wouldn't have pushed him to put it out at that particular moment, it would just continue to molder somewhere."

As Brian was very much into immediacy, he and Michael Vosse (another member of the new entourage, whose father had printed one of the first books about LSD) took the dubbed-down record to KHJ and went on Sam Riddle's teenage rock TV dance program, *It's Boss*. As Anderle recalls, "They went down, and they actually got on TV and played it. And Brian was eating carrots while it was [playing] . . . he was doing his whole vegetable thing to Sam Riddle. That was the beginning of the moment. And it was tremendous watching it on TV. And we all know what happened to 'Good Vibrations.'"

Despite initial resistance from radio programmers who were concerned that it might be both too long and too progressive, 'Good Vibrations' became an instant hit, sold four hundred thousand copies in four weeks and became the Beach Boys' *first* and *only* million-selling single. [Author's note, 2022: Until 1988's 'Kokomo.']

By the fall of 1966, the Beach Boys led by Brian Wilson had musically gone past the Beatles. In October of that year, the Beatles had permanently quit touring, were working on separate projects, and *Sgt. Pepper's* was barely in the beginning stages. With 'Good Vibrations' Brian surpassed everything current in popular music. "They've Found the New Sound at Last" claimed one British paper. That one song captured the emerging sensations of the almost-acid generation, and the title of the song soon became a clichéd byword.

At the same time, the Beach Boys toured to universal (outside of the United States) acclaim. It was the Beach Boys who on their English visit were greeted by screaming mobs tearing at their clothes. It was Brian Wilson in L.A. who was driving around in a Rolls-Royce that had once been owned by John Lennon. To top it off, the Beach Boys (by a vote of 5,373 to the Beatles' 5,272) were named the number-one "world vocal group" in a year-end poll conducted by the *New Musical Express*, a British rock newspaper. It was all coming together rapidly for Brian.

What David Anderle calls "the beginning of the moment" was a period of creativity that burned and died with supernova brilliance. It was a time when Brian ignored all artistic limits and boundaries and was operating in another area of consciousness. For a brief time, he captured it in his music; whatever he saw scared him enough to retreat from all he had created. Brian may have simply gotten too close to the edge, and when he glanced over the side his sense of self-survival was strong enough that he turned and ran. But for a tentative, tantalizing time, he did have it.

Although many people have pointed to 'Good Vibrations' as Brian's greatest achievement, in 1966 it was more of a plateau to Brian. For David Anderle, Brian had no "sense of it being a pinnacle. I think he really had a sense of it being a beginning. I don't think Brian ever had a sense of anything being the pinnacle. Which is what I loved about him." Was Brian afraid of putting something out that he couldn't top? "No way! During that period, there was no way. And I was certainly trying to help him to think that there was no end to it. Everything was just the beginning."

For Brian Wilson, those months of feverish creation centered around an album, first called *Dumb Angel*, that came to be known as *SMiLE*. Although *SMiLE* was just one part of the cascading creativity, it is the part of the period that received the most attention, showed the most promise, and caused the most heartbreak when it disintegrated. Many of the songs that were part of *SMiLE* have surfaced, some in edited, bastardized form. What are we missing by not having a completed and released *SMiLE*?

According to David Anderle, "We're missing what I felt was going to be the revolutionary step in pop music . . . Instead of getting that, you're getting pieces, you're getting hints of what it could have been . . . It's as if a classical composer [wrote] a four-movement symphony, and he has all the music written out somewhere, he has it all recorded somewhere. But instead of the composer putting it into the logical order in which he views a symphony, somebody else [in this case, the Beach Boys] is coming in and grabbing certain pieces and putting them in some kind of chaotic order. That's why I say that we will never know what *SMiLE* was supposed to have been, because Brian had composed the music but he was still in the process of putting it together.

"I don't want to say it was classical because I think that's pretentious. And I don't think Brian thought of it as classical at all. But it was. It was a step. And I think had *SMiLE* been concluded and put out, I think it would have been a major influence in pop music. I think it would have been as significant if not a bigger influence than *Sgt. Pepper* was. When *Sgt. Pepper's* came out, good, bad or indifferent, everybody started making records that sounded like *Sgt. Pepper's* . . . Everybody said, 'Whoa, let's do this!' I mean, the concept of an album was created, I believe, with *Sgt. Pepper's*. Put it on in the beginning and it has a movement all the way to the end. And I know everybody wanted their sounds to sound like that album. That album was just startling. And I think *SMiLE* would have been even more startling."

SMiLE, never completed, never released, has become the most enigmatic project in rock history. What it was, what it could have been is left to legend and speculation. What it did become was an everlasting musical albatross for Brian Wilson as well as for the Beach Boys' career. In *SMiLE*, Brian was creating his own American gospel from a Southern California point of view. When his dream was shattered, so was his artistic *raison d'être*, and he embarked on a retreat into a battle with his own personal demons that has lasted to this day.

In examining the myths that have grown up around *SMiLE*, it is important to understand the atmosphere that surrounded Brian Wilson as he went about making his new music. As our chief guide, we have David Anderle, a man who was there when everything was working and watched it fall apart until he too became a victim of the collapse.

To begin with, Anderle explains that *SMiLE* wasn't just one album; more correctly it was an era of creativity that encompassed more than the single album project. Anderle starts "with *Pet Sounds* through 'Good Vibrations' to *SMiLE*. It was that period of time. Definitely, it was all part of one thing . . . *Pet Sounds* was a break from your standard Beach Boys fare. I think it was the exercise of Brian Wilson as a major musical composer or a major musical force, not just a person who can write hit songs. *SMiLE* was an extension of *Pet Sounds* in the fact that it took one step even further into the nature of exploring the musical idiom with a sense of pop." Both Anderle and Brian felt that *SMiLE* was as different from *Pet Sounds* as *Pet Sounds* was from *Summer Days (and Summer Nights!!)*.

"We're talking about significant steps," Anderle emphasizes. Or as Dennis Wilson put it in 1966, "It [*SMiLE*] makes *Pet Sounds* stink—that's how good it is."

In explaining exactly what *SMiLE* was, Anderle outlines all the projects that were being talked of in 1966 and notes that "this is really important. Brian was so creative at this time it was impossible to try to tie things up . . . we were talking about doing humor albums . . . there was the *SMiLE* talk . . . there was 'The Elements' talk." There were film ideas and TV ideas and health food ideas and entire recordings of just water sounds, all part of an atmosphere of "anything goes."

What Anderle is pointing out is that there were many different interchangeable concepts floating around. "All the various projects that never happened that were all part of that . . . very intensely creative period of time. Every day, something was happening . . . the humor concept was separate from *SMiLE*, originally." To Brian, laughter was a special kind of medicine, and he wanted to incorporate a kind of shimmering joy within his music. It was Brian's belief that humor had restorative properties for an ailing soul. In the surviving fragments of that time, *SMiLE* has become Brian's humor album because, according to Anderle, "That's all that's left of the whole thing . . . *SMiLE* was going to be the culmination of *all* of Brian's intellectual occupations . . . People don't know about the other projects that were total humor."

Anderle further explains that, along with the humor concept, spiritualism was important, almost the flip side of the humor concept. "Brian was one of the more spiritual people I've known," Anderle wistfully remembers, "and we would spend a great deal of time looking at the sky at night 'til the morning and talking about planets . . . Brian had a real innate sense of spiritualism without the knowledgeable part that you learn by reading . . . I would say he was deeply into spiritualism as a person. Whatever manifestation it took was whatever that was. There was numerology for a while; there was astrology for a while. Then we got into the I Ching [an Oriental occult forecasting device]. We did that for a long time. Those were just the things. The foundation was a real, very, very deep spiritual . . . I just always felt Brian was in touch with the cosmos."

It is important to recognize this polarity in Brian's personality and realize that there was often a precarious balance between the outrageously funny and the incredibly serious. Brian loved to have fun, but he also loved to talk about life and the stars and search for some meaning in all of it. Scientific evidence in support of many of the spiritual fields is still sketchy, and it may seem that Brian was involved in areas that provided immature amusement but had no foundation in reality. Logic, however, has little to do with emotion and creativity, and it was this openness to new thoughts that made Brian a special person and a special creator.

At first Anderle's role was that of supportive friend with whom, night after night, Brian would play or compose music or discuss his musical plans and all his ideas. Those all-night sessions, aided by Desbutols (a type of upper), were very serious; there was no fooling around or any of the legendary pranks and put-ons that Brian would soon become known for. Anderle thinks that Brian's put-ons arose from a feeling of "being unsure of yourself at certain times. It's much easier to do that." When Anderle and Brian were alone, there was no need for mind games, because there was an intense trust between the two men. "It was Brian and I together [alone] a lot of the time and there was never any of that put-on. I mean, we never even joked with each other. We would have very serious conversations, and we would spend an enormous amount of time just planning and talking and probing. But as soon as people started coming around, we would definitely get into games."

Brian's practicality in dealing with business problems was mostly fleeting, and Anderle was there to help Brian through the maze of business that stood in the way of his emerging "pure" artistry. There was no concern, on Anderle's or Brian's part, as to whether these ideas were commercial. Anderle felt that what Brian was doing was so important that it had to find an outlet. So, urged on by Brian, Anderle began to set up a channel for Brian's overflowing creativity.

It was named Brother Records (for obvious reasons), and it was designed for all the projects that Capitol Records wouldn't want because they wouldn't sell. As Brian's music was ahead of the Beatles', in 1966, so were his business ideas. The formation of Brother predates the Beatles' Apple Records by over a year.

As Anderle notes, "Brother Records was an avenue for Brian to vent his creative spleen, as it were, in directions other than the Beach Boys. Initially, we weren't really concerned with Brother being distributed through Capitol . . . Brother was for the humor albums . . . the sound effect albums . . . making records with Jasper [Dailey, who was not a singer, was much older, was hanging around and taking pictures]. It was for doing 'whatever you want to do, Brian. You want to make an album of water music with water sounds? You want to do an album that has no lyrics?

Fine, Brian, it'll be on Brother Records.'" Brother was for the projects that were special to Brian, and Anderle remembers that "I wasn't even sure at that point that I thought the Beach Boys should be a part of Brother Records."

Brother was designed as Brian's creative oasis, and, in 1966, Brian didn't consider himself a Beach Boy. Anderle insists, however, that "I was not there to break the Beach Boys up. That had nothing to do with anything in my head at all. It was not my plan to do that. As a matter of fact, I was concerned with trying to keep it together 'cause I knew if he had hassles with his brothers and cousins and so forth, it was not going to be healthy for him."

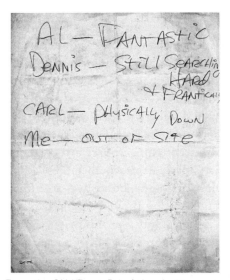

From the *SMiLE* era, Brian's handwritten note.
Credit: Courtesy of the Jonathan Anderle collection

Anderle anticipated the difficulties that Brian's projects would cause with the family, and he remembers having several conversations with Brian about the group's involvement with *SMiLE*. "Don't have them as part of *SMiLE*. Do it on your own, man," Anderle argued with Brian. "Make this the Beach Boys and that Brian Wilson . . . real division . . . like a Brian Wilson album."

SMiLE was Brian's personal vision, and in describing the creation of the music, Anderle points out that "so much of what was going on was in his head. He doesn't share the vision that much. We were just hearing the music as an end result," at which point Van Dyke Parks began to create lyrics that would match the feel of the music without getting in the way and still remain clever and intricate.

Van Dyke Parks: "I was really intent on working for him, and I didn't change the melody one note . . . I think I had a difficult collaborative responsibility. It took a great power of inference that becomes at once melodic. You have to understand the melody and support it with words and things . . . it's a more difficult challenge than people would imagine . . . I think that Brian's a better musician and knows how to incorporate more revolutionary aspects into recording than anybody I've ever met. That he's more curious and that there's something really sweet about what he does. I mean insouciant, something truly sweet."

Those end results were startling to Anderle, not only musically, but in the way Brian was composing. Like *Pet Sounds*, it wasn't straight-ahead songwriting. Anderle explains that "Brian was cutting sections of music as they were coming to him. He was going in and recording them. He wasn't doing them as 'this is this song, and this is that song.' Things were happening to him [people, feelings, new ideas], and he was recording these pieces of music" that were in part a reaction to the new experiences. Then, Brian began "putting those pieces of music together." The music evoked strong "emotion and colors and moods, movements. It had a sense of classic music without being obviously classical music. It felt extremely American to me, like Aaron Copland or something like that. But I think it was the approach, his approach to the music" that was so innovative.

Anderle explains Brian's unique talents by noting that "during the period where the Beatles and other people were starting to use a lot of electronic effects to get certain kinds of sound, Brian was getting the same kind of effects, only he was doing it with music. He wasn't using electronic effects at all. He was just writing music in very strange patterns and ways so that he was getting organic [natural] sounds that were just like what people were getting by reverse tapes and so forth. He was just writing them. It's real hard for me to describe verbally."

One man who did capture the music in words was writer Jules Siegel. Originally commissioned by the *Saturday Evening Post* to write an article about Brian Wilson and his new music, Siegel became so excited by Brian's creativity that he became part of Brian's entourage. His article, turned down by the *Post* for being too positive and sincere, eventually surfaced in the first issue of *Cheetah* magazine, and it is *the* classic piece on Brian and *SMiLE*.

> Using a variety of techniques ranging from vocal demonstration to actually playing the instruments, he taught each musician his part. A gigantic fire howled out of the massive studio speakers in a pounding crash of pictorial music that summoned up visions of roaring, windstorm flames, falling timbers, mournful sirens and sweating firemen, building into a peak and crackling off into fading embers as a single drum turned into a collapsing wall, the fire engine cellos dissolved and disappeared. "When did he write this?" asked an astonished pop music producer who wandered into the studio. "This is really fantastic! Man this is unbelievable . . . I just can't believe what I'm hearing," said the producer and fell into a stone glazed silence as the fire music began again.

According to Siegel, Brian worked on the recording of the music for over three hours, and after twenty-four takes, he was finally satisfied and invited the musicians to hear what they had just recorded: "'What do you think?' Brian asked. 'It's incredible, incredible,' whispered one of the musicians, a man in his fifties, wearing a Hawaiian shirt and iridescent trousers and pointed black Italian shoes. 'Absolutely incredible.'"

What was being put on tape, depending upon who you listen to, ranged from "incredibly artistic" to "startling" to "revolutionary." To David Anderle, "It was just the nature of the way he was writing the music plus the synthesis of his music with Van Dyke Parks's lyrics which made it revolutionary at that time to me."

The hardest facets of the *SMiLE* legend to pin down are determining how close to being finished the album was and what songs were actually to be included on the record. Bruce Johnston notes that "I don't know how close it was to being finished because, with Brian, you were almost overdubbing as you went to the lathe to cut the [mechanical] parts so you just don't know until it's out. I thought it was pretty close."

Although the back cover created by the Capitol Records art department has twelve titles, that listing isn't definitive because, according to Anderle,

"He was always interchanging parts. At one point, he'd say, 'OK. This is "Surf's Up." Or this is "Bicycle Rider." Or "Vegetables."' And then a night or two later, maybe the first verse and chorus of what had been 'Bicycle Rider' was all of a sudden the second verse of something else. It was continually changing at that point . . . I was always being thrown because I would hear something, and then I'd come back the next night, and he'd be shuffling around" the pieces.

Anderle describes an incredible scene. With the lights out, Brian would sit by the turntable with acetate discs of the sections of the music. They didn't have any labels on them, but Brian could tell from the subtle differences in the grooves which disc was which piece of music. So he would sit and play them for Anderle, explaining how he saw the puzzle on that particular night. Anderle remembers saying, "'God, Brian, why don't you leave it already? Just leave that, that's perfect that way.' And I'd get real frustrated, and then he would play . . . he'd say, 'Well, listen to this. This is going to be this, and that'll go into that . . . 'And I'd say, 'Well, of course that's perfect [too].' That was the excitement of working with Brian Wilson. It was all his personal vision."

The listing of potential *SMiLE* songs contains over twenty names, and according to Anderle, there was enough music for as many as three albums. Some of the titles were just short segments of music that hadn't been fully developed or were going to be fitted into part of another song. Anderle also explains that "a lot of those titles were at that point really just the tracks without the lyrics put on. That's why it was so easy to interchange." Had it reached the point where it was obsessive tinkering on Brian's part? "No," insists Anderle, "it was searching for the right combinations . . . it wasn't tinkering at all."

Nobody except Brian knows what pieces of music were attached to each other; the public's confusion was shared by the other Beach Boys, particularly when they would try to piece something together. The perfect example is 'Cabinessence,' which was finally released on 1969's *20/20* album. Reportedly, there were twenty-five different mixes and combinations of that song all put on separate acetate discs before they put out one version. To add to the confusion, the song in its released form contains portions of 'Who Ran the Iron Horse' and 'The Grand Coolie Dam.' Brian, who has been called the Orson Welles of rock, also at one point supposedly recorded and destroyed large quantities of music.

While Anderle spent his nights with Brian on a personal and musical basis, he spent his days setting up a business framework. "My whole feeling [of] what I wanted to do in relation to Brian was that I wanted him to be totally free, to just have everything come out. And I just wanted to try to keep some semblance of organization going so that things would move in a forward direction so that at some point we'd say, 'OK. This is this; this is that; and this is how we handle this,' so he wouldn't have to think about any of that stuff." Anderle repeated his next point to underscore its importance. "I wanted to try to keep him feeling that everything is possible, nothing is impossible. Nothing is so silly that we can't pull it off; nothing is so serious that we can't pull it off."

This juxtaposition of the serious and silly played an important part in the mythology surrounding Brian Wilson. The stories that leaked out are marvelous tales of eccentricity. For instance, Brian had a giant sandbox built around his piano and filled with sand so that he could get the feeling of being at the beach while he was writing. He put up a huge tent in one room for meetings; he turned the living room into a gymnasium when physical fitness became important. Sometimes he drove his own limousine. As David Anderle remembers, "I was there for the sandbox; I was there for the tent . . . I was there for him sending his car down to pick up the ping-pong table" late one night when Brian decided he needed to play ping-pong. And there was another desperate search when Brian wanted a telescope at three in the morning. Brian's solution was "Let's buy a telescope place, man, we'll have it open twenty-four hours a day." Brian was "really freaked out on astronomy when I was a kid."

All of these activities were just part of an artistic blowing off of steam. Brian would spend many hours in intense creation, and to "come down" from that, he would look for immediate release. Most definitely, it had to be immediate. If it didn't happen right away, for Brian, it wasn't going to happen. There were whipped-cream fights and corny dives into the swimming pool. It was adolescent stuff, and it was a very healthy, unselfconscious kind of fun. For the moment, Brian forced his friends to forget how "hip" they were supposed to be, and he got them to do what were, for the time, some pretty outrageous things. It wasn't making fun of other people; the idea was to make fun of yourself. In that respect, Brian hadn't changed at all from his high school days when he loved to be the center of attention and the butt of his own practical jokes. It was all silly and childlike, but it was freedom . . . the whole crowd doing all these things for fun, forgetting their self-image. Some nights, they would ride around the Beverly Hills Police Department in Brian's limo, smoking marijuana in the back seat of the car, but nobody could see in because the car had tinted windows.

David Anderle remembers that swimming was extremely important in Brian's life. "It started off by having meetings in the pool 'cause it was healthy. And it went from there to a couple of times we had meetings in the pool 'cause he thought the house was bugged, and he knew that there was no way to bug a swimming pool. So we'd get in the middle of the pool and whisper." Brian felt putting people in the water forced them to tell the truth, and if people started bullshitting or boring him, he would just start splashing around. As Anderle remembers, "I used to hate all those things until I got into them, and then I loved them."

That's the way it was with all of Brian's creativity. His ideas didn't include only music and film; he was interested in all forms of communication. According to Anderle, Brian wanted to change radio, wanted it light and humorous and gentle and no framework. In a marathon *SMiLE* post-mortem conversation with writer/editor Paul Williams, which first appeared in *Crawdaddy* in early 1968, David Anderle noted that everything Brian said during this period "struck our ears as totally insane." Brian's personality was so forceful, so dominating that he could convince the whole group that he was right. "Anything he said was right, no matter how outlandish it seemed." Anderle also points out that Brian's thoughts were so unique that "he never had one idea that was simple . . . Every single idea he would say had no foundation except for his head."

Nothing was too "far out" for Brian in '66. As Anderle remembers, "Brian got very much into chanting. Not just Hawaiian chants but chants in general. Chants were a big part of the formation of Brother Records . . . We used to chant around the dinner table." On the B-side of 'Heroes and Villains,' there is a chant called 'You're Welcome.' Anderle felt that the music released was a poor imitation of what they had been doing.

Brian was full of energy, and he loved to entertain people whether it was with chanting or with his music. Mark Volman and Howard Kaylan (the core of the Turtles and now "Flo and Eddie") remember going to a large dinner party at Brian's house in the fall of 1966. Everyone was seated at a long table, and at each place there was a set of headphones. When all had donned the phones, Brian proceeded to play parts of *SMiLE* to the astounded gathering.

Another of Brian's favorite dinnertime games was creating music with eating implements. Anderle remembers that he would get "maybe fifteen people all doing different rhythms," banging their plates with spoons. "Then he would come and sing over them . . . non-verbal things, just these chants, and they were absolutely stupendous." Whether it was the chanting or Brian's spoon musicale, "it was a daily routine," Anderle noted, "to have your mind blown by something Brian was coming up with."

David Anderle's favorite non-musical moment centered around the swimming pool. CBS TV's David Oppenheim, fresh from producing an award-winning documentary on composer Igor Stravinsky, was in Los Angeles to film a TV program about Brian Wilson's new music. One night, they were at Brian's house, and as Anderle remembers, "They just came up as a crew to do this filming. I think we filmed a while in the living room, and they did the piano in the sandbox deal. And then Brian said, 'OK. I want you to take pictures of all of us swimming underwater.' And they all had to borrow bathing suits and get into the water and take pictures of us in the water. He made Oppenheim strip down and get into the pool too. It was just this one night of all these straight people in the middle of winter in a swimming pool, taking pictures of these lunatics underwater. I liked that a lot when they weren't ready for it, for getting them into the swimming pool to film."

On occasion, Brian would push too far, and even Anderle would pull back. Once Brian wanted the whole crowd to go into a bar and start a fight because he wanted to record the sounds of a real fight. That was going too far. Anderle's problem was that, from his "point of view, how do you deal with somebody and you give them as much room as you can, but still hold it in check so that you can get something accomplished? That was my position, to try to see these things happen. It's one thing to be able to sit around and talk about what you want to do, and it's even another thing to maybe go in a studio or go out to a pool hall or whatever and do some crazy thing. But at some point, it's got to become an actuality, and my position was to see that become an actuality. And I had the experience of dealing with the other side of the street . . . and that's what I tried to do. I would try to let Brian have his head, but then at some point say, 'That's enough. Let's do it man, and let's get it to the people.'"

Sometimes, Anderle and Brian would clash over Brian's ideas. Like a spoiled child, Brian often made incredible demands, and as unreasonable as they seemed, Brian didn't understand the word "no." He only wanted to hear "yes."

"That was Brian in those days. 'Why? What do you mean, man, we can't have that? Let's do it!' And I'd spend my time going, 'Brian, the reason we can't do it is because . . . ' knowing that what he wanted was correct." Brian was so absorbed in his own world that he never could have understood that there were people who didn't have the force (or the cash) to indulge their whims. Brian, Anderle recalls, "was just very active. Instead of being bored, he just wanted to move on to something new. All the time."

David Anderle paints a subjective and fascinating picture of Brian as a searching and growing artist. With the perspective of time and objectivity, all of Brian's actions can be taken in a totally different light. All of the delightful eccentricities that made Brian loved can be construed as the actions of a man in serious trouble. As Anderle admits, "He may have been going through problems, and I didn't recognize it," but he insists that Brian was only "crazy in the purest sense of the word. I thought he was as crazy as you have to be to have the visions that he had. I don't like that word, 'crazy' . . . The kind of behavior that was going on at that time, I thought, was real healthy insanity, craziness or madness or whatever. I mean, it was fine . . . I would never cut that kind of thinking off because, for me, it takes that kind of extreme thinking to get something done. And Brian was one of the great extreme thinkers."

The contradictions in Brian's behavior remain confusing to this day, even to those who know him intimately and are around him constantly. Brian is renowned for the "put-on," but there were few people who really knew when Brian was being serious or seriously insane. Derek Taylor laughingly recalls how Brian "used to talk a lot of totter about health food [while he was] digging into a big, fat hamburger. And gymnasiums! I was fitter than he was, and I was only just a wet rag. Going on about vitamins. I thought maybe he was just being amusing, you see. Having a meal with him was like the Mad Hatter's tea party: 'Have some tea, there isn't any tea.' I could understand that, and I quite liked it. But when it got serious, when he pointed at me and said, 'You're not taking me seriously,' that's when I got nervous. Because then I realized that it was a possibility that here was real insanity." Derek feels that, to Brian, he was "something of a comforter. 'Is it going to be OK, Derek?' 'Yes, it's going to be OK.' 'What?' 'What is it you're worried about?' 'You know what.' 'Let's go for a drive.' A fine madness, I must say."

Derek and Brian spent hours in conversation. As Derek notes, "In addition to being a great producer, he was also a very great talker. It put strains on my marriage because his hours were not ours. He lived like a vampire. He got up at night, and he wanted to talk. It seems [in retrospect] that he was also taking rather more acid than I would suppose.

"What was difficult for me was that he wanted to know was it [*Pet Sounds*] the best album in the world? . . . I had the problem, 'Who was the fairest in the land?' Brian was always grumpy about Beatles releases if they were good." Brian wasn't mean or jealous. "He got the grumps, grouched and said, 'Yeah, well . . . I can do as well as that.' Indeed he could, but in a different way."

Brian did most everything in a different way. Acquiring a reputation as a reclusive, eccentric genius, there appeared to be a little more madness than method, but Brian wasn't really hiding from people. Derek Taylor recalls that "he wanted company. He wanted the company of the Beach Boys . . . Marilyn, Marilyn's sisters, his mother, [his friend] Arny Geller, Nick Grillo, the Beatles, most particularly Paul McCartney. Of anyone with whom he could have some sort of dialogue about music or himself or life or fitness or anything. He needed people very much indeed. It was tough keeping up with him. But when he was in good form, he was terrific." Derek adds, "One of the most awkward people I've been privileged to work with, yes."

Awkward, yes, but also lovable. And not reclusive, just shy. Not institutionally crazy, just highly imaginative. Brian was a loner who surrounded himself with people, but he was not a Howard Hughes. He thrived on verbal stimulation. The way David Anderle remembers it, "It was definitely not a reclusive thing, quite the opposite. [We didn't go out much] because we were with each other and most of the planning and organization was happening in the house. All the playing of music was in the house. There was no particular reason to be out on the street. We were enjoying each other so much. 'We' meaning Vosse and everybody. We met at Brian's house and hung out. But I always thought the going-out part was violating our being together in a way. It was bringing the external things into force."

It was the "external things" that eventually came between Brian and Anderle, Brian and Van Dyke, Brian and his music. Those external things were the record business, the Beach Boys and his family. As Terry Melcher later noted, "They really nailed him. That poor motherfucker."

Circa Fall 1966. L–R: Engineer Chuck Britz,
Brian and Van Dyke Parks in the halcyon days of the *SMiLE* era.
Photo by Jasper Dailey, courtesy of the David Leaf collection.

CHAPTER 9

HEROES, VILLAINS
AND NO SMILES

FROM THE POINT OF VIEW OF HIS FAMILY, BRIAN WAS ALMOST A BENEFACTOR rather than an artist. He wrote the hits and made the records, and the group sang them and toured and were rich and lived in the manner they had become accustomed to, all thanks to Brian Wilson.

When they saw that Brian was heading in directions that didn't always include them, they rebelled. It was this rebellion, this dissonance in Brian's life, that was in part responsible for the creeping paranoia that eventually resulted in the collapse of *SMiLE* and all the other ambitious creative projects. Brian could handle the music. He could take on the Beatles. He could charm and thrill the media. As a creative leader, he was virtually unchallengeable. But when it came to business decisions, that's when the trouble started. Brian's new circle of friends would be banished one by one, and, in the end, his family would have him again. Unfortunately for all concerned, by then, Brian had retreated from most everything, including the music.

Back in '66, though, all of Brian's dreams were becoming a reality. Anderle was forming Brother Records, and at the same time, he hired attorney Nick Grillo to institute a lawsuit against Capitol Records to force renegotiation of the Beach Boys' contract. Anderle "got the feeling they [Capitol] thought this is just another one of the Beach Boys' deals, and it'll pass over . . . if we can weather it, it'll go away. I wasn't real impressed with the deal that the Beach Boys had with Capitol Records in relationship to the success they had achieved. I felt it was time for them to get a better deal for themselves, certainly a better deal for Brian."

The accounting for record sales and royalties (centering around a disputed and outdated "breakage" clause that existed when 78-rpm records were very fragile) that Grillo and Anderle demanded became a labyrinthian task. Capitol tried to blame a fire for lost accounting records, and the suit became an interminable debacle. That suit was the first serious "bad blood" between the group and Capitol and contributed greatly to the difficulties the group would soon encounter.

While Brother was coming together, the critical praise that had followed the release of *Pet Sounds* and 'Good Vibrations' was providing just the kind of acceptance that Brian was hoping for. It firmly established him as the foremost composer/producer on the music scene, surpassing even Phil Spector. There were transatlantic phone calls and an ultimate summit meeting between Paul McCartney and Brian Wilson. And when they met, the two bass players had an immediate affinity and rapport that transcended the commercial battleground and their musical common ground. Brian blew Paul's mind with his music *and* his eccentricity, and that meant a lot to Brian. Paul, Brian felt, was *the* Beatle.

In his bid for acceptance by the "hip community," Brian was meeting and winning over all the "underground" press. David Anderle brought writers like Jules Siegel, Paul Williams, Tom Nolan and Richard Goldstein into the inner sanctum to watch Brian Wilson's magical creations. They were all duly amazed, and their writings were the beginning of the *SMiLE* story from a publicity point of view. The word was getting out: Brian Wilson was making important music.

Eventually Brian attracted the attention of the more established media, and CBS TV's David Oppenheim came to town to do a documentary about Brian Wilson. By the time the program (hosted by Leonard Bernstein) aired in '67 it had become a special about many pop music artists because Brian's and the Beach Boys' fame had begun to wane. One segment did feature Brian, alone at the piano, singing 'Surf's Up.' The voiceover narration begins: "There is a new song, too complex to get all of first time around. It could come only out of the ferment that characterizes today's pop music scene. Brian Wilson, leader of the famous Beach Boys, and one of today's most important pop musicians, sings his own 'Surf's Up.'" After Brian performed the song, the viewer heard "poetic, beautiful even in its obscurity, 'Surf's Up' is one aspect of new things happening in pop music today. As such, it is a symbol of the change many of these young musicians see in our future."

'Surf's Up' was the one song above all that was the perfect synthesis of Brian and Van Dyke Parks. It was written in one night, and in the midst of all of the craziness that was going on, Van Dyke named it with perfect simplicity. With Van Dyke and Brian working well together, the team of Wilson/Parks/Anderle seemed to have all the bases covered.

Artistic creation doesn't happen in a vacuum and Brian was reaching new heights of artistry and heading in uncharted directions, spurred on by his new group. In '66, Brian had assembled a world of friends and associates that he directed with Academy Award-winning skill. Brian and his troupe were like a modern-day Robin Hood and his merry men and Marilyn Wilson was Maid Marian, keeping the hearth warm or stocking the refrigerator with the mammoth quantities of sweets that Brian consumed. Despite whatever personal difficulties existed between Brian and Marilyn, during the SMiLE period, she was a good artist's wife. She denied Brian little, and his whims in those days were sometimes harder to follow than a pregnant bear's.

As Brian awaited the return of the Beach Boys from their English tour, he was concerned as to how the band would relate to the new people. David Anderle thinks that Brian "knew there would be resentment toward all of us new guys. I think he innately knew that they were not going to dig the lyrics to some of the songs." Brian also wasn't sure that they would "be able to pull the music off the way it should have been pulled off, that they were going to resist it . . . and be very leery of us new people."

To a certain extent, the disagreements were part of a self-fulfilling prophecy. As Anderle watched, "Brian wasn't really doing that much to help get it [his new ideas] over. He really did back away from it in a style which is not uniquely his own, but one which he does well, which is just back off and go to the bedroom or whatever. I mean, he just wouldn't face up to it. I didn't think he faced up to it."

The Beach Boys, back in town from their amazing tour of England, were having their minds blown by all the activity. The formation of Brother Records was to give each of them a chance to exercise his creativity and let each one sign and produce artists he was interested in. There were twice-weekly "chalk talks" with teams of business experts explaining how the group was going to make millions. That part was understandable. The music, however, wasn't quite what they expected, and while the group got bogged down in corporate business, they lost the creative impetus of Brian's *SMiLE* concept. The "moment" was beginning to slip away.

As the days passed, and *SMiLE* wasn't completed, the pressures from all sides bore in on Brian. Capitol, which had planned *SMiLE* for release before Christmas '66, was unhappy with the delays. They were also concerned by reports that Brian was getting "further out" with his music and spending hundreds of hours of expensive studio time, booked day and night in month-long solid blocks for Brian's convenience.

The doubts and fights that had plagued *Pet Sounds*' creation were getting stronger both within Brian *and* within the group. The inaccessibility that had hurt *Pet Sounds*' sales seemed to be even more present in the new music, and the group and the record company were concerned that what Brian was doing wasn't going to be commercial. Brian knew how good the music was—in his words, he felt that he was "writing a teenage symphony to God"—but there was always the slightest seed of uncertainty that maybe he was going too far. Once the Beach Boys were back in town, they may have heavily "watered" that fear. As Brian found himself locked in a fearsome struggle for his artistic freedom, his doubts grew. Reportedly, the group resisted the experimentation and resented the way Brian treated them as a musical instrument; but most of all, they didn't like Van Dyke Parks's words. It was the fighting over Parks's lyrics that eventually made Brian, who loved what Van Dyke had created, begin to question the songs.

To try and explain the Beach Boys' resistance, David Anderle played devil's advocate: "When they came back from England, their physical reality [i.e., the great success] had nothing to do with creating something new. It has to do with being recognized for what you have done. So when they came back, the last thing they would want to do would be to become experimental. Justifiably so, from their point of view. I think that there was a certain degree of short-sightedness on their part. I'm not really sure that they really saw what Brian was doing, not totally. I mean, I know they have ears so they could hear the music. Maybe from where they're coming from, the Van Dyke Parks influence was not a healthy influence for them lyrically. It was not Beach Boys lyrics."

Anderle told Paul Williams that there were nights when Brian would "go through a tremendous paranoia" before going to the studio "because he knew there were going to be arguments. Brian would come into the studio uptight," and when he would give out the vocal parts, there would be considerable resistance. After endless takes, Brian would just junk all the tape, and after they had left, he would go back into the studio and record all the parts himself. "All the parts," Anderle emphasized. "But it was very taxing and it was extremely painful to watch." Anderle felt that "a great wall had been put down in front of [Brian's] creativity."

In 1968, David Anderle explained to Paul Williams that Mike was the one Beach Boy who opposed Brian's "experimentation stronger than anyone else. He's the one more divorced of the family relationship . . . Mike was continually fighting Brian." Mike and Brian's studio scuffles would often end with Brian's stomping out of the studio in frustration because he couldn't control Mike and couldn't relate to Mike, and there was a lot of lost creative time. Anderle remembered that he and Mike got along well on a business level because Mike (of all the guys) best understood what Anderle was trying to accomplish. Artistically, it was another matter.

Brian and Van Dyke Parks had put together an incredible amount of music while the Beach Boys were in England, and when the group finally got to the studio, they didn't relate to what Brian was creating. As Anderle noted, "They were hearing things they never heard before, [and] you've got to remember that none of this Beatles stuff was happening then." The Beach Boys felt that Brian had created something that was not within the framework of the Beach Boys: "You're going too far now, Brian, this is too experimental. I can't sing this part." There was one song that Brian wanted to sing lead on, but it had apparently been promised to Mike. Mike was doing it beautifully, but it still wasn't what Brian wanted. After wasting almost a week of studio time, Brian finally sang the vocal.

In examining the entire period, even with the passage of ten years, Anderle's emotions remain strong whenever he discusses *SMiLE*. The passion is still there, but the years have added perspective. "Sure, I was an interloper, and I'm sure they saw me as somebody who was taking Brian away from them. And somebody who was feeding the fuel to Brian's weirdness. And I stand guilty on those counts . . . I was an interloper, and I was definitely fueling his creativity. No holds barred. No rules. 'There are no rules, Brian, you can do what you want to do. As long as the music is good, then there's no rules to what you should be able to do or not do.' I think [what happened] is unfortunate 'cause I really liked the guys.

And I really thought it could have all happened as a Beach Boys situation. I suggested to Brian at the time that a certain duality could exist. That he could still create for the Beach Boys, and then he would create his own thing on his own. Which to this day, I will fight anybody on. I don't think the Beach Boys should have been involved with *SMiLE*. From where I came from, that was Brian's mistake."

The Beach Boys were a part of *SMiLE*, according to Anderle, often unwilling and uncooperative participants, particularly in those intense and frustrating vocal recording sessions. It should also be noted that by this time, Brian didn't have much patience for mistakes or objections to the lyrics. Because so much of Brian's communicating had become non-verbal, the group was left to try and discern Brian's plans without ever getting a full explanation.

Brian could have broken up the Beach Boys very easily at that time by doing *SMiLE* on his own. Brian, however, put his brothers first, before the music, and it is a shame that they couldn't have understood this. The "duality" could have existed, but both camps were too uptight and paranoid for there to be any compromise that would satisfy Brian.

Depending upon which accounts you believe, the fights over the lyrics ranged from uncomfortable to brutal. Van Dyke Parks and Brian had created at a "hot" pace, but they split up, got back together and eventually split again.

In February of 1967, Van Dyke was offered a solo contract by Warner Brothers Records, and he left the Beach Boys and Brian behind. Van Dyke Parks: "Mike Love asked me what the lyrics meant, 'Over and over, the crow cries, uncover the cornfield.' And I said, 'Quite frankly, Mike, I don't know what this means. I can't tell you.' And I split on that, went out to Palm Springs with an advance from Warner Brothers and wrote my first album."

Van Dyke left Brian to deal with the Beach Boys on his own. It has been suggested that their parting was both tragic and predestined because both creators were very strong-willed, and Parks resented being dominated by Brian. Anderle remembered that they "were two people who absolutely did not want to separate but knew that they had to separate." Parks's departure only worsened the situation for Brian. With some of the lyrics incomplete, Brian now had the added, realistically impossible task of trying to write words compatible with Van Dyke's. It was when Parks left that

Brian's creative spark began to wane, and rather than creating new music, he began obsessively to rearrange the pieces of the *SMiLE* puzzle, at this point still trying to form a coherent picture.

According to Anderle, "If he can't get it done like that [he snapped his fingers], if he can't act upon it immediately and see it happening in front of his eyes, it's not gonna work. If he has to wait until morning, it's not gonna happen. That's what happened to *SMiLE*." With the return of the guys from England, and their reaction to the music, Brian had lost that immediacy; he had to try to explain the music to so many people. Parks's subsequent leave-taking only became an additional obstacle. More obstacles soon arose, but there had already been one disturbing incident, one of the first indications that not everything was right in Brian's world.

One of the most famous events in Brian's career revolved around a piece of music known as 'Fire' or 'Mrs. O'Leary's Cow.' The music, brilliantly described by Jules Siegel a few pages back, was to be part of 'The Elements' concept that Brian was creating—Earth, Air, Fire, Water. Brian had spent a week in Big Sur to get away from the city's artificial atmosphere and really taste the surrounding nature in unspoiled form. The music that was emerging was astounding to everyone who heard it. 'Fire' was described as a "terrifying internal whine"; the music wasn't pretty. Just amazing. A few days after the session for 'Fire,' Brian heard of a number of fires in Los Angeles. Maybe there were more fires than usual. Whatever, Brian felt that the music was the cause of the fires, and he, according to the legend, destroyed the master tapes. One tale notes that he tried to burn the tapes, but, ironically, they wouldn't catch fire, so he just dumped them in the garbage. Actually, he locked the tapes in a vault. Brian told Jules Siegel, "I don't have to do a big scary fire like that. I can do a candle and it's still fire. That would have been a really bad vibration to let out on the world, that Chicago fire. The next one is going to be a candle."

As understanding as one might try to be, it would be generous to call that behavior anything less than unusual. A person rooted in a world of common sense and logic, as Jules Siegel noted, would begin to speak of neurotic or psychotic behavior. Brian in those days, however, was always spiritual. He was creating emotional, religious, spiritual music, and there was no room for everyday reality.

Unfortunately, it was that type of thinking in which Brian began to wallow as winter dragged on. When Parks left, Brian got out of the studio altogether and devoted his attention to the business aspects of Brother Records' formation. And there was all the media attention. Besides the CBS documentary, writers from all sorts of papers and magazines were coming by. Brian had always been shy, and all these new people and kinds of people that Brian hadn't ever met were coming around. Anderle remembered that Brian began to question Anderle as to the validity and importance of the critical community and of certain people. He was, Anderle recalled, having difficulty separating "who was real and who was not real . . . because he'd not been exposed [to the media] in the past." The business, the media, the film for 'Good Vibrations,' the fighting with the guys all kept Brian from finishing the music. Brian, Anderle felt, "was clinging on to excuses."

Events were becoming overwhelming, and Brian was evidencing more paranoid behavior, as this next tale illustrates. Brian went to the movies one day and returned in a fevered state, desperately seeking reassurance. He had seen the psychological horror film *Seconds*, and upon entering the theater, the first words from the screen he heard were, "Hello Mr. Wilson." That really upset Brian, but what followed was equally disturbing to him, and he later claimed that the movie included his entire life, his birth and his death and rebirth (and even the beach). Brian felt the movie was the work of "Mind Gangsters" who had been hired by Phil Spector to upset and scare him. After his friends calmed him down, Brian repaired to his psychedelically decorated den and went over to his jukebox, which was filled with Spector and Beach Boys records. Brian punched the numbers and out jumped 'Be My Baby' at top volume. Then, Brian explained to Jules Siegel why he felt that Spector was out to get him.

"Spector has always been a big thing with me . . . I heard that song three and a half years ago, and I knew that it was between him and me. I knew exactly where he was at, and now I've gone beyond him . . . he was the first one to use the studio. But I've gone beyond him now. I'm doing the spiritual sound, a white spiritual sound. Religious music. Did you hear the Beatles' album? Religious, right? That's the whole movement. That's where I'm going. It's going to scare a lot of people."

On another occasion, Brian kept a studio filled with violinists waiting for a session, waiting to find out if the vibrations were right. They weren't, and three thousand dollars went down the drain. Besides the money, the incidents are revealing as to Brian's relative stability (or lack of it) during the *SMiLE* period.

In the midst of all this "unusual" behavior, there were, as always, pressures from the record company for a new single and the completed album, and from the guys not to use Van Dyke's lyrics. There was pressure from Murry that all of the music was just too darn weird. On top of all that, Brian was now having trouble getting studio time when he wanted it (often in the early morning hours). Also, the studio operators were hassling Brian for violating union regulations because Brian was often engineering his own sessions. Nobody but an engineer was supposed to touch the control-room board, but Brian didn't want to have to try and communicate his ideas. He wanted to implement them; in addition to all his other talents, Brian is an excellent mixer and engineer. The combined studio problems may have been why Brian built a studio in his home in mid-1967.

In the spring of 1967, the Beatles released their conceptual production masterpiece, *Sgt. Pepper's Lonely Hearts Club Band*, a record that brought the Beatles back to their position of supreme leaders of the rock world. A number of people have speculated that the release of this album, hailed as *the* new sound, convinced Brian that it was too late to have an impact with *SMiLE*. It was probably only another contributing factor. 'Heroes and Villains' was released after *Sgt. Pepper*, and if Brian had decided to scrap *SMiLE* only because of *Pepper*, then he probably would not have released the highly progressive new single that was an integral part of *his* new sound.

As it was, the negotiations with Capitol Records had reached a crucial stage, and it was necessary for the Beach Boys to get a single out. David Anderle remembered, "I told Brian he had to have a single. It was the hardest thing I ever did." The business was coming between Brian and Anderle's friendship, but Anderle knew that if Brian wanted Brother Records to become a reality, a single had to be released. 'Heroes and Villains' was chosen because it was the closest to being completed.

Actually, it had been finished in December, but Brian, caught up in his puzzle, continually edited the song, creating new pieces and scrapping them, until it emerged in its sharply shortened form. Chuck Britz, who engineered the original recording in late 1966, noted that "it was done like 'Good Vibrations'; it was just one hell of a song. It was a great song.

Then, I understand, they went up to his home [studio], and they did a lot of things. They cut it and inserted an organ down at the bottom of the [swimming] pool to get the pool quality [all the water was out]. They did all kinds of things, but I think basically it could have been as good a classic as 'Good Vibrations' or better . . . Our [version] ran about five or six minutes . . . it was just a further step from 'Good Vibrations.' It had some great melodic lines . . . the arrangement was so full, and it was just something that I was very disappointed in when I heard the final product."

According to various accounts, there are many longer versions of 'Heroes and Villains,' some reportedly as long as twelve minutes. All those who heard the original are of the opinion that the released version is missing, as Jules Siegel wrote, "entire sequences of extraordinary power and beauty . . . sacrifices to the same strange combination of superstitious fear and God-like conviction of his own power he [Brian] displayed when he destroyed 'Fire.'" What was released is still an incredible piece of harmonic and lyrical wizardry.

At this time, there were significant changes in Brian's life. Anderle left because it was impossible to run the business without decisions from Brian, and as Anderle remembered, "We couldn't find where his head was at for a whole long period of time." Anderle was gone, shut out of Brian's life in a heartbreaking finale when Brian refused to leave his room while Anderle pleaded with Brian to come out and see him. Reflecting on their creative relationship and friendship, Anderle explained that all the new people and the writers and the demands were very difficult for Brian because "he is a very shy person. Not a real social person. Brian was bombarded with newness. And he was on his own. The guys were not around when this was happening. He definitely was handling it all by himself. When something like this happens, you have to start trusting people. You either trust someone around you or trust no one. You either become paranoid or you can trust people. I think for a long period of time, Brian trusted a lot of us. Then it went from that to, from what I could tell, paranoia. Where he didn't even trust us anymore."

What remained of Brian's trust resided in uncommon, occult places. Numerology may have caused an irreparable rift in Brian and David Anderle's friendship. Inspired by Brian's boundless creative energy, David painted a picture of Brian. When Brian saw it, as writer Tom Nolan commented, "the whole room went on an acid trip." Brian then went over to the picture and began to count the objects in it, and Brian was freaked, as was David, by the coincidences of numerological significance in the painting. Brian partly felt that Anderle's portrait had captured his (Brian's) soul. Anderle may have crossed an inviolable line in Brian's mind, a mind that was becoming increasingly confused.

Astrology dictated the release date of 'Heroes and Villains.' Brian was waiting for the astrologically correct moment to let the world hear his new record. Terry Melcher colorfully recounted the scene (in Nolan's '71 *Rolling Stone* article). A string of Rolls-Royce limousines went to KHJ radio to give them a worldwide exclusive premiere of the next Beach Boys single. Brian prepared the moment carefully, presented the acetate disc to the DJ who turned to Brian and said, according to Melcher, "'Can't play anything that's not on the playlist.' Brian almost fainted . . . It really killed him." Even when the program director finally straightened things out, it was too late. The spell was broken, and the damage to Brian had been done.

One of Brian's friends recalls that Brian had become "like a petulant child. 'It's my ball and we'll play by my rules or we won't play at all.'"

The death of *SMiLE* was reported by Derek Taylor in the May 2, 1967 issue of *Disc and Music Echo* magazine: "In truth, every beautifully designed, finely wrought, inspirationally welded piece of music made these last months by Brian . . . has been SCRAPPED. Not destroyed but scrapped. For what Wilson seals in a can and destroys is scrapped."

The Beach Boys' time, too, seemed to have passed. It had only taken a matter of months, but the delay in following up 'Good Vibrations' with something of equal impact had damaged their commercial momentum. With the release of *Sgt. Pepper* and the arrival of San Francisco psyche-delia and the Summer of Love, the Beach Boys had become incredibly passé. They had one final chance to create a bridge with the new "hippie" audience, and they may have sealed their own doom when they failed to play at the Monterey Pop Festival, which was the predecessor of Woodstock.

With Brian on the festival's board of directors, the Beach Boys were slated to appear on Saturday, June 17. It was Brian who eventually decided that the group wouldn't perform. Among the "official" reasons given for the cancellation was that the group needed to finish 'Heroes and Villains' because of the crucial status of the record company negotiations; that reason wasn't too "hip." The other excuse was that Carl, who had been indicted for refusing to join the army, was so upset that he wouldn't be able to sing.

Through the years, a number of additional explanations have surfaced. One is that the group was initially supposed to be paid for the concert, but when it became a non-profit event, their fee was withdrawn and they felt they were being "ripped off" and used to make money for someone else. Mike Love offered another explanation, remembering "a meeting in the backyard, and I don't know what was happening, but I guess we were wrecks. Brian was really shattered by some really bad trips. He'd been taking acid and some uppers and smoking some hash and was out of control. Dennis was in some weird place [he was getting divorced from his first wife Carol] . . . "

John Phillips, leader of the Mamas and Papas, one of the festival's organizers, felt that "Brian was afraid the hippies from San Francisco would think the Beach Boys were square and boo them." It is possible that the Beach Boys, in their short hair and striped shirts, would have been subjected to ridicule at the festival. The music? It's hard to believe that the audience wouldn't have been moved by the music. It hadn't failed before, and it might not have at Monterey. But that, as they say, became academic when the group pulled out.

Probably it was just one of Brian's capricious career moves, which were so much a part of that wildly illogical summer of 1967. Before pulling out of Monterey, Brian had finally decided to shelve *SMiLE*, to relegate it to the land of limbo. What brought about the final decision nobody but Brian will ever know, but it seems that it was forced upon him by incredible negative pressure. It was Brian who chose not to release *SMiLE*, but that choice was hardly a free one. All around him, people were saying "NO!"

Bruce Johnston now thinks that the fights over *SMiLE* were "like a slap in the face to Brian. You have all these coat-and-tie people up at Capitol saying, 'Hey, Brian, you're breaking the mold of something you did really well.' He's a guy who did things [made hits and great records] very well, and he wants people to trust his judgment. And here you have people saying, 'No.' He's a very fragile person, he's a special person, and he didn't understand that kind of 'no,'" particularly when he had produced so much success. Bruce feels the "no" came "a little bit from Murry and a little bit from the record company."

It has always been publicly unthinkable for the Beach Boys to acknowledge that their resistance was partly responsible for Brian's freak-out and the ultimate destruction of *SMiLE*. They blamed it on the new people he was hanging out with, like Van Dyke Parks and David Anderle and the others, and the drugs they were all feeding Brian. Through the years, the group has always had to answer the question, "What happened to *SMiLE*?" Their answer, which became the official line of the Beach Boys family, was that Brian, in Mike Love's words, "freaked out completely in the last stages of *SMiLE* and stepped back and said 'I can't handle that production race thing that was going on between the Beach Boys and the Beatles' . . . Subliminally, it was a competition thing, and Brian just stepped back, and the production war collapsed, and we did a very light album. It was his withdrawal, a reflection of his withdrawal, and our withdrawal from that confronting thing on a production level . . . our music was one bass note in 'Vegetables,' and that's how psychedelic it was, but it sure was in a freaky way . . . Brian was so out of it, though. He was taking acid and uppers."

David Anderle is convinced that "the music was definitely so focused that I would have to say that drugs had nothing to do with anything . . . the drugs may have had something to do with his searching . . . I don't know. I never thought of drugs in terms of the music with Brian, *ever*. I would never think of taking LSD with Brian."

There has never been a public (or private?) acknowledgment that the Beach Boys have felt the least bit guilty for fighting with Brian over the new music. The drugs are the scapegoat for Brian's retreat, but what forced him to take drugs?

Anderle's drug experiences with Brian were confined to "soft" drugs. Brian had taken acid before meeting Anderle, and Brian's use of LSD reportedly didn't increase until *SMiLE* was unraveling. If Brian sought refuge within drugs, in reaction to all the pressure, then everybody must share the blame—the record company, the family, the Beach Boys, and Brian's entourage. Brian was spurred on by what Bruce Johnston called Brian's "vertical, temporary friends dropping all sorts of drugs on him. 'Try this, smoke this, eat this, take this, burn this.' You had that happening, and then everyone else saying, 'Yes. No. Maybe.' I think it got very confusing for him."

David Anderle had eliminated the rules for Brian as long as "the music is good," and that type of thinking may have provided Brian with the impetus to search for his outer limits. The family's and Anderle's love of Brian and his music could not, and did not, include a personal vigilance. There was no way to tell Brian to slow down; he's always been too powerful for that.

In looking at that period in retrospect, Brian seemed to be heading in one direction—self-destruction. Brian did survive the *SMiLE* era, and even if he may have been an "acid casualty," his very existence is a triumph of personal survival. Brian was one of the first rock stars to "burn out," and he could very easily have destroyed himself completely, as so many others did, like Jimi Hendrix, Janis Joplin, Brian Jones and Jim Morrison. Those people, tragically, did not come out on the other side of their personal hells.

Fortunately, Brian did pull back just in time, and as he explained in 1976, he had to destroy *SMiLE* because "it was destroying me."

In determining the ultimate cause of *SMiLE*'s demise, it is possible to speculate endlessly. Possibly, at one point, Brian could have forced the issue and insisted that *SMiLE* be released. That act might have destroyed the Beach Boys and splintered the Wilson family. David Anderle feels that the support that Brian didn't get from his new friends and from his family forced Brian to kill *SMiLE*.

Anderle explained to Paul Williams that all the "Nos" were a big shock for Brian. "It's like taking a person, exposing him to something he's always wanted to be in, taking him right to the brink of it and leaving. And saying, 'Geez, Brian, how come you haven't followed up with that whole thing? Why have you fallen down?' He zoomed right up there, alienated from a lot of things that had been his strengths in the past. Those strengths were ripped away, shown to be shallow and phony, [and they were now] taken away from him . . . but no [new] foundation put under him. And the foundation that we all had, that we were trying to supply him with, was us! And when we went, there was nothing left there. Just him, hanging . . . perhaps we should have never gone in the first place."

Without the exposure to the new people, Brian would never have reached some of the extremities of *SMiLE*, but Anderle realized that unless this whole new group was prepared perpetually to support Brian, then they might have been wrong in showing him this new world. Still, Anderle believes that the music would have transcended all those difficulties if Brian had made a break from the Beach Boys and demanded his artistic freedom. Yes, he could have forced *SMiLE*'s release, but it might have cost him what was left of his precarious hold on reality, and, in that respect, it is much better to have Brian than to have *SMiLE*.

Whatever turned this creator into a paranoid pop star is what killed *SMiLE*, and those causes are complex and still unresolved to this day. In the end, it was Brian's decision not to release it. Because his decision-making process had become bizarre and illogical, he cannot in any way be blamed for his choice. Brian knew then and knows today how important that music was both to his art and to the world of music. He's aware of its power. The buck stops with the artist, and in this case, Brian Wilson decided to pass, *but* he backed down from his artistic impulses to save himself. There can be no art without responsibility to an audience. Art without responsibility is self-indulgence. In the case of *SMiLE*, Brian had to choose between himself and a responsibility to others. His decision was very human, understandable, and necessary.

David Anderle, who watched it all come together and fall apart, remembers that he "had the feeling that at one point, Brian just wanted to back away from the whole thing and forget about it. It was just too much for him. The formation of Brother Records . . . all of a sudden, attorneys were around. He was having to make major decisions. He had the group on another hand, everybody wanting him not to experiment. Then he had people like me who were pressing him to continue to experiment and 'Fuck the rules, Brian. This is more important than what you've already accomplished.' I felt that what he was doing was too important to have his mind messed up with the other thing.

"I also thought, by the way, when I first met him, started hanging out with him, I thought he had the capacity to handle a full range of activities. Apparently, I was wrong. He didn't have the ability. All the things we talked about, I came to realize he couldn't pull off . . . But that's OK, 'cause I could have helped him."

Once Anderle and the others were gone from the scene, Brian was a lone (and often paranoid) warrior fighting for his music. The battle was more than he could handle, especially when he realized that he wouldn't be allowed to create away from the Beach Boys as Brian Wilson, solo artist. What Brian couldn't comprehend then (and it is as true in 1978) is why the family wouldn't allow him the freedom to create apart from them. It is clear that they were scared; all they'd ever been was Beach Boys—straight from high school to rock stars. While their insistence that Brian remain a

Beach Boy is understandable, it was not then nor is it now excusable. The man is an artist who has something to say on his own.

As Anderle claims, "I just felt it could survive next to each other. I thought it could. I didn't understand why nobody else could see how easy it would be. But again, maybe from their point of view, they just saw all of us as people who were in there to get what we could get. I think that came from the father [Murry]. People coming into the situation to get what they could get. And probably, to some extent, that was true. But it wasn't in mine, and I just resented being thought of as anybody else 'cause I knew I was different. I knew my motivations were good motivations for all of them."

What is inexplicable is that Anderle, who was putting together the record company, never got a chance to explain his vision to the group. "We had meetings," he recalls. "They had as many meetings as any band I've ever seen in my life. But these meetings were always so strange." Despite prodding from Anderle that Brian create apart from the group, Brian at one point made it very clear that all the ideas had to include his brothers and that he would not break up the group. Anderle often wondered if the family ties were really strong, but he came to realize that the Wilsons "really do have a strong bond . . . it's a strange family, but it is a family indeed. When it came down to it, they're Beach Boys. That is their thing. Which is what I came to learn; above and beyond everything else, that is their thing. Dennis's [1977] solo album is a much more critical move than people think. That's amazing that he actually did it. It is significant because it's something that Brian couldn't even do. The baby of the family came through . . . It's really what I thought *SMiLE* should have been. Just a separate album. Dennis is still a Beach Boy. Brian could still have been a Beach Boy. 'Just do *SMiLE*, man!'" Ironically, ten years after *SMiLE* almost destroyed Brian and the Beach Boys, Dennis Wilson's solo record was a key factor in their temporary breakup in the late summer of 1977.

The legend that has become *SMiLE* is a mystery that to this day has never been satisfactorily explained. One of the hopes that has intrigued Beach Boys fans for years is that the group might one day complete and release *SMiLE*. After the Capitol lawsuit was settled in '71, the group began to claim publicly that *SMiLE* would be forthcoming. They said that all the tapes that had supposedly been lost or destroyed actually existed and that *SMiLE* would be released. Reportedly, the group did piece together a still-unreleased album that included 'The Elements' and many of the original musical segments grouped under the overall subtitle of 'Heroes and Villains.' *SMiLE* never did surface, though, and there is a distinct possibility that the 1971/1972 promises were designed to stall the record company's demands for a new album. It was also a clever extension of the *SMiLE* myth, which garnered the group a lot of publicity.

What actually remains to be released is a mystery. One current member of the group's staff thinks that it's all "a big story and that all of the things have been released, and all of the things that weren't worth releasing are in the can but no one would want to hear them anyway." Through carelessness, a lot of the master tapes have been lost. Others were allegedly erased or put in a storage vault by Brian. A lot of the music does still exist, and a number of the participants have acetates of still-unreleased *SMiLE*-era Beach Boys music.

Bruce Johnston, however, claims that "most of *SMiLE* is available now." While it is true that many of the songs that were intended for *SMiLE* have been released (particularly on *SMiLE*'s replacement, *Smiley Smile*), the original instrumental tracks, lyrics and vocals to those songs (e.g., 'Wind Chimes,' 'Wonderful,' and some of the missing segments of 'Heroes and Villains') have never come out.

Rock writer, Beach Boys observer, and now record company executive Ben Edmonds: "The main thing to consider is that it may have been great for its time. Once you remove a period piece from its place in history, a lot of times it just doesn't make sense. Chances are, if there was a brilliance to *SMiLE*, it was a conceptual brilliance that Brian never could get the mechanics right on. 'Cause I'm sure that his ideas at that point in time were mind-blowing. But I'm sure that between the drugs and the hassle with the group, he found it very difficult to translate those brilliant concepts into brilliant music."

Still, it would be fascinating to hear and analyze the music for ourselves so that we might know how great the loss of *SMiLE* was. Taken together, the songs intended for *SMiLE* that have been released constitute a mind-boggling collection and surpass everything else the group has released with the possible exception of *Pet Sounds*. Of course, it can never be completed as Brian intended, so a compromise solution might be to release the surviving tapes and outtakes in a series of records called *The SMiLE Sessions*. Like Elvis's *Sun Sessions*, it would be an invaluable opportunity to analyze Brian's working methods during the time of his life that is always considered his most creative.

The possibility exists that the release of any of that music (if any does exist) would ultimately be disappointing, which may be why it hasn't been released. Van Dyke Parks said (in 1978) that if *SMiLE* were finally released, "that would either expose us all as idiots or really give us a lot of ammunition. I'm ready for the gamble. It's a high roll, but I would take it if I were he . . . I really mean that. I know it's real good. It's heavily massaged music, within the confines of that fidelity."

Bruce Johnston believes that a modern-day release of *SMiLE* "wouldn't be a good idea. Sometimes, when you talk about something, you're kind of let down. Say you discover the tapes and you say, 'Oh yeah?' It's been talked about so much . . . It would live up to your expectations if you were Zubin Mehta analyzing a young composer's work. It's the kind of music you almost need a Ford Foundation grant to make. It was really a clever album, [but its release today] would [only] be important for Brian artistically. If you put that album all together, there would be an incredible artistic value . . . but for keeping a band alive, no."

Bruce also thinks its release in 1967 "probably would have hurt our careers in terms of working and supporting ourselves . . . I think the *SMiLE* album would have done worse than *Smiley Smile*. It was really good, but it was a little esoteric. There's a little [commercial] bridge you can cross," and Bruce thinks that *SMiLE* would have been that bridge for the Beach Boys. "I think it was better to squeeze it out rather than put it on one album, which we were going to do. Sometimes, I don't think people are ready for something that heavy, but now, when you look back at what's happened in the ten or eleven years since *SMiLE*, it's not as heavy; it's kind of a prototype of the idea that people can experiment more, even though it was never one album." And it probably never will be. *SMiLE* is a vibration that will remain locked away, at Brian Wilson's insistence.

Brian was a kind of guinea pig for the record industry in his fight for artistic freedom. His biggest mistake was coming along just a few years too soon. He was always ahead of most of the rock world in his creative thinking, but he was virtually consumed by the battle by the summer of 1967. Brian's timing was tragic because that summer was the turning point for the record industry. By the fall of 1967, the artist had finally become important, and it was the artist who was beginning to call all the shots.

Brian missed that creatively free period by only a few months, but that miss is what created the *SMiLE* myth.

David Anderle has always felt that it was a great loss that Brian has never shared the beauty and the power of the *SMiLE*-era music with the world. He has the final word on *SMiLE:* "I think it's just a crime. As a person who enjoys listening to music, I think it's a real tragedy. I think it's a tragedy that it was bastardized by the guys. That music should not have been Beach Boys music. And I'll always feel that way. I think that not because I don't think the Beach Boys pulled it off or whatever. But I think it was just such a personal vision of Brian's that I don't think anyone should have been allowed to mess with it. And I felt that way when it was happening. I remember Brian told me he wanted the guys to sing on it. I thought it was a mistake, not 'cause they couldn't, but why should they? It was very personal. It was created all by him. But so be it. But I think it's a giant hole that will never be covered in Brian's musicality."

CHAPTER 10

BEACHED

"YOU'LL NEVER HEAR SURF MUSIC AGAIN." THAT OFT-QUOTED LYRICAL observation was made by Jimi Hendrix, one of the legendary stars to emerge from the Monterey Pop Festival.

The Beach Boys' non-appearance at Monterey, combined with the release of *Smiley Smile* (*SMiLE*'s replacement), pretty much ended the group's importance within the rock world. *Smiley Smile* was greeted primarily with great disappointment by an audience that had been hearing promises of *SMiLE* for over a year. The fights over Brian's progressive experiments were over but this latest artistic about-face just didn't cut it, particular compared with the production masterpiece of *Sgt. Pepper's*. It is only in retrospect that this record has been given its due and recognized for being a great "head" album. At the time, it was considered strange, and, for the most part, it was treated with little respect by the critics as well as by a baffled public, who stayed away from the album in droves.

'Heroes and Villains' was one of the most highly publicized single records in rock history. Because it was the follow-up to 'Good Vibrations,' expectations were high. Restless anticipation increased to such a peak that the record's actual release could only seem anti-climactic. So while it was a successful single, it wasn't a big enough hit to turn the tide.

Brian Wilson, meanwhile, mostly watched as his old group fell out of favor with the public. The Beach Boys would again have hits, they would again play for cheering audiences. The late 1960s and early 1970s, however, was not their time. Those were the lean years . . . years of creative inertia, financial chaos and personal difficulties. The Beach Boys, unfortunately, had become dinosaurs.

★   ★   ★   ★

177

By the end of 1967, although it may now be hard to understand, the Beach Boys were no longer important to the music world. With Brian Wilson at the group's helm, their records had been among the most innovative in popular music. With Brian in retreat, it took the group but a few months to go from the heights of 'Good Vibrations' to a banishment imposed by the new rulers of the rock kingdom.

The summer of 1967 was the media event billed as the Summer of Love, the official coronation of the psychedelic era. San Francisco was the home of the new music, as the rest of the world tripped over itself trying to catch up. If that meant psychedelia was now a marketable commodity, that was OK with San Francisco's hippie "merchants." They didn't mind selling instant, tie-dyed hipness to a new generation which was just beginning to flex its economic muscle for the first time.

The San Francisco scene and the Monterey Pop Festival were the combined birthplace for a new set of musical leaders. The Jefferson Airplane and the Grateful Dead were San Francisco's hometown bands, but Monterey was a showcase for the world's talent. Out of the festival burst Hendrix and Janis Joplin and the Who. The Mamas and Papas' singing of 'California Dreamin'' seemed to more than make up for the absence of the Beach Boys' 'California Girls.' All of those acts and myriad others gained a new and wider audience just by being part of the festival. By not appearing, the Beach Boys missed a perfect opportunity to make their peace with the San Francisco consciousness. Instead, they alienated the hip audience that had just begun to accept them because of music like *Pet Sounds* and 'Good Vibrations.' By not appearing, the Beach Boys quickly found themselves in exile as pop relics.

Ben Edmonds has been a longtime observer of the Beach Boys' career, and he explains why the Beach Boys were so scorned in their home state. "When everything got very much 'hipper than thou,' people, to a certain extent, found the Beach Boys embarrassing. Because the Beach Boys definitely were not hip. People out here, I think, saw them as being the antithesis of everything that was hip. And just viewed them as like the disabled member of the family that you lock away in the attic and don't tell people about." Bruce Johnston, who was part of that clean image, thinks that a lot of it was just a generation "growing up and throwing away a lot of traditional kind of behavior; it was like *Leave it to Beaver* [the family situation comedy] or something. It was just too straight. It was the kind of music where maybe the parents had said years before, 'Now, the Beach Boys, that's nice music. Why don't you look like them?'"

As Bruce Johnston once noted, "People look at the Beach Boys, and think we're surfing Doris Days." *Rolling Stone* magazine began publishing in the late fall of 1967 and quickly became the arbiter of hip for the emerging acid generation. *Stone* was "underground" press in those days, and because playing or listening to music was a main pastime of the hippies, *Rolling Stone* concentrated on the doings in the rock music world.

What this meant was that when *Rolling Stone* put down the Beach Boys, a lot of people picked up on that and spread the word that it was no longer cool to like the Beach Boys. That stigma lasted a long time, and it was the product of comments like these excerpts from a December '67 article by *Rolling Stone*'s founder and editor, Jann Wenner. "In person, the Beach Boys are a totally disappointing group. (At the last minute, presumably afraid of a sophisticated audience, they pulled out of the Monterey Pop Festival) . . . Brian Wilson actually is an excellent writer and composer and a superb producer, however his genius is essentially a promotional shuck . . . The Beach Boys are just one prominent example of a group that has gotten hung up in trying to catch the Beatles. It is a pointless pursuit. A lot of people talked about it, but the Beatles have so far been the only group to come up with a fully orchestrated and interiorly cohesive symphonic or operatic piece."

Wenner, of course, was ignoring *Pet Sounds*. For reasons unknown, he dismissed their entire body of work with the next sentence. "Their surfing work continued for about ten albums with little apparent progress. 'Sloop John B' was stupid but transitional. John Lennon said he really dug 'God Only Knows' [it was Paul] and the world perked up." Wenner's insight into Brian Wilson's growth as an artist appeared to be minimal. There was no way anybody could have really listened to *Surfin' Safari* and then *Pet Sounds* (besides all the intermediate steps) and not seen growth. Hip prejudice had gotten in the way of legitimate criticism, and this is one prominent reason the Beach Boys' career began to wane in late 1967. People weren't bothering to listen; it was cool to just put the group and Brian down. If there were any hang-ups involved, it was on the part of the hip generation. A new set of prejudices gained favor, one that centered around the length of your hair, the clothes you wear and the chemicals you ingest. The ultimate irony is that underneath the Beach Boys' surface image were some very bizarre people who were often into the latest thing before it became the latest thing.

Brian and Dennis in a heart-to-heart conversation. In the late 1960s, following in his big brother's footsteps, Dennis would emerge as a genuine artist, writing some of the group's best post-*SMiLE* songs.
Credit: Michael Ochs Archives/Getty

The Beach Boys, though, didn't exactly help heal the communications breakdown. Their stage outfits were still pretty silly even though they finally abandoned the striped shirts. Unfortunately, they replaced the shirts with suits that were only a small step in updating their onstage appearance. The Beach Boys were clinging to the old image out of a sense of security, and their hesitation in changing cost them a generation of popularity. By the time the Beach Boys realized this in early '68 it was too late. Time had passed them by.

Brian Wilson, meanwhile, was moving physically but not musically. The Wilsons had moved from Beverly Hills to a beautiful Spanish-style home in Bel-Air that had once been owned by Edgar Rice Burroughs. According to Terry Melcher, when Brian first moved in, he painted the house a bright purple. "The neighborhood went crazy. He lives on Bellagio in the heart of Bel-Air. There was a Bel-Air residents citizens' committee, and they were up in arms. It was funny. It was a shitty color, I'll have to admit. You wouldn't want to live in it."

Brian and the Beach Boys recorded *Smiley Smile* in Brian's gigantic home studio. Although that album was the beginning of a long decline in popularity, at least they had put out an album. For a while the Beach Boys had ceased to exist.

Amid all the weirdness and drugs, there didn't really seem to be a functioning band. In August of 1967, Brian and the group went to Hawaii, where they filmed and recorded a concert for a possible live album. They were all wasted on one drug or another. (Bruce Johnston didn't go on this trip; it had become too bizarre for him.)

Next came a great deal of hashish, which influenced the making of *Smiley Smile*. To begin with, *Smiley Smile* was and is a very peculiar album. Some of the songs that had been written for the *SMiLE* album were used on this album, but the instrumental tracks that Brian had spent months recording had been replaced mostly by Brian at his Baldwin organ. Watered-down versions of several of the Wilson–Parks songs were recorded, Brian and Mike worked on a couple of tunes, and Brian wrote a few songs that were pale reflections of his musical experimentations. These bastardized versions are evidence of Brian's composing skills, but they are ultimately disappointing in light of the promise *SMiLE* once held.

This album was, as Carl Wilson put it, "a bunt instead of a grand slam." One writer called *Smiley Smile* "do-it-yourself acid casualty doo-wop." Actually, it was an artistic cop-out and disaster. After months of resisting Brian's experimenting, the group produced this lollipop of psychedelic simplicity. At the time, the album was totally incomprehensible to the public. After almost a year of *SMiLE* hype, *Smiley Smile* was more than a mere disappointment. It was a broken promise. Brian Wilson was going to expand the boundaries of popular music. Instead, he had quit, given up, just when the new horizon was almost behind him.

Nineteen sixty-seven was a bleak year in general for the Beach Boys. They had always relied on Brian for creative direction, and in the process of resisting his leadership, the Beach Boys had become a rudderless democracy. *Smiley Smile* was a hastily assembled, minimally produced effort that took less than a month of recording. The Beach Boys were often so stoned that they sang the vocals lying down on the floor. The album credit read "Produced by the Beach Boys," and with the exception of 'Heroes and Villains' and 'Good Vibrations,' none of the other songs were elaborate

Brian Wilson productions. Brian didn't even want 'Good Vibrations' on the album; Capitol Records dictated its inclusion.

Smiley Smile contains some great Brian Wilson songs (e.g., 'Wonderful' and 'Wind Chimes'), but in comparison to *Pet Sounds* and the two previous singles, this record didn't seem to be much more than a half-hearted effort. It was as much "product" as it was "art," and back in '67, it didn't succeed on either level. Only after years of listening has this record become "art"; it has finally been embraced by the fans and understood by the critics. Brian and the Beach Boys had advanced "ahead" of their audience, but they were going in the wrong direction for all but a very small, intense cult. With the passage of time, it became OK to admit that it was a good record. It was just disillusioning to those who were enrolled in the "Brian Wilson is a genius" school of thought. And that disillusionment translated into poor record sales, a trend that wouldn't be reversed for a long, long time.

In the fan magazines of the time, there were numerous stories that the group might be breaking up. Carl was under indictment for refusing to be inducted into the armed services, Brian was in outer space, and Dennis was going through one personal crisis after another. If they had broken up at the time, Brian might have been able to regain the creative momentum that had been slowed down when he was forced to remain solely within the group situation. However, the Beach Boys did remain together. In fact, *Smiley Smile* had been such a disaster that, in one respect, it brought the Beach Boys closer. When these guys were hit in their collective wallets, it was a message that wasn't missed.

Within two months of the release of *Smiley Smile*, the Beach Boys had put out another album, *Wild Honey*. Bruce Johnston has very positive memories about that record. "I loved that album, honest to God, I loved that album because I thought it was getting us back on track again. It was probably the funkiest Beach Boys album, very little production, but a lot of music without any complications. I just remember we wanted to be a band again. The whole thing had wiped everyone out, and we wanted to play together again."

Wild Honey was a very primitive album, even in comparison to *Smiley Smile*, but it was no better accepted than its predecessor. This Beach Boys soul album was in part a response to critics' claims that the group consisted of ball-less choir boys. Critically, it was viewed as more lightweight fare, it didn't set the charts on fire, and it further alienated the rapidly shrinking legions of American Beach Boys fans. According to Carl, "*Wild Honey* was music for Brian to cool out by. He was still very spaced." The record was more coherent than *Smiley Smile*, but while it was competent and enjoyable, it wasn't very important. There was no artistic pretension on this album. It was a return to the fun and simplicity of earlier albums, but that return wasn't particularly welcomed by the fans after all the previous advances. The title cut, 'Darlin',' and a few others are great tunes; still, it's hard to listen to it and feel that Brian's creative heart was really in it. *Wild Honey* is the kind of music he can throw off the top of his head. Very nice but unspectacular.

Some tried to claim that this return to simplicity was another example of Brian's leading the way. This theory emerged following Dylan's release of *John Wesley Harding*, which is a bare production. More likely, Brian had begun to ignore the outside world and was writing songs because it was his job, not out of any sense of artistry. Brian was tired of dealing with the demands of artistic leadership. Now, he was going to make records that reflected his lifestyle.

Although Brian was no longer interested in being a leader of the pop music world or the Beach Boys, he still enjoyed making music with his friends. Even these desires would be foiled by the group. Brian was producing a group called Redwood, led by Danny Hutton. Redwood went to work on 'Darlin',' and all the instrumental tracks had been recorded. As Bruce Johnston noted, "Brian had written and produced 'Darlin'' for them [Redwood] and we [the Beach Boys] used it." [More on this in the 2022 Epilogue.]

"In December of 1967," Bruce Johnston recalls, "we played a concert for UNICEF in Paris. Everyone from the Beach Boys to Marlon Brando, Elizabeth Taylor, Richard Burton, Johnny Hallyday, Ravi Shankar, Maharishi [Maharishi Mahesh Yogi, the guru of Transcendental Meditation] was there." After the concert, the group flew to London, but Dennis remained behind and met the Maharishi. Dennis called the group in England and told them to fly back. Bruce Johnston remembers telling himself, "Oh, God, here we go again," and Bruce stayed in London while the rest of the band went back to Paris and were initiated into the ways of TM.

Unfortunately for the Beach Boys, their timing was way off. In 1968, the Beatles adopted the Maharishi and then scorned him as a false prophet;

because of that, the Beach Boys could ill afford to be associated with Transcendental Meditation or the Maharishi. *Friends*, an album influenced by Transcendental Meditation, was the first result of the association, another quickly made, gently produced LP. Brian's involvement was still decreasing, but he managed to spin out some gorgeous jazzy melodies. What was missing was the adventurous spirit. *Friends* is laid back, which gives an accurate insight into what Brian Wilson was up to in 1968.

The title cut includes the lyrical plea "Let's be friends," but the standout autobiographical tune was 'Busy Doin' Nothin'.' Backed by a bossa nova beat, Brian's solo vocal describes a very mundane existence. Brian had mellowed somewhat in his retreat, and he'd found a certain peace away from the hectic demands of creation. Through the years, Brian has always named *Friends* as his favorite Beach Boys album. "It seems to fit the way I live better—it's simple and I can hear it any time without having to get into some mood. *Pet Sounds* carries a lot more emotion, at least for me . . . [*Pet Sounds*] is by far our very best album. Still, though, my favorite is *Friends*." The lack of emotion in *Friends*, the very reason it is Brian's favorite, is what makes the album such an important statement. Brian did not want to deal with emotions by 1968, particularly his own.

Meanwhile, the Beach Boys, who had risen to success rapidly, found themselves having trouble meeting the payroll after their nearly five-year ride at the top of the charts ended. Starting in 1968, the Beach Boys began to "pay their dues," a rather novel approach to hitting the skids in that most major groups have their bad times before they make it big.

Friends, for the Beach Boys, brought yet another decline in sales, so the group took to the road to shore up their sagging finances. The disasters that befell them were impossible to predict; their timing and luck were incredibly bad.

The first fiscal disaster of 1968 occurred in April. The Beach Boys set up a tour of the Southeast with Buffalo Springfield, Strawberry Alarm Clock, and the Soul Survivors as supporting acts. A few days into the tour, Dr. Martin Luther King was murdered. The Beach Boys were in Nashville, setting up for that night's concert. That show and the rest of the tour were canceled, and the group lost a small fortune.

The next tour was even worse. The Beach Boys had agreed to tour with the Maharishi to help him sell Transcendental Meditation to the world. Originally planned as a tour of colleges, the Beach Boys were booked into huge halls like Philadelphia's Spectrum. The Maharishi, meanwhile, decided to back out of the tour, and the Beach Boys had to threaten him with a lawsuit to get him to fulfill his obligations. Bruce Johnston recalls "the Maharishi giving his lecture and the audience screaming for the Beach Boys . . . It was probably Mike Love of all the guys who was trying to promote the Maharishi . . . We would charter a plane and have a funky band in the front of the plane, drinking and carrying on, and Maharishi in the back." The tour cost the Beach Boys between a quarter- and a half-million dollars. As Al Jardine noted at the time, "If anybody benefits from this tour, it'll be the florists."

Besides the monetary loss, the tour was also damaging to their image. Suffering from a lack of relevancy, the group was accused of trying to appear trendy because Transcendental Meditation was still an "in" thing. The truth was that the Beach Boys (except Bruce) were playing music for what they believed to be a good cause. The Beatles (listen to 'Sexy Sadie') would soon desert the Maharishi but the Beach Boys stood by him. Whether the Beach Boys were right, naive or misguided, they were again ahead of much of the country. The Beach Boys and TM were an item long before (talk-show host) Merv Griffin gave it his seal of approval.

In '67 and '68, the Beach Boys seemed to be heading into all the wrong areas, whether it was Transcendental Meditation, health foods (*Wild Honey*), or vegetarianism ('Vegetables'). In the summer of '68, though, the group did strike a chord in the American consciousness. With a summery song called 'Do It Again,' the Beach Boys had a single based on nostalgia. For those who were not being "Clean for Gene" (McCarthy, the anti-war senator running for president) or demonstrating in the streets of Chicago, 'Do It Again' was a perfect call to arms—sun-tanned arms. It was irresistible, and it made it as high as #20, the highest a new Beach Boys single would get on the American charts until the summer of 1976. The record proved that Brian Wilson hadn't lost his magic touch; he just wasn't all that interested in using his wand on recycled "formula" records. He'd already done that years ago. Why did everybody want him to keep doing it again?

In an era of assassinations and anti-war protest, the group's apolitical image became a serious problem. And that was despite Carl's "conscientious objector" status. His courage in standing up to the draft board could have been "used" to make the group hip. That didn't happen. So while America's "Woodstock Generation" was just around the corner, the Beach Boys were alienating that generation's tastemakers because of what was perceived to be a lack of sociological or political relevance. That's what doomed them in the late sixties. The ferment of the "revolution" victimized many established figures, and the Beach Boys were an appropriate target. There was no pretense on their part. It was "accept us as what we are or don't accept us at all." America at that time had no use for the Beach Boys, so they became wandering troubadours and ambassadors of "good times" to the rest of the world, particularly England, Australia and Western Europe. Eastern Europe too. A few months after the Russians invaded Czechoslovakia in 1968, the Beach Boys played at a Prague music festival. Of the Beach Boys' thousands of concerts, Mike Love remembers that show as "the epitome of the event transcending the music. The reception was probably the most unbelievable we ever got anywhere."

It was a difficult time for the group. Bruce Johnston recalled "a time in 1968, believe it or not, when the Beach Boys drew two hundred people in New York City. And we went to England right after that and sold out a whole tour." Ignored or dismissed in the United States, the group had a growing international following that would sustain them until the mid-1970s when America needed the Beach Boys' musical optimism.

Brian Wilson lyrics have almost always consciously reflected his state of mind at the time of a song's creation. It's interesting to note that two of his next released songs were 'Time to Get Alone' and [with Carl] 'I Went to Sleep.' Those songs were on the Beach Boys' *20/20* album, the group's last LP of new material for Capitol (it was their twentieth album release, including *Stack-o-Tracks* and greatest hits albums). The record was mostly a collection of recent singles, and Bruce Johnston remembers it as "a very un-Brian album, the first album where all the members of the band got to do what they really wanted to do."

Although it did not flow well, it was a strong album musically. 'I Can Hear Music,' Carl's first production, is fabulous, and side two in particular has some great vocals—a shimmering "deep and wide" on 'Time to Get Alone,' and a beautiful a cappella 'Our Prayer' (cut at Capitol's studios while they were finishing up *20/20*). The highlight of the album, though, was the appearance of a portion of *SMiLE* under the title of 'Cabinessence.'

With the album's release in January 1969, the Beach Boys' career, in the parlance of Hollywood directors, appeared to be "a wrap." Without a record contract at home, and United States concert crowds getting smaller and smaller, 1969 was a bad year for the Beach Boys in America both artistically and financially. Personally, Dennis Wilson's involvement with Charles Manson, Mike's divorce and the strain of failure were beginning to tell within the group. Although they continued to record, there was no outlet for the music except for the one single they owed Capitol.

Because the group was still big in Europe, England and Australia, they concentrated their efforts in 1969 overseas. In fact, things were so good for them in Europe that Deutsche Grammophon offered the group a contract that was very lucrative, considering their inability to sell records in the United States. Besides a huge advance for six Beach Boys albums, the contract also provided the group with money to produce other artists. The deal fell through for a number of reasons, not the least of which was Brian's surprise press conference in late May of 1969.

On the eve of the Beach Boys' British tour, Brian called the press together to announce that "we're pretty low on money. We owe everyone money, and if we don't pick ourselves off our backsides and have a hit record soon, we will be in worse trouble . . . Nick Grillo, our business manager, says if we don't start climbing out of this mess, he will have to file bankruptcy in Los Angeles by the end of the year . . . Things started deteriorating eighteen months ago. Thousands of dollars were being frittered away on stupid things. We spent a heck of a lot of [Beach Boys] corporation money on Brother Records . . . When our records started to bomb, we looked around desperately for something to save ourselves . . . [One hit] isn't enough to pay for our tremendous overheads . . . We all know that if we don't watch it and do something drastic, inside a few months, we won't have a penny in the bank."

Brian had written and produced a new single, 'Break Away,' which he thought might change the group's fortunes. "It's the kind of disc that will either be a smash or a miserable flop . . . The British tour, I hope, will help our waning popularity. I've always said, 'Be honest with your fans.' I don't see why I should lie and say everything is rosy when it's not. Sure, when we were making millions, I said we were. Now the shoe is on the other foot."

The overhead that Brian referred to was the group's huge office complex/rehearsal hall on Ivar Street in Hollywood. That office was necessary to keep up a corporate image of a prospering business, but the Beach Boys, never a thrifty bunch, hadn't saved a lot. As one associate explains, "they never thought there would be a time when they wouldn't be popular and making lots of money." Nick Grillo has been accused of making bad investments on the group's behalf, including a large piece of property in California's Simi Valley. It wasn't that it was a bad property. The Beach Boys corporation just couldn't meet the mortgage payments after a while because there wasn't a big enough cash flow, and they eventually lost their investment. There was virtually no income from records, and the profitable American concert scene had dried up for the group.

Daryl Dragon, of Captain and Tennille fame, joined the Beach Boys as a touring member in 1967 and remembers how bad things eventually got for the group. "On that first tour in 1967, it was Ron Brown on bass and me on keyboards. We were the only outside musicians at that time. They had Cadillacs, and I thought, 'Boy, this is really first-class, limousines to the gig, and the kids were beating on the windows, just like you hear happened to the Beatles.' I thought, 'Wow, it can only go up from here,' and then they started to go down a little bit, and they started to rent Chevrolets instead of Cadillacs. They just couldn't afford it. All they could afford to do was to promote the group . . . mostly it was hard times."

According to Dragon, the English tours were successful in filling seats, but those sellouts didn't make much money. "I toured with them in England, and the major reaction of the audience was curiosity. A lot of the younger kids just wanted to see the Beach Boys and think the sun was out. England doesn't get much sun. They didn't make any money there. It was more to keep their name going, in the public eye. The worst thing you can do is stop everything. They could always play their hits."

Those tours weren't exactly a lot of fun, the way Daryl remembers it. "We went out for three weeks in 1970, and it felt like four months. I was really tired because they used to do two and three concerts a day in two different cities and stuff like that. One year, they had two different PA systems and one would jump by the other. They'd alternate, so one could be in one place and the other in another place . . . We'd do one concert during the afternoon and another at night . . . just jump in the car or on the plane and go to the next one. There were days when Carl would have to sing four hours in one day, and he'd lose his voice."

And these weren't major metropolises the group was playing. Bruce Johnston recalls being booked at such places as the Corn Palace in Mitchell, South Dakota. According to Bruce, the guys for a while really scraped "the bottom of the barrel."

By the end of the decade, the group had so little money that Fred Vail (who had returned to work for the group after a lengthy absence) financed a Beach Boys' tour out of his own pocket. The group had exhausted all available credit, and Vail charged twelve thousand dollars' worth of flying and dining and hotel rooms on his personal credit cards to keep the Beach Boys on the road so they could generate income. A sympathetic Beverly Hills banker ignored the fact that the mortgage payments weren't being met. Otherwise, the Beach Boys corporate members (Brian, Dennis, Carl, and Mike) would have probably had to sell their homes.

None of this was ever made public, but Brian's mid-1969 press conference alerted the world to the group's financial troubles. That's one reason the Deutsche Grammophon deal fell through. The other reasons are more hidden. When the Beach Boys played their new material for Polydor (Deutsche's American affiliate), Polydor refused to sign the Beach Boys because they didn't like the music, or they didn't like the Beach Boys personally.

Meanwhile, 'Break Away,' the song Brian thought might save the sinking ship, was released and ignored in the United States, although it did well overseas. Bruce Johnston feels that it was Murry who "forced the song to be a good track." Bruce also marks that record as "when Brian stopped singing high . . . He had been singing lower and lower. The way it's voiced, it sounds like a bunch of old men. It doesn't sound like the Beach Boys." It remains one of the great unnoticed Brian Wilson arrangements and productions; the lyrics (co-written with Murry, disguised as Reggie Dunbar) are another autobiographical effort.

> Time will not wait for me
> Time is my destiny
> Why change the part of me
> That has to be free
>
> The love that passed me by
> I found no reason why
> But now each day is filled with love
> That very same love
> That passed me by
> And that is why

I can break away from that lonely life
And I can do what I want to do
And break away from that empty life
And my world is new

Lyrically, it seems that Brian was considering a break from the group, as the release of 'Break Away' marked the end of the Beach Boys' contractual obligations.

Murry's source of income through the years had been the Sea of Tunes Publishing Company. As the group's records stopped selling in the late sixties, Murry's income dried up. Sometime in late '69 or early '70, Murry sold Sea of Tunes to A&M Records for approximately $700,000. At the time, the Beach Boys' corporation didn't have the money to purchase Sea of Tunes from Murry, but what upset the Beach Boys was that Murry didn't even tell them he was selling their work until after the fact.

A&M's Chuck Kaye, who was responsible for the purchase, found that he had a problem when he began reading the lyrics to Brian's songs. He felt it would be unlikely for middle-of-the-road singers to record a song like 'Don't Worry Baby' because of the lyrics. Tony Asher recalls that he was asked by Chuck Kaye if he would be interested in writing new lyrics to some of the songs. While no revisions were ever made, this incident remains notable as an indication of how Brian felt at that time. According to one account, when Chuck Kaye called Brian to find out if it would be OK to rewrite the songs, Brian expressed supreme disinterest. Today, Chuck Kaye insists that the earlier report was inaccurate. Brian, according to Kaye, was enthusiastic about the changes and was "all for anything that would improve the songs."

A more poignant (and undisputed) example of Brian's state of mind is related by Hal Blaine, who received an unusual visit from Brian one day. Brian came "over one afternoon with a box filled with (his gold) records, and wanted me to have 'em all." Blaine couldn't convince Brian to keep the records for himself, and a number of the records hang on the wall in Blaine's home, "A couple that Brian insisted I take." Brian was seemingly disassociating himself from his past.

By that time, the media had created an image of Brian as a reclusive genius whose life revolved around paranoid reminiscences of his former musical greatness. Nothing, however, could have been further from the truth. Brian had basically abandoned a full-time career in music; he'd found a new niche, as part-owner and proprietor of a West Hollywood health food store called the Radiant Radish. The image of Brian Wilson as reclusive genius is especially ridiculous when you consider that on most any night, one could just walk into the store and see and talk to Brian Wilson. He would even give you advice on what vitamins to take. Like many of Brian's passions, this too was short-lived and lasted only a couple of weeks.

In early 1970, the group (following talks with CBS and MGM Records) finally secured a record contract with Warner Brothers. Mo Ostin, the President of Warners, believed that the Beach Boys represented an important part of American music. The deal even included a reactivation of the Beach Boys' dormant Brother Records. Beach Boys albums would be released on Brother/Reprise and non-Beach Boys Brother product was to be channeled through Starday/King, an independent record label. This new contract succeeded in reactivating Brian's recording interest, and he became very much a part of the proceedings as the Beach Boys began to produce their next album.

Around that same time, there was another striking example of the inaccuracy of the myth that Brian Wilson was a reclusive non-performing Beach Boy. In the winter of 1970, Brian went on a short tour with the group. Brian recalled: "When Mike Love was sick, I went with the group up to Seattle and Vancouver and the Northwest for some appearances. I was scared for a few minutes in the first show—it had been a while since I was in front of so many people. But after it started to cook, I really got with it. It was the best three days of my life."

While Brian's 1970 tour is a little-known fact, Mike Love's illness is even less known. According to Tom Nolan's 1971 *Rolling Stone* article, Mike was hospitalized following a three-week fast that allowed him to have only water, fruit juice, and a little yogurt. As Nolan wrote, "Everything got very amplified during the fast, he became quite sensitive to all positive and negative forces around him. He began to look at things rather metaphorically. The birds in the sky seemed to have a purpose in flying southwesterly, and if he could try a little harder perhaps he could talk to the birds . . . As he protested, 'I'm fine, I'm going to Hawaii to mellow out,' his brother drove him to a hospital and said, 'You'd better check this boy over.' They simply found that he hadn't been eating. Once he started to eat and meditate again, he was out in four or five days." Former members of the Beach Boys entourage remember that Mike was hospitalized much longer.

For years, the group has allowed the tale to be told that Brian Wilson was the crazy, drug-using Beach Boy. That image is inaccurate when the lives of the other Beach Boys are examined. While Al Jardine's life has been smooth and clean, the rest of the band have indulged in considerable drug use from time to time. Dennis's involvement with Charles Manson and Mike Love's absence from the road are usually glossed over, as is the fact that both Dennis and Mike have had a number of unsuccessful marriages. Carl's marriage to Annie Hinsche has survived some incredibly hard times.

The group's near-obsession with Transcendental Meditation is particularly understandable when one sees that their personal and professional lives have been full of stress. Still, at times, the group seems almost to have hidden behind Brian's "insanity." Brian had reduced his participation and visibility, and it was assumed he was hiding because he was crazy. Actually, Brian was out and about, but if that fact were well known, then the Beach Boys would have to explain his limited involvement with their records. The "unspeakable" truth was that Brian wasn't all that interested in being part of the Beach Boys' records. Rather than assess the group's problems objectively, it was always easier to point in one direction. Brian's misfortune was to be the man that everybody was pointing at.

At this juncture, it might help to get back to the more typical insensitivity of the record industry. The business must take its fair share of the blame for creating commercial problems for the group as well as contributing to Brian's emotional problems. It has already been noted that Capitol went out of their way not to promote *Pet Sounds*, and that Capitol released 'Barbara Ann' without asking or telling the group. Capitol wanted more fun songs from the Beach Boys, and when Brian refused to provide them, Capitol decided to concentrate on the past instead of the future. As the Beach Boys' music grew artistically in '66 and '67, Capitol released two haphazardly compiled greatest hits packages as well as the first of the endless succession of repackages, *The Beach Boys Deluxe Set*. In 1967, in the middle of the acid days, Capitol was promoting the Beach Boys as if it were the summer of '64. The Beach Boys were no longer surfers (not that they'd ever been), but Capitol kept pushing 'Fun, Fun, Fun.'

Capitol, of course, wasn't happy to watch the Beach Boys decline as a hitmaking machine, but they never seemed to have any good ideas as to how to slow the group's slump. For instance, just after *Friends* was released, Capitol released *Stack-o-Tracks*. This is a fun and fascinating collection of backing tracks of Beach Boys songs, but it couldn't have helped sell *Friends*.

On top of their poor promotion of the group's post-*Party* LPs, Capitol also made it hard to purchase the Beach Boys' new records. Sometimes, within months of an album's release, it was no longer on sale in the record stores. Capitol also put together numerous repackages of the early Beach Boys LPs and the original releases became collector's items. They almost forced the fans to buy the repackages of hits by making the original albums unavailable. It is ironic that, in 1974, Capitol would create a new Beach Boys repackage called *Endless Summer* that would help the group find a brand new and very large audience.

After eight years of cold Hollywood business from Capitol, the group was ready for the more gentle Burbank treatment of Warner Brothers, which had a growing reputation for taking care of their artists. There was no way to predict that the Beach Boys' relationship with Warners would be almost as stormy as the one with Capitol.

As the seventies began, the Beach Boys were in Brian's home studio recording many new songs. The first music to emerge was a wonderful single, 'Add Some Music to Your Day,' backed with 'Susie Cincinnati.' Warners wanted to impress their new artists and prevailed upon distributors to purchase large quantities of the single. It was soon reported to be the fastest-selling 45-rpm record in the company's history. The only problem was that there was nobody coming into the stores to buy the records. The Beach Boys' new records in those days got virtually no airplay, except by stalwart fans like Peter Fornatale at WNEW-FM in New York, but one DJ at one very progressive radio station doesn't make hits. The group and Warners were not very happy with the results, and the relationship was off to a bad start.

Things only got worse when Warners rejected the album the Beach Boys submitted. The company wanted a stronger album so off came a number of cuts ('I Just Got My Pay,' 'Carnival,' 'When Girls Get Together,' 'Two Can Play,' 'Lady' and 'Susie Cincinnati'), and they were replaced with more "acceptable" material. Finally, the album came out. Originally titled *Add Some Music*, the name was changed to *Sunflower*, and it was cleverly packaged as a very humble "album offering." It garnered great reviews, and was a terrible sales disaster, possibly the worst-selling album in the group's history.

A *Sunflower* era publicity picture. (L-R) Carl, Bruce, Mike, Brian, Al and Dennis.
Credit: Michael Ochs Archives/Getty

That was especially devastating because, quite simply, the group had come up with an incredible record. It was the first album that could come close to equaling *Pet Sounds* on a production level, partly the result of studio engineer Steve Desper's fine work. The Beach Boys' harmonies were present in a way that had been missing since *Summer Days* . . . and it was probably the truest group effort ever in that it was a showcase for all the individuals in the band. Brian's presence was obvious, but the others, particularly Dennis, contributed some very strong material. It was, claims Bruce Johnston, the last real Beach Boys album because it was the last one to have been produced with both Brian's interest and active participation.

Brian's work on *Sunflower* was on a par with some of his best efforts. One song in particular, 'This Whole World,' was an amazing composition. Daryl Dragon, who is a classically trained musician, said, "From a harmony standpoint, I've never heard a song like that since I've been in pop music. I've never heard a song go through that many changes and then come back." Brian also provided some transcendental doo-wop with the background vocals, "*OM* bop dit it." One tune on the album was disturbing to Brian. He said, "In 'Cool, Cool Water' there's a chant I wish we hadn't used. It fits all right, but there's just something I don't quite think is right in it."

The chant that Brian was referring to was recorded during the *SMiLE* era, reportedly once part of *SMiLE's* 'Elements' section. Originally titled 'I Love to Say Dada,' it was supposedly the water segment. Brian's discomfort at its inclusion on *Sunflower* was understandable. *SMiLE* was still very special to him, and he didn't like to deal with it, particularly out of its proper context. It was also an indication that Brian *still* didn't have control over his music.

The critical praise the record received hardly paid the bills. Brian, who had shown new interest with *Sunflower*, was very hurt by its sales failure. That, on top of the old, unhealed scars, was a hurt he really didn't begin to get over until 1976. For the Beach Boys, it was a great disappointment too, but the setback didn't make them any less determined to forge a comeback. So they went back to Europe, where they were loved. The story, in a music trade publication datelined London, read as follows:

> The Beach Boys were mobbed in London on a recent Monday night as they arrived for a seven-week European tour. More than 100 reporters joined with admirers in braving a chilling wind and rain to meet the Beach Boys at a press reception . . . The group answered questions mostly centered on their new album release in England, *Sunflower*, which British critics call "The Beach Boys' *Sgt. Pepper*." The album has been out less than one week, and it already is indicated to be their most popular recording in history, according to EMI Records.

Upon returning from that overseas tour, the Beach Boys took the first steps toward realigning themselves with the "peace and love" generation that had reached a peak at Woodstock. The Beach Boys were about to settle an account that was long overdue.

CHARLES MANSON

"Charles Manson." Those three syllables shattered the late night/early morning silence at Dennis Wilson's beach house. Without any prodding, Dennis had steered our marathon conversation to the one topic that has been taboo in every interview he's granted since the Tate/LaBianca murders in 1969. He has steadfastly refused to discuss his involvement with the Manson Family and has usually become upset whenever the subject was mentioned. For some perverse reason, he himself had brought it up. "You probably want to know all about that," he continued. "I guess it's time to talk about it.

"You see, when I knew Manson it was no big thing. We were friends; we lived together. That was long before the murders. And we'd talk every night, just like you and me. We'd really talk about important things."

The obvious question is, "Do you know why Manson organized those murders?" Dennis stares into space, and softly reveals. "I know why Charles Manson did what he did. Someday, I'll tell the world. I'll write a book and explain why he did it." Dennis realizes that isn't a satisfactory answer, and with a fearful sigh, goes on. "Over the years, people have always wanted to know what happened, what my relationship with Charlie was." Dennis again insists, "We were just friends." There is no evidence to contradict that statement. Dennis Wilson was in no way involved with the Manson Family murders, nor did he have any knowledge of what had occurred.

Years after the murders, the memory of his fear remains strong. The Family allegedly made numerous threats on Dennis's life, and Dennis would pick up the telephone and hear, "You're next." Still, Dennis does have intimate knowledge of Manson's thought processes, and it is this insight that Dennis to this day refuses to share. "I didn't testify at the trial. I couldn't. I was so scared. You know, the writers really raked me over the coals for not testifying." As he didn't testify in 1970, Dennis doesn't reveal any more on this occasion. His opening comment was no more than a tease.

Dennis first met Charles Manson in the late spring of 1968. According to prosecuting attorney Vincent Bugliosi in his book *Helter Skelter*, Dennis "twice picked up the same pair of hitchhikers while driving through

Malibu. The second time, he took the girls home with him." At the time, Dennis was living at 14400 Sunset Boulevard near Will Rogers State Park.

The evening he picked up the hitchhikers for the second time, Dennis went to a recording session. Returning at 3 a.m., Dennis was met by a stranger, Charles Manson. When he entered the house, Dennis found out that he had nearly a dozen houseguests, most of them girls.

To understand why Dennis Wilson, a rich and famous rock star, would get involved with the Family is a question that is hard to understand. By one account, Dennis in 1968 was feeling guilty about his material wealth. He didn't think he deserved it, so he reportedly gave away his money to total strangers. Dennis also had recently divorced his first wife, Carol; Scotty, his adopted and beloved son was living with Carol.

At first, Charles Manson and his Family must have appeared harmless to Dennis and his friends. Dennis introduced Manson to many people including Terry Melcher and Gregg Jakobson. Gregg, a close friend of Dennis's, spent many hours talking with Manson and reportedly felt a certain affinity for Manson's philosophies.

Besides the appeal of the male-dominated lifeway that Manson directed, both Dennis and Gregg supposedly felt that Manson's preachings were correct. For Dennis, Manson was a spiritual guru. While they lived together, Dennis appeared to be very much under his spell. In an article in England's *Rave* magazine, Dennis spoke of his "wizard." "Sometimes," Dennis admitted, "the wizard frightens me." The "wizard" Dennis referred to was Charles Manson. That fear wasn't overpowering, not yet. Manson's talking was just ideas at that time.

In the late summer of 1968, Dennis tired of the Manson Family's exploitation (which reportedly cost him about a hundred thousand dollars) and moved into a small room in Gregg Jakobson's Beverly Glen home. Dennis left the task of evicting the Family to the Beach Boys' business management.

Even though Dennis wasn't living with Manson anymore, a friend of Dennis's remembers that "Dennis was still hypnotized enough by Manson to think he was going to do something tremendous. Dennis used to draw lots of symbols in his notes, all the time practically quoting verbatim what Manson had been saying." This friend recalls that "Dennis and Gregg were scared off long before the murders happened. They finally had realized that they were involved with someone who was different than what they had first thought. They still saw him, but they were becoming afraid of him. It was only weeks before the murders that they became aware that Manson was really dangerous. That's when they tried to have nothing to do with him."

Just after the August 1969 murders, Manson visited Dennis and demanded money ($1,500) so he could go to the desert. Two friends of Dennis's remember that night as "the first time we met him. We were at Gregg's, down in Dennis's little room. Dennis was playing the piano. All of a sudden, the door flew open and he [Manson] came flying through the air, jumped into the room. His eyes were just like on fire." Dennis greeted Manson and nervously asked him where he'd been lately. Charlie replied, "I been to the moon."

Dennis's friends recall that Manson's hair was standing straight out on its end, and there was a tremendous amount of energy in the room. "His eyes were so magnetic. This was the night Manson told Dennis that he was going to kidnap Scotty if Dennis didn't give Manson money." According to Bugliosi's account, Manson said, "Don't be surprised if you never see your kid again." By some horrible coincidence, Scotty ran away from home the next day. Naturally, everyone assumed the worst, but Scotty came home unharmed.

The Tate/LaBianca murders were terrifying to the whole country, but to those who lived in Los Angeles, there was a special fear. Although it took the police a long time to connect the two cases, the bizarre murders had people buying guns and guard dogs and hiring security agencies. When Manson and three Family members were charged with the murders, the fear in Los Angeles remained because so many of the Family's members were still on the streets. Nobody knew where they might strike next.

The night of Manson's arrest in the fall of 1969, he apparently tried to contact Dennis for help. That night, Gregg Jakobson's wife was giving birth, and Gregg and Dennis had taken her to the hospital. Dennis's live-in friends had stayed home, and one of them answered a "collect phone call for Dennis, and it was from Manson. I had already gotten instructions from Dennis and Gregg that they wanted nothing to do with him. I said, 'No, I'm sorry, he's not here.' And Manson yelled, 'I don't care, anybody accept the charges,' and he started screaming like a wild man. He said, 'You're going to be fucking sorry if you don't—' and the operator cut him off as soon as he cursed. The next morning, I said to Dennis and

Gregg, 'By the way, you got a phone call last night from Charlie, and he was at a police station.' They were so upset about Gregg's wife losing the baby that they just didn't want to hear anything about it. And I said, 'Well, he's in jail.' And they said, 'We don't care,' and that was it."

In the Family's attempts to stop Dennis from testifying at the trial, there were threats made on Dennis's life. Besides these direct threats, the Family supposedly intimidated Dennis by "creepy crawling" Dennis's home. This consisted of sneaking into Dennis's home while he was asleep and moving the furniture around at night. It was like a calling card—the Family's way of letting a person know that, despite all the security, they could penetrate his defenses and get inside his home.

Another friend of Dennis's remembers how all this was shaking Dennis up. "It was really weird to see someone who seems to be in control of things get really spaced out by a noise in the bushes. He was very nervous. He couldn't sit for more than two minutes at a time." This fear wasn't Dennis's alone. The entire Wilson family reportedly feared for their lives.

Dennis never did testify at the Family's trial but did have an extensive conversation with prosecutor Bugliosi. Dennis's testimony wasn't essential because Gregg Jakobson was willing to publicly testify and corroborate what Dennis had revealed only in private.

The Manson connection with the Beach Boys provided a certain unwelcome notoriety, but it also was one indication that the 'Fun, Fun, Fun' image had new and more bizarre meanings. Dennis offered Bugliosi one final observation on his whole involvement with Manson. "I'm the luckiest guy in the world, because I got off only losing my money."

CHAPTER 11

SURF'S UP

ALTHOUGH *SUNFLOWER* HAD RECEIVED GOOD REVIEWS IN THE ROCK PRESS, including *Rolling Stone*, there was still a stigma attached to the group's image, particularly from the point of view of the "West Coast consciousness" that was centered in *Rolling Stone*'s San Francisco offices.

From the moment the Beach Boys failed to show up at the Monterey Festival in 1967, until the day they played the festival in 1970 at Big Sur, the Beach Boys were outcasts in California. Ben Edmonds points out that "during that period out here, the Beach Boys were still regarded as outdated teen relics. They [the Californians] didn't see the connection between the Beach Boys and Buffalo Springfield and Crosby, Stills and Nash. To them, West Coast culture *was* CSN, the Springfield and so on. On the East Coast, there was always a great intellectual appreciation of the Beach Boys and Brian Wilson. Paul Williams in *Crawdaddy* really understood the implications of the Beach Boys, while at the same time, *Rolling Stone* on the West Coast was dismissing them."

The Beach Boys were about to shock their homeland and begin the long climb back from obscurity.

In October of 1970, the Beach Boys finally did something right for the folks at *Rolling Stone*. They played the Big Sur Folk Festival and stole the show. People who had been putting down the Beach Boys as an anachronism when the concert started were dancing in the aisles by the end of the first set. The response was so strong that, after closing the afternoon segment of the festival, the Beach Boys just left their equipment onstage and opened the evening portion of the concert. And blew the audience away with music.

Jann Wenner's article in his own *Rolling Stone* was almost an apology. "The Monterey International Pop Festival finally ended. The Beach Boys,

200

the very first of the California groups, closed the show . . . the occasion was the eighth annual Big Sur Folk Festival . . . and the Beach Boys—the one act that didn't show up at Monterey, the group that went right to the genesis of California Music . . . " Finally, the Beach Boys had been forgiven. Finally, they were understood by the man who controlled the most powerful rock magazine in the United States. *Rolling Stone's* acceptance of the group was belated, but they helped make up for that by playing a major role in the group's renaissance.

The key to the group's comeback was a man named Jack Rieley. Rieley appeared virtually out of nowhere one day, claiming that he'd worked for NBC News and won a Pulitzer Prize. Somehow, he convinced Brian to do a radio interview for a show that Rieley hosted on L.A.'s Pacifica public radio station, KPFK. Rieley, sensing a once-in-a-lifetime opportunity, quickly presented his ideas to the group and became an important cog in the Beach Boys' operation, directing their career on a creative level and then taking over the group's business affairs.

In a six-page memo to the Beach Boys dated August 8, 1970, Rieley outlined a plan to revitalize the group's career in the United States:

> As you all have no doubt learned, I've been very much into the group's music for a very long time. Perhaps our paths should have crossed earlier . . . I don't believe I'd be presuming too much to say we all agree generally that the Beach Boys face a continuing problem with the image . . . predominating in this country . . . For the purposes of this friendly little note, I have decided to label the problem simply: HOW TO LET THE FOLKS OUT THERE IN RECORD-BUYING LAND KNOW WHERE THE GROUP IS AT MUSICALLY AND TO TRANSLATE THAT KNOWLEDGE INTO INCREASED RECORD SALES AND POPULARITY FOR THE BEACH BOYS.

Rieley then outlined the group's career and explained how the Beach Boys should convince the public that the group was ecologically and politically aware.

However Rieley may have eventually damaged the Beach Boys finances, his initial ideas were the perfect solution to their image problems. Jack got the group to play many politically advantageous concerts, changed the focus of the lyrics to reflect the concerns of the day and basically made the Beach Boys more relevant. It was a clever public relations effort. Rieley remembered that "one of the things was to just say it right out in a series of advertisements, 'It's safe now to listen to the Beach Boys.'" More and more, people were beginning to believe that.

Another of the Beach Boys' new interests was a South African group called the Flame. The Beach Boys had discovered them playing in a London club, and Carl in particular thought they had great potential. The Flame were signed to Brother Records, and their album, described by reviewers as Beatlesque, was the only record ever released on Brother that wasn't a Beach Boys' disc. The members of the group were black, and this gave the Beach Boys an additional boost in "hipness," although that wasn't the motivation behind the association. The Beach Boys really felt that the Flame were going to be big. Unfortunately, the first album flopped, and the second was never issued due to personal and personnel problems. The Flame, however, would be the training ground for two future Beach Boys.

In 1970, though, the Beach Boys were really pushing the Flame. When the Beach Boys' resurgence first began, they insisted that the Flame be their opening act, a plan that they first implemented after the Big Sur Festival, when they returned to Los Angeles and played a four-night stand at the Whisky a Go Go nightclub. It was the group's first formal L.A. appearance since they had played the Hollywood Bowl in '66. Bruce Johnston remembers those shows fondly.

"The Whisky gig was great. It was just to remind people that we were still around—they thought we'd broken up. The line went three blocks up the mountain. Brian played one set." There are various accounts of how many sets Brian played, but his return to performing was cut short, supposedly because the onstage volume began to hurt his one good ear. More, it was another case of stage fright. The audience response was fantastic at the Whisky, but the onstage vibrations weren't all good. Daryl Dragon recalls, "I didn't feel it was any kind of reunion for them, just a gig because it was close to home." Daryl also remembers that there were still "a lot of weird things going on between Brian and Mike, just old things that haven't been resolved."

The next big step was a concert at New York's Carnegie Hall ("Playing in the myth," as Bruce Johnston put it), and this was a show with a unique story. The Fillmore East wouldn't book the Beach Boys because the group had drawn such a small audience on their previous appearance. Three Beach Boys fans, who worked in the music business, decided that if they wanted to see the Beach Boys, they'd have to hire them. Mike Klenfner, Chip Rachlin and George Brown (as Krab Productions) rented Carnegie Hall for a February evening in '71, and, as Rachlin remembered, "It eventually sold out the night of the show."

The Beach Boys' performance was quite remarkable. Opening with 'Heroes and Villains,' they proceeded to play a two-hour set that included a smattering of hits but concentrated on the artistic material from *Pet Sounds* onward. That approach was new for the group, mostly the result of their dissatisfaction following their fall 1970 overseas tour. The Beach Boys were tired of being a fifty-minute jukebox of hits.

Carnegie Hall was a revelation for the Beach Boys. As Bruce Johnston remembers, "We were absolutely astonished at the reaction. After having people tell us how boring we were, and how out of time we were, we did this concert and everybody just went 'Ooooh!' They just loved the Beach Boys." Following that show, the group returned home and, according to Bruce, "The concert at the Santa Monica Civic was fabulous, that's probably the best L.A. gig ever." For Bruce, 1971 was his favorite time with the group musically because they were playing so many songs that had never been played before, and the oldies were mostly in the encores. Bruce points out: "Unfortunately, it's not that way now." The oldies are now the body of the show. Back then, the new material worked.

The 1971 Beach Boys concerts were the best from a true music fan's point of view. With a full horn section, extra percussionists and the exciting spirit emanating from the stage, their '71 concerts had an exceptionally full and moving sound. The hits were reserved for a compact portion of the program at the end, but the opening song was often 'Good Vibrations.' That's how good they were; they could open with a peak, and still get better. The best moments included satisfying versions of songs like 'Cool, Cool Water,' 'Heroes and Villains' and 'Country Air,' and emotional, touching love songs played by Dennis at the piano (the still-unreleased 'Barbara' and 'I've Got a Friend'). Nothing could top Carl's magnificent rendition of 'Surf's Up.' Backed by a great horn arrangement by Daryl Dragon, there was a definite magic to Carl's performance. That song connected with the audience of hardcore fanatics, who gave Carl a standing ovation.

In the midst of this artistic recovery, there was a severe organizational shake-up. Jack Rieley, according to Bruce Johnston, "somehow stirred everybody up." Rieley has been accused by his victims of using backstabbing techniques. Supposedly, Rieley would create dissension within the ranks by talking behind people's backs, and then establish himself as the one central figure they could all "trust." Nick Grillo and Fred Vail were both squeezed out of the operation, without much thanks. Grillo left in a cloud of accusations that he was a crook and a liar, suddenly fired one day with little notice or chance to defend himself. And there were strong accusations that Nick had "lined his pockets" with Beach Boys money. One participant politely noted that "Nick had taken advantage of the situation he was in." Others claim that he failed to pay the group's bills and that the IRS once padlocked the Ivar Street offices for failure to pay taxes. All of this was allegedly Grillo's fault. For a man Brian had once called "one of the family," things had gotten very unpleasant.

Derek Taylor explained that the Beach Boys were always "very aware of and very silly with money. And they all needed it . . . huge spenders. Nick Grillo," Taylor felt, "was in the hottest seat in the world. I never saw a man under more pressure than Nick Grillo in my life. There were so many of them, first of all." The four corporate Beach Boys were all "buying, selling cars, houses, whatever. And all changing their minds. God, for mind changing . . . Nick Grillo, a work freak . . . poor Nick . . . never a complaint. Nick thought whatever he did for them or whatever sort of hell he went through, that the reward was somewhere in heaven." It was always OK, whatever the Beach Boys did, because "it's just the boys, y'know boys will be boys."

Grillo himself gave one example of what he had to deal with in describing an idea of Mike Love's that centered around a floating hospital in the shape of a pyramid off the coast of Florida. Grillo, however, refused to say anything else about the Beach Boys because they've already been through one lawsuit together.

With Rieley leading the way, the Beach Boys continued to build good-will, playing benefit concerts and making a triumphant return to the Fillmore East. That was April 27, 1971, when they jammed with the Grateful Dead. It was really a great move. The Dead are the ongoing symbol of San Francisco, and appearing with them was like the Dead saying, "Hey, these guys are all right. They make good music, and they're

pretty cool. Forget your old prejudices. These are the new Beach Boys."
As one reporter noted, in the middle of the performance, Bob Dylan said
to Jack Rieley, "You know, they're fucking good, man."

The group followed this show with a May Day appearance at an anti-war
demonstration in Washington, D.C., the only major group to show up.
People were shaking their heads in disdain when it was announced that
the Beach Boys were going to play. After all, the Beach Boys at an anti-
war rally? There were also ecstatic reactions to their performance. It
didn't hurt that the group was doing a formative version of 'Student
Demonstration Time,' a song based on 'Riot in Cell Block Number Nine.'

All of a sudden, the Beach Boys were relevant. They played an anti-war
benefit for the Berrigan brothers' defense fund and appeared at the closing
night of the Fillmore East. The Fillmore's founding owner, rock impresario
Bill Graham, introduced the Beach Boys by saying, "There are very few
groups that have had more influence on what is going down today than
this one. I really don't know of any." In the summer of '71, a TV special,
Good Vibrations from Central Park, featured the Beach Boys.

Through all of this, however, the Beach Boys' basic problem hadn't really
changed. In the late sixties, they had been put down for playing all the
oldies, but at the same time, the concert audiences were demanding to
hear the hits. Reportedly, there were shouting matches between the audience and Mike Love. With the new acceptance of the Beach Boys in the
seventies, the group was faced with the dilemma of how many oldies to
play. The audiences that they were now attracting were split between the
remnants of the longtime fan cult and the brand-new fans who were
college-aged and came to hear the hits because they'd never bothered to
see the Beach Boys when they were growing up. The latter group of fans
wanted nostalgia, and there were some depressing nights when their cries
for 'Help Me, Rhonda' drowned out the applause for 'Caroline, No.' The
audiences had an amazing effect on the Beach Boys in those days. If the
crowd was attentive and appreciative of the newer material, the group gave
out a positive energy that made all the songs sound better. On the nights
when the rowdies disrupted the show, the band would shorten the program,
leave out some of the slower songs, play the hits, and get out of town.

It was probably at Jack Rieley's insistence that the program stayed in
its long form. It was a true joy to hear 'Wonderful' or 'Let the Wind Blow,'
but a time was coming when the shouts for 'Surfin' U.S.A.' would win

out. In 1971 and 1972 and into 1973, however, the group was committed to creating a new audience by playing the more recent material.

The recording of the *Surf's Up* album was the first false start in the group's resurgence. Brian's involvement was minimal. In fact, the album was initially titled *Landlocked*, but it was changed after a battle within the group resulted in the inclusion of the song 'Surf's Up.' That *SMiLE* jewel was put on the LP against Brian's wishes, and Bruce Johnston remembers that the entire album was designed to fool the public into thinking that Brian was part of the group. "I think it was sort of a sham, not intentional. I felt that Jack Rieley had to make us look like a unit to pull us in a direction he was pulling us." Besides Brian's unhappiness, another internal feud resulted in Dennis's not having any songs on the album, one reason that the record isn't nearly as strong as *Sunflower*.

The vocal arrangements on *Surf's Up* weren't as full as those on *Sunflower* either, and that is mostly because Brian wasn't working on the album. Bruce recalls, "It was strange to be doing vocal arrangements to make it sound like the Beach Boys when we were the Beach Boys. That's a little weird to me."

The resurrection of the song 'Surf's Up' is a confusing tale. Part of the album track was from a recording Brian had made for the 1967 Leonard Bernstein special; other segments were recorded in 1971 to fit in with the old track. Bruce: "I remember thinking, 'Well, if I voice this chord into Brian's part from the end of Carl's part, it'll sound OK and no one will know about it.' We ended up doing vocals to sort of emulate ourselves without Brian Wilson, which was kind of silly."

Bruce again: "And yet, the last great Brian Wilson song was on that album. ''Til I Die.' I remember Brian playing it for the band and one member of the band didn't understand it and put it down, and Brian just decided not to show it to us for a few months. He just put it away. I mean, he was absolutely crushed. This other person just didn't like it, but Brian cut it anyway. I think that song was pretty meaningful in expressing where he was at that point in time. I think it's his heaviest song, even though I'm probably wrong."

> I'm a leaf on a windy day
> Pretty soon I'll be blown away
> How long will the wind blow
> Until I die

Heartbreaking lyrics, beautifully arranged and sung, this song was an artistic triumph, like the best of *Pet Sounds*, a window into Brian's heart and soul. The offered glimpse is quite sad, and it was the last time a Beach Boys album would include a Brian Wilson song that so openly expressed his emotions.

The title song was all that the *SMiLE* legend had promised and maybe a little more, and it was when a song like 'Surf's Up' was finally released that one could really begin to understand what the collapse of *SMiLE* had cost the world of music.

The one cut on the album that defies explanation is 'A Day in the Life of a Tree,' which features an unexpected lead vocal by Jack Rieley as well as a guest appearance by Van Dyke Parks. Ben Edmonds: "Now, that probably was one of Brian's classic put-ons. 'Cause I remember Jack Rieley telling me after he did the vocal that he went into the booth and Brian was crying. 'Was so choked up.' *You* listen to it. How can anyone get choked up listening to that with anything but laughter?" The vocal does have an oddly appealing, sensitive quality. As one friend of Brian's theorized, Brian was "choked up" because "he really related to the song. It was about him."

The rest of the album was marred by musical inconsistency and pseudo-important Jack Rieley lyrics. Bruce's 'Disney Girls' was a perfect piece of pop, and Carl's work showed his emerging composing and producing talents, but the triteness of the lyrical themes expressed in the ecology and anti-war songs was almost embarrassing. The group's sudden relevancy was hard to take for many who had observed the Beach Boys' basic political silence over the years. Few knew that Carl had been a draft resister before that was common. Nineteen seventy-one, though, was a turning point in the entire "counter-culture revolution" and the Beach Boys would be caught up in the eventual return to nostalgia that followed Vietnam and Watergate.

The *Surf's Up* album did quite well for the group, critically and commercially, especially in light of the *Sunflower* debacle. The Beach Boys, though, were going in different directions, which created a basic instability within the band that has lasted to this day. Dennis was constantly quitting or getting fired and then rejoining. He was in a movie, *Two-Lane Blacktop*, with James Taylor; he'd stopped drumming due to a hand injury suffered during a drunken temper tantrum and was giving serious consideration to a solo career. In December of 1970 he released a solo record in England with Daryl Dragon; by February of '71, both he and Bruce were talking of doing solo albums, talk that continued for five years before seeing fruition. In late '71, the Beach Boys, on the verge of a new success, were in danger of losing their sex symbol (Dennis), and his leave-takings would continue throughout the decade. For that matter, all the members of the group periodically quit.

The one member who never wanted to leave the band was let go in the spring of 1972. An Earl Leaf gossip column noted that: "On the seventh anniversary of attaining his official status as a Beach Boy, guitarman Bruce Johnston got the axe. Carl Wilson, Mike Love and Al Jardine voted unanimously to drop him from the group due to hostile vibes his lifeways caused them." Bruce claims that he left the group by mutual consent, but regardless of how "mutual" the decision was, there is no question that it was Jack Rieley who forced Bruce out of the group.

Bruce: "I don't know if he was trying to get rid of me; I think he was just trying to redirect a band." Ben Edmonds notes, "Bruce was the one member of the group that was beginning to have some doubts about Jack Rieley's intentions. And at that time, I seem to remember people pointing to the fact that he was the one Beach Boy who didn't meditate and wasn't a vegetarian and wasn't part of their lifestyle. Whether that was just the official line or the reality of the situation, I don't know. Bruce was definitely the one who most clearly saw exactly what Jack Rieley was up to." Although this is not one of Bruce's favorite topics of discussion, he does credit Rieley. "All I can say is that at the beginning, I thought what he was trying to do was absolutely right on the money. He helped the band become aware of what our niche was in pop music."

Many of the group's employees and entourage hadn't liked Rieley from the beginning, and one office worker reportedly hired a private detective who found out that Rieley had never worked for NBC, won the Pulitzer Prize, or done anything else he'd claimed. His actual background allegedly showed a lack of stability.

One humorous note in the Jack Rieley affair is that Brian and Jack's friendship lasted only a few weeks before Brian got bored with Jack. As Ben Edmonds recalls, "Even when the rest of them were apparently being fooled by his [Rieley's] come-on, Brian really knew what was going on. Brian made up a little song called 'Is Jack Rieley Really Superman?' So

Brian knew what was going on. But at that point in time, he obviously had no desire to control the situation."

It was Rieley who was in control, and he was still making the right career moves even if his intentions weren't pure. Ben Edmonds remembers that "Jack saw Brian as being one of the big keys to reviving the Beach Boys. Which was an extension of Derek Taylor's 'Brian Wilson is a genius' hype. For which I can't fault Derek because at that time he meant very well. Unfortunately, it's been one of those things that has come back to haunt Brian like a curse. At the time, it certainly seemed valid, and Derek, bless his heart, was certainly doing his job as a press agent.

"I think that Jack Rieley saw an extension of that as being very critical to bringing the Beach Boys back. Which was very correct. Because the whole playing on the Brian Wilson mythology, whether it be for that point in time or for 1976, has always been crucial to manipulating the Beach Boys image."

The Brian Wilson legend was reborn in the fall of 1971 with a two-part article *Rolling Stone* called "The Beach Boys: A California Saga." Writers Tom Nolan and David Felton managed to capture all the bizarre elements of the group's history and, at the same time, concentrated on the legend of *SMiLE* and its lost glories. Combined with the group's growing appeal as a concert attraction and the success of the *Surf's Up* album, the Beach Boys were firmly on their way back. If it involved exploiting Brian and dredging up a lot of bad memories, so be it. The Beach Boys came first.

Brian was well aware of that, and he wanted less and less to do with the group. He had expressed how he felt in his music, ("'Til I Die'), but the family seemed to ignore his feelings. They had come to tolerate Brian's eccentric behavior. One observer notes that the family was totally "condescending in their love and support. They were giving off feelings like, 'Considering how messed up you are, you're OK.' Instead of saying, 'Brian, you're OK, but these things bother me,' they say, 'Brian, you're not OK, but this thing here is nice about you.' If you love him, then he is OK. They were communicating that you're a lovable person in spite of yourself." That same observer recalls the tremendous hurting that was going on between the brothers. "Brian would hurt them, not by being a mean person, but by copping out, backing down from his commitments. They would strike back at him, not understanding that he was having trouble keeping a commitment to himself, let alone anyone else."

209

According to this longtime friend of Brian's, "He wasn't always communicating with them what was bothering him. But even when he did, they ignored him and passed it off as his crazy behavior. At that point, Brian's eccentricities didn't seem to be hurting anybody, except himself.

"Brian was crying out for help," this friend recalls, "but nobody was really sure whether he meant it or not." Another observer remembers that even Brian's suicide threats became a joke, like the time he touched off a mad dash by announcing that he planned to drive his Rolls-Royce off the Santa Monica Pier and into the Pacific Ocean. That got some attention. Brian was even rumored to have once dug a grave in the backyard; he wasn't being subtle, but somehow it was all tolerated. Brian's actions have always been hard to understand, and there are only a handful of people who are able to discern whether he is playing games or being serious.

Because Brian didn't relate to the Beach Boys' situation, he created a new world of friends, much like the people he had surrounded himself with during the *SMiLE* era. Danny Hutton (a founding member of Three Dog Night) and Van Dyke Parks were still around from the old days and Tandyn Almer (he wrote the Association's first Top Ten hit, 'Along Comes Mary') had been added to this circle of far-out creators. In 1970 and 1971, Brian wasn't a recluse. He could be found at his health food store, or at the Troubadour bar, or at one of two health food restaurants, H.E.L.P. or The Source. Brian wasn't especially happy, but at least he had friends whom he could trust and people to hang out with. Besides that, these people didn't care whether Brian would have five songs ready for the next album. They liked Brian Wilson the person, not Brian Wilson the Beach Boy. These people and others became Brian's family.

In the early 1970s, Brian was reportedly getting kicked out of the house or just leaving for days at a time. One member of Brian's new entourage remembers that "Marilyn got up at six in the morning, made breakfast, and ran the house, took care of the kids and all that. Brian got up at six in the evening and went off to his own separate world. Marilyn had no idea what Brian was into."

Brian: "Danny Hutton was a major influence in my life . . . he's got such a touch about him. I admire a lot of people, but he's just a special person in my life . . . being around a strong person like that was good for me." For Brian, Danny Hutton's house was a refuge, a place where he could go to escape the pressure. Brian never felt used at Danny's; he knew that Danny wasn't going to try to "get" something from him. At Danny's, Brian could just relax and be himself.

One interesting trait of Brian's is that he always dominates whatever situation he is part of, even when he is not overtly exerting his influence. When he chooses to lead actively, he can be incredibly forceful and decisive. Brian constantly enjoys the power trip of testing his friends' commitment, often coaxing them into taking part in one of his unusual activities, which are often bizarre mind games. The irony of such happenings was that Brian's friends would be blamed by the family for being a bad influence on Brian and always getting him into trouble, when quite the reverse was true. Consequently, these friends were never welcome at the Wilson house.

Musically, Brian's dwindling output found a new outlet with the reformation of his wife's singing group. This time, it was just Marilyn and her sister Diane, and they called Spring. Ben Edmonds says, "A lot of people have different points of view on the whole Spring trip. I mean, some people will tell you it's a situation where Marilyn and Diane bullied him into it. And he was doing it out of a sense of obligation. Other people will tell you he was really into it. The only thing I can ever recall Brian saying about his wife was that she was a great singer, one of the great singers, and he was going to let everybody know that." Marilyn is a capable background singer, and her lead vocals are pleasant. Brian's productions framed her voice perfectly.

Spring (later changed to American Spring to avoid legal hassles) secured a contract with United Artists Records. David Sandler, the newest arrival in the Wilson camp, went to work with Brian on the *Spring* LP. It should be noted that Sandler's contribution to the album and the subsequent single on Columbia was greater than Brian's. Sandler's talent for singing and producing in Brian Wilson's style is remembered as remarkable by observers—some people couldn't tell the difference. The *Spring* album has become a cult favorite, probably because the production and the background vocal arrangements were so good. Even if Brian's involvement wasn't as great as the publicity surrounding the record led listeners to believe, it still served as a reminder that Brian's skills were intact.

Brian and David Sandler were also planning another album (without Spring), and they even talked about it with Warner Brothers Records.

In early '72, Blondie Chaplin and Ricky Fataar (both formerly of the Flame) were officially made Beach Boys. The first album they worked on, *Carl and the Passions*— '*So Tough*', was a disjointed affair, definitely the result of the Beach Boys' recording in three different studios at once—Dennis Wilson and Daryl Dragon in one, Carl, Mike and Al at another studio, and Blondie and Ricky at a third. Brian's involvement in the recording of this album was virtually invisible; Brian called it phantom singing. It was even suggested that Brian refused to pose for a group picture, and the inside album photo was put together to make Brian appear to be one of the group.

Brian's musical contribution was the smallest he's made to any of the Beach Boys albums in their entire career. He wrote only two songs, but now, a new wrinkle had been added. Jack Rieley was changing Brian's lyrics. 'You Need a Mess of Help to Stand Alone' was written by Brian and Tandyn Almer; it was originally titled 'Beatrice from Baltimore.' The original lyrics included this verse: "She got a hole in her stockin' / She do a whole lot of rockin' / She do the shake down at Bumbles / She do the Chi-ca-no rumble."

Rieley decided to write a new set of lyrics that would make the song more "relevant" and "hip sounding." Brian's other song, 'Marcella,' was about a masseuse who had been an understanding friend to Brian. In those days, Brian had taken to frequenting massage parlors for human contact. And despite all that had transpired through the years, Brian still managed to get himself into funny situations, often unintentionally. Dean Torrence says that "Brian has always been funny to me visually, a walk or an expression. Sometimes I just look at him and crack up. He used to tell me seriously about something that would make me laugh . . . a massage parlor he used to go to. He couldn't figure out why they treated him so poorly just because he was walking along in a hallway and tripped in a hole in the rug and fell into this room and scared the girl and whoever she was 'massaging.' And they kicked him out. He said all this with a real straight face, and I'm just dying."

Reportedly, 'Marcella' was also rewritten so that it wouldn't sound like Brian had been hanging out in massage parlors. Despite those lyrical changes, it is the most "Beach Boys" – sounding song on the record.

Dennis's two contributions were fine but neither were as good as *Sunflower*'s 'Forever'; the TM song, 'All This Is That,' worked because of the group's solid singing, Carl's great lead vocal and the beautiful fade. Longtime Beach Boys fans were unhappy that two of the eight cuts were by "outsiders" (Blondie and Ricky).

Another problem for *So Tough* was that it was released in a package with *Pet Sounds*, and it could only suffer in comparison. That coupling helped make *So Tough* seem like the Beach Boys' worst album ever.

The addition of Blondie and Ricky did add a new, very soulful dimension to the Beach Boys' records and concerts, but some purists were displeased at the sound of Blondie Chaplin singing 'Wild Honey.' It was certainly different. In fact, Blondie's voice was a welcome addition to the Beach Boys, and his vocal on 'Sail on Sailor' would make that song one of the best records the group released in the 1970s.

Brian Wilson, entering one of the worst periods of his life, received the unwelcome news that the group had decided to record their next album in Holland, and like it or not, Brian was going along. For a man who really was only at home when he was at home, the trip was not something to look forward to. As Audree Wilson remembers, "Brian didn't want to go to Holland. He didn't leave when everybody left."

The story of how Brian finally got there was recounted in the group's *Holland* booklet, which was a history of the entire project. According to that tale, Brian's trip was "a miasma of false starts and silences. His wife, kids, and housekeeper went over first. Twice, Brian got as far as the airport and turned back. The third time, he appeared to get on the plane. A phone call went through to Amsterdam to confirm it. But three hours after the plane landed, there was still no sign of him. A search of the aircraft yielded Brian's ticket and passport, abandoned on his seat. Oblivious to the panic, Brian shuffled off the plane and fell asleep on a couch in the duty-free lounge, where he eventually was found."

The one point that this story glosses over is that everybody went over without Brian and left him behind. As Audree Wilson remembers, "My opinion on seeing Brian was that he wasn't thrilled with Holland. He was there, but I think he would have preferred to be home."

The Holland trip was a Jack Rieley idea, and with Carl's support, the group made plans to spend a number of months abroad, touring and recording a new album. The whole affair was disrupted by the ineptness that has frequently marked the Beach Boys management. In Holland, they couldn't find housing in a central location, so everybody was scattered over a large area. Then, the group learned that there was no studio that could accommodate their demands for time, so the Beach Boys had an entire studio built in Los Angeles and flown over piece by piece to Holland where it was reassembled. The stay in Holland, what with the studio costs and living expenses for dozens of family, friends and staff, ran into the hundreds of thousands of dollars. To top it all off, when the group submitted *Holland* to Warner Brothers, it was rejected for lack of a strong single. That caused more than a bit of grief.

Holland, like its predecessor, was a disjointed album because the song-writing chores were shared by so many people. This time, however, the quality of the songs and the more involved production made *Holland* a successful effort, but not before Warners and the group fought a bloody battle. Finally, a mediocre song, 'We Got Love,' was replaced by the album's real gem, Brian's 'Sail on Sailor.'

'Sail on Sailor' has a curious history, and there are several "definitive" versions of the birth of the song. Regardless of its origins, it is known that Jack Rieley again added his own lyrics which were used in place of some of the original lyrics.

'Sail on Sailor' wasn't the only creative stumbling block for Brian on the *Holland* album. While in Holland, Brian had written a bizarre fairy tale, inspired by Randy Newman's *Sail Away* album. Although the musical segments are short, they have a power that was missing from the rest of the album. The music comes from that faraway place that Brian has always gone to for his special sounds. The group, however, was not prepared for the fairy tale's length and refused to put it on the album. A compromise was reached, and it was included as a special seven-inch bonus record with the *Holland* album. Recently, Brian developed the 'Pied Piper' theme into an entire song, 'Lazy Lizzie,' and it is very good.

The fairy tale itself was another statement from Brian Wilson as to his current situation. He knew that he had retreated into something of a fairy-tale world out of a sense of self-preservation. The storyline is about a prince who had a magic transistor radio, and how the prince had trouble hearing the music from the radio. The not-very-hidden meaning of the story touched on Brian's family difficulties, and Brian's problems in creating music. Metaphorically, the magic transistor could be considered Brian's muse, and he was telling the world that he was having trouble tuning into his station.

Following the financial debacle that was *Holland*, the Beach Boys realized that maybe Jack Rieley wasn't all he was supposed to be. Carl went to Amsterdam where Rieley had remained and fired him. Despite all the claims that Rieley took advantage of the group, his contribution should never be underestimated. Ben Edmonds, himself a victim of Rieley's false promises, puts Jack's efforts into perspective. "As much of a liar and a possible crook, or whatever Jack Rieley might have been, he was also responsible for bringing the Beach Boys back out of obscurity, something they could never have done themselves. They never had the kind of direction and guidance to be able to really do it. They have always had to depend on outside sources to keep them in contact with the real world.

"Al Jardine," Edmonds remembers, "so believed in Jack Rieley that Jardine once claimed, 'Well, I suppose that we have some talent, but I just don't know where we'd be without Jack Rieley.' He had duped them to the extent that Alan was obviously reflecting the group's attitude that they owed it to Jack Rieley. Which on one level is true but on another level is absurd. However Jack Rieley may have misled them and used them, or whatever, you still can't deny that he was responsible for the 1971 resurgence of the Beach Boys. He did engineer that. There are probably a lot of negative things that people have to say about Jack Rieley, my own included, but you also have to give him credit where credit is due. He pulled it off very well. He made a place for the Beach Boys again, and you can't take that away from him."

In Holland, Brian's depression deepened, and his weight, which had been an occasional problem, began to rise out of control. To Brian's always fragile ego, this heaviness made him publicly unacceptable, so, once he had returned home, he tended to remain behind the closed doors of his Bel-Air mansion.

Brian was unable to record at home. Marilyn had removed the home studio because she wanted to live a more "normal" life and not be in the middle of a constant traffic jam of musicians and record makers. To Brian, this was a devastating blow. As Brian later noted, "If I could have anything in the world, I'd have a studio in my house again. That's the one thing I want more than *anything!*"

Because of his weight problem, Brian didn't like to travel to a studio in Hollywood, so his recording ambitions were effectively stymied. Tandyn Almer, one of Brian's closest friends at this point, sincerely felt that Brian needed help. One friend of both Tandyn's and Brian's remembered that Tandyn "encouraged Brian to see a psychiatrist. The family wouldn't hear of it." Tandyn eventually got Brian to meet a well-known Los Angeles psychiatrist, as this friend recalls, "and he refused to treat Brian as an outpatient because he said that it was 'his environment that is his problem.'" "The family," another friend of Brian notes, "wouldn't even admit that there was a problem. It was like an alcoholic that people ignore. The whole Beach Boys trip revolved around their closing their eyes to Brian's problems. Brian was part of the woodwork, like a disabled child that everyone ignored."

While it may be true that the family would ignore Brian's problems, it is important to understand that illness isn't easy for any family to accept. With Brian, nobody was ever quite sure how sick he was. Also, it should be noted that all the Wilsons were experiencing personal difficulties of one sort or another, and they didn't spend all their time worrying about Brian. Their concern may not have appeared on the surface, because in order to survive in a household or a family business with a "sick" person, it is sometimes necessary to ignore that person. That doesn't mean that each and every one of the Wilsons wasn't heartbroken to watch Brian's difficulties. The Wilsons may have lacked understanding of his situation, but there was plenty of compassion, particularly from Dennis and Carl.

Their treatment of Brian's friends, though, wasn't the least bit gracious or understanding. As one of those friends recalls, "The family thought that Tandyn and Danny and Van Dyke and all the others were crazy." To an objective viewer, that was a reasonable conclusion, but this other friend points out that "Brian's friends got Brian actively interested in creating, thinking, writing. They could make Brian sane sometimes, but everybody resented them." Their resentment didn't center around the creative area. As one observer put it, "Brian and Tandyn explored new realms of eccentricity together." A close friend of Brian's called Tandyn evil and says that on balance "I think he damaged Brian."

The next event shook the entire family: Murry Wilson died of a heart attack on June 4, 1973. Audree Wilson remembers that "Brian was extremely upset when Murry died. It was very hard on him." It was so hard that Brian left town. As Audree recalls, "Carl said something like a leading remark about Brian, and I said, 'What's wrong?' And he said, 'I'm really pissed at Brian; he went to New York.' And I said, 'It's OK, Carl.

He can't handle it. I really totally understand. He just can't handle it. And the first thing he could think of was to go pretty far away.'"

Diane Rovell [Marilyn's sister] was dispatched to New York to bring Brian back, but before they returned, Brian dropped by WNEW-FM for a chat with Pete Fornatale and visited *Record World* magazine for a rare print interview. The visit to WNEW was incredibly strange. Fornatale, who counted Brian as one of his idols, was crushed to meet him finally in his overweight, overwrought shape. Their on-the-air interview was filled with mostly irrelevant chatter about a visit to the zoo and a gorilla named "Pattycake" and the maids at the Americana Hotel. Brian noted, "They'll get you in trouble every time." There was a hilarious (although perfectly serious) comment from Brian about American Spring's performing on *The Ed Sullivan Show* (which was off the air by 1973). As he made the comment, Brian realized his mistake, and his embarrassed laughter rang out at such volume that it's echoing in the halls of WNEW-FM to this day. Brian did make one comment that was particularly revealing. "My group for the last few years has been American Spring." Brian said it right out. He wasn't a Beach Boy. His comment only hinted at what was really going on.

In the *Record World* magazine interview that took place that same afternoon, Brian discussed the impact of Murry's death, and said that since Murry had died, "I feel a lot more ambitious . . . I'm gonna try a little harder now . . . He died just before we could record one of his tunes, 'Lazzaloo' . . . And then I got a call that he was gone . . . It's makin' a man out of me. Makes me want to produce a little more."

Even at this depressing time, Brian's humor shone through. During the WNEW interview, Brian had claimed, "I've never been a hype . . . but I'll eat my hat, if I had a hat I'd eat it, if that record doesn't really get some kind of action. I'm talking about 'Shyin' Away'" by American Spring. Talking to *Record World* a few hours later, Brian noted, "I said on the air that if people would buy the record, I'd sell my wardrobe. Yeah, my wardrobe, two shirts and a pair of jeans. That's my whole wardrobe."

"My father's dying," Brian would later recall, "had a lot to do with my retreating." For Brian, 1973 was the start of a period in his life that all would like to forget. For the Beach Boys, it was the start of a major resurgence. In '73, the traveling band finally began to reap the financial rewards of persistent touring. All the years of playing small, often half-filled school gyms and local auditoriums were paying off in grand style so that, by the end of 1973, the group could headline major arenas like Madison Square Garden. At that concert, Bruce Johnston joined the group onstage for the encore. This mini-reunion came about, according to the then road manager Rick Nelson, "because he [Bruce] had always hoped that the Beach Boys would play the Garden, and when they did he wanted to be there. That was one of his goals as a Beach Boy."

The new and growing acceptance of the Beach Boys' music on the concert scene was documented in the December '73 release of a two-record live album. It isn't a memorable record, but nobody could ignore the fact that this record of mostly old hits became the group's first gold record for Warner Brothers, even if it took an accounting maneuver to gain it that status.

Nineteen seventy-three was the last year the group struggled financially, but the internal problems raged on. Rick Nelson remembers that Dennis was pretty inactive: "He would just wander around the stage, plink a little piano, stand at the mic. He was lost. There was no musical reason for him to be there except that he was Dennis Wilson." Blondie and Ricky were beginning to tire of playing the Beach Boys' music and not enough of their own.

In those days, though, before the big success of 1974, as Rick Nelson remembers, "They were united then. They had fights, but it was like, 'Here's another shot. Let's make the most of it.' They were actually humble, a little bit. We were traveling coach class, and we were renting cars and everybody had to drive, and we weren't staying in the fanciest hotels. As spoiled as they'd been, that was hard for them to acknowledge that they had to go back a little bit. And they did it." When they did start on the upswing, "They forgot about [the bad times] real quick."

Money in 1973 (or most any year) ruled the Beach Boys, and Rick Nelson thinks Steve Love (Mike's brother) "was really instrumental in keeping it tight. Economics were the key because they didn't want to blow it all on the road; they wanted to have something left over. Everything was, 'Well let's take this one little step.' In some big cities, we'd get limos. It was a slow transition." The Beach Boys had taken charge of their own business affairs. Rick Nelson recalls, "They insisted on making the money decisions because they wouldn't rely on a manager. It was always interesting to do that because I would have to call them up individually and say,

'Here's the issue, what's the vote?' 'What did Dennis vote?' 'I haven't talked to him.' 'Well, you call him, and then you call me back.'"

The group's live program was also slowly starting to include more of the hits, the result of backstage "battles" between Carl and Mike. Mike is the man who makes the live shows work, who knew the impact of the hits. His commercial instincts would be vindicated in 1974, when the Beach Boys had their first #1 record in many, many years.

MURRY WILSON

Brian Wilson: "The biggest figure of authority is the parent. I had an extreme experience of living with an authoritative father. It's enabled me to see the injustice authority creates. The teenager's scapegoat existence sort of proves that there is a great lack of communication between young people and adults. Their [adults'] antagonism [toward their children] basically is a misunderstanding of themselves. It's awfully easy for them to come home from work and to jump on and annihilate teenagers emotionally just to get rid of the anxieties, failures and frustrations of the day. They feel the necessity of taking them out on someone who isn't in a position to fight back. I had a real struggle when I was a kid. I used to think my folks were pretty much out of it, didn't even know where it was at. But how are you going to tell your parents where it's at? . . . When they're out feeding you . . . and meanwhile you're going to be the first one to eat all the ice cream. I'd like to see the day when parents and teenagers can just get along with each other . . . why don't they like each other?"

That mid-sixties plea from Brian was the result of growing up with Murry Wilson as his father. Murry had a multifaceted personality. He could be a brutal parent, a dedicated manager, a "man of the world," a generous and thoughtful friend, or an inconsiderate and relentless adversary. As father of the Beach Boys, it was Murry's drive that instilled a competitive force within Brian that fostered his desire and need to succeed. Brian feels that it was Murry's attitude of "Don't slough off, get in there and fight" that taught him a lot. One associate of Murry's noted that Murry was very "Bomb Hanoi-ish." According to Brian, Murry said, "'If you're going to do it, do it good.' He didn't believe in halfway business. Of course, we learned this from him, and it's helped us out."

Though his methods were sometimes crude, Murry did instill a sense of pride in his sons and eventually in the Beach Boys. The group needed that; they were just kids when it began. Sometimes, they would curse offstage (or on), and Murry would fine them for swearing and teach them that this was unprofessional. According to numerous reports, Murry often taught the Beach Boys with physical and verbal abuse. Audree Wilson remembers that "Murry was a taskmaster; he really was. He was tough. I used to think he was too tough, but I tend to be very easy."

Gary Usher recalls that "Murry and I didn't get along especially well. I was constantly getting in Murry's way, and I opposed a lot of his ideas. I would influence Brian in ways that would take him away from his father's thinking, and to Murry that was high treason. He'd like to shoot traitors, I'm sure." When it came to Murry's treatment of his sons and the other Beach Boys, Usher notes: "He was doing what he thought was right for the boys, driven by an incredible energy source. He truly believed that everything he did was right for the boys. He tried to teach them to be men the only way he knew how. The sons were a little bit more sophisticated. Murry's philosophy was 'aim high, and if you miss low, you're still higher than a lot of people.' So he would push as hard as he could for those kids, even though it may have been clumsy and it may not have been up to the standards of those days, somehow it worked. Even though he sometimes had bad judgment in the way he conducted himself, the train still went forward. Strange combination of energies."

As Bruce Johnston recalls, "Murry was kind of like a set of jumper cables. He'd get it rolling, but that's as far as he would go; yet he'd keep sending current in, which would be the wrong current, but he would get it started."

From the very beginning of their career, Murry was there to make sure things went right; even when his way clashed with what everyone else wanted, Murry persevered . . . until the Beach Boys finally fired him. At the start, though, Murry was in charge. According to Bruce Johnston, Murry "had a thing about making sure that the guys sounded high in terms of pitch, because it sounded young. If you listen to 'Surfin',' that was sped up to make the guys sound younger. He didn't want them to start their careers sounding like old men. He was right there. Murry is a lot like Dennis; they both operate more on feel."

Murry's creative talents as a composer and a record producer were not responsible for the Beach Boys' success. Gary Usher remembers that Murry's "musical tastes were from a little before our time." Murry's music was pure schmaltz, sentimental and romantic, sometimes overblown and melodramatic. That style was out of fashion by the early 1960s, and the Beach Boys were definitely a rock 'n' roll group, not a big band. All that, however, did not prevent a crossover into Brian's and eventually Dennis's music. The emotional intensity of Beach Boys' music, as a reflection of Murry's personality, helped make the "hit records" powerful enough to survive the years, even though much of the lyrical content is by now irrelevant. 'Surfer Girl' still works. There is an emotional, almost spiritual quality about Brian's music that transcends lyrical simplicity. *Pet Sounds* is as emotion-packed today as it was a dozen years ago, maybe more so in light of what Brian has been through. Dennis Wilson recalls that Murry would cry like the Cowardly Lion from *The Wizard of Oz* when he would hear certain chords or Brian's singing on songs like 'Caroline, No.'

Murry's fights with Capitol Records on the Beach Boys' behalf had an immeasurable effect on the group's career. While Murry's persistence kept the people at Capitol alert, the possibility exists that Capitol may have grudgingly complied with Murry's demands, and, at the same time, only half-heartedly performed those tasks. One unsubstantiated report claims that when Murry insisted on putting out his own album, Capitol finally submitted but buried the expense of the record in the Beach Boys' accounts. Effectively, this source claims, the Beach Boys paid for Murry's album. When the Beach Boys' hitmaking machine began to sputter in 1967, some people at Capitol must have secretly smiled. Without hits, Murry Wilson was totally powerless and could be completely ignored.

The mercenary aspects of the record business were particularly prominent in the late fifties and early sixties. The rock 'n' roll explosion meant huge sales for the record companies that had, before rock, done quite nicely with Broadway show albums and singers like Sinatra. In 1961, when the Beach Boys first started making records, the music industry was still geared toward the adults. Elvis may have sold bunches for RCA, but there was a pervasive hope that the rock 'n' rollers would go away. Along with that failed prayer was the idea that these rock bands were an insignificant commodity. Few groups at that time were writing their own material or producing their own records. As long as the record companies' in-house producers and writers controlled things, the new rock group with their big smash hit was unimportant. There would be a bunch of kids along the next day to take their place.

A further handicap for young talent was the dishonesty of the business. Artists were consistently being cheated by their record companies, their managers, their publishers, or all of the above. It was this system that the Beach Boys were up against. With Murry's help they fought it. Unfortunately for Brian and the boys, Murry Wilson didn't have the innate shrewdness or slickness to combat the executives. His bombastic behavior only succeeded in alienating them.

Roger Christian remembers that "Murry Wilson was an honorable man. His word was his bond. He was one of the finest men I've ever known. A lot of people will say he was a hardhead; he was only a hardhead because he knew what was right, and he was very protective of his family. Whatever he told you, you could put in the bank. He was as honest as they come."

Murry's managerial stint with the Beach Boys lasted less than three years, years that saw the Beach Boys become one of the biggest recording and performing acts in the world. As Audree Wilson recalls, those years weren't always filled with the joys of growing success. "They went through a lot of tough, tough times together. Murry would pick on Denny. Denny taught himself to play the drums. He was at that point learning all the time. He used to beat the hell out of the drums, and Murry would be signaling to him to 'tone it down, tone it down,' and Denny would ignore him. And then Murry would say to me, 'You go tell him to stop playing so loud.' Things like that, just dissension."

When the Beach Boys grew tired of Murry's tyrannical control, they fired him. Audree Wilson remembers that Murry was terribly hurt, but "the funny part of it was that he said he wouldn't work for them anymore; he couldn't take it, said he couldn't stand it . . . He did so many jobs. He wanted to be everything and take care of all the facets, and that's pretty hard to do when a business grew as fast as that did." When Cummings and Current, an accounting firm that took over the management of the group, asked Murry to assist in setting up the tours, he refused. According to Audree, "He was very stubborn about that, and yet he would give advice. Wanted or unwanted, he gave a lot of very good advice. They would say years later, 'Why didn't we listen to him?' I've heard Carl say, 'We were punks.' They were just kids, they really were."

When the Beach Boys fired Murry, his pride was very hurt, and as

Chuck Britz explains, "Murry wanted to prove to them that he could make another group as great as they were," which is why he formed the Sunrays.

Murry was doing the best he could though, and it should be noted that, in those days, there weren't any professional management firms for rock groups as there are today. Everybody was just finding their way in the business, and most talent was eventually exploited. Murry can only be praised for trying to protect his kids. It was a difficult task, as Audree Wilson notes: "He used to call them young stallions. It was a very hard job for him, having three teenage boys and a nephew." It was more than he could handle. A number of associates felt that Murry was just simply out of his depth, out of his element.

In business dealings Murry was, as Gary Usher remembers, "A hard person to get along with. He knew what he wanted, and he pushed really hard to get it. Murry was basically dated in the record business; he was from another era and had learned what he had learned from another era. It wasn't really applicable to what was coming down in the early sixties. The sons, of course, were very progressive, so Murry in some respects was like 'a bull in a china shop.' His personality was so overwhelming; he could aim it at you like a ton of bricks, wham! People would talk to him, and after he left, they'd say, 'What was that? Is he for real?' I'd hear that all the time. He was blind to all of that; he'd just push forward—get out of the way!

"It was him barging into doors and pushing ahead that created a mystique, an awe about the whole thing. He had his own moral codes that he followed, and he felt that everyone else should follow them. The truth of the matter is that some of those moral codes left something to be desired. Murry would miss certain subtleties that were involved, especially in dealing with his sons. He wasn't aware in certain areas where they were, that was the main thing. Murry wasn't sensitive enough in some respects and overly sensitive in others. That's why it was so tough in that family; it was hard to communicate with Murry."

Fred Vail is one of the most loyal, dedicated and level-headed employees and friends the Beach Boys have ever had, and he is one of Murry's staunchest defenders.

"No one will ever beat Murry as far as the Beach Boys are concerned. He's my idol, I guess. He's looked on with disfavor by a lot of people, but when you get right down to the nitty-gritty, he was great. People think he held them back, bruised Brian's ego, stuff like that. Very few people, however, recognize or even realize the importance of Murry's contribution, particularly when you consider the politics of the industry and the [fight] for survival."

According to Vail, Murry was "a pusher and a doer. He would camp out in front of the office of Capitol's executives until they would see him. The world couldn't neglect the Beach Boys as long as Murry was around." While he was the group's manager, Murry effectively used the group's records to complement the live performances. Vail notes that "Murry made sure that the local radio station always had the latest Beach Boys records to play. He covered all the bases."

Murry's chief source of income was that he administered and eventually owned the publishing of the Beach Boys' songs. Frequently, Murry went to Europe to take care of the foreign publishing. As Fred Vail recalls, "Murry would buy gifts in bulk. Then, when the boys were on tour, in each city he'd have a gift for the disc jockey and the jock's wife. Murry would go to the station, and when he'd see the DJs he would ask them about their families. He would even remember their wives' names. And then he would give the guy some French perfume to give to his wife. Murry was a very generous person."

Rick Henn was a classmate of Carl's at Hollywood's Professional High School, and Carl introduced him to Murry. Rick had a group, and Murry took them over, dressing them in striped shirts like the Beach Boys. Chuck Britz thinks Murry used the Sunrays "to prove to the Beach Boys he didn't need them for harmonies. He could make these guys do it. And they couldn't. They weren't that good singers. They were a bunch of good guys, but they only had two hits, 'Andrea' and 'I Live for the Sun.'"

Murry did his best to copy the Beach Boys, but without Brian's talents, the Sunrays were just the latest in a string of imitators of the Beach Boys' sound. As the organizer of the project, Murry's creative limitations shone through because he had to hire producer/arranger Don Ralke. According to Britz, "Don Ralke did all the coaching. He put it all together. He did the arrangements; he did the vocal things. He'd even sing with them to help out."

Murry's basic distrust and dislike for outsiders was absorbed by the group, and they too became wary of people who weren't part of the "family." The family eventually grew as the guys got married, and the organization grew with the group's success. Many of the employees were part of the Beach Boys family. Murry had warned his kids not to trust people because people would use the boys to achieve their own success. Ironically, an entire organization grew up around Brian Wilson's talents, a huge family of people, all with their own families and all depending upon the Beach Boys' continued success for their own personal security.

Somewhere along the line, this lack of trust that had been fostered by Murry was "rewarded" with financial disaster when the group began to trust the wrong people. The Beach Boys' basic innocence was destroyed by dishonest management in the early 1970s.

In the mid-sixties, Murry's involvement with the group tapered off. Still, he was their publisher, and because his income depended upon the continued commercial success of the Beach Boys' records, he reportedly had many negative things to say about the new type of songs that Brian was writing in 1965 and 1966.

The Wilson family business was not a smoothly operating machine by 1966. Murry wasn't managing the group anymore, nor was he exerting parental influence over his boys. The Wilson brothers' use of drugs served to further divide the family. Audree Wilson painfully recalls that time: "I remember Carl coming to me and telling me that he had smoked marijuana. Brian and Carl both told me at the same time. We were walking through an airport, and I just choked, because at that time it was such a new thing to me. I knew nothing about it except 'Stay away! Dangerous! Bad!' And, of course, their father, oh, he just went wild, because they all told him. They were very honest, and I used to wish they had never told. We talked about that later and Carl said, 'No, we had to do that, we had to be honest about it.' They were very upfront.

"So there was a time when that was going on when Murry wouldn't let them come to our house. It was a terrible time in my life. He wouldn't let them come over until the day they would tell him, 'I'll never touch another marijuana cigarette again.' And I only got to see them— really, it was sort of sneaky. He didn't want me to go to their houses, and instead of asserting myself and saying, 'Go to hell, they're my sons,' I did what he told me to do. It was on a Christmas Day when he said, 'You can have the family over for Christmas.' I was ecstatic. I was thrilled, and they all came over and had a wonderful day, a wonderful dinner. And I don't remember if they ever said to him [that they wouldn't smoke mari-juana anymore]. That's very vague. What is very prominent in my mind is the pain of the months he wouldn't allow them to come to our house. That's how strongly he felt about it, not wanting to see his own sons. He really loved them dearly, in his own way."

His love often had a negative effect, though. Derek Taylor, a Beach Boys publicist in the mid-sixties, and now a major record company execu-tive, observed that Murry "was a daft man. He really scared the hell out of his boys." Taylor remembered that Mike Love had some great stories about Murry and "I was always trying to get them out of him." Taylor also felt that Murry "knocked them about emotionally to the point where they became the image he'd set up for them. Carl had to take so much weight, be so calm. Dennis had to be such a crack-shot son."

In the late sixties, Murry's involvement with the group was almost nonexistent. Fred Vail thinks that Murry's absence was one of the principal reasons for the group's decline. Nick Grillo, who managed the group's corporate finances for the second half of that decade, has been blamed for the Beach Boys' money problems, as was his successor, Jack Rieley. Audree Wilson recalls that Grillo "seemed to be a good manager, and my husband was the first one to point out that things weren't the way they should be. He used to tell the boys, 'Do this; do that; don't do this; don't do that.' They didn't listen. They have all said since that he was right. Nick Grillo invested the money very unwisely and lost a fortune. They were really worried, they were in trouble, damn near broke. Maybe not broke-broke, but they weren't where they should have been." As for Jack Rieley, Audree Wilson dismisses him by saying, "I think Jack is very prone to exaggeration, that's putting it mildly. I always liked Jack very much. He had a lot of nice qualities."

In the early seventies, Murry and the Beach Boys had pretty much gone their separate ways. Road manager Rick Nelson recalls that "Carl or Dennis would invite Audree on tour, 'Come on, Mom, it'll be a nice tour, you can spend a couple of days with us.' They would invite Audree but not Murry. They didn't get along with him basically. There was more fear than anything else."

Although Audree and Murry had a very difficult relationship, they seemed to reach a peace in 1972, and reportedly were living together more harmoniously than ever. At that same time, Dennis and Murry grew close, sharing a passion for fishing as well as a realization that they were very much the same person.

Murry Wilson's imprint on the Beach Boys and especially his three sons has been immense, and the ambivalent relationship between father and sons shaped much of their personalities. Most people agree that Dennis is the one most like Murry, but Brian seems to have been the son most affected by his father. One minor indication of how Murry got on Brian's nerves—Brian once wrote a song called 'I'm Bugged at My Old Man.' The musical reason for Brian being upset was, "He don't even know where it's at." As Murry later noted, Brian meant the song as a put-on, but he meant it. Brian recalled, "There was a lot of his critical mind . . . I learned from it. I learned to be highly critical of myself, and I am with myself, very critical because of that." Murry's criticism of Brian's work was a sore point between them 'til the day Murry died.

CHAPTER 12

ENDLESS SUMMER

RECORD COMPANIES REGULARLY REPACKAGE OLD SONGS BY ARTISTS WHO are no longer on their label, so nobody was surprised when Capitol released *Endless Summer* in 1974, a two-record set that was Capitol's umpteenth attempt to cash in on their Beach Boys catalogue.

What was shocking was the album's success. Spurred on by a massive TV campaign, the album went to #1 on the album charts, the first million-seller for the group in a very long time.

The success of *Endless Summer* was only a part of the group's new appeal. Between the endless touring and the changing social climate in the country, it was only natural that the Beach Boys' music would catch on with a whole new generation. Besides that, the old records had been so well produced by Brian that they still sounded fresh; and they lyrically captured a time in America that was a focus for the growing trend toward nostalgia.

The fans weren't asking anymore, "What happened to the Beach Boys?" It was more like, "Hey, where have you guys been all my life?" Discovered by new teenagers, and never abandoned by a fanatical older cult, the Beach Boys had their largest audience since the mid-sixties. Surprisingly, a large number of rock critics turned out to be big Beach Boys fans. Suddenly, they came out of the closet, admitting that they knew the Beach Boys were great all along, and that they were the original thing and it sure is good to have 'em back.

The Beach Boys were back, but where was Brian Wilson? Very simply, Brian was hiding from a hurtful world. It was a curious combination . . . the Beach Boys' resurgence and Brian's retreat.

★　　★　　★　　★

Brian Wilson in 1974 was a deeply troubled man, depressed, self-destructive, and given to long bouts of drink and drugs. The result of this "condition" was that Brian, for the first time in his life, made a public spectacle of himself.

There was one night at the Troubadour when Brian, in his bathrobe, unexpectedly jumped up onstage to sing 'Be-Bop-a-Lula.' The only problem was that the band playing was Larry Coryell's jazz group. Brian was ejected from the club, dejected at having embarrassed himself. David Anderle, when he heard of incidents like that, was very upset. "He never went through those public displays when we were together. The thought of Brian even drinking—I can't believe that."

Then there was Keith Moon's birthday party at the Beverly Wilshire Hotel. Ben Edmonds: "I saw him at that; somebody, it must have been Michele Myer [long a part of the Los Angeles rock music scene], called Brian and said, 'Oh, Brian, it's a fabulous party. You have to come down.' And I think he just walked out of the house, got in the car and drove down, which was incredible 'cause he wasn't supposed to drive at that point in time. He didn't have a license [Brian was involved in a number of accidents]. I saw him, and he just walked in with this bathrobe on. In the Keith Moon scheme of things, that certainly isn't a major outrage by any means. He fitted in perfectly."

In view of the fact that this behavior was disturbing, one wonders where the Wilson family was at times like this. In '74, Brian had moved out of the main part of his house and moved into the "chauffeur's quarters." Those around in 1974 note that Brian was weighed down by both personal problems and his physical condition. He was being made to feel guilty by at least one family member, and, at the same time, Marilyn was not always around. If Brian was in as bad shape as some people observed, then why wasn't there any effort made to help him? As Audree Wilson remembers, "It would get to the point where Marilyn really thought Brian needed help, then he seemed OK, and she'd sort of forget about it, not necessarily talking to him about it at all."

When Brian began granting interviews in '76, one of the most frequently asked questions was "What did you do during the last few years?" Brian's simple answer: "Drugs and hanging out with Danny Hutton. He was one of my best friends . . . It was a Danny Hutton period. It wasn't because of him that I did drugs . . . it was a matter of seeing people like Van Dyke

Parks and Danny Hutton." Brian did the drugs "with Danny, shared a lot of stuff with him."

The Wilson family despised Brian's friends as leeches who only came around to get money from Brian to spend on drugs, or what one member of the family described as "their imaginary projects." To Marilyn Wilson, these people were the "drainers."

One of Brian's friends claims "it was Marilyn and Diane who were really the 'drainers.' At least Brian's friends had creative projects. Marilyn and Diane's ideas weren't the least bit clever. They were always jealous because Danny Hutton or Van Dyke Parks could get Brian thinking and interested in creating, and they couldn't do it even with incessant pleading and threats.

"There was also this double standard that really bugged me. If Brian wanted to buy some musical equipment for one of his friends, that caused a big stink, but it was OK if Marilyn bought matching fur coats for herself and her friends. After all, it was Brian that made the money. It was his to throw away if he wanted to. They were always getting down on him for doing things that they would turn around and do themselves."

Another friend described the situation around Brian as a "malicious matriarchy with people like Mike Love, whose name belies what he really is. Brian is not able to express himself due to the Machiavellian politics around him that lay waste to his prodigious talent."

From the family's point of view, people like Danny and Van Dyke were just indulging Brian's increasing appetite for drugs and weirdness. Regardless of who was right, everybody was powerless to prevent Brian's downward spiral of self-destructive behavior.

Brian's musical interest in 1974 was still strong, but he had virtually no desire to share it with any but a select few friends. Brian recalled, "People kept asking, 'What's your next song going to be, Brian?' I didn't know, and it got so that I didn't want to know . . . I got to a point where I couldn't even go to a piano—I was too afraid." Apparently, he did spend a lot of time, in private, at the piano, because one friend of Brian's remembers a night when Brian played twelve new compositions (none of which has ever been released). The dozen songs were complete, melody and lyrics, and included two very emotional songs, 'Spark in the Dark' and 'Just an Imitation.' The latter was written about Murry.

Terry Melcher has likened a visit to Brian's house in the mid-seventies to a visit to see Aesop to hear the latest fable. Bruce Johnston: "Brian went through a period where he would write songs and play them for a few people in his living room. And that's the last you would hear of them. I don't know what Brian did with these songs. I've heard things of Brian's all the way along. I can play you things that never even got recorded that I think are hits. A lot of the times, it's not always what he writes, it's the way he voices [vocally arranges] what he writes." To Bruce, Brian was just writing the songs, and not developing them: "He may make these little sketches knowing that he'd never be able to do a canvas, but I think if we offered him the canvas, they'd be done. Take it separate from the Beach Boys, separate from anything he's been doing. Don't make it Brian's solo album, you just make it Brian Wilson's project," and something would get done. "Don't even announce it, just say, 'Brian, if you want to do this, you can do it. You have three years to do it, and if you do it, you can perform it or have it played, and if you want, you can have it recorded. And there are no strings attached.'"

That opportunity was never concretely offered to Brian. Occasionally, Brian would be motivated to record. Brother Studio engineer and record producer Earle Mankey remembers the first time he worked with Brian in the mid-seventies. "At one session of Carl's, somebody said to Brian, 'Let's cut a track,' and he said, 'I have this great song, it's called 'Ding, Dang.' It was a legendary track, and it was around, as I understand it, for a long time."

In late August 1974, Brian made one of his rare media excursions to KRTH-FM radio in Los Angeles for an interview with Jim Pewter, a longtime L.A. disc jockey and keeper of the surf music flame.

Brian discussed his Beach Boys career as Pewter played many great hits and album cuts. Pewter also showed Brian a record industry trade magazine that showed the success of *Endless Summer* and 'Surfin' U.S.A.,' which was becoming a hit again, eleven years after it first went Top Ten. Brian commented: "It's going to be a little freaky for me to see that, but, nevertheless, I can accept that. It definitely makes me think I'm dreaming, because I see the title [on the charts]. Now, I've seen that title before on another chart sometime in another year somewhere before. And then I see it again, and I think, 'Huh? That again?' But with a new kind of thing happening. It seems weird. It gives me a shock, and when I go through shocks I go [makes funny noise]. I go through shocks."

231

Pewter asked Brian if he had any plans for performing live. "If I could lose some weight, I'd be onstage. I'd do it, I really would. But I'm overweight, it's my problem at the time. And that can be a problem."

Brian was also disturbed by the memories that 'Good Vibrations' and 'Heroes and Villains' evoked, and when Pewter played those songs, Brian walked out of the booth.

Significantly, an article in the *L.A. Times* that took note of the interview was headlined "Ex-Beach Boy Revisits Waves."

Brian explains his contribution to the group in the mid-seventies. "I was supporting the group in thought and communicating with some of the members. And I was thrilled that they could release repackages like *Endless Summer*, and, of course, the old songs took off with the new generation. I was very much into that. I can't say I contributed all that much . . . to the group . . . at that time."

Meanwhile, the Beach Boys' battle between the oldies and the newer material was in its last round. The release and subsequent success of *Endless Summer* created an increased demand for the hits. It was James William Guercio (the guiding light behind the group Chicago) who finally established some order in the chaotic situation. Rick Nelson remembers, "They always internally had big discussions and arguments about what songs to play. Mike always wanted to do all the oldies, as many as they could, because he knew the effect of them. Carl, along with Ricky, kept on saying that the creativity was in the new material. They'd come up with a compromise and a couple of days later, they'd change it. It wasn't until Guercio came along and started touring [he played bass] that there was a person who could say, 'Yeah, Mike's right and Carl's right,' and make the show totally work.

"Jim was more than the bass player on the tours. He'd get them to sit down and do critiques after the show, which they'd never done. They used to just all go off in their own direction. He'd have meetings after the show, 'What happened during this song? Why didn't that work? Carl gets mad when you call him Cousin Carl, so don't do that anymore, Mike,' . . . all sorts of bizarre things like that. That was about the time Ricky left. Blondie went first. They were comfortable doing the music and getting paid well, but they just felt something inside. The result of that might be drinking too much or temper flare-ups. Ricky and Carl were really close and when Ricky wasn't there anymore to back him up on playing the new stuff, Carl had no alliance."

During their 1964 European promotional tour, they took in all the high spots, including the Eiffel Tower in Paris. L-R: Carl, Brian, Al and Dennis. MICHAEL OCHS ARCHIVES/STRINGER

he Wilson boys. Carl is standing behind Dennis (on the ft) and Brian on the right. COURTESY OF BRIMEL ARCHIVES

rom the 1962 cover photo session at Malibu's Paradise Cove for the Beach Boys' first album, *Surfin' Safari*. MICHAEL OCHS ARCHIVES/GETTY IMAGES

Circa 1964, all looks ideal in The Beach Boys world. Clockwise from upper left: Mike, Brian, Carl, Dennis and Al. GAB ARCHIVE/GETTY IMAGES

(Left) Circa fall 1966. Inside Brian's infamous living room tent, Banana stands atop the six Beach Boys. GAB ARCHIVE/ GETTY IMAGES

(Right) Brian shares his fries with Louie. Banana and Louie the Wilson family dogs, are the ones heard barking at the end of *Pet Sounds*. MICHAEL OCHS ARCHIVES/GETTY IMAGES

In his Laurel Way home in Beverly Hills, Brian's at his Hammond B-3 organ. JASPER DAILEY/DAVID LEAF ARCHIVES

The 45 RPM picture sleeve for the record that became the Beach Boys first million-selling #1 single. In 1994, 'Good Vibrations' was inducted into the Grammy Hall of Fame. MICHAEL OCH ARCHIVES/GETTY IMAGES

...ian at Gold Star studios in Hollywood, November 1966, ...sting a musical spell as he works on *SMiLE*.
SPER DAILEY/DAVID LEAF ARCHIVES

Brian directs the 'Good Vibrations' promotional film. His 22-year-old cameraman, Caleb Deschanel, became a director and a world-class cinematographer, nominated 6 times for an Academy Award, once for a BAFTA. His daughter Zooey has collaborated with Brian. *She and Him*, her duo with M. Ward, toured in Summer 2022 and performed selections from their Brian Wilson tribute album, *Melt Away*. MICHAEL OCHS ARCHIVES/GETTY IMAGES

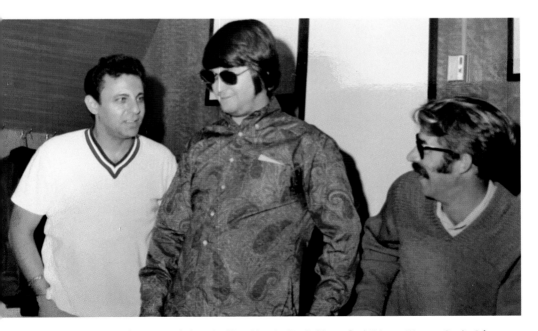

...egendary session musicians, drummer Hal Blaine (Left) and bassist Ray Pohlman, flank Brian at Western Studio 3 for a *MiLE* session in January 1967. JASPER DAILEY/DAVID LEAF ARCHIVES

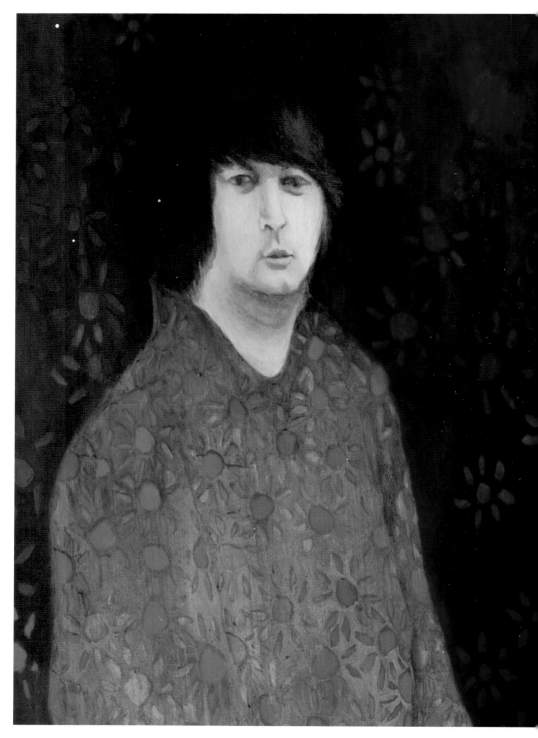

David Anderle's fabled portrait of Brian.

In the music room of Brian's home, the two greatest record producers of the 1960s. Brian and Sir George Martin got together in March 1997 for the taping of George's TV series, *The Rhythm of Life*. MELINDA WILSON

Sir Paul McCartney and Brian Wilson perform together at the second annual *Adopt-A-Minefield* benefit, September 2002.
KEVIN MAZUR/WIREIMAGE

At rehearsals for *An All-Star Tribute To Brian Wilson*, March 2001. Clockwise from upper left, Brian with Elton John, Paul Simon, show day with Wilson Phillips and Carly Simon (as Jimmy Webb observes).

Fall 2003, (L-R) Brian, Darian Sahanaja and Van Dyke Parks at work on *Brian Wilson Presents SMiLE*. MELINDA WILSON

ebruary 20, 2004. Following the triumphant world remiere in London, Brian and Melinda's daughter Daria resents her father with flowers as (L-R) sister Delanie and and members Darian Sahanaja, Probyn Gregory, Nelson ragg and Jeffrey Foskett watch. JON FURNISS/WIREIMAGE

Van Dyke Parks and Brian, the creators of *Brian Wilson Presents SMiLE*, receive a tumultuous standing ovation after the world premiere. J. QUINTON/WIREIMAGE

Brian on tour. Above, he embraces the audience;
below, he bows as the audience returns the love.

With Ricky no longer on drums, Dennis became a more integral part of the show again. As Rick Nelson noted, "I think the greatest thing that ever happened for him was to get back with playing drums. His whole attitude changed; he really felt vital to the group again."

The Beach Boys were apparently pleased with the way things were running with Guercio around, so they agreed to have him manage the band. Rick Nelson remembers that "Brian wasn't around during those days, Brian was a nonexistent Beach Boy. One of Guercio's projects was to get Brian involved again. He promised the guys, 'I can do it.'" The group did spend some time at the Caribou Ranch recording studio in late fall of 1974, but there was no significant progress made toward the recording of a new album. The group's last record, *Holland*, had been released in January of 1973 and with the success of *Endless Summer*, Warner Brothers was pushing the group for some new "product." None was forthcoming, because the Beach Boys felt that a new album would have to be exceptional to match the quality of the earlier hits, and that quality could only be achieved by Brian Wilson.

Brian wasn't particularly interested in doing a Beach Boys album, but in December 1974 he did record a new single. Unfortunately, it was a yuletide song, 'Child of Winter,' and by the time the record company could release it, Christmas was past. Aside from that one record, there wasn't much music emanating from the Wilson house, although one friend remembers that around Christmastime in '74, Brian wrote one beautiful composition that was a lot like 'Surf's Up.' That song, too, was not for public consumption.

The Beach Boys' new popularity wave was just cresting, and with Guercio leading the way, the future looked bright. Guercio, according to Rick Nelson, "was the one who put together the Chicago/Beach Boys tour, which wasn't an easy thing to do. It was his idea; he was looking at both sides." Still, the tour greatly benefited the Beach Boys, while at the same time, it made Chicago seem not quite as exciting in comparison. Nelson remembers that "there was some tension between Guercio and Chicago because it was the first time he'd done anything but them since they got together. It was not an easy time for him, but he was very interested in revitalizing the Beach Boys. A big part of that was that he believed in Brian as an important musician."

Another Capitol repackage, *Spirit of America*, bulleted up the charts in the summer of 1975, and Rick Nelson recalls that all the new success gave the Beach Boys renewed confidence, and they fired Guercio. "The Beach Boys felt that they didn't need anyone and made comments like 'Guercio just happened to come along at the right time; he just lucked out.' They would never give credit to anyone."

With or without Guercio, it was a successful time for the group. They were named *Rolling Stone*'s Band of the Year (for 1974), and although they weren't the headliners, the Beach Boys stole the show from Elton John at a Wembley Stadium concert in the summer of 1975. To be fair, the Beach Boys' portion of the show was a big hit on the strength of the oldies machine, while Elton, to his credit, was introducing an entire new album, the autobiographical *Captain Fantastic and the Brown Dirt Cowboy*.

All this time, Warners was still clamoring for a new album, and with none forthcoming, they reissued a lot of Beach Boys material from the post-*Pet Sounds* days. Warners' reissues had only limited success, and the Beach Boys were asking questions like "How come Capitol can do so well with our records and you are our present company, and the records aren't selling?" Rick Nelson explains, "They blamed the record company. It's never the group's fault. They always blame it on either the record company or the management." Warners was really paralyzed. They were the Beach Boys' current label for *new* material, and they were getting a lot of flack for not selling old records. The Beach Boys, with the past staring them in the face, looked to Brian to help them match their former glory. Brian, meanwhile, was looking elsewhere to exercise his creativity.

Bruce Johnston: "I don't think Brian had a friend he could trust in the band, and that's why he developed a little bit of a relationship with Terry Melcher." Terry, through the years, has been one of Brian's closest allies. In 1971, Terry told *Rolling Stone*: "He's as good as anyone I've heard. He writes fantastic melodies . . . but he isn't a lyricist so he's put down . . . The people who put him down, if they were really musicians, they'd forget the words and get into the structure . . . his [music] has a depth that other people can't touch. He knows more about music than anyone who's at present on the music scene. He knows a lot more. He left the music, yes, but he left it, it didn't leave him."

In 1975, when Brian wanted to get back to making records, he went to Terry. Bruce and Terry had formed a production company called Equinox, which was associated with RCA. They told RCA that they were going to allow Brian to use their company as his own and agreed to turn over all royalties to Brian for whatever he produced. At that time, Brian had no money of his own. The family had taken away his credit cards and cash because he was giving people money for drugs, but Brian also had no money for everyday things like taking a taxi or eating dinner. One longtime friend of Brian's remembers, "He had no personal freedom, let alone musical freedom." It was good that Brian didn't have the money to buy drugs, but if he was in so much trouble that the family took away his money, then just preventing his buying drugs wasn't the solution to his problems.

Brian, Bruce Johnston recalls, "told Terry, 'I need some of my own money for my own bank account.'" Brian didn't want a handout. He told them, "I need to earn my way back." Terry helped Brian open an account, but Brian left the bankbook around the house, and as Bruce remembers, "Eventually the money was transferred to an old business account, right away from him, which was kind of strange."

There was one point where one of Brian's friends was functioning as a personal manager, when Brian decided he wanted to make a complete break from the Beach Boys. This person was trying to acquire copies of all the contracts that Brian had signed because Brian "doesn't have any idea what deals he's a party to." That desire to quit the group that had galvanized Brian's friend never became positive action.

Hal Blaine, who had drummed on so many of the Beach Boys' hits, remembers the session when Brian came in to work on a record with Bruce and Terry. "We were doing a session for Terry Melcher at RCA . . . Terry said, 'Brian's coming, and I think he's gonna make it.' Brian did come in; he was a little strange. It wasn't standoffish; I think he was frightened to death. I think he was panicked. Brian walked in, his hair was rather long, and he sat down, and he started playing 'Good Vibrations' at the piano. And a kind of chill went through me, and Brian looked at me and said, 'Do you remember this song?' And I said, 'Do I!' And then he just hugged me . . . gave me a hug and said hello. And we got on with it; that was that."

Terry Melcher later recalled that Brian "wouldn't go all the way. He wouldn't even touch anything in the control booth; he acted like he was afraid to. He'd offer suggestions, but he wouldn't go near the board. He knows his reputation, so he makes a lot of unfinished records; sometimes,

I feel that he feels that he's peaked and does not want to put his stamp on records so that peers will have a Brian Wilson track to criticize."

Brian produced only one record under the name of California Music, a fictitious name that Bruce and Terry had "for him to do anything he wanted with." Bruce explains that "Brian spent a day and night talking to us about it; he was really desperate for an outlet, because basically the deal at Warners was for the Beach Boys . . . Eventually, he just sent the money back to RCA. I think that if Brian had gone to Mo Ostin and said, 'I want to produce my own things without the Beach Boys, give me a budget,' he would have gotten it. I just don't think he knew how to speak up for himself or realizes that he's an important spoke of the Beach Boys' wheel." A Warner Brothers executive remembers discussing recording projects with Brian, but notes that Brian was very "hot and cold" and he never seemed to keep up his enthusiasm for a project for a long enough time to get anything accomplished.

The very serious intense depression that Brian was caught up in by the latter half of 1975 was the absolute low. One observer claims, "He was suicidal, and this time, he was quite serious." Dennis Wilson, after Brian came out of the depression, said, "He was really sick; it was terrible. I could sit here and tell you atrocity stories of things that have happened to Brian . . . I thought it was permanent brain damage. That's how I was living for a while. That was frightening, to think that somebody you love very much will be permanently damaged. If you'd have seen him just a year ago, you would have been convinced that he was permanently ruined. It's phenomenal, the way he is. It takes a lot of guts for a guy like Brian to come back, put himself in the public that way . . . The turning point is making an attempt to seek help."

In late 1975, Marilyn Wilson finally decided to get professional assistance. The man she found, Dr. Eugene Landy, a showbiz psychologist, was the man who brought Brian back to the "normal" world of being a Beach Boy. It was Dr. Landy who made Brian Wilson presentable as a public figure so that, in 1976, the Beach Boys could claim, "Brian is back!"

CHAPTER 13

BRIAN IS BACK

THE RUMORS BEGAN IN LATE 1975 AND GREW MORE PERSISTENT AS FALL broke into the winter of 1976. The Beach Boys were at work on a new studio album. Of course, there had been talk of a new album for years; the difference this time was that Brian Wilson, for the first time since *SMiLE* died, was going to produce the album.

Brian's return was the capstone to the Beach Boys' big comeback and helped make 1976 the biggest and probably most profitable year in the group's history. Because of Brian's presence, the group was again important enough to merit extensive coverage in the mass media. There were cover stories in *New Times*, *Crawdaddy*, the *Village Voice*, *People*, and *Rolling Stone*, and many other feature articles in publications like *Newsweek*, *TV Guide* and *New West*. The Beach Boys also starred in their first-ever network television special on NBC, and a six-hour syndicated radio documentary on the group's history was widely distributed throughout the U.S.A.

This hoopla produced impressive results at the box office—the group's first Top Ten hit single in eight years, their first gold album of new studio material in eleven years, and a huge sold-out concert tour of major stadia around the country. All of this served to reconfirm that the Beach Boys were an important part of American music, just in case anybody had forgotten.

This return to prominence was centered on one slightly inaccurate but highly successful phrase, "Brian is back!" The Bicentennial year was often criticized for over-commerciality. The Beach Boys, the ultimate American band, did their part to keep in step with the country. They were very involved in an offensive effort that might be called "The Selling of Brian Wilson."

★　　★　　★　　★

237

The architect of Brian Wilson's re-emergence into public view was Dr. Eugene Landy, a "Hollywood" psychologist who was known for getting quick results with outrageous methods for exorbitant fees. If anything was going to make Brian Wilson become a Beach Boy again, it would take the total domination of a man like Landy.

It is important at this point to make a distinction between what is good for Brian Wilson and what is good for the Beach Boys. The group needed Brian to rejuvenate their recording career. They also knew that his presence would get the band a lot of publicity, and publicity sells records. Brian, on the other hand, was an unhappy man who needed love and attention. As one friend of his insisted, "Brian didn't need the attention of an adoring public who loved him for his music. He knows that he's a great musician. And he didn't need to have hits, even though some members of his family loved him better when he was having hits. The family felt that what Brian needed was to have a couple of hits, perform in concert and then he'd be all right. What they were ignoring was the fact that a slew of hit records and claims of 'genius' hadn't prevented Brian from having a series of nervous breakdowns in the 1960s. To Brian, the shallowness of success was something he was well aware of, and something he didn't want to be engulfed by again. He already knew that hits wouldn't make him happy."

Dr. Landy first came into the Wilson family's life when he was called by Marilyn. In David Felton's 1976 *Rolling Stone* story, Marilyn discussed Brian's problems. "It was difficult to find somebody who could help him 'cause I didn't know what needed to be helped. Sometimes I really thought to myself, is it me? Am I the one who's not seein' things right? And it was also difficult for the family to see it the same, and the close friends, because everyone loved Brian and just said, 'Oh, he'll get over it.'"

When someone in your family is unhappy or sick, it is not easy to accept that fact, because admitting that the problem exists can mean accepting part of the blame for causing the troubled situation. It is hard to watch somebody you love wasting away, and in the Beach Boys' case, this was compounded by their knowledge of how talented Brian is. Still, a pretend game of "Everything's all right; it'll be better in the morning" can be played for only so long.

As Marilyn noted, "The thing that made me go to Dr. Landy was I couldn't stand to see Brian, whom I just love and adore, unhappy with himself and not really creating . . . When I met Dr. Landy, I knew I'd met someone who could play Brian's game." By "Brian's game," Marilyn was partially referring to Brian's skill at manipulating people toward his own desires. Brian is incredibly perceptive and aware of everything, even when his expression is frighteningly blank.

Right away, Landy's game-playing with Brian was considered a mistake by one of Brian's close friends. "Dealing with Brian on a human level isn't playing his game. It's getting past it. There's no value in playing games with Brian. He wants people to get past the games. Those games are only played for survival. To really relate to Brian, to be his friend and give him support, you have to get one step beyond the game-playing."

Marilyn Wilson had one other observation that finished off an earlier quote. "But I'm the one who had to live with it." Marilyn is Brian's wife and the mother of his children, although she wasn't totally involved in Brian's personal care. One friend of Brian's observed that "Marilyn wasn't there all the time to take care of him. She'd go off to Hawaii or out of town to see a Beach Boys concert, and Brian would be home alone. By the way, Marilyn isn't exactly a pure martyr. She digs being Mrs. Brian Wilson and the money and status that goes with that."

Yet, as Ben Edmonds points out, "In a lot of respects, Marilyn probably put up with an awful lot. Just in the sense that she was left pretty much to raise the kids by herself. And having to take care of Brian almost as if he was another one of the kids. And indulge Brian and make sure that Brian was OK. And then, having to raise the girls herself. That's not an easy job for anyone. I would think that she held all of that together is incredibly to her credit." Yes it is, except that all that was really done was to hold it together. Like the Beach Boys' false image of harmony, the family sometimes seemed to be more concerned with their image in the outside world than whether Brian was happy.

Dr. Landy was given complete charge of Brian's life, and a team of people was put together to direct his daily activities and to help in the "rehabilitation" process. There were a therapist and a live-in bodyguard (the ever-present Scott Steinberg) as well as Landy. Stan Love (Mike's brother and a former professional basketball player) was Brian's constant companion, chauffeur, physical fitness director, and, as it turned out, a sympathetic friend who truly was concerned with Brian's well-being. A rigid schedule was imposed on Brian's life, a nine-to-five existence that was totally the opposite of everything he'd been living since the Beach Boys came into being.

According to a number of accounts, Landy first diagnosed Brian as a paranoid schizophrenic from Marilyn's description of Brian's behavior. Aside from the merits of any diagnosis that isn't the result of careful interaction with a patient, Dr. Landy's professional ethics also appear to be questionable. His public discussion of Brian's personal problems could not have helped Landy and Brian build a relationship founded in trust and confidentiality. The public airing of Brian's difficulties must have embarrassed Brian while it created sensational stories for the hungry media machine.

Still, Landy's approach got through to Brian. As Landy explained, the whole point of all the activities was "to prove that he's not really crazy, that he's not sick, but that he's just not acting in an acceptable way. We've just been enculturated to define people who act differently as being sick. If Brian wants to act normally, he can." Landy insisted, "There is only room enough for one crazy person in Brian's head and that's got to be me. I have to be the ultimate power in this situation . . . Brian said, 'Make me.' I said he had to get out of bed and start living a normal life and he said, 'Make me.' How do you make a guy get out of bed after so long? Explain it to him first? No. You throw water on him first. That's just what I did. I warned him, and then threw water on him and he got up.

"I can't let Brian blackmail me. He's manipulated everybody for a long time, and I have to confront him at every turn." Landy's methods were indeed unusual, but they got results quickly.

What didn't make sense was the rush to make Brian a Beach Boy. From what Landy saw, Brian was scared of facing life. "He was not able to deal with being frightened or even have a response to being frightened," Landy explained. As much as is possible, Brian had withdrawn from emotion, had withdrawn from any activities that might cause him pain. Those painful experiences, to Brian, often came out of being involved with the Beach Boys.

Landy, however, forced Brian to confront those hurtful situations. Then road manager Rick Nelson points out, "In Landy's evaluation of the situation, what was necessary to treat Brian was to make him an active Beach Boy, to make him write and perform music, seeing the fans' response, relating to the people. Just doing it, whether it scared the shit out of him or not, that's what [Landy] made Brian do." Landy claimed that he "was working for Brian Wilson to have something that he has not had, and that's an alternative . . . that if he chooses to withdraw and be scared, that's as good as choosing not to, but to have a choice."

The choice that Landy offered, however, seemed often to be directly at odds with Brian's basic personal and artistic problems. "Brian doesn't want to be a Beach Boy because he *has* to be," one friend pointed out. "Brian only wants to share his music with the world on his own terms. It's not that he doesn't want to work with the Beach Boys; that's not the point. Brian loves working with his brothers when *he* wants to. Not when they make him. Brian wants and needs a base of operations of his own. He wants to be Brian Wilson, person and solo artist, and not have any musical obligations to other people. Then, if he chooses to, he will work with Dennis and/or Carl or the Beach Boys. For Brian to want to create music, it has to be his desire, and not because he feels he owes it to his family."

Although Landy claimed to be working for Brian, he often seemed to have the Beach Boys' interests in mind. Nobody would argue that Landy's physical fitness efforts didn't result in a more physically attractive and healthier Brian Wilson. That was an important step, because Brian's self-image as an eyesore needed to be eradicated. The only way to do that was to whip him into good condition. But if Landy was interested in Brian's self-image, why did he put him on public display before Brian's physical state had improved? When the ceaseless publicity parade began, Brian had lost only a few pounds, and he didn't look great.

From an objective point of view, the emotional help that Landy offered seemed very strange. Landy consistently had Brian encounter all the things that make him uncomfortable—the recording studio with the Beach Boys, concert tours, interviews, television—but Landy apparently didn't first equip Brian to deal with the emotional responses to those scary situations. Brian coped. He chain-smoked cigarettes (when he could get his hands on them), and he talked and sang out of the side of his mouth like comedian Buddy Hackett on speed. In effect, Brian went into those hostile environments, went through the motions, and did his best not to allow them to affect him emotionally.

Landy's methods were a much-discussed public item, but he certainly got quick results for the Beach Boys. Rick Nelson says, "Gene Landy is definitely an individual; he has his own way of doing things. The only thing that can be said about them is that they work. He happens to be very successful and gets very bizarre cases. From a fan's point of view, looking at how Brian was suffering was very disturbing, but," Nelson explains, "for so many years, Brian was sheltered from everything, and whatever Brian wanted, Brian got, and that just pushed him further away. They didn't tell him any of the problems. He didn't have to deal with any reality."

Rick Nelson observes that a lot of the pain Brian experienced in 1976 was justified because, until then, Brian had been living in a place that "was closer to a non-world than anything. And being sad is a reality. Landy was trying to do it in a very short span of time . . . one of [Brian's] biggest things to overcome was to get him to be a Beach Boy again." Of course it was; Brian didn't want to be a Beach Boy again or deal with their reality. As Brian noted, the submergence into the Beach Boys' world was "a shock" to his system. "I'm going through shock right now."

"Brian Is Back!" the magazine headlines screamed. Timothy White's two-part story in *Crawdaddy* in particular held out the promise that the musical return of Brian Wilson was not only imminent but would be quite momentous. That anticipation was based on White's reaction to a brand-new Brian Wilson song, 'California Feeling.' Actually, the song was one of the tunes Brian had written during his "reclusive" period. Whatever its merits, it still hadn't been made publicly available as 1978 began, although it was finally recorded. Brian may have returned to the studio, but he didn't have total control over what music would be released.

Aside from the musical rejuvenation that article virtually guaranteed, the Brian Wilson that White wrote of was a man who was, to say the least, uncomfortable to be "back." All the interviews and the work in songwriting and recording were ostensibly designed to get Brian well, but the immediate goal seemed to be to get Brian into the studio to produce a new Beach Boys record. It was an extension of Brian's role as family benefactor. From the family's point of view, putting Brian into the studio situation was the right cure.

Landy claimed his work was to give Brian an alternative to his basic do-nothing existence, yet it was becoming increasingly obvious that Landy's presence wasn't totally motivated by the family's desire to see Brian well. Nineteen seventy-six was a big public relations game with Brian as the chief pawn. With Landy pushing Brian from behind with a pitchfork, Brian went out into the world. Landy apparently understood Brian's problems, but his solution was bizarre for a man "suffering from scared." It was like throwing a quadriplegic former Olympic swimmer in the pool; he once knew how to swim, but the muscles didn't work anymore. Or as Bruce Johnston put it, "It's like someone who's not over the flu yet and [people put] him out where there's no heat, out by the ocean."

The making of Brian's comeback album, *15 Big Ones*, was full of conflicts that sometimes even managed to seep through to the public in articles in *Crawdaddy* and *Newsweek*. The original idea of the album was to do a record totally filled with "oldies but goodies," so that Brian could ease back into the recording process without having the pressure of coming up with new material. To make things like the "old days," the Beach Boys arranged recording sessions with all the studio musicians that Brian had loved and trusted so much back in the hitmaking days. As Steve Douglas (one of the original session players) noted, "I figured if I got Brian back in the original studio over at Western Three with all the original guys playing and Chuck Britz engineering, I'd get him off his ass; that and Landy, I guess that combination worked. We did 'Blueberry Hill.' He was really nervous and emoting. I thought *15 Big Ones* was more therapy than anything else." If it was supposed to be therapeutic, it was a strange kind of help. Douglas continued, "As soon as we got a couple of days there [at Western], the whole pressure started, all the bullshit. The pressure was just enormous on him. So he didn't really seem to want to take the time to do it."

Brian recalled that he "felt a lot of pressure from the Beach Boys because I told them that I'd produce an album and started to change my mind." It was just like the old days, all right; the old days when the pressure to create drove him into himself. The talk centered around the absence of Beach Boys hits, and how Brian could again make hits for the group.

Underneath the public relations veneer that "Brian Is Back," and the Beach Boys are happy to have him, there was a tremendous battle raging within the group. In Brian's absence, the Beach Boys had become a functioning democracy based on one man, one vote, as opposed to the monarchical control Brian had once had over the group. As Brian described it, "We voted on oldies but goodies on *15 Big Ones*." In *Newsweek* magazine it was reported that "Jardine and Love were all for letting Brian take full charge, even though Love makes no secret of resenting him. Love, who jumped rope to get in shape for the tour, recently declared, 'I'm not going out on the road like some broken-down rock star.'" It seemed that the simmering feud between Mike and Brian was already at full-tilt strength, only a few months after Brian started working with the group again. The *Newsweek* story was one of the first public indications that not everyone in the group was totally pleased with Brian's return, despite their public relations protestations to the contrary.

Carl explained that "Dennis and I had a picture of doing an album of oldies, just as a warm-up, and then doing another album. But as it happens, we started to do the new stuff and then Brian said, 'Well, I've recorded enough. I don't want to record any longer and the album's finished.'" Dennis opines, "The album should have been one hundred percent original. We had enough Brian Wilson material to do it . . . Steve Love [by 1976, the group's business manager], Mike Love and Alan Jardine were pushing to get it out—it was a big push. They'd rather just get it out there than take time with it and develop it. Carl and I were really upset."

Somehow, the three brothers seemed to have been victimized by their own band. None of them were happy with what was going on. Rick Nelson remembers that "Dick Duryea [a Beach Boys road manager in the sixties and by the mid-1970s an executive at Caribou Records] had an expression, SNAFU. **S**ituation **N**ormal, **A**ll **F**ucked **U**p." What is amazing is that the group hadn't learned anything during Brian's long absence. The battles over material were constant, and there still seemed to be no indication that there was any increased sensitivity to Brian's needs as a human being. If *15 Big Ones* was supposed to bring Brian back, it succeeded remarkably well in bringing him back to all the group's old hassles. In the *Newsweek* article, Dennis claimed, "It was a great mistake to put Brian in full control. He was always the absolute producer, but little did he know that in his absence, people grew up, became as sensitive as the next guy. Why should I relinquish my rights as an artist? The whole process was a little bruising." For everyone involved.

Earle Mankey (chief engineer at Brother Studio) remembers, "It was really tense in the studio. Brian would come in around nine or ten in the morning. One day, they would get something done, and the next day they would do nothing except fight." Mankey's role in Brian's comeback is often ignored, but Earle has displayed exceptional sensitivity in his working relationship with Brian, and the two men have developed a strong trust. Mankey observed Brian's tentative return to the studio and thinks that Landy's strict scheduling of Brian's activities was "necessary at that time. Otherwise, Brian would have gone home. Brian had writing sessions a couple of times a week, and he'd write two or three songs in a morning. Landy would say, 'OK, you have to have three songs written today because on Thursday and Friday, we have two recording sessions, and you won't have anything to record.'" As Rick Nelson noted, "He was just grinding it out because that's what he was instructed to do, write songs . . . ten songs in a day, if that's what they told him to do, but they weren't worth much." Some of the songs were quite good, however, but the songwriting game was pretty silly. Brian had written a lot of songs in the mid-seventies, and he frequently dipped into his melody stockpile when he was confronted with the need to produce songs quickly for the group. Prominent examples of this game are 'Ding Dang,' 'It's OK' and 'Back Home,' all written before Landy's arrival. Nobody was especially fooled by this, except for the public, who were told that Brian's creative return was current. Some of the "Aesop's Fables" that Brian had played for a select audience (including Van Dyke Parks, Bruce Johnston and Terry Melcher) were now becoming Beach Boys songs. Besides all that, Brian was beginning to write a lot of new songs.

Still, as *Newsweek* magazine reported, all the Beach Boys "shared misgivings about Brian's competence"—enough, according to Jardine, to "sneak into the studio at night and add extra background vocals to the songs which Brian had wanted done 'dry' (without echo)." Their respect for Brian as an artist seemed to have hit a new low in private, while they continued to tell the media that "Brian is back and he's really gonna blow minds when he starts to stretch out."

The recording of *15 Big Ones* was a difficult effort. Brian's interest was fleeting, and it made the record an unfinished, somewhat underproduced affair. Chuck Britz remembers how nervous Brian was: "We did 'Palisades Park' in one take, and then I could see he was completely nervous so I said, 'OK.' I realized that to get another take out of him would have been disastrous. I just said, 'Well, either good, bad, or indifferent, you're only going to get one take out of him so we might as well take it.'" Besides the lack of production time, Brian hadn't fully returned to serious songwriting. As Earle Mankey recounts, "Brian would throw out really catchy melodies in no time. It's a shame that sometimes he only spends five or ten minutes on a song." Steve Douglas examined those first public Brian Wilson songs in years and noticed that "there's some little hook or charm that really should be developed," but hasn't been yet.

Brian's singing also became a matter of concern. In those early 1976 vocals, Brian sounded hoarse, and his vocals had a quality that reminded one friend of Randy Newman. Another friend noted, "Brian's been smoking like a chimney to get that husky sound. Also, he rushes everything. He doesn't want to be singing with all of them." Bruce Johnston theorizes that Brian's singing was in a lower register because "singing up high must represent some kind of anti-masculine macho thing to him, and that's why he stopped."

All of those reasons are part of it, but Brian himself explained the motivation behind the change this way. He noted that when he heard those early happy songs, "I'd cringe at some of the falsettos. 'I sang that?' It made me cringe because I realized where I was at, at that time, and I was in a very emotional place, very hung up, highly scared, fearful, and very withdrawn."

The strangest aspect of Brian's new public singing style is that, in private, Brian's falsetto is intact. It's a little thinner than it used to be, but otherwise as beautiful and expressive as ever. Brian's current public voice sometimes sounds like a cross between Louis Armstrong and Dean Martin, a gravelly, macho sound. In the studio, Brian can still sound like anyone he wants to sound like, including Brian Wilson. The most prominent examples of recent falsetto singing remain in the tape vaults; 'You've Lost That Lovin' Feelin'' and 'Sherry She Needs Me' have very good vocals.

15 Big Ones was released in June 1976, and it was treated with critical kid gloves by both the reviewers and the fans. It contained a Top Ten hit single, 'Rock 'n' Roll Music,' the Beach Boys' first big hit since 'Do It Again' in 1968. There was also another Top Forty hit, 'It's OK,' which could have passed for 'Do It Again, Part Two.' The rest of the album is filled with a bizarre selection of oldies, odd new songs, and a *Sunflower* reject, 'Susie Cincinnati.' For some reason, the Beach Boys left much better material in the can. As Rick Nelson explains, "It was a case of fighting it out and coming up with some compromise. Mike wanted this and Carl wanted that. It's always like that."

Among the unreleased oldies that are better than what has been released are 'Ruby Baby' (featuring a great vocal from Brian), 'Come Go with Me' (an intriguing arrangement and powerful Al Jardine vocal), and 'Sea Cruise,' which is a lot of fun. Also, there is an original mix of 'Rock 'n' Roll Music' with clashing guitar licks and an extra verse that was remixed because Brian felt it wouldn't sound right on AM radios.

Even in its unfinished state, the record has a feel that had been missing from the Beach Boys' albums for years. This definitely is a Brian Wilson production. It's not something that can be articulated. It was just obvious that Brian was back at work. The problem was that because it was his first record in years, people were expecting a masterpiece. It wasn't, and the fans who had been patiently awaiting the return of Brian Wilson felt betrayed and disappointed following all the media hype and build-up. We were all expecting miracles too soon. "How can you turn it on after seven or eight years," Steve Douglas wondered, "and expect all this wonderful stuff to come out? I think he's trying not to let anybody down. Everyone's demanding stuff out of him, and he's trying to satisfy everyone."

Bruce Johnston is quite outspoken about the hype of '76. "I thought the whole 'Brian Is Back' campaign was disgusting, manipulative and disgusting. It's the wrong kind of career move, it's bad business. Everyone loves Brian so much. They were all waiting for this incredible game that was going to be played. And it was a real disappointment, that album, I think." In an insider's evaluation as to why *15 Big Ones* (and its follow-up, *The Beach Boys Love You*) aren't up to previous Beach Boys standards, Bruce Johnston offers this explanation and excuse: "I think Brian decided about seven years ago that the Beach Boys were over. I think he decided, and then made the statement that he didn't want to carry on with it. But he was kind of forced over the years to keep it going, and I don't think he's done a very good job, because he's not really interested." As far as the Beach Boys are concerned, Bruce feels Brian is "a little bit emotionally and physically burned out. I don't think he wants to do it, but he's not a strong person that way . . . I think he's doing something he doesn't want to."

Willingly or not, Brian is carrying on; some people claim that Brian is producing mediocre records in a perverse plan to destroy the Beach Boys so he can gain his freedom. Ben Edmonds, however, thinks that "if it was all just a game that he was playing, it would have stopped with *15 Big Ones*. I mean, that album was obviously the product of a damaged artist on some level. If he was in control, then that would have been a brilliant album as opposed to the half-baked piece of shit that it was." As for the sabotage theory, David Anderle doesn't agree. "Brian is just confused. I don't think Brian would purposely go out to ruin the Beach Boys, ever. Although he could. I don't think he would purposely go out to hurt any of his brothers, ever. Although he could. But not from a maniacal point of view or not even from a sitting-down-and-planning-it-out point of view. I don't think he would ever do any of that. Just like I don't think Brian would ever purposely create music that was less than what he could do. I think that Brian may be forced into doing things he's not ready to do. And the result may be what we hear. I think that maybe Brian at times has a real desire to want to get in there and do it."

Anderle watched the "Brian Is Back" campaign with a personal interest and his assessment was violent. "Disaster! Fucking disaster! Stupid. I couldn't believe what happened with the Brian Wilson renaissance. In the beginning I was real thrilled 'cause I thought this is all a reflection of his reappearance onto the scene. For a long time, I think we all felt that was actually what was happening; we were led to believe that was what was going on. Brian Wilson belongs in the music business, and I think that—not the business but music—can only benefit from Brian Wilson. But from Brian Wilson, not from the bastardized version of Brian Wilson, not from the skeleton version of Brian Wilson, not from the controlled version of Brian Wilson."

Next on Brian's schedule was the filming of a TV special produced by Lorne Michaels, the producer of *Saturday Night Live*. Michaels felt that the Beach Boys were the perfect metaphor for California. The program, broadcast in August, looked like a lot of fun, except Brian was obviously suffering, particularly when he was made to surf or sing 'I'm Bugged at My Old Man.' It was marvelous and perverse entertainment to watch Brian in bed talking about his problems or—in a sketch with comic actors Dan Aykroyd and John Belushi, dressed as California Highway Patrol, "Surf Squad"—getting arrested for "failing to surf" and then being forced into the ocean to surf. Still, it seemed to be another instance of Brian's being put on public display, putting him through his paces.

Brian's next bout with the world came on the concert stage, a step that was really frightening to him. On July 2, at the Oakland Coliseum, Brian joined the group onstage after the first few songs; and on July 3 at

Anaheim, Brian came out with the rest of the group. To even the most casual of observers, it was immediately evident how uncomfortable Brian was. He sat stock-still, as if he were frozen. He rarely sang or played the piano. When he did sing, his beautiful voice was lost in a nervous croak.

Midway through the concert, some fans in the crowd held up a banner which read, "Welcome Back, Brian." Mike Love exhorted Brian to stand up and take a bow, and wave to the fans. Brian dutifully half rose and waved his right hand like a giant bear's paw. The whole thing had the aura of a circus trainer forcing one of his star animals to do his trick.

The return to live performing did have an important goal behind it: the concerts were to show Brian how much he was loved, for him to bask in the glow of fan adulation. Rick Nelson remembers that Brian's nervousness only lasted for a few shows "where it was shaky, but that didn't last long. He started going over and playing bass and waving and talking to the kids. He really grew fast from that." Those benefits seemed transitory, and Brian's dislike for performing and the pain involved in playing before a big crowd appeared to overshadow the gains.

The first shows were embarrassing for all; the group's sound suffering because, as Rick Nelson notes, "Brian would be at the piano, and he wouldn't even be playing the same songs. He was just so scared up there; I think he was unconscious of how bad it sounded. He was very nervous and very paranoid at concerts, but he was onstage. The group's love for him overcame the lessening of the quality of the show. I know Dennis was really inspired by that. I'm sure they were disappointed he didn't do very well, but happy to have him there. It generated a lot of excitement. Kids who were screaming for Brian didn't know about him. That was incredible too, to see a fourteen-year-old kid with a sign that says 'Welcome Back, Brian.' They weren't around when he was around." Besides all those benefits to Brian, Rick adds, "He was an angle to use for publicity that was fabulous."

Throughout the year, Brian dove headfirst into the world of media, and he was interviewed by dozens of relatively sensitive people. Brian's revelations were alarmingly honest, to his credit, but many of the journalists didn't exercise editorial responsibility, particularly when it came to discussion of Brian's sex life. Brian was generously sharing his innermost thoughts with the public, yet the guardians of the free press didn't always accord Brian the respect he deserved as a human being, occasionally treating him as just this month's dissection.

There were three important TV appearances, besides the group's own special. First, there were the Rock Awards. Brian had been nominated for the "Hall of Fame," and when he came out with Dennis to present an award, he was greeted with a standing ovation. Brian: "The standing ovation was one of the highlights of my life. Without a doubt. I've never, I almost cried. I didn't expect it."

Next, Brian taped the Mike Douglas program, and in their interview, Brian bared his soul and troubles to the public in a touching and disturbing display of honesty. Brian described the handicap of his partial deafness, his difficulties in coming back and his long involvement with drugs: "I used to think that that was the positive way to go. I mean, drugs can be positive, but unfortunately there's usually a negative effect associated with drugs. A lot of hippies in the sixties said, 'The great messiah was supposed to come in the sixties and it came in the form of drugs.' Which I agree, there's a certain amount to be said for that. But in my personal story I have to tell, it really didn't work out so well, so positively, because I began to depend on the drugs. The cocaine was a beautiful high, I mean I could write songs, get in an elated state, but the comedown was *so* God-awful. You've got at least two hours of a high, but then you've got an hour and a half of nothing but garbage. It's called heaven and hell. I mean, drugs are a definite balance of heaven and hell, you go to heaven and then you go right to hell."

Mike Douglas wanted to know what brought Brian back. "My brothers encouraged me to get out of the sack. 'Come on, Brian, start writing, get off your butt' . . . A little voice said, 'Hey, you're getting a little bit thin in the pocketbook' [Brian has earned millions], and I tend to react very personally to something like that. I'm a believer in monetary security, I believe that money can buy happiness, opposed to what a lot of people think. If you can get something with money that makes you happy, well then, by God, money made you happy. Let's face it, when you can get money, you're a lucky person, like I was. Drugs were expensive, but I could afford it. I can't afford it as much as I could. Thank God, I don't need them as much as I did." As Brian admitted, "I did my dose of LSD. It shattered my mind, and I came back, thank God, in I don't know how many pieces."

One of the most humorous moments in any of Brian's interviews took place when Brian gave a half-serious propaganda speech for Transcendental Meditation. In discussing his TM mantra, Brian noted that "you're not supposed to say a mantra, especially on national TV. Maharishi says keep it to yourself." Brian continued obliviously, "But mine is . . . " and he revealed his mantra. Pow! Was it a little blow to Mike Love, who had been using the Beach Boys to sell TM for almost a decade?

The experience was a positive one for Brian. He performed two songs, 'Sloop John B' and 'Back Home,' and his voice was considerably better than it had been on *15 Big Ones*. Brian later recalled that it was "the first time I've ever done a talk show. I wasn't nervous. I thought I would be nervous. So I sort of knocked down some fear there. [Like in the movie] *Fear Strikes Out* . . . It's good to know that there's an audience out there that can experience a Brian Wilson alone without the Beach Boys. It's good to know that you can . . . do these things, kind of individually . . . that you have the freedom . . . I'm glad that they said I can step out of the Beach Boys . . . I'm very proud of it."

In explaining his long absence from the music business, Brian noted that he saw himself "like some Maharishi in the hills, hibernating in his bed, snorting cocaine, meditating, all these weird things." It is a fascinating self-portrait, and like many of Brian's public revelations, it indicated a self-awareness that he is rarely credited with. Brian, in whatever troubled state he's in, has never forgotten who he is and what he's done. Always enamored of his various masks, Brian once said that he was proud to have created so many legends.

The steps away from the Beach Boys were very small, dictated by Landy's control, which caused a great deal of resentment from Brian. "I go through periods where I think, 'God, I'm thankful that I have a doctor,' you know? Then I go through periods where I think, 'Goddam, he's doing nothing but restricting my mind!' It's paradoxical, I know, and I feel an inner battle." As David Anderle theorized, "I think Brian just needs his mind."

Brian's behavior, unfortunately, was still filled with contradictions. All of his "eccentricity," whether it was put-on and/or real insanity, had come back to haunt him. Brian had created a vision of a "mad creative genius" and he was now being victimized by that image. Brian told David Rensin of *Out* magazine, "Today, I want to go places . . . Danny Hutton's house, but I can't because of the doctor. I feel like a prisoner, and I don't know when it's going to end." Brian submitted to Landy's treatment because "he'd put the police on me if I took off . . . and he'd put me on the funny farm." Brian, who reportedly had briefly been hospitalized earlier in the decade, feared institutionalization more than almost anything. "He's always got that threat of putting me on the funny farm." If Brian needed institutionalization, then why wasn't he getting that treatment? And if he didn't, what kind of professional treatment allowed a patient to be told how to behave, "or else"?

Brian admitted that he was handling all those threats by "waiting it out, playing along. That's what I'm doing . . . I have a pretty good poker face . . . Do you have any uppers?" Brian's continuous "public" asking for drugs was another game. As one friend notes, "If he had really wanted to get drugs, he would have known where to get them." Landy's treatment of Brian wasn't penetrating Brian's game-playing. In one interview, Brian described Landy's ideas for self-nourishment and concluded his explanation with the comment, "I thought the guy was crazy."

Landy's next move seemed to be one step too far for everyone as Brian guested on *Saturday Night Live* in late November. For the first time since the Leonard Bernstein special, Brian performed solo on national television (the Mike Douglas program was videotaped and wasn't shown until December). On Brian's 1967 appearance, he had introduced 'Surf's Up' to the world. Nine years later, he played 'Love Is a Woman,' and it wasn't one of Brian's better performances. The really discomforting part of the program was when Brian performed 'Good Vibrations.' Not that the vocal was bad. It was fascinating to see Brian alone at the piano singing one of his most famous songs, the way it must have been when he had finished writing a song and hadn't yet shared it with the world. What was cruel was that Brian sang the song seated at a piano in a giant sandbox. Trading on his legendary eccentricity, this making fun of Brian would have been amusing in 1966. Not only that, Dr. Landy was reportedly standing behind the camera and holding up cue cards for Brian with such directions as "Smile."

This appearance on *Saturday Night Live* brought outrage from Brian Wilson lovers everywhere. *Crawdaddy* magazine's Peter Knobler editorialized: "There was a moment on the telecast as he sang 'Love Is a Woman' when Brian hit a phrase and began to go with it. There, for maybe three seconds, you caught a glimpse of what Brian at one time could command at will. His voice moved the melody and the melody moved me." Despite that moment of lucidity, Knobler wondered, "Where's the humanity of the people in charge of Brian's health? Brian doesn't need more solitude. But he certainly can do without public trials and humiliations—whether he is aware of them or not, we are, and the more one cares about both the music and well-being of this troubled giant, the more one has to wonder why he is being exhibited when he could be being helped." As David Anderle feels, "It was not something you do if you love him."

In the fall of 1976, Brian had actively returned to the studio, and he produced two complete albums of material, one to be titled *New Album* and the other called *Brian Loves You*. Earle Mankey engineered Brian's recording sessions, and he recalls that "Brian played nearly everything on the tracks himself, at least eighty percent of the instruments. On nearly every song, Brian was in the studio by himself, doing the basic tracks. A lot of the things he finished and sang all the parts himself. He was running smoothly. He just came in and did it . . . When the guys came back from tour, they'd come in and sing vocal parts."

One of the best sessions was the recording of 'You've Lost That Lovin' Feelin'.' Earle Mankey remembers, "It was like the song was ingrained in his mind. He really had it down. He went through and played every part, without looking at the music or anything. And then he went out and sang the vocal all the way right through, singing both of the Righteous Brothers' parts." Earle describes Brian seated at the piano, singing the high and low parts. When he had a high part, he would lean to one side of the microphone; a low part, the other side; and when he got to the vocal conversation at the end of the song, his head was going back and forth pretty fast. It is a very good production and performance.

Brian was really beginning to come back. All the media noise was behind him, and he got down to the music. As Earle Mankey noted, "Now, when he records, it's his idea. Brian came [into the studio] and did it instead of being forced into it."

Brian had also resumed regular touring with the group by late November of '76. Rick Nelson remembers that "Brian made an agreement that he's a Beach Boy, and when they tour, he tours. There were times when the input was so spectacular from the audience," Nelson recalls, "that he was touched by it, and he said, 'That's the purpose of the music. That's really why I'm here.'"

Brian was also playing bass onstage for a couple of songs (including a wailing and impressively fun version of 'Back Home'), and Earle Mankey recounts how Brian rehearsed for the tour. "In the studio, he was practicing for playing live. He got out his bass, and he was playing in the studio, and he didn't have anything to play, so we put on the Ronettes' album, and he played every song on the album. That was his practice for playing on the road with the Beach Boys." Still, it wasn't totally voluntary on Brian's part. The concerts still scared him, and he was being forced into performing.

On December 31, 1976, the Beach Boys played their fifteenth-anniversary concert at the Los Angeles Forum, and the capacity crowd reveled in the oldies. That show also included one of the early public indications that Brian was again sharing his personal music with the world. Even if the singing was off, the performance of a song called 'Airplane' was exciting. It was a genuine thrill to hear a good, new song.

In late December, Dr. Eugene Landy was fired as Brian's psychologist/Svengali for reasons that remain unclear. Audree Wilson notes that "Dr. Landy did a lot of wonderful things for Brian. He, as many others have done, became very greedy. I think exceedingly greedy." Rick Nelson recalls, "They fired Landy because they thought he was going too far; they thought he wanted to manage the group. He was actually trying to get involved in selecting tunes for the album." The most curious element in the firing is the use of "they." If Landy was there to help Brian and had been hired by Marilyn, why did the group have the right to fire him?

As 1977 began, the Beach Boys were again splintering. Mike traveled to Switzerland for six months of meditation and levitation training with the Maharishi; Al returned to his Big Sur estate to enjoy the quiet life of a gentleman farmer. Dennis finished up his solo album, and Carl finally completed co-producing (with Billy Hinsche) a record by Ricci Martin (Dean's son), a project that had been begun in 1974.

That left Brian in the studio, mostly by himself, which was the way it had been in the "old days." Except that the early records had been made with a studio filled with musicians. Now, Brian seemed to be carrying the entire musical load. An electronic drum kit and a Moog bass don't make up for the absence of Steve Douglas, Hal Blaine, Ray Pohlman and company. Dennis and Carl did help on those sessions, but Mike and Al were rarely around. The result was a group of songs featuring the Wilson brothers that became most of an album called *Adult Child*. It included two beautiful ballads, 'It's Over Now' and 'Still I Dream of It.' Those songs and a few others featured the string and horn arrangements of Dick Reynolds, who was the Four Freshmen's arranger and had arranged *The Beach Boys Christmas Album*.

In January of 1977, *The Beach Boys Love You* (the name was changed to make it seem more like a group effort) was submitted to Warner Brothers. Rick Nelson says, "Most of the people at the company liked it, but Mo Ostin thought that it should be touched up. He didn't think it was finished. It wasn't that he didn't like it musically. Somehow, word that Mo felt that way got back to Brian and hurt him deeply." It was the everyday insensitivity of the record business that had driven Brian away once; this time, he weathered the static.

Surrounding the latest Warner Brothers/Beach Boys battle were widespread rumors that the group would follow Dennis and sign with Jimmy Guercio's Caribou Records. There was even talk that Caribou/CBS Records might release *Love You*. Although Warners didn't particularly want "the product," they decided to release it on April 1. That very day, it was leaked to the *Hollywood Reporter* (by Warner Brothers?) that the Beach Boys had signed with Caribou Records. The timing was incredibly bad, and with the group now officially leaving the label, Warner Brothers put out very little promotional effort, and the record died a quick death.

The commercial disaster that was *Love You* can't really be blamed on lack of promotion, though. It was an uncommercial record, and as Mo Ostin had noted, unfinished. This time, however, it couldn't be put down to Brian's lack of patience. By now, there were lots of finished songs in the can. Excluding the oldies, there were very nice productions like 'Lazy Lizzie,' 'Marilyn Rovell' and 'Diane.' The songs were considerably more sophisticated and fulfilling efforts compared to what was released. 'Lazy Lizzie,' in fact, includes the 'Pied Piper' theme from Brian's *Holland* fairy tale, but 'Lizzie' is a fully realized production as well as a strong example of Brian's songwriting ability. *Love You*, in its incomplete form, is still a personal album from Brian, almost a solo record. Even the teenage themes that Brian examined were those that he still related to, although there was some indication that he was being "asked" to write songs that would appeal to teens. On side two, Brian had composed a number of songs that were directly related to his current existence, and these lyrics were more interesting. The best combination of words and music occurred in 'The Night Was So Young,' which included a heartfelt story and a soaring, if still slightly thin, falsetto line from Brian. The ending harmonies on 'I'll Bet He's Nice' were especially reminiscent of the fullness of *Sunflower*, and 'Let's Put Our Hearts Together' was a touching, if slightly banal ballad.

The album also contained Brian Wilson music that indicated he hadn't lost his love of the eccentric or his musical sense of humor. Both 'Johnny Carson' and 'Ding Dang' (at last) were obviously the products of only one person—Brian Wilson—and his remarkable and delightful musical lunacy.

As winter melted into spring, the Beach Boys began to gear up for another big summer, but all the career momentum of the previous year had been dissipated. The decline happened very quickly; *15 Big Ones* hadn't been nearly as big as anticipated, and the TV special broadcast in August had been the peak of the group's media hype. There were no cover stories on the Beach Boys in 1977, although interest in Brian Wilson was still relatively high. The Beach Boys had missed their chance to re-establish themselves firmly as ongoing artists, and their concerts seemed to be mired in the continuing conflict over whether to play oldies or newer material.

As the group began rehearsals for a European/English tour, Mike was still in Switzerland, Carl's back was again giving him trouble, and Dennis was working night and day on his solo music. The practice sessions for the tour were extensive, and there seemed to be the promise of a new musical excitement. Dennis was going to have his own spot within the show to perform some of his songs, and the group was also going to perform tunes from the forthcoming *Adult Child* album.

What happened next was a disaster for the group. They canceled their European tour, giving reasons that didn't seem to jibe with the reality of the situation, since the group then traveled to London to play at the CBS Records convention. After "postponing" the tour due to "lack of preparation," it was a real slap in the face to the overseas fans when the Beach Boys played a show for the record industry. Those fans had supported the Beach Boys faithfully through the bad years, and they were disillusioned by the group's actions.

Bruce Johnston was at the CBS convention. According to Bruce, the show "wasn't a disaster for the audience. They loved the Beach Boys."

From Bruce's point of view, "you had an insider watching the band, knowing too much to enjoy it. The band was stiff, was not ready to be doing a concert, but there they were.

"Brian looked like he was drugged, not that he was, but he was just in some strange state, and Mike was a little uncomfortable, and then later that night [during the concert], I saw Mike get upset at Brian in front of all these people. It was just very unpleasant. I saw [Brian's] piano moving. I don't know if it was toward Brian or toward the stage." One member of the touring band recalled, "It was unbelievable, Mike started lifting the piano like he wanted to pick it up and drop it on Brian. The guy can really act crazy. He had just come back from six months of meditating, and was supposed to be more evolved, but he freaked out there on the stage." Rick Nelson explained that Mike had a "girlfriend who was killed in a car wreck toward the end of the six months, and I think that sort of startled him into reality real quick."

As Rick Nelson (himself a TM teacher) observes, Mike "still has a bad temper and gets hostile, but the only thing I ever thought about that was 'imagine if he never meditated.'"

That incident was only one public display of the war among the Beach Boys. The release and subsequent success of Dennis Wilson's fine debut solo album created much jealousy among the non-Wilson faction in the band. Their reaction seemed to be, "OK, Dennis, you have a solo career, now leave the Beach Boys to us." As Audree Wilson notes, "Mike and Al have always had a competitive thing with the Wilson brothers. I think the

Brian, circa Summer 1977.
Credit: Lester Cohen

Wilson brothers have always been a threat to them in some way, like they had too much power."

The group's management set-up became the next battlefield, with Dennis insisting that Steve Love be ousted as the group's business manager. All the problems came to a head at the end of the American tour in the late summer of 1977. When the blowup was reported in *Rolling Stone*, the talk of a Beach Boys breakup became pervasive.

This latest fight wasn't over the petty things that had caused scuffles in the early days, nor over the artistic issues that had rocked the group in later years. This one was a very basic disagreement between the two factions in the group, Mike and Al on one side, Carl and Dennis on the other, and Brian, very much in the middle, as always, just wanting to make music and not be bothered with the corporate affairs.

The Wilson brothers had once enjoyed control over the direction of the group because, in the four-man corporation, they had three of the votes. With Brian often absenting himself from the proceedings, Dennis and Carl got their way by virtue of a two-to-one vote. In the mid-seventies, Al Jardine finally became a member of the corporation, and the voting now would be split two against two, with Brian holding the decisive vote and almost always refusing to break the deadlock in non-musical matters. When Brian was pressured for a business decision, he often left town. Other times, the pressure would be unbearable, and Brian would just give his vote to Mike to stop all the hassles.

In August, Mike Love gained control of the group, and the messy breakup took place in September, with Mike and Al threatening to replace Carl and Dennis with two other musicians. It wasn't the first time the group had disbanded, and it wouldn't be the last, but it was probably the most bitter fight. Also, it was the first time that the public got a real glimpse of the Beach Boys' dirty laundry.

The much-reported split in the group almost cost the group their Caribou/CBS Records multimillion-dollar contract, but it was saved by reaching a very uneasy truce. It was another example of how money, rather than family, was the chief binder in keeping the group together. The public and private hostility was more blatant than ever, but the "harmonious" Beach Boys somehow stayed together. Or, in the words of one inside observer, "The Beach Boys have managed to exist all these years in spite of themselves."

The fall of 1977 was a busy time for the Beach Boys as the group's always complicated business puzzle took on added wrinkles. Mike Love and Charles Lloyd (with help from Al Jardine) formed a group called Waves and gave a number of benefit concerts to raise money for the Age of Spiritual Enlightenment, an offshoot of the International Meditation Society. Transcendental Meditation, which the group had often credited with helping them over the stresses of career problems and family fights, was ironically the new divisive factor. Mike Love was now running the group and he proceeded to get rid of almost all the non-meditating members of the Beach Boys' touring band, people and musicians who had loyally worked for the group for years.

The musicians were replaced by meditators, and Mike and Al holed up in Fairfield, Iowa, the home of Maharishi International University, where they had set up a studio for the purpose of producing Transcendental Meditation-oriented records. They flew Brian to Iowa to produce records for them. Working all fall, Brian wrote a lot of new material. One informed source reports that the new songs were not very good and will never be released. Another of Brian's friends offers the explanation, "Brian didn't want to be there with Mike and Al, so naturally the music wasn't very good." There were also a half-dozen songs (including 'California Feeling') recorded with American Spring that might someday be on a new album by that dormant group. Those songs are reportedly excellent, and as Marilyn and Diane noted in a recent interview, they can't reveal the names of the songs because "The Beach Boys are dying to get them, but we are going to keep them for ourselves."

There was still no word of a Brian Wilson solo album. Brian explained the problem. "They want to keep the material for the Beach Boys—a solo album would take away from the Beach Boys' sales."

Despite that observation, Brian continued working on a lot of personal material that belongs only on a Brian Wilson album. The two most exceptional new songs (written in late '76/early '77) are both stark and darkly sung love ballads. They are the most personal tunes Brian has recorded since "Til I Die."

'It's Over Now'
The flame of love we had has finally died
Can't take this emptiness it left inside

It's over now
And though I played the role
I lost my soul
It's still within your heart

'Still I Dream of It' contains the chorus:

Still I dream of it
Of that happy day
When I can say I've fallen in love
And it haunts me so
Like the dream that's somehow linked
To all the stars above
I'll find my world
Someday, I'll find my world

These were the kind of songs that Brian had been writing all along and hadn't been sharing with the world.

As 1977 came to an end, Brian was still trapped within the Beach Boys' whirlwind, unhappily performing in concert and disinterestedly making mediocre records. The group's traditional sixteenth-anniversary concert in Los Angeles on December 27 was one of the worst shows they'd ever given, and the bitterness and hostility within the band were so thick that even the harmonies failed to cut through. Twice, when songs were played that Mike or Al had written, Dennis stalked offstage, the second time taking Brian with him. Mike Love brought his three sisters onstage, making it four Loves and only one Wilson (Carl). Mike told the audience, "This kind of evens things up for all those years" when he'd been outnumbered.

The group's singing wasn't at all lively, and the oldies were flat. One writer commented that it "looked like they were giving their final concert." Brian's discomfort was more than obvious; if the point of his being onstage was to soak up love from the audience, that had been accomplished long ago, and now the concerts had just become a torturous chore. Brian was back with the Beach Boys, but he certainly didn't seem to be a willing participant.

The two albums that Brian has produced since his return have been forced out of him, and that is one reason they aren't polished gems. Both records are very difficult to listen to unless you are involved in Brian Wilson's musical and personal psychodramas. As one friend of Brian's noted, "The records are interesting only when the content is taken within the context of Brian's life. I love those records, but then, I'm biased."

The new music that Brian has created which remains unreleased is a strong indication that he is planning to share himself with the world; but his personal life seems to be a very confusing situation. Brian Wilson still lives in his own personal haunted house, and it does not appear that any steps are being taken to alleviate his difficulties. The solution, according to one friend, lies mostly within Brian. "Brian must respect someone before he can let that person help him. The support he got from people he respected is what drove him to the heights of creativity. He needs that kind of support to get well as a human being, and the people around him aren't giving it to him. Not because they don't want to. They just don't understand him. Brian does not think he's worthy of good things, so he's surrounded himself with people who are using his talent to make money for themselves. Have any of those people ever said to him that he is a good human being, that he is a kind and gentle and special person? I don't think so.

"Brian *is* a special person, but until he really believes that, he isn't going to get much better. Most of that knowledge must come from himself. The rest has to come from his brothers, his family, his friends, even a doctor. Whatever. Until Brian is treated as a human being instead of a money-maker, nothing will change."

What makes the entire situation so complicated is that, as David Anderle explains, "Like Howard Hughes or other people like that, Brian is so dominating. In his whatever state, nobody is going to mess with Brian. Who the hell's going to, which one of those guys in the band is really going to mess with Brian? None of them, for fear that he may be faking it. I can't see any of those guys dealing with Brian at all."

In trying to understand Brian, there remain two unanswerable questions—what is left of Brian's talent? And how much damage has he suffered as a human being? Cursory observations will reveal that Brian at times is totally lucid; other times, he appears to be totally out of touch with reality. A number of Brian's close friends insist that Brian is in control of his situation and is pretending to be crazy. Dennis Wilson's comments show the contradictions inherent in any analysis of Brian Wilson's psyche. "Brian is crazy. Brian is fine. Brian is my master. Brian has real problems." How much of Brian's behavior is evidence of real difficulties and how much of it is an act? Regardless of the cause of the unusual behavior, his comeback on a personal level is nothing short of heroic.

At one December '77 concert, Brian left the security of his piano and played bass the entire show, the first time he's done that since 1964. On another night, Brian was so bored that he played the wrong songs to amuse himself. The band, however, was not amused.

That boredom, though, is possibly the best indication that Brian is really coming back. The initial shocks over his return to a "normal" existence are wearing off, and Brian appears ready to confront all the problems that have held him back the past dozen years. Those problems center on the Beach Boys. It will be difficult for the group to face up to Brian. For nine years, their public pronouncements claimed that Brian is fine. He's always writing and someday soon, he's going to stretch out again and really shock everybody. There was never any public admission on the group's part that Brian was lonely or troubled or hurt or that he might have desired to be released from his Beach Boys obligations.

Audree Wilson: "I think there must be something about becoming so famous and so acknowledged . . . There has to be pain with that. I've talked to Brian about the millions of people his music has affected . . . He'll say, 'Oh, I know it; I really do know that.' But I don't suppose [that takes away from the pain]. So many people think he's the greatest. He is the greatest, and that's very hard to live with."

Mike Love: "Sometimes you can quit a group, but you can't quit your family very easily . . . even if you have a horrible disagreement, he's still your brother or your cousin. So I think that has been one salvation for the group . . . I don't know what I'd have done if I hadn't been in the Beach Boys. I would probably have made money doing something because I have a strong competitive urge and desire, and I relate to making money with my family."

The family ties that have kept the Beach Boys together are incredibly strong. One friend of Brian's points out that, regardless of all the hurt Brian has received from his family, "they are just about all he's got. Sure, he's got a few close friends who would take him in, but then what? It's that fear of the unknown that keeps Brian there."

One friend of Brian's explains this blindness. "For them, there is a terror involved in the Beach Boys ending . . . a basic fear of survival as to whether they could make it without the Beach Boys. It's all they've ever known, and they went from being kids to being Beach Boys. They've had to do their growing up within their career, and it has been very hard. Carl has been a Beach Boy for more than half his life. Almost the same with Dennis. They've never known anything else. That is why they couldn't allow Brian to break free."

This disregard for Brian hasn't been malicious. Brian Wilson has always been an enigma, even to his family. David Anderle thinks their insensitivity toward Brian "is based on a Hawthorne mentality . . . the surfer mentality. Insensitive to other people, to an extent insensitive to what Brian was going through. I don't think they're stupid. I just don't think they know too much. I just feel that their approach to the present of that presence is extremely narrow, therefore shallow. I just never had a sense of them being real worldly."

Bruce Johnston, a Beach Boy for seven years and always a knowledgeable observer of the scene, thought that Brian "was always surrounded by a bunch of average, ordinary, monaural group of friends. They're the sort of people who, if they didn't know how to swim, would probably take a shower instead of taking a chance. Brian's genius is sort of vertical, which is great when he is locked in the studio. And, this is my opinion, I always felt that because of them, the rest of it is horizontal. There are all these nice ordinary bowling-league people in his life who would never go 'Great!' for the right reasons or stimulate him, encourage him to reach beyond some of his lyrics or these ideas that he throws out. Most of the people who have always been around Brian are maybe related; I don't mean the brothers, but distant cousins and things, people who somehow got on the payroll and sort of keep him company."

Where does all this leave Brian? Brian: "All I want is something new . . . physical health . . . something that feels like life, or anything."

David Anderle: "I have no idea what Brian is left with. I just keep getting Howard Hughes vibes. This guy just tucked away somewhere with all these people doing business for him. And no matter what condition he's in, everybody is still fearing him. That's the way I see Brian Wilson. Yes, I can see the parallel between the eccentricity of Howard Hughes and the eccentricity of Brian Wilson. But I'm saying that behind the eccentricity is the power of a *human being*! That awesome power that is there, whether Brian exercises it or not. And the fear that power causes in other people around him 'cause Brian does do that, even with his family." Still, Anderle thinks that Brian must be suffering, even if he is playing a game. "I can't believe a person could be putting on and going through the agony he must be going through. I mean, he's not having fun, is he? He's not having a good time." One friend of Brian's explains that "he has amazing adaptability. No matter how bad the situation, he manages to survive."

EPILOGUE, 1978

Aside from the personal issues at stake, it is very hard to understand why Brian Wilson would be forced to play a charade that he is a Beach Boy, almost fourteen years since he quit the road and over ten years since he stopped producing their albums. In many respects, Brian's current situation is much like the conflict that engulfed him during *SMiLE*. Brian himself stated, "Sometimes, I really feel like a commodity in a stock market." Brian indicated that he wants "freedom and I want to do my own album. Either I'm going to stay and produce only their stuff or go on my own and do an album by myself . . . I haven't decided which to do yet."

Just as in 1967, there seems to be no reasonable compromise in the Beach Boys situation, and the same issue exists. There doesn't seem to be any reason why Brian couldn't do both, produce the Beach Boys and make records of his own. If that was what he wanted. Van Dyke Parks asked this rhetorical question of *Crawdaddy*'s Timothy White: "Don't you think that the man has done enough for the industry that he could put out his own album? . . . I do . . . I would say in any court in the land that you would find Brian Wilson is quite sane, capable, ready, willing and able to put out an album . . . He would want to, but it's not in the works.

"You can quote Hugh Downs on Jack Paar. 'He isn't inflicted with mental illness. He is a carrier.' I think that's a good thing to say about Brian . . . For two Christmases in a row, Brian has come over to my home. On those two occasions, I found no difference between the Brian Wilson I saw then, and the Brian for whom I worked so long ago. No difference. Brain damage? Hell no. I've seen those bumper stickers. I don't stop for Brian Wilson . . . I think the guy can afford to sit it out . . . Sooner or later, he's going to see a project that ignites his interest, and he's going to hit it . . . I believe that he will have a lot of public interest in his favor to command the attention that it will take to catapult him into the center ring, if he wants it again. At this point, I should imagine he is bored. Why, I don't know. It may have something to do with the Louis B. Mayers of the record industry, those awful people . . . I used to think he was very, very strong . . . As a friend of mine who is also a very close friend of Brian's said, and it may be true, 'Brian is spineless.' I'd like to catch Brian out in the yard so I could get into a little kickass with him, to be quite frank. I think he's misbehaved. It's as simple as that. He's just very talented, and . . . I think he's perpetrated a great myth."

People like Van Dyke Parks and Danny Hutton, once inside but now banished from Brian's presence, observe that Brian is trapped. Brian's strengths as a musician have never translated to other parts of his life. He can lead in the studio, but when it comes to standing up for his personal freedom, he backs down. As one close friend admitted, "That's the one aspect of Brian I have trouble understanding or accepting. I love everything else about him, but I find it hard to cope with the fact that he's just sitting back and not fighting his way out of the trap."

It would not be an easy thing for Brian Wilson to break out of the Beach Boys. How do you leave the Ford Motor Company when you're Henry Ford? Career-wise, the move would be easy, and there are many record industry people who are standing by, ready to help and publicly applaud the move. For Brian, it is a personal move of incredible signifi-cance and would involve his leaving the security of his present life. Brian is not a person who seeks out trouble. He creates it, he is a magnet for it, but he also doesn't enjoy not being free.

Most of the people who want Brian to make the music that is in his head believe that Brian will never create that important music within the Beach Boys situation. They all firmly believe that when Brian decides he's had enough, and that he wants to run his own life, then he will leave the group.

Daryl Dragon thinks that if Brian is ever going to get back "to that creative thing again, I think what he needs is a spark for writing. The excitement is gone; I think the family's been together too long, has been a business too long, you know?" Many of those who have loved Brian Wilson's music through the years think that Brian's music is too important to be tied into a group formula for making hit records and paying the bills. Again, Daryl Dragon: "A lot of people who have natural gifts can't take criticism. Brian should be out on an island, playing for natives, writing music for kids to be happy and not worrying about people saying things about him, putting him down for 'Let's Go Surfing.' He's not writing on that level, he's writing on a gift level."

Bruce Johnston: "My idealistic solution would be that someone should go and get Brian a grant. Brian is a serious musician. Someone should commission a live performance and recording of Brian's [future] music for orchestra or a combination of orchestra and voices . . . do something that's adult Brian Wilson instead of trying to recapture the things Brian's already done. They [the Beach Boys] should allow him to grow and go ahead. I'm sure he has something to say [musically] . . . At this point in Brian's life, I think he should be making music and not worrying about making records . . . maybe a commissioned work in a three-year period that would be underwritten. I think that if you took away the 'make it in the old mold, make it commercial' pressure from Brian, he might come out with something incredible." Bruce feels that Brian doesn't know how to ask for his freedom. "I don't think he knows how to pull it off. He's kind of trapped." Brian's leadership ability, Bruce claims, is "all in one area. His 'Here's what we should do' is mainly in his music."

Steve Douglas: "He's a great musician. What I'm sure has been a big problem in his head is all these people that are dependent upon him coming through. Maybe he'll get off wanting to make Beach Boys records. He should make his own records. Maybe he'll get to the point where he'll make records with other kinds of music and it won't necessarily be Beach Boys-oriented. I think of Brian as a great orchestrator . . . I think he could do a fabulous symphony of some kind. It would be great if he would put all those orchestrating and arranging chops into a full symphony—it would be astounding."

Many people understand the importance of Brian's musical freedom, and they all hope that the Beach Boys will soon allow Brian to create whatever he wants to. Those same people, however, believe that the family won't let go. As one friend noted, "What else can they do? Dennis has a lot of talent, and Carl could sing on records, but otherwise, they'd be lost. They've been Beach Boys almost all their lives."

Brian Wilson is the Beach Boys, even in his unwilling, disinterested state. His musical creations and productions have been responsible for well over ninety percent of the group's hits. Their gross income has reached into the multimillions. "It is their egos that won't let Brian go," another friend claims. "They could tour without him; they have for years. And they should keep touring if that's what they want to do. Just leave Brian alone." The Beach Boys have made and continue to make most of their money from touring. There doesn't seem to be any legitimate reason for Brian to be part of the nostalgia show.

Brian Wilson has earned the right not to be part of that parade. He earned that more than a dozen years ago. He's made all the Beach Boys and his family very rich.

The Beach Boys themselves have been almost totally responsible for keeping Brian's music in front of the public for all these years. Their perpetual touring in the face of incredible difficulties, both personal and financial, is an example of tremendous perseverance. The Beach Boys *have* stayed together through all the fights and problems, and that is very much to their credit. If the Beach Boys had quit back in 1969, it might have been a long time before the music of Brian Wilson again became important. With the group performing in concert, the revitalized interest in Brian Wilson only took a half-dozen years.

Besides the entertainment value of the Beach Boys music, Brian has created a type of popular music that influenced much of what has been created in the past dozen years. Groups like Crosby, Stills, Nash and Young, Queen, the Electric Light Orchestra, 10cc, and many others have all incorporated Beach Boys harmony into their music. It was Brian and the Beach Boys who established the validity of harmony in rock music. In addition to all of that, Brian's creation of a California myth has had a significant sociological impact.

What should be understood is that this book isn't aimed at minimizing the importance of the Beach Boys' contribution. The group has given the world sixteen years of joy, and Brian's work with the band has often resulted in artistic achievement that stands out above much of the world of popular culture. What is sad is that the Beach Boys group always came before the individuals. All of their personal problems, Brian's included, have been secondary to keeping the group together.

Audree Wilson admits, "There have been times when I thought, 'Is it really worth it?' I think about Carl, he really missed out on his teenage years. He was fourteen years old, and Dennis was sixteen, and that's so young. They've all had their share of glory and the good life, but money does not buy happiness. I know that."

Many people have been waiting patiently and faithfully for many years for Brian to become an artist again, as opposed to a benefactor. Few people realized the seriousness of Brian's personal difficulties or the complexities of the situation.

There are no easy answers for the Beach Boys or for Brian Wilson. There are no easy answers for any artists. The people around Brian were doing what they thought was best for all, as misguided as their ideas often appeared to be. The only aspect of this tale that has a right or wrong is that Brian Wilson needs love and support as a human being, and he doesn't seem to be getting it. The rest of it is, of course, very judgmental, and everyone has his own motivations for seeing the story as he does.

Bruce Johnston wishes for "an incredibly funded foundation" that would pay for artists like Brian to make music. Once, many years ago, Brian Wilson himself created that very foundation. It's called the Beach Boys. In 1967, it could have been the base for Brian to branch out from, but in 1978, it has become the anchor that holds him back.

In late 1967, David Anderle observed, "The next big Brian Wilson thing will not happen with the Beach Boys." There hasn't been a "big" Brian Wilson happening in the ensuing eleven years, in or outside of the group. Brian wasn't even a Beach Boy for many years, but, as Anderle notes, "He hasn't been anything else."

Before any new creation begins, though, Brian must be respected as a human being. Then he must be freed as an artist. The first is much more important. Even if Brian Wilson never writes another note of music or chooses never again to share his music with the world, he has already left the world an incredible legacy of his creations, music that has made millions of people around the world happy.

THE BEACH BOYS AND THE CALIFORNIA MYTH

1985 Update

From June 1980, (Clockwise from upper left: Mike, Brian, Dennis, Al, Carl and Bruce.)
It was one of the last times the three Wilson brothers
would be photographed together as Beach Boys.
Credit: Michael Putland/Getty Images

CHAPTER 14

CODETTA, 1977–1985

THE *HARVARD DICTIONARY OF MUSIC* DEFINES *CODA* AS A "CONCLUDING section or passage . . . added . . . to confirm the impression of finality." That same book describes *codetta* as "a short coda . . . a closing passage at the end of an inner section." To the ear, a codetta is a false coda; it makes the listener think that the musical piece is over when, in fact, it only signals the end of a specific movement.

In 1977, the year I wrote this book, what appeared to be the breakup of the Beach Boys proved to be a false ending. As Carl Wilson later told Geoffrey Himes of *Musician* magazine, "that was a very rough time for all of us . . . what we had to do was just let everything fall apart, and then . . . see if we really wanted to be a group or not . . . It became clear that we should put it back together."

However, this book was written during that period in which the Beach Boys were imploding, which partially explains its downbeat tone, particularly as it relates to the group. In 1977, the Beach Boys' future seemed so unpromising that it made more sense to discuss what Brian's career could be without the group.

But 1977 wasn't the Beach Boys' first codetta (nor would it be their last), and in 1978 they looked ahead to their new Caribou/CBS Records contract. However, before the Beach Boys could approach the future, there remained one final obligation.

The fall 1978 release of the *M.I.U.* album marked the end of the group's eight years as a Warner Brothers recording act. In 1970, the label had taken a chance on a fading group, helped the band achieve its most effective non-Brian work, and waited patiently for Brian to return to action. Maybe more than anything, Warner Brothers' faith (and money) might have kept the group intact in the early 1970s. But Warners had been

271

unable to turn the Beach Boys' albums into big hits, and when CBS outbid Warners, the Beach Boys departed for greener pastures.

M.I.U., like many of their Warners' records, was assembled after numerous songs (including a new, mediocre Christmas LP) were rejected. Ironically, as a record, *M.I.U.* sounded more like a real group album than anything since their Warner Brothers debut, *Sunflower*. Unfortunately, *M.I.U.* was an effective fraud, since Mike, Al and Brian did almost all of the recording. The only way to get Dennis on the disc was to redo 'My Diane,' a track that Brian had originally produced during 1976's "write a song, get a hamburger" days. Carl's presence on the record was felt only in terms of his always solid lead singing. Dennis's songwriting had made *Sunflower* consistently strong, and without him, *M.I.U.* was just a stylistic rehash.

Still, the album does contain some of the best and most "Beach Boys-sounding" material of the decade. Happily, 'She's Got Rhythm' marked the return of Brian's somewhat scratchy falsetto, and 'Match Point of Our Love' proved that his compositional skills were intact. However, the dirge-like production of many of the tracks was completely out of step with 1978's commercial demands, and the album made nary a dent in American consciousness.

Brian's extensive involvement with the group, from *15 Big Ones* through *M.I.U.* plus his work on the title song for the 1978 film *Almost Summer*, made it seem like he might be ready to take control of the group's records. But with the exception of the cult status of *Love You*, his inconsistent efforts weren't well received, and Brian's active period, originally stimulated by Dr. Landy, seemed to be at an end. By the late summer of 1978, he was ready to step back from the Beach Boys—a feeling that prompted him to call ex-Beach Boy Bruce Johnston and ask him to work with the group. At the time, Bruce thought it was a temporary "distress signal," but he has since become a more-or-less permanent member of the Beach Boys' family. Joining the group at Criteria Studios in Miami, Bruce was back with the band from which he'd been separated six years before. And this time, with Caribou/CBS Records' support, Bruce was enlisted to make the Beach Boys "commercial."

First, Bruce went into the studio with producer Curt Boettcher with the idea of steering the Beach Boys into the then-popular disco arena. And that duo, along with James William Guercio (an advisor to the group and the head of Caribou Records), set out to produce an album behind which CBS could exercise its considerable muscle.

The result, *L.A. (Light Album)*, proved that in groups, democracy is not necessarily a good thing. Each member contributed at least one song, with Brian's lone "new" composition, the oft-talked-about 1974 track, 'Good Timin',' a beautiful ballad written with brother Carl which felt like the "old" Beach Boys.

The album's success hinged on the extended disco version of 'Here Comes the Night' (a song from 1967's *Wild Honey* LP). In the past, Brian had been the one to popularize fads, not jump on bandwagons. With 'Here Comes the Night,' Bruce and Boettcher had tried to make the group current by hopping on a hip happening, and the crassness of the concept hurt its commercial chances, the musical merits of the track aside. Actually, I liked it, particularly the short version; at least Bruce was *trying* to contemporize the group's sound. It didn't work.

Released in March 1979 to coincide with a big promotional push by CBS and a four-show, SRO (standing-room only) engagement at Radio City Music Hall, the album peaked at #100 in the *Billboard* charts. 'Here Comes the Night' didn't crack the Top Ten. The follow-up single, 'Good Timin',' spent only a week at #40 before plunging off the charts. Initial sales of the LP were only in the neighborhood of 100,000 copies, a low-rent district the Beach Boys have too often occupied since 1967. But the release of 'Good Timin'' turned a disaster into a relative success, pushing album sales over 300,000.

Unfortunately, neither CBS nor the group were able to build upon the modest momentum provided by 'Good Timin',' and subsequent single releases in 1979 would produce only two more disappointments for the group. Al's 'Lady Lynda,' a surprise Top Five smash in England, where the group's fans have always been intensely loyal, failed to cross the ocean. And 'It's a Beautiful Day,' one of the band's best upbeat songs of the seventies (from the *Americathon* soundtrack), didn't find a home on the hit parade.

Regardless of the results, CBS had invested so many millions in the Beach Boys that there was little to do but send them back into the studio. And this time, CBS wanted more involvement from Brian Wilson.

Nineteen seventy-nine's most interesting sessions tried to put Brian into a "time machine" at Western Studio Three, the site of the original hit recordings. Engineer Steve Desper (who had run Brian's in-home studio from 1968 to 1971 and mixed the group's concerts during the same period) teamed up in midyear with Carl to create a recording atmosphere in which Brian would feel comfortable. Enlisting the help of Chuck Britz, still an engineer at Western, the threesome resurrected the old electronic tube recording equipment, found the appropriate period microphones, and installed the "ancient" studio monitors, all aimed at making the studio like it was in 1964. The original session players from the sixties were booked. Desper stepped aside so that Britz (who had turned the knobs on virtually all of Brian's triumphant records) would again engineer Brian's sessions.

A similar effort had been tried in 1976, and, as before, the yield from 1979 wasn't large: only four songs, two of which had no vocals. The quality was good, but Brian's interest quickly waned.

An interesting footnote to the proceedings was that, according to Desper, there was some sense that this might be the last time Brian would be actively involved in Beach Boys sessions, and when Brian was in the control room, an audio recording was made of his every word for posterity.

The other half of the get-back-to-the-old-days game was teaming Mike and Brian for songwriting sessions. Mike had written the words for quite a few Beach Boys classics, but this creative relationship wasn't necessarily the most inspired choice. However, Brian and Mike did collaborate on a half-dozen new tunes, including the highpoint of *Keepin' the Summer Alive*, 'Goin' On,' a song that incorporated a theme from the *Almost Summer* soundtrack.

As Carl later recalled for *Musician* magazine's Geoffrey Himes, "Brian got hot for about three days in the studio. He was singing like a bird. All the protection he usually runs just dropped; he came out of himself. He was right there in the room." The results of this activity weren't overwhelming to the listener, possibly because the songs didn't connect with an adult Beach Boys' audience or to the teenage throngs that still came to the concerts to celebrate the old music. And if *L.A. (Light Album)* had the least Brian involvement in Beach Boys history, then *Keepin' the Summer Alive* may have presented him with the most uncomfortable sessions. Because Brian had written so many songs, he was keenly interested in how they would be recorded. Unfortunately, Brian wasn't willing to take charge.

Steve Desper, the chief engineer for *KTSA*, observes, "Brian lost control of the records in 1967 when he said that it should say on the credits,

'Produced by the Beach Boys.' After a period of the records being produced by committee, it then evolved to where whoever wrote the song produced the track."

Desper points out that not only had the Beach Boys grown musically from the days when Brian told them what to do, but Brian "isn't the same person he was then. He's not twenty-two. He's had success and excess. Back then, he had nothing but confidence, innocence and command of the group . . . If Brian could've metamorphosed into his former glory, they would have stepped back. But by *Keepin' the Summer Alive*, they had concluded that he wasn't going to do it, at least not for that record. And while they still recognized his talent, they felt their judgment was superior to his."

Cruel and unfair as it may sound, Desper feels that at those sessions, "Brian was tolerated" by the group. However, Desper doesn't think the group was wrong in ignoring Brian's wishes in the studio.

Another observer of the sessions recalls, "The truth is, Brian wasn't there all that much. The Beach Boys weren't overriding his decisions. It was more that he couldn't or wouldn't finish the work." Steve Desper concurs: "In the past, the group had violated the sanctuary of Brian's songs." While those kinds of changes continued to take place in 1979, Desper notes, "There was no sanctuary to violate." In Desper's opinion, what Brian had created was often incomplete, and as he was "unwilling and perhaps incapable of 'properly' finishing it, it fell to the group to shape his [musical] ideas into finished productions."

For *Keepin' the Summer Alive*, the Beach Boys recorded nearly three dozen tracks, in months of sessions at Western, Daryl Dragon's Rumbo Recorders, and on Al's ranch in Big Sur, using a twenty-four track mobile recorder, both in the woods and in Al's barn. At least for the Big Sur sessions, the group were almost all together, for the making of the record and for the optimistically titled *Goin' Platinum*, a pilot for a short-lived television series. But that film neglected to address the fact that for the recording of *Keepin' the Summer Alive*, Dennis wasn't involved.

In June of 1979, during a series of concerts at L.A.'s Universal Amphitheatre, Dennis's onstage antics kindled the always smoldering resentment between Mike and Dennis, leading to a reported backstage confrontation between the two cousins. Shortly afterwards, according to a former employee of the group, Dennis received word that he was no longer welcome to be a part of the Beach Boys until he began behaving himself. After eighteen turbulent years, this dismissal from the family band may have seemed cold, but it was hardly undeserved. His unpredictability had frequently disrupted shows. As one longtime associate admits, when Dennis was drinking a lot, "he would get out of control." Although he continued to receive income from the Beach Boys, it was rumored to be considerably less than what his share was when he was touring. Dennis, in the midst of a torrid romance with Fleetwood Mac's Christine McVie at the time, would return to the group almost exactly one year later, in June of 1980.

Dennis's payroll cut came at the same time the group was having money troubles. The latter half of 1978 saw the first significant slippage in the Beach Boys' concert grosses, and a severe cash crunch in 1979 reportedly threatened the Beach Boys' survival. In the past, according to one former employee of the group, Brian had bailed the band out of other money troubles. In this case, the group had reportedly received a multimillion-dollar advance from CBS Records, and not being able to pay back the advance was a strong glue in keeping the Beach Boys together.

New records were the key to keeping the deal alive. Bruce, in a sense, saved the Beach Boys by getting the first two CBS albums made, even if that occasionally meant functioning as a travel agent. For the *L.A. (Light Album)* in particular, Bruce drove up and down the coast to get the vocal parts from Al and Mike, who no longer lived in L.A. But the records did little to enhance the Beach Boys' reputation, either inside CBS or with the world at large.

With the lengthy sessions for *Keepin' the Summer Alive* over and Brian humorously captured on videotape (Question: "Brian, what makes you laugh?" Answer: "Arguments . . . [listening to] other people's arguments"), the Beach Boys returned to the road. Not only were they without Dennis, but it was decided in late 1979 that for Brian's well-being, he should be hospitalized. That meant a lonely Christmas: Brian was in the process of getting divorced from Marilyn, and his relationship with his longtime, off-and-on girlfriend was nearing the end—even though Brian was considering marrying her when his divorce was final. His next significant relationship would be with Carolyn Williams, a psychiatric aide he met during this hospitalization.

On the musical front, things were equally grim. In 1979, the *Light Album* had enjoyed qualified success, but *Keepin' the Summer Alive*, released in March of 1980, was a major failure. Like its CBS predecessor, it had the appropriate slickness, but the public ignored the music that was bordering dangerously close to self-parody. As one current associate of the group recalls, "the promotion for *L.A. (Light Album)* was terrific, but by the time *Keepin' the Summer Alive* was released the record business (like the entire economy) was in a slump, and they didn't really put a lot of money behind it."

Five albums in five years had failed to re-establish the band as contemporary hitmakers. As the 1980s began, there was little left for them but to settle into the oldies groove. The one saving grace for the band was a change in the political climate in the country which would make the Beach Boys' old-time image not only acceptable but desirable.

If the new records were deemed unlistenable by the masses, at least the Beach Boys seemed to be emerging as social statement. They played a 1980 fundraiser for then-presidential candidate George Bush. And on the Fourth of July, the group journeyed to Washington, for their first, free holiday concert. As 1980, their nineteenth year as a group, came to an end, the Beach Boys received a star on Hollywood Boulevard's "Walk of Fame." The next night, they played their twentieth-anniversary concert, a show "highlighted" by the return to the live act of their very first song, 'Surfin',' and at one point, Al and Bruce appeared with "out-of-the-mothballs" striped shirts.

Nineteen eighty-one would be the absolute nadir in the band's history. Dennis had returned, but his brother Carl had decided to pursue a solo career, stating he did not "plan on touring with the Beach Boys until they decide that 1981 means as much to them as 1961." Carl said he would return to the band if the group promised to make a record of *new* songs, to properly rehearse before every tour, and to agree to no more extended dates in gambling resorts like Lake Tahoe.

His absence proved conclusively that Carl was the one absolutely essential *musical* element in the group's live shows. Without Carl, a seemingly lost and oblivious Brian was forced to attempt Carl's vocals, and Brian's nerves betrayed him. Bruce or sideman Adrian Baker had to rescue the still-troubled Beach Boy whose onstage singing could only be described as humiliating for a man who had once made sound-perfect records.

Through the years, Carl had evolved into Brian's "voice to the people," and the concerts without him could be shoddy. On July 4, the Beach

Boys earned immeasurable goodwill with their second annual free show in Washington. The next day's show, a nationwide broadcast from the *Queen Mary* in Long Beach, was a disastrous follow-up. As Bruce Johnston admits, "the sound was totally out of balance. The monitor mix I heard onstage was fine, but when I later listened to the TV broadcast, I had to leave the room. The TV mix had only parts of the vocal mix . . . only Al, Mike, and [backup musician] Adrian Baker. Everything we sang went on tape, but only the three parts went out live."

If you heard or saw the show, Bruce's alibi just doesn't wash. First of all, other groups on the same show, especially Three Dog Night, sounded great. And while the Beach Boys sound mix is more complicated, bad mixing can't excuse a lifeless stage presence or Brian's unstable and disturbing performance. My phone rang that night, from fellow Beach Boys' fanatics asking if I'd seen the show; I wondered aloud, "Won't they put themselves out of our misery?"

Without Carl, the Beach Boys of 1981 were like a tired old magician who is so bored with his one great trick that he doesn't do it very well anymore. It had always been hard work to sing Brian's songs well in concert, and the group had pulled it off for years, doing a more than credible job until Brian returned to the road in 1976. But by 1981, the Beach Boys' once-sparkling vocal display had broken down. Without Carl, the key voice, the Beach Boys were almost unwatchable, desecrating Brian's creations as if *they* no longer cared.

After a particularly unpleasant onstage incident at their Greek Theatre, L.A. appearance, local headlines read like obituaries for the hometown band. "Is it time for the Beach Boys to hang 'em up?" wondered one paper. "Beach Boys' Public Psychodrama" heralded another. Like an old mule on a dust-bowl farm, the Beach Boys of 1981 blindly plowed ahead, and, if nothing else, must be credited for surviving this "career codetta." Ironically, during this period the Beach Boys enjoyed two Top Forty hits. Capitol Records' medley of Beach Boys' favorites bolted into the Top Twenty. And a single from a fine CBS compilation LP, the Beach Boys' version of the Del-Vikings 1957 hit 'Come Go with Me,' made the charts in late 1981.

In the meantime, Brian and Dennis were more and more drawn into a downward spiral. Their presence fulfilled contractual obligations but little else. As 1982 began, both were showing the effects of uncontrolled intake—be it of food, alcohol, or drugs. In the midst of their personal crises, Brian and Dennis worked in the studio in brief but productive bursts. While nothing has been released from those sessions (in fact, little was completed), the brothers displayed a heartfelt propensity to create as a team outside of the Beach Boys. For a vaporous moment, the tantalizing prospect of a Wilson Brothers album was an unspoken possibility, but it disappeared in that same wisp.

Unfortunately for the third brother, Carl's solo album and tour didn't really generate a substantial career. Only the beautiful 'Heaven' got much airplay, and even as he finished his second album, the way was being paved for his return to active Beach Boyhood. Rejoining the group in mid-1982, Carl eventually brought the band back to life, rediscovering new ways to sing the old songs, rehearsing the band to its most precise playing in years and, by 1983, even injecting more than a half-dozen songs into the standard live menu.

As for new music, Carl told writer Geoffrey Himes, "I'd like to see the group take another shot at making one more good record. That's the thing we keep trying to do, but can never quite pull together all the elements. But I don't think we'll make another Beach Boys album until Brian's healthy enough to produce again. I know we could make a real strong commercial record with an outside producer. So that's possible, but if you're talking about a great record, 'Good Vibrations' class, you're talking about Brian with us. Anything else is bullshit."

Carl's time away from the band had given him a fresh perspective. He didn't "mind if he [Brian] doesn't make any more music. I don't care if he makes hits or not. My interest in Brian is that I love him as a human being and a brother, as I love all my family. I want him to have some joy and satisfaction in life, and he's not getting that. I'm not discouraging him [from writing] by any means, but the main thing is that he have a nurturing, loving life. That's all that matters anyway."

Carl's concern was well timed. By the end of 1982, Brian seemed to be drifting away from the group. Weighing nearly 300 pounds, he was living with former psychiatric aide Carolyn Williams and her children. Dennis, his scorching affair with Christine McVie ended, was now living and traveling with a teenage girl by the name of Shawn Love, whose primary appeal to him may have been her (disputed) claim to be Mike Love's illegitimate daughter. If Shawn was Mike's daughter, that would make her the Wilson brothers' cousin. More significantly, if true, it would make Mike Dennis's father-in-law and the grandfather of Dennis's last child, son Gage. Mike Love denies the paternity. But the story is an indication of the animosity between Dennis and Mike.

There was no way to control Dennis's behavior. But by early 1983, fearful that Brian was perilously close to becoming the next big rock 'n' roll death, the Beach Boys' management had rehired Dr. Eugene Landy to straighten out Brian. As Carl told *Musician* magazine in the early 1980s, "Brian [in 1976] was getting back on his feet. He had been with Gene for more than a year. He was becoming a lot more productive. But Gene and Steve Love [Mike's brother and then the group's and Brian's business manager] disagreed about what Brian should do. Gene was doing it from a therapeutic angle, and Steve had business considerations. So Steve terminated Gene. It was really a shame. Brian regressed pretty much after that."

That regression would be immediately checked by Dr. Landy's return. The Beach Boys, dedicated to saving their former leader, reportedly pledged the net proceeds from one concert a month to pay for Landy's services. This charity raises the question of what happened to the millions of dollars Brian had made through the years. He didn't snort that much cocaine.

At a fee reportedly in the neighborhood of $1,000 a day, Landy now had the opportunity, as he put it, to complete his canvas. Landy pointed out that Murry Wilson had never given his sons guidelines—the same action could provoke punishment or evoke love. Landy called that kind of upbringing "a little schitzy" and blamed Brian's acid-taking for expanding the problem.

Landy's stated goal was to be the "good father." As he told the *L.A. Times*, he planned to teach Brian "ways, methods, and functions to become self-sufficient, competent, adequate, logical," able to make his own decisions and, in the long run, be independent of Landy. Landy noted that their previous relationship had been interrupted before he could finish his work; now, Landy's controversial twenty-four-hour therapy again controlled every moment of Brian's life—eating, sleeping, exercise, music making, social encounters and cultural activities—all designed to bring Brian into the "real world," give him songwriting input, and show off how much progress he was making. All of the activities were directed by Dr. Landy.

Thus resumed one of the most curious partnerships in rock history, what has become a doctor/patient songwriting collaboration. However, in early 1983, it really didn't matter if Landy had any ulterior motives. Brian was clearly in trouble, and Dr. Landy may have saved his life. Not that another doctor couldn't have done the job; but Landy was able to control Brian effectively and once again steer him onto the road to physical fitness.

Dennis, unfortunately, didn't have the temperament to listen to reason or take advice. His 1983 "acting up" had a desperate edge to it, as if Dennis knew he had just about used up his nine lives. He had once felt invulnerable, but when he needed throat surgery to salvage what was left of his voice, even the most carefree and careless person had to be aware of the damage he was doing to himself. On numerous occasions, he made futile attempts to stop killing himself with alcohol, but nothing worked for any length of time. As in 1979, Dennis wasn't even welcome at Beach Boys' concerts. He could be so disruptive that the group was again paying him a reduced share—in effect, to stay away.

In a last-ditch attempt, the Beach Boys reportedly expressed a willingness to fund an arrangement similar to Brian's. But for Dennis to put himself under Dr. Landy's control was an impossible consideration.

Ironically, Dennis's final decline came at a time when the Beach Boys were again on the rise, thanks to Carl's return and the increasingly professional approach to their concerts.

On April 5, 1983, Secretary of the Interior James Watt stated that the Beach Boys would not be welcome at the Washington Monument to play a free, Fourth of July show because, in the past, rock groups had attracted the "wrong element." Watt's attack was actually aimed at rock music audiences, but the Beach Boys themselves became a cause célèbre, and Watt never really knew what hit him. By shooting from the hip at the group's supporters, Watt had created the kind of career impact that can never be bought or faked. By presidential fiat, the Beach Boys became *the* American band, playing a show at the White House for President Reagan and the First Lady.

In mid-1981, the Beach Boys had looked to be near death. Thanks to the media firestorm surrounding Watt's remarks, their career was full of life, and they were now ready to seriously think about reactivating their recording career. With Brian healthier and the commercial debacles of the seventies receding into the past, the Beach Boys and the record company could approach the studio with renewed enthusiasm. Would

Brian be ready? Landy's discipline had Brian working. And while the first songs (e.g., 'The Boogie's Back in Town') were simpler than much of Brian's previous work, the "return to the roots, doo-wop" vibe of 'It's Just a Matter of Time,' with its flavor of the Beatles' 'This Boy', showed that Brian was tuned in to his hitmaking station. Nothing astonishing yet, but in his work, Brian was again exposing the raw nerve of the lonely life that he leads.

And if his writing wasn't yet inspired, his live performances were beginning to elicit excitement. In the past, his mere presence had earned standing ovations. Now, his singing could stir the crowd, be it his belting out of the new songs or his solid presence on the classics. As 1983 came to an end, there finally seemed to be reason to be optimistic about both the Beach Boys' and Brian's future.

That positivity was short-lived. On December 28, 1983, three days after checking himself out of a substance-abuse program in Santa Monica, California, Dennis Wilson drowned in the waters of the Marina Del Rey harbor where he had often lived on his beloved boat, the once aptly named *Harmony*.

The details of Dennis's "final days" will be found in other books about the Beach Boys. I won't dwell on the painful, pathetic, tragic end to a wild roller coaster of a life. Daryl Dragon, who worked with Dennis during his most inspired period, remembers Dennis's "willingness to express the real sensitivity that most people work a lifetime to hide away," even though, as Daryl points out, Dennis had trouble reconciling his "sensitivity with the macho thing he saw with groups like the Stones."

Ironically, in death, Dennis was at the center of a new Love–Wilson battle. The Wilson family, led by Carl and Dennis's ex-wives and children, hoped for a burial next to the brothers' father, Murry. Shawn Love Wilson insisted that Dennis wished to be buried at sea.

As Dennis's widow, Shawn got her way, and through presidential intervention, Dennis was buried at sea in January 1984. One simple phrase described how the Beach Boys felt about his death: "He will be missed."

As one former employee of the group believes, "when Dennis died, the soul of the Beach Boys died with him. Even though no part of a group is greater than the sum total, they are still all diminished. There was a certain magic when they were all together, and you can't break that circle without breaking the magic."

After a suitable period of mourning, the Beach Boys returned to their work obligations, sobered but determined to carry on. If losing Dennis had taken away the spontaneity and sex appeal from the live shows, the band could now perform at a more emotionally even level.

By the time of their triumphant return to the Washington Monument on the Fourth of July the following year, it seemed that the Beach Boys had put Dennis's death behind them, and for one day at least, had found the perfect substitute drummer—Ringo Starr.

In 1984, the Beach Boys enjoyed their status as a full-fledged concert attraction, and during the Los Angeles Olympics, the Beach Boys were part of the festivities as patriotism peaked during what were called the most successful Olympics ever.

One of the bizarre incidents that makes the Beach Boys' story always unpredictable occurred in August at the 1984 Republican Convention. According to the *L.A. Times*, the Saturday before the convention began, the Beach Boys played a $100-a-person fashion show as a promotional event for the host city of Dallas. On Sunday, August 19, Brian and two other men—whom the news report called "medical assistants employed by the group"—were arrested when they wandered into a high-security area without credentials. As the *L.A. Times* reported, the two men with Brian were arrested for possession of "bags of pills found in their pockets." Dr. Landy has refused to explain or comment upon the newspaper account to this writer.

Nineteen eighty-four saw the Beach Boys return to the studio in earnest. An earlier attempt to make a record with a collection of outside producers had fallen through. When it appeared that Brian wasn't going to step up as producer, the Beach Boys and CBS Records knew they had to find somebody to fill his shoes.

In the late 1970s, Bruce Johnston and Curt Boettcher had co-produced an album by the British group Sailor. The engineer on that project was Steve Levine, a young Englishman who by 1984 was the producer of the multiplatinum records of Boy George's Culture Club. Bruce suggested to CBS that Levine might be the right producer for the Beach Boys, and Levine eventually agreed, signing on to become the first non–Beach Boy since Nik Venet to produce the group. (A curious footnote: Levine had been assistant engineer on Chris Rainbow's 1978 song 'Dear Brian,' not only the best Brian Wilson tribute record ever made, but a track which also captured the Beach Boys' studio sound as well as any record in the past ten years, even better than many of the group's efforts.)

Throughout 1984, Levine worked extensively with Carl (and Brian, too) in his London studio, laying down instrumental tracks to create state-of-the-art, digitally recorded sounds. By the fall, Levine had recorded enough basic tracks that the Beach Boys could begin vocal sessions in L.A.

When Brian Wilson and the Beach Boys sing as they know how, it is, as Brian once called it, "the sound of heaven." Unfortunately, if Brian doesn't write great songs, it doesn't really matter how well they're singing. It all starts with Brian's chord changes, and those he wrote for this album, as he himself admitted, were very simple.

In a recent interview, Brian said he has written seventy songs in the past two years. The ones he's performed in concert and on the new album aren't of the complexity we expect from Brian. Having had his more adventurous material rejected in the past, he may see no point in expressing his ambitious artistic vision.

However, before the return of Dr. Landy, inspired by Dennis in 1981/1982, Brian was making exciting, deeply spiritual music on songs like 'City Blues' and 'Oh, Lord.' Other reports indicate that Brian has been writing beautiful ballads in a 'Caroline, No' mold. If, as I claim, Brian still has his incredible gift, why isn't it evidencing itself publicly?

The convoluted excuse for his recent mediocrity is that, because Brian resents Landy's control—who, according to the *L.A. Times*, Brian playfully calls "Napoleon"—Brian may be hiding his creativity so as not to let Dr. Landy get credit for returning him to the state of "musical genius." Brian's passivity generally means that he won't initiate a direct confrontation, but this bizarre theory can't really account for Brian's unimpressive compositions.

More likely, Brian has been stockpiling his best new songs for a solo album, which may be recorded and released within the year. In the fall of '84, Brian recorded demos for eight new songs. According to an informed source, these tunes were not offered to the group for inclusion on the album.

At this point, it may be necessary to explain the ambiguities inherent in Dr. Landy's dealings with the Beach Boys. Whether his decisions are right or wrong, whether he's solely concerned with his patient or also interested in feathering his own nest, Dr. Landy is helping Brian establish an independent beachhead away from the group. For Brian, the choice has always been "be a Beach Boy or stay in bed." Working with Dr. Landy has emerged as a third alternative, and for the time being, it may be the best of the three. While Landy's actions may cause tension in his relations with the group and CBS Records, at least somebody is exercising power on Brian's behalf. Landy's determination and ambition may get him fired, but he has a lot of nerve, and he's on Brian's side. The two men show a curious devotion to each other; unfortunately, his lyrics are terrible. Brian writes far better lyrics.

In the last three years, Brian's spirited singing has brought his personality back into the music. If he brings that energy to his solo album, it will be a success. Events will someday make me a fool or a prophet, but I'm part of a small cult that has complete faith that the creative resurrection of Brian is imminent, and that he will always be able to move us with his music. For Brian Wilson fanatics like myself, the long-awaited prospect of an official solo record has been the pot of gold at the end of the musical rainbow and the hoped-for reaffirmation of Brian's renewed creative interest.

However, regardless of Brian's solo activity, 1985 and 1986 shape up as the Beach Boys' last go-round in the big top for a long time. Nineteen eighty-five began with the release of Van Halen lead singer David Lee Roth's version of 'California Girls,' complete with an unashamedly salacious and sexist video and beautiful vocals from Carl Wilson and Christopher Cross. The record literally jumped up the charts to #3, the highest position of a Brian Wilson/Mike Love song since 'Good Vibrations' was #1 back in 1966.

On the evening of January 19, 1985, the Beach Boys were the lone rock group to take part in the nationally televised Presidential Inaugural Gala. Watching at home, when they were introduced, I looked at the screen and silently counted to myself, "1, 2, 3, 4, 5. Who's missing?" I wondered. I'm still not used to Dennis's absence, but the Beach Boys' moving a cappella rendition of 'Their Hearts Were Full of Spring' was their best public moment in nearly two decades. When Brian put his arm around Carl, one could see and hear the magic of the Beach Boys.

Growing interest in the group was reflected in every medium—from books to film. In early '85, a terrific hundred and three minute collection of the group's television and film appearances, *The Beach Boys: An American*

Band, was released by Vestron Video. If you've read this far in the book, you'll definitely want to seek out the tape because the fabulous film clips, particularly from the *Pet Sounds/SMiLE* era, are visually fascinating when you already know the story.

However, it's no more than *The Beach Boys' Greatest Hits* on video. The narrative offers no strong point of view or historical context, and the inaccuracies, omissions and unconscionable sound remixing make this tape a sadly wasted opportunity to show how important Brian's music is. As a historical document, it's better than nothing, but not by much. Even some of the Beach Boys, who were heavily involved in this project, have expressed dissatisfaction with the results.

The Beach Boys, meanwhile, were back on the road, and turning their attention to the memory of a lost brother. In late March, the group played a benefit concert in Dennis's name, with proceeds earmarked for the Special Olympics (Dennis's favorite charity) and a newly established Dennis Wilson Memorial Special Olympics fund to help athletes with disabilities and to promote medical research. At a press conference announcing their plans for the show, Mike Love said, "Dennis had a lot of personal problems, but the very best thing about him was his compassion."

Brian, too, was doing his bit for charity. He made the first live solo appearance of his career at the "Trouble in Paradise" benefit concert to raise money for the homeless, and his brief set of 'Da Doo Run Run,' 'Sloop John B' and 'California Girls' was well received.

In May 1985, I saw Brian at another benefit, this one for the Malibu Emergency Room. For this headlining stint, he was in great shape, and his five-song set was dominated by strong, confident vocals. In addition to the three songs he did at the "Trouble" show, Brian added two new tunes, 'I'm So Lonely' and 'Male Ego,' the latter available only as the B-side of the 'Getcha Back' single. His performance that night showed off his adult voice, and if it's not as sweet and innocent as his youthful timbre, Brian is now working with power and energy. His full vocal presence is much more important than his choice of pitch.

The most memorable musical moment of the night was Brian's singing on 'Sloop John B.' Onstage with rock veterans Stephen Stills, Dave Mason, and John Stewart (whose Kingston Trio version of 'Sloop' had inspired the Beach Boys), Brian really came alive. His lead vocal was clear and perfect, and his high harmony "de-doo-be-doos" were the most exciting notes he's sung in years. For a few magical minutes, he was lost in the music, and he took the audience with him. In nearly two decades of being a fan, it was one of my true emotional highlights.

Between that show and the 'Getcha Back' single, my hopes had been raised that Brian would play a dominant role on the new album. Brian's singing on 'Getcha Back' was a true delight to hear, and his vocals turned a most mediocre song into a very listenable hit record. I'd never expected to hear Brian's high falsetto on record like that, and it raised expectations that the new LP would indeed mark the real return of Brian.

Released in June 1985, *The Beach Boys*, the group's first new album in over five years, was an initial disappointment because if it has any Beach Boy's personal stamp on it, it's Carl's, not Brian's. But in comparison to their last five albums, *The Beach Boys* is both a commercial step forward and proof positive that when they work on their vocals, the result is enjoyable music. It's their most coherent group record in over a decade, and their first album since *Holland* (1973) that has the potential to win them new fans and satisfy the old ones.

'Getcha Back,' released in May, jumped into the Top Forty before peaking at #26, and the album also quickly moved into *Billboard*'s Top 100, but the jury is still out as to whether this will be *the* record that could make the band something more than a nostalgia act. Ironically, one of the reasons 'Getcha Back' might not have done better is that it so strongly echoes the hits from the sixties.

And while there's really nothing on *The Beach Boys* that can stand alongside their greatest work, there's also very little that's embarrassing, a fact that all by itself may help reignite their recording career. The main question to be answered in the sales department is whether a Beach Boys album can succeed without any great Brian Wilson melodies.

Whether the album is a hit or not, Steve Levine has done a fine job. The vocals are full and impressive, and given the limitations of the material, most of the tracks hold up under repeated listening. Even though Brian's songs, as he himself admits, are not much more than simple song-writing exercises, Levine's gotten a lot out of the tunes with a clever harmonica here and a ballsy sax intro there.

The unqualified musical highlights for me are Carl's wondrous 'Where I Belong' and his inventive 'It's Gettin' Late,' both of which should become radio and concert staples. Throughout the disk, Carl's vocals stand out.

What's missing on the record is more of Brian's spirited lead vocals, the kind he's been doing in concert. On 'Getcha Back,' Brian reportedly worked hard on the backing vocals out of respect for his old friend, co-writer Terry Melcher. Brian's background singing, particularly his Billy Joel-like "wo, wo, wos," shows how vital his musical presence is to the group's sound and commercial appeal. There's a new-found exuberance in his vocals, kind of an adult *Wild Honey* middle-class R&B, perfect for today when the music industry is dominated by black sounds. But then again, Brian has always been ahead of the game, as he demonstrated on the (unreleased) big-band *Adult Child* LP in 1976, and on the synthesizer/drum-machine production *Love You* in 1977.

With Steve Levine at the controls, the group has made an album that fits in with today's commercial style, not tomorrow's. 'Male Ego' doesn't have great lyrics, and in no way could it fit on *The Beach Boys*, but it's full of fun and spirit, the key ingredients. I'd prefer an album of those kinds of tunes because they make the connection from Brian's heart to the listener's gut. The calculated appeal of *The Beach Boys* isn't wrong; it would just be more interesting if the group would follow Brian's instincts. Then again, he has to be willing to lead.

What there is of Brian on the new album shows that the visceral element in Brian's music remains so strong that even his slightest songs jump out. Even when his chord changes aren't that great, Brian's sound can be emotionally overwhelming. The lack of Brian's strong hand may be why this record probably won't have that timeless appeal.

For eighteen years, the Beach Boys have been faced with an insurmountable problem: record buyers compare the new albums to the classic hits. What might make this record the exception is the remaining joker in the deck.

How might a hit record affect the group's future? If it does well, the Beach Boys may see they can make it without Brian, and that might free him to pursue his muse without commercial constraints. Or the group might push Brian to produce one final "ultimate" Beach Boys' record, or a hit might give Brian and Carl the impetus to make a record that would be more artistically expressive. If past history means anything, the Beach Boys have always been most united in failure, and success seems to be the catalyst to disagreement.

It's really unreasonable to expect or demand that Brian produce material similar to what he did in his youth. That's not what interests him. But the great old songs will continue to get in the way until Brian comes up with great new songs, because without Brian, strange as it sounds, the Beach Boys' records can only simulate the Beach Boys. As engineer Steve Desper puts it, "the sensitivity that the old music had came from Brian, and it won't be there unless he puts it in. The Beach Boys, as an act, have learned to perform with sincerity. Sensitivity can be acted out. That will fool the mass of people for a long while. But when you compare 'acted out' sensitivity with the real thing, you blow its cover." In other words, there's a big difference between emoting and emotion.

Off and on, for over a decade, Brian has remained mired in a musical malaise. The question has often been posed, to the Beach Boys and Brian alike, as to when the public could, if ever, expect to hear records like the hits from the 1960s. Writing songs to satisfy others wouldn't work, as Brian noted: "Cranking it out doesn't satisfy *me*."

In the future, Brian will feel the pressure to produce more complete works than just a song fragment here and a pretty vocal part there. Everybody wants the full Brian Wilson treatment applied to new music. And if I'm not just offering false hope—if what I'm told is indeed accurate—if Brian's creative spark has truly been rekindled, then we can all look forward to new Brian Wilson music filling not only Beach Boys' albums but Brian's own records.

The truth is, when Brian sits down at the piano, he can't help but write beautiful music. However, translating his ethereal chords into hit songs is a task that Brian may not be interested in or capable of. It will be Brian's decision as to how much he wants to work within the constraints of the Beach Boys.

The momentum of public interest should carry them through 1986, their twenty-fifth-anniversary year, but it's hard to imagine the group continuing with its current lineup for much longer, although the same could have been said ten years ago. The listening public is receptive to a "great" new Beach Boys' album, and a complete Beach Boys' rebirth depends on a new record not being an expensive disappointment.

Nineteen eighty-six will either be a new beginning or another codetta. Either way, what will probably always exist is a Beach Boys' performing unit, in which Mike, like Frankie Valli and the Four Seasons, could carry on as long as the fans are eager to hear the hits and the $urf is up.

REQUIEM FOR THE BEACH BOY

In November 1983, after the Beach Boys' opening night concert at the Universal Amphitheatre, I spoke with Brian Wilson backstage. During a long conversation, Brian asked me whether I liked the way the group had performed 'Surfer Girl.' As their harmonies had been mediocre, and as I've never deliberately hurt Brian's ultrasensitive feelings, my answer was evasive. But it was also the truth.

"Brian, I don't know why, but it was on that song that I missed Dennis the most. You know, the way he stands at the microphone, with his hand in his ear, his eyes closed, singing and swaying with the music. It's just not the same when he's not there."

Dennis would never perform with the Beach Boys again. He died just a month later, weeks after his thirty-ninth birthday. And if you had seen Dennis in the last year, his death really wasn't a surprise.

I last saw him in April 1983 at the Meadowlands Arena in New Jersey. It was obvious that something serious was wrong. He could barely speak, let alone sing, and his once muscular surfer's body seemed doughy. Describing it to friends, I called it "beer bloat."

Whatever the L.A. County coroner finally concludes, my belief is that Dennis's death wasn't from alcohol or drug abuse so much as a cumulative overdose of life. Nobody I've ever known lived a more intense existence. When Dennis Wilson worked, it was nonstop, for days at a time, until he would collapse from exhaustion on a studio control-room couch. And when he played—well, let's just say that in recent years, he was more a "player" than a worker.

The night Dennis died, a South Bay newspaper reporter asked me to characterize Dennis. I told him that Dennis's most fascinating personality facet was his intense curiosity. Dennis wanted to know everything through *experience*, and he attacked life with a combination of blind faith and childlike innocence. He lived his life with a freshness and vitality; all that really mattered was this one, wonderful moment of *now*. Dennis was a perpetual bad child, but he could always win your forgiveness with his smile.

Incredibly, it was not an act. Dennis had never been taught how to deceive people, and he was genuine. In his dealings with the media, Dennis

290

was easily the most candid and revealing member of his family and the group. A rare combination—intensity and honesty; and Dennis didn't lie—except maybe to himself. As with Keith Moon and other dead rock stars, chronology is relatively meaningless. Dennis Wilson lived more life in a month than most people do in a lifetime; we need not feel badly just because he died so young. We mourn not for his youth but for the waste. He had much to give, and he only tapped a fraction of that. On albums like *Sunflower*, Dennis bloomed, and his emotional artistry would later see its first (and last) major expression on his impressive debut album, *Pacific Ocean Blue*. His music was adult and maturing, and there was the promise of more to come. Sadly, he never really knew how much his music was appreciated.

Dennis seemed uncomfortable with his talent (who wouldn't be, in the shadow of Brian?), and while insisting that his brother "Brian is the Beach Boys," Dennis overlooked the fact that he, Dennis, was *the* Beach Boy. He, with his sandy hair and winning grin, was the one the girls screamed for.

In his personal life, Dennis acted as if he feared nothing, including death. Some people said he was self-destructive, but from what I saw, Dennis approached almost everything he did as a challenge. Maybe he pushed himself beyond the limit so that he could prove that for himself there were no limits. And for Dennis, there was so much to try that it was inevitable that he would cross the boundaries of "acceptable behavior."

Not that this is an apologia for Dennis. He could be rude and irresponsible. But when he was sober, Dennis often exhibited to his fans a modest charm and unexpected thoughtfulness. He made everybody he was with think they were the most important person in the world at that single second. He was sincere, but, like a child, would move on to a new toy. Maybe worst of all, Dennis didn't know how to say *no*.

There were qualities he kept hidden, too. Perhaps most moving was the remark one of Dennis's children made after Dennis died. "Mommy," he cried, "things will never be the same again. No one can make me laugh like Daddy can."

When I heard that Dennis had died, I was determined not to dwell on the sadness; and when *BAM* magazine asked me to write a reflective memoir on what Dennis Wilson meant to California music, I began to flash back to the times when I had seen him or been alone with him. Like the day I had watched him vigorously perform his promotional duties for his pride, *Pacific Ocean Blue*; that night, he took me and a bunch of other writers into Brother Studio to sing on 'He's a Bum,' teaching us that making records was hard work.

Later that night, Dennis was at the piano in his beachside house. He pounded out 'Heroes and Villains' at the piano, and then, smoothly and with a musical wink, moved into 'River Deep, Mountain High.' By three in the morning, he had me writing lyrics to a new song of his. And as the night wore on and I fought sleep, he told me a little about his time with Charles Manson, and the fear he still lived with. As dawn broke, he was on the phone, rousting friends.

There were also the concerts in the early seventies when Dennis would sit at the piano and humbly play his beautiful, haunting love songs like 'Barbara' and 'I've Got a Friend,' as if to say, "I know they're not as good as Brian's, but . . . " Or at the end of the show, when caught up in the crowd's excitement, he peeled bandages off his hand and jumped onto his rightful perch—the drums.

I certainly don't claim to have been a close friend of Dennis Wilson's, but the time I've spent with him and his music has always been precious. I hope that I've absorbed just a little of his spirit. He was *alive*.

In death, I pray he finds his peace.

(Note: This section is adapted from an article that originally appeared in *BAM* (*Bay Area Music*) magazine in January 1984.)

CHAPTER 15

RETROSPECTIVE, 1985

I USED TO HAVE THIS STRANGE DREAM. THE BEACH BOYS ARE PLAYING A concert at the Hollywood Bowl on one of those perfect Southern California afternoons. Just before singing 'Good Vibrations,' Carl Wilson announces that this is the final concert the Beach Boys will ever play. Usually, I woke up just as the tears began streaming down my face.

It's been nearly eight years since the Beach Boys last invaded my sleep, eight years since I created a labor of love originally titled *The Beach Boys and the California Myth*, the updated version of which you're reading now. From the quietude of time gone by, my publisher asked me to look back upon and enhance what I consider the most important work I've ever done. The time has come to look within myself to reveal how my perception of the Beach Boys has been tempered by events of the past eight years.

The key difference is that now, instead of writing about the Beach Boys in a feverish determination to "save" Brian Wilson, I more calmly examine what has become a dormant although still easily aroused passion. How did it all happen? Why did I *have to* write a book about Brian Wilson and the Beach Boys? It will add to your appreciation of both the original text and this update if you understand why I was originally driven to create this personal monument to Brian Wilson.

Like many of my generation, I was a Beach Boys fan as a teenager, but the Beatles were my musical gods in the sixties. By the end of the decade, the Beach Boys' continued existence had become a cultural anomaly. In the fall of 1971, I read Tom Nolan's two-part investigation of the Beach Boys in *Rolling Stone*, and from that moment on, I was dedicated to exploring the real story of Brian Wilson. Based on just that article, I developed the naive belief that if I told what I, in my obviously limited view, saw as the truth about Brian's situation, the people responsible for his creative "imprisonment" would suddenly see the light and free him to make "important" music again. This unswerving, self-serving faith, coupled with what I soon discovered to be an unparalleled body of musical work, carried me through the completion of this book.

What I couldn't know in 1971 and wouldn't learn for many years was that I was destined to join a long list of people who had tried to alter Brian's determinedly downward course. What I also didn't fully understand was that there was nothing "wrong" with Brian. It's just hard to heal a heartbreak.

In 1977, I began publishing *Pet Sounds* magazine, a periodical devoted to promoting the music of Brian Wilson and the Beach Boys. That's when I started to meet Brian's friends, a handful of true believers who were greatly concerned with Brian's well-being. It was then I first realized that I was not alone in my quest; each of these people had a plan to "save" Brian. The essential truth I wouldn't grasp until years after I had finished the book was that Brian didn't really want to be saved, and that the solutions we offered could never relieve the pressures affecting this troubled man and the puzzling contradictions with which he lived. Our long-term artistic vision for Brian often obscured the present-day reality of Brian's enormous sense of responsibility to his family.

I dreamed of writing a book in which I could expound upon Brian Wilson's life and times but didn't think the world at large cared. It took a six-month chain of coincidences, triggered by the first edition of *Pet Sounds*, to lead me to a book contract in the fall of 1977. It was the opportunity of a lifetime. With three months to produce the promised revelations, I attacked my work with missionary zeal, with my unbridled, self-righteous moral outrage in high gear. After all, I was part of a crusade to free the man who made music that was as close as I had come to adult religious experience.

Dangerously, at least in terms of my journalistic credibility, I had become intertwined in the inner sanctum, and while I had been admitted to shine the printed light on Brian's circumstances, my objectivity, if I'd ever had any, quickly evaporated. The cause was to help Brian as a person and a creator, and I was to be the messenger. Presumptuously, I decided that my role was to be his unofficial Boswell and self-appointed scribbling savior. I was determined to tell Brian's story *and* change his life.

In advocacy journalism, there is an almost fatal tendency for the writer to give greater weight to evidence supporting his basic hypothesis; undoubtedly, despite my best efforts, there are places in the book that are one-sided and could have profited if the Beach Boys had been willing to offer more input.

Not that they could have told me the deep truth. They couldn't afford to and maintain their image. For the "truth," I was forced to rely on those who had lived inside the Beach Boys' universe. As a biographer, my goal was to put together a fair representation of the Beach Boys' story, but that job was made most difficult because nobody, not even the Beach Boys themselves, really agrees on much of anything. The realization that a definitive history was almost impossible helped confirm my belief that the only tale worth telling was the life of Brian—of what had happened to him and his "gift."

I pursued the "storyline" relentlessly, in dozens of interviews over hundreds of hours, augmenting these personal recollections with several meetings with the Wilson/Love clan plus the vast library of previously published and broadcast material. Capitol Records' publicist Earl Leaf's private archives yielded unexpected insight into Brian's early years.

In researching the book, I came to call myself "the Beach Boys' Exorcist." People who had been involved with Brian and the group were hesitant to reflect upon what had been a very painful period in their lives. Dwelling on the frustration and hurt of working with the Beach Boys was like psychiatric treatment, and, for many, it seemed that telling me their truth had great therapeutic value, particularly when the tape recorder was turned off. As memory is often imperfect and self-serving, I had to exercise extreme caution to weed out comments born out of bitterness or personal disappointment. The "truth" in this story often proved to be elusive.

Out of this endless research psychodrama came the original edition of this book, the tip of the iceberg of the story, completed in the midst of the most public squabble the Beach Boys have ever had. If one of my intentions was to counterbalance the public image of the Beach Boys as the harmonious gods of 'Good Vibrations,' the group did the job itself, tearing down their facade with a bitter internecine feud that became public in *Rolling Stone* in 1977.

This book was first published in late 1978, after two tension-packed years in which the group had almost completely wasted the momentum of their comeback. More than that, a career's worth of goodwill was slipping away. The Beach Boys appeared to be a dying entity.

I had been hoping that a great public outcry would force those in control of Brian's life to relinquish their power to more benevolent forces . . . that the public exposure of a private hell would change Brian's reality for the better. Of course, the book had virtually no immediate impact. But my disappointment was muted by a turn of events that I had dreamed of, but never envisioned really happening.

The book opened the door that allowed *me* to become part of Brian's extended support group, and Brian and I became friends. Once he saw that I wasn't out to "get" him in print, our encounters turned from awkward conversation to rewarding meetings. As his wariness faded, he would play me a new song in his home, or chauffeur me to a Sunset Strip record store.

The private reaction of the rest of the Beach Boys' world was a mix of anger, resentment, jealousy and resignation. At a Beach Boys' fan convention, perhaps I was being oversensitive, but it felt like Mike Love was trying to burn a hole in my head with an icy stare; and it seemed, to me at least, that he began his speech with acerbic remarks aimed in my direction. Heads in the room turned to see my reaction. Al Jardine wondered why his role in the Beach Boys' story had been glossed over, then refused to talk to me. Brian's brothers found it hard to read about their dominating, unpredictable father. Even though mother Audree Wilson was a primary source for the book, she was naturally hurt by the close examination of her family's turbulent history. Possibly most hurt by the book was Brian's ex-wife, Marilyn. The public dissection of their difficult marriage inevitably seemed cruel.

However, I think the Beach Boys' unhappiness comes more from what I implied than what I wrote. I've tried to "spill the beans" without resorting to the often embarrassing specifics. I detailed private behavior only to explain how personal problems overwhelmed Brian's musical ability. To those who know the secret truths, my book may have seemed to be a tremendous invasion of privacy. Those readers were projecting their own experiences into my between-the-lines commentary. I guess when you have a lot of skeletons in your closet, it makes you nervous if somebody starts rummaging around in there, even if they're only looking for a broom.

Because of my obsession with the "truth," when my publisher asked me to do this update, my first call was to offer the Beach Boys the opportunity to correct any errors I made. My attempts to get their comments for this edition fell upon angry ears. From what I understood, the main reason for the Beach Boys not being a bigger part of this book is that several of the members of the group didn't agree with what I've written. The reader should be aware that while some of the Beach Boys' extended family supports this book, some find my conclusions to be wrong.

It's too bad that the non-Wilson faction of the band so heartily disapproves because more "inside" insight could have helped me avoid overdramatizing Brian's story. However, even without the group's full participation, I believe I've accomplished my main objective. I trust that in telling Brian's story, your appreciation of his music will be enhanced. When we fully comprehend the mountains Brian has climbed to bring us his gift, it helps us understand why he might be reluctant to climb again.

After the book was first published in 1978, a number of Beach Boys fans wondered if I even liked the group, given the tone of my writing and my view of their past decade. The only way I can answer that is by explaining my motives in this section and to be as hard and judgmental on myself and my work as I've been in my analysis of the Beach Boys' career. I recall how, when I began the book in 1977, I already felt I knew too much, but the pain of Brian's life has made my love for his music even deeper. Besides, his reaction to the book has made it all worthwhile.

As one of his friends explained to me, Brian acknowledged the book's worth by allowing me into his life. It is always difficult for Brian to verbalize his feelings, but in 1979, he seemed to be saying, "I know what you've done, and I appreciate it, and the only way I can show it is by letting you get to know me." Ever so sweetly, Brian would ask, with serious concern, how the book was doing and express disappointment that it wasn't selling as well as my Bee Gees biography. He seemed satisfied when I reminded him that his book was done out of pure love.

Relationships with Brian are hot and cold affairs. There was frequent contact followed by long stretches of silence, but he was always happy to see or speak with my wife and me. He welcomed our friends who wanted to meet their musical hero.

At Christmas in 1979, we visited Brian in the hospital where he was spending the better part of the winter just prior to his divorce. The next year, Brian was "home for the holidays," and we set up a Christmas tree with all the trimmings in his otherwise spiritless, empty, rented house.

One of the most unusual visits was when Brian came to my home to borrow a tape of one of his unreleased songs. He wanted to work on a new arrangement of the still-unreleased 'My Solution' and needed to hear how the old version went. I'd never told Brian about my tape collection. He just *knew* that I had it. Brian's behavior consistently demonstrated an uncanny omniscience which extended far beyond his musical gift and was most surprising, given his public playing of possum.

His sensitivity to life is so acute that even the smallest, unintentional slight can cause unbearable pain. That knowledge makes being his friend one of the most difficult experiences of my life. I'm not complaining. I cherish the times when Brian called upon me for help, and for all the joy his music has given me, it was a small price to pay. And now that I have experienced his discomfort on an intimate basis, I measure my words with the weight of knowing how easily he can be hurt.

Originally inspired by George Gershwin, Brian once noted that he felt that both he and Gershwin made their major musical statements in their mid-twenties. But his own personal masterpiece, *Pet Sounds*, unlike Gershwin's *Rhapsody in Blue*, was released to a heartrendingly lukewarm reception. At twenty-four, Brian's revolutionary *SMiLE* was stillborn, and Brian has never fully recovered from the double disappointment. In a sense, Brian, like his idol Gershwin, died young. Except it wasn't a brain tumor that "killed" Brian; it was a broken spirit.

Finally, my long-ago dream about the end of the Beach Boys makes sense. I once feared the group's internal struggles would diminish the public's appreciation of Brian's music. I should have known better. Through the years, the Beach Boys' solid and sometimes spectacular success as a concert attraction has shown that the sounds created by Brian Wilson are indestructible. And fifty years from now, when musical historians remove the music from the social context, they will see that what Brian accomplished in the studio all by himself makes him, not Paul McCartney or John Lennon or Bob Dylan, the most important musical artist of this era. The *feeling* of Brian's durable music has outlasted all the songs of revolution.

As the Beach Boys themselves approach their twenty-fifth anniversary, it's almost inappropriate to discuss the timelessness of the music when the group's performances during the past decade often are a bit like a mobile jukebox. But the power of the music is so strong that, as I've finally come to accept, it no longer matters whether the men onstage like each other or hit the high notes or even want to be performing songs they've sung literally thousands of times. The Beach Boys have gone beyond the normal rules of show business; the flat singing and shaky harmonies are irrelevant to an audience that hears the records, calling up the soundtrack of our minds, playing our personal videos as the Beach Boys provide exactly what is demanded of them—their physical presence.

In a world of plastic and ersatz goods, of Beatlemania and *Dream Girls*, the fact that those are the *real* Beach Boys onstage seems to be more than enough. And that's because the Beach Boys are no longer just a group of men standing on a stage playing those old familiar anthems. Rather, the Beach Boys have become year-round summer—shimmering, irresponsible summer—the same way that Bing Crosby and 'White Christmas' auto-matically evoke memories of holiday seasons past. Even those who know that the Beach Boys are unexciting, chauvinistic relics can't resist the music. It's almost un-American not to like 'em.

So, as an audience, we are left with two very different, almost separate Beach Boys stories. One is about a band that during the last three years has re-emerged from obscurity to become everybody's, including the President's, favorite group. That's a story about winners, and America loves to love a winner.

The other Beach Boys' odyssey follows guiding force Brian Wilson through his up-and-down life. That's the story of this book—which makes the Beach Boys' resurgence a bittersweet tale. Having been on intimate terms with failure, the Beach Boys have finally and understandably accepted their niche in our culture. The price of that commercial capitulation, of playing only for the crowds, has almost completely obscured Brian's still-revolutionary artistic vision.

To their credit, they're still trying, with their first new album in over five years. Whether or not that record succeeds makes little difference to the cultural shrine the Beach Boys have become. Even if they don't have any new hits to sing, their old ones will always attract an audience. There are few things in this world that can evoke simple pleasure, and the Beach Boys, despite all their karmic baggage, can still do that. A portable California to the world, our American band provides blissful fantasies in an ever

more stressful environment. The Beach Boys are the universal representative of an old-fashioned fun that is endlessly attractive and difficult to
recapture. The vows have been taken. For better or worse, the Beach Boys
have become the "Spirit of America."

David Leaf
Santa Monica, California, May 1985

SHADES OF GREY

Fourteen years after I first became interested in Brian Wilson as something
other than a hitmaker, my search for the "truth" in the Beach Boys story
has come to an end with the understanding that no such thing exists. If
their story is a puzzle with a million pieces, I've collected several thousand
and painted an impressionistic picture of the troubled life of an artist.

Since this book was first published, many people have asked me how
it would be different were I writing it today. Let me assure the reader
that there is little of substance I would change. I believe that what I wrote
in 1977 is as valid today as it was then.

However, I now know that, with Brian and the Beach Boys, there are
no black and white answers, only unanswerable questions and shades of
grey. How much harm did LSD and alcohol and cocaine do? How much
permanent damage was caused by the prescribed tranquilizers given to
Brian in the late seventies and early eighties? What's left of his incredible
gift and will he ever fully use it again? This section of the book is designed
to address those issues, based on the new information I've gathered since
this book was first published.

I once drew a picture of Brian as a prisoner of circumstances, the victim
of an insensitive world. That's a big part of the story, but now I know
that there is a side of Brian that needs to be manipulated. Having seen
first-hand the frustrations of dealing with a person as powerful as Brian,
I no longer self-righteously indict the world of being "bad to Brian,"
when it's apparent that *Brian* has been hardest on himself.

Actually, it's amazing that Brian withstood the heat for so long before
caving in. Too often, Brian has been viewed as a money machine, and has
felt strong resentment when he has refused to use his "gift" to fuel the
bank accounts of those less talented. Complete retreat is the only way

Brian knows to prevent people from "using" him. But what I failed to make clear is that Brian not only allows leechlike behavior, but by eccentrically not taking control of his life, he virtually guarantees that there will always be those who attach themselves and literally drain him dry of his creative resources and his money.

It's always been a cruel irony that Brian, who may bring more pure, uncomplicated joy to the world than any other contemporary musician, has found so little personal happiness in his achievement.

That may be why Brian is so reluctant to put himself fully into the music again. However, the special dispensation artists receive disappears when the hits stop coming. Failure turns eccentricity into weirdness and maybe even into insanity.

Brian's hiding from reality and avoidance of responsibility are not healthy operating modes—however understandable they may be. Brian was always "different," but for a time, he was in control of himself and his work. The flip side for Brian has been total inaction. But if physical health, constant music making and commercial obligations didn't make him happy in 1964, why should new success be his goal when success only tightens the noose?

Will Brian ever get psychological treatment that will address his problems without simultaneous re-entry into the pressure cooker? Dr. Landy has stated that he's working to give Brian a choice, but does Brian have the right to choose who his creative collaborators will be? In the healing, there also seems to be a great amount of wheeling and dealing. As Brian bounces back and forth between forced participation and numerous cop-outs, one waits for an alternative that Brian can sustain for the balance of his life. Maybe it's naive to think that Brian will ever be on solid ground, but we can hope that, creatively, Brian will become more consistently active.

One former employee of the group theorizes that Brian's relative creative disappearance since 1970, and particularly in 1973–1975, can be partly attributed to the diminished presence, then death, of Murry Wilson. "After Murry died, the scary motivation that had made Brian work left the planet, and Brian felt like he could relax for the first time in thirty years. That's the kind of power Murry exercised over his sons."

This same person also speculates that "Brian's come to the realization that he needs outside discipline. He has no self-motivation. With Landy, he's organized and people are giving him a purpose. The effect of Landy is Murry's, but in a more genteel way."

This is a key point. For fifteen years, everybody has wanted Brian to try. Only Dr. Landy has been able to make Brian actually do it. Dr. Landy moved Brian out of his slothful world into a universe of more meaningful and stimulating experience, giving Brian the chance to fill up his artistic tank.

The harder question to answer is how much Landy, like Murry, actually helps or hurts in the long run. As one associate of the group recalls, "Murry only appeared to be dominating, like a blowfish. But there was no substance. His mere presence could disrupt a recording session without adding anything to it. When he would finally leave, it could take an hour before the guys had sufficiently recovered to get back to work."

For the Beach Boys, there remains an unresolved dichotomy; as there was with Murry, there is also conflict with Dr. Landy. One of the prime causes of this tension may be Landy's determination to separate Brian from the Beach Boys. If so, he must be careful not to make the same mistake I made in the first edition of this book.

Many of my sources suggested that, to be an important artist again, Brian would have to move away from the Beach Boys—that they were in his way. Unfortunately, I missed a key subtlety in Brian's relationship to the band. While he may feel that they are an obstacle to his artistic expression, I misunderstood this to mean that Brian didn't want the group to exist. As one friend of Brian's recently explained, "It's not that Brian doesn't want to be a Beach Boy. He just wants to run the show the way he did in the old days."

In the first edition of this book, I didn't fully appreciate how much the Beach Boys' approval means to Brian, and how vital the band is to his self-image. As one former employee of the group points out, "Brian halfway committed suicide so the Beach Boys could go on. He destroyed himself for the group. If he didn't care about them, he would probably be a sane man today. Or dead. He would either have never gotten so involved with drugs or gotten so involved that he would've ended up dead. Drugs were an escape from the responsibility of being the big, head Beach Boy . . . but now, all he has is the Beach Boys. Nothing is as close to him as the concept of the Beach Boys."

In a 1984 interview in *Blitz* magazine, Carl Wilson explained that the source of Brian's trouble was that "basically Brian just wanted to be acknowledged. He practically killed himself doing it. He really put his heart and soul into it. He wanted to be OK. He just needed the validation."

One person who has been extremely helpful in explaining Brian's relationship with the Beach Boys has been engineer and studio designer Steve Desper, one of the major characters in the story who I didn't locate until after the first book was completed. As the man who ran the studio in Brian's home, he has been able to provide me with a treasure trove of insight into that period of Brian's creative life.

In my original writing, I ignored the total disruption the studio caused in the Wilson household, and envisioned Brian's home studio as this terrific environment in which Brian could be creative. My first mistake was in assuming that Brian even *wanted* a studio in his home. As Desper explains, in mid-1967, to the Beach Boys, the first obvious sign that something was "wrong" with Brian was that he had stopped going to the studio. So, as Desper recalls, the Beach Boys brought the studio to Brian, hoping that the proximity of the equipment would stimulate him.

Up to that point, Brian had usually written his music at home and recorded in outside studios. In a way, the reclusive pattern that would mark Brian's next eight years was partly aided by the studio's immediate presence.

The record company was screaming for a record, and in 1967, Brian was so important to the Beach Boys that his personal privacy was of little concern. Even if Brian didn't want to make records, the home studio would confront him with the obvious fact that he was no longer productive. The simpler records Brian made in 1967 and 1968 proved that a piece of Brian Wilson was better than most everybody else. And after it became apparent that Brian would at least do some work, the decision was made to build a permanent system.

Steve Desper supervised the building of an elaborate PA system for the group's live performances, one that was cleverly designed for the piggyback concerts the group needed to perform in the late 1960s to stay financially afloat. And when the Beach Boys were off the road, the equipment would be installed in Brian's house as his home studio. Desper points out the irony of this set-up: "Traditionally, when the Beach Boys went on the road was when Brian wrote his songs and recorded the tracks." But now, when they toured, he was without his home studio. So, by 1970, if Brian liked the convenience, he had no guarantee the equipment would be there when he needed it. It was like telling a housebound painter he could use the sunroom, but only at night.

As Desper recalls, "the studio was directly below Brian and Marilyn's bedroom, which meant that when a session was going on, and a session was always going on (including the Manson sessions), Brian and Marilyn woke to the sounds of recording and went to sleep to the same sound."

Fortunately, there was some creative benefit to this inconvenience. For weeks at a time, during Beach Boys sessions in 1970, Brian would slip out of the house early in the morning, come home late at night and sneak up to the bedroom without coming into the studio to work. But then, Desper relates, "Brian might suddenly appear and say, 'I was lying in my bed, listening through the floor, and I think you should add this part.'" Desper describes a harried attempt to keep up with Brian: "He worked very fast. He would pick up the guitar and record the guitar part. Then, he'd play the bass part. Then, the organ. Another guitar. Then the group would gather around the piano, and he would teach them their parts. They'd rehearse, but only for a couple of minutes. Brian was very impatient. They would record their vocals. And Brian would leave. He would rarely listen to the playback of any of it. He just knew how it should sound, and it all did fit together perfectly."

From watching Brian work, Desper saw that Brian's ability was all instinctive. "He just has this natural gift to master keyboards and strings, and he's even good at the drums. I used to rent all sorts of exotic instruments for Brian. In just a couple of days of experimentation, Brian could completely grasp any instrument. Then, a couple of months later, he would remind me of a particular one and tell me to get it for the next session. And I'd rent it again, and Brian could play it. It was incredible. The only thing he wasn't good at was horns. He didn't have the lip for it."

As one who has observed Brian at close range for many years, Desper firmly believes that Brian is playing a gigantic game and that "all those instincts are intact. They're just dormant." But Desper also talks of Brian's courage in the face of static. As Desper recalls, Brian didn't want the song 'Surf's Up' included on the album of that name ("he was superstitious about the SMiLE stuff"). But "Brian still tried to sing the lead vocal. The lyrics were taped to a music stand in the studio, and any number of times, Brian tried to sing it. He just couldn't pull it off to his satisfaction."

Working with Brian, Desper was also first-hand witness to the effect of drugs. "I've probably erased more Brian Wilson than most people have heard. Many times, he would come into the studio, apparently not himself, and try to improve upon [by recording over and erasing] a track. His altered state of awareness made him do it worse, which meant we had to scrap the entire track."

Adding to the legend of Brian's unreleased music, Desper remembers that the original lyrics to "Til I Die' were "much more personal and relevant to where Brian was at that moment in time. But one day, Brian came in and said he wanted to record a new lead vocal with a new set of lyrics. There were no empty tracks on the tape." There was no time to set up a "slave." There was no dissuading Brian. "So we had to erase the original lead vocal with the original lyrics. What we ended up with was, in my opinion, nowhere near as great as what it could have been." Desper doesn't blame drugs for this change. "I think Brian just felt that the lyrics revealed too much of himself, and he felt too vulnerable."

Before Brian's retreat, he had never hesitated to expose his soul, and on *Pet Sounds*, he wore his heart on the Beach Boys sleeve. Unfortunately for Brian, he was a victim of being born in the wrong era, and he knew it. Just listen to 'I Just Wasn't Made for These Times.' This master of popular music during a rock 'n' roll time, Brian wrote the most emotionally evocative and personal music of the 1960s, a decade in which lyrical "meaning," i.e., sociopolitical "heaviness," was paramount.

If anyone had bothered to look closely, the lyrical expression, written by himself or with his collaborators, was often terrific, and on hits like 'California Girls,' 'When I Grow Up' and 'God Only Knows,' it could be memorable. For a brief moment, following the critical success of *Pet Sounds* and the commercial masterstroke of 'Good Vibrations,' Brian had enough power to override any objections to the pursuit of his creative whimsy. Except that the "hip" critical establishment, whose approval Brian wanted, felt that if Brian were to make important "artistic" records, he would need better lyrics.

As one of Brian's friends from that time remembers, "Brian was suffering from the 'Orson Welles syndrome' . . . the media pressure to top himself. He was on a roll," but he needed more firepower. In a sense, this friend thinks, "Brian enlisted Van Dyke Parks to appease the critics."

Regardless of the motivation for the collaboration, it was really the only time that Brian has worked with a creative being who, if not his equal, could give Brian positive feedback, bring out his most creative and adventurous ideas, and support the ambitious music with clever lyrics.

What Brian was writing was not typical Beach Boys music. In fact, he often wasn't writing songs at all, just musical pieces, making Parks's job even more difficult. However, Parks expressed Brian's musical concepts in words, and if his lyrics seemed inscrutable, all the better, because like the complex music, it wouldn't all be grasped upon first, or even twentieth, listening.

After this book was first published, I finally had the chance to hear the unreleased recordings from the *SMiLE* era, the remnants of the Brian/ Van Dyke sketchbook. Virtually all of these tapes are incomplete, but two pieces of music are particularly meaningful. The first is the original version of 'Wonderful.' Even in its primitive "demo" form of Brian alone at the harpsichord, the pure power of his performance provides ample aural evidence of how *SMiLE* was Brian's baby and *Smiley Smile* was the Beach Boys' miscarriage.

The other is 'Can't Wait Too Long / Been Way Too Long,' a song that wasn't intended for *SMiLE*, but a production that shows how Brian's gift could effortlessly evidence itself. Like a true wizard, Brian took a simple phrase and turned it into a dazzling musical montage that is as revolutionary today as when he wrote, sang, arranged and produced it eighteen years ago. All of these tapes have helped me to personally understand what was lost when *SMiLE* died, unfinished. And I remain convinced that a collection of the still-unreleased fragments pieced together with the music that has come out would make for an unparalleled collection of pop music experimentation. More than that, given the group's image, Brian's move from 1965's *Summer Days . . .* to 1966's *Pet Sounds* and *SMiLE* was far more radical than the Beatles' simultaneous shift from *Rubber Soul* to *Revolver* to *Sgt. Pepper's*.

However, the time may have come to stop crying over the tragic spilled milk of *SMiLE*. Maybe even a greater tragedy has been the years in which Brian has done comparatively little work, let alone seriously collaborated with anybody approaching Parks's skill and support. Our only current hope is that Dr. Landy exerts just enough influence over Brian to get him motivated and help the solo album become a reality without straying too far into the creative process. Nearly twenty-five years after co-founding the greatest American band, Brian Wilson still has little artistic freedom.

"Suddenly, I found myself chained to the dungeon wall, and I was cranking out little gems to pay for the cost of keeping a guard on my door. And I just thought I wouldn't give anymore, but I knew someday I'd overcome that . . . you've got this unfinished canvas, and you've got to put something there."

Those words could have been spoken by Brian Wilson. However, they are the thoughts of another legend from the 1960s, a man who found success filled with pitfalls and, like Brian, withdrew from the world. The difference is that John Fogerty, the guiding force of Creedence Clearwater Revival, re-emerged in 1985 with a smash solo album and a fresh outlook on his future. Brian still seems caught up in his past. In the balance of this chapter, those who know Brian best have offered their insight into his thought processes to help understand where Brian's been and speculate as to where he might go.

"Brian," according to a former associate of the group, "is a knight in shining armor in a world where fancy sports cars are more important than what you do. Brian is the royal flush of romantics . . . a hothouse orchid. Brian wants everybody to be happy, but he's profoundly tired. All he cares about is his music, and everybody else is doing business. He's just a simple man at the piano, writing the way he feels. His withdrawal is a sane reaction to an insane world. Who would want to deal with it?"

Others suggest ways to move him out of his inertia. One close friend acknowledges that "Landy has done his job and done it well. Brian would probably be dead if not for Landy. But now it's time for Brian to get back to the real world. He may still need someone to guide him, but I don't think Landy is that person. In fact, I'm beginning to think that Landy and Brian are changing places through osmosis like in that old Dirk Bogarde movie, *The Servant*. If I had any influence, I would keep Brian at the beach, keep the physical fitness thing going. Then I'd get him into a relaxed co-writing situation with creators he respects and with whom Brian can be himself. That would get him back in the habit of communicating and exchanging ideas.

"Then, I would put him with hot songwriters . . . it would really help Brian to have a hit record *now* so that he can sense that he can succeed today. I wouldn't put him with hit producers. I really believe that the way out of his current situation is through good, hard work. He can break his old routines by starting new ones.

"So I would get him back with creative people. And instead of keeping him away from old influences and bad memories, I think it's OK for Brian to confront them." This person fondly describes Brian "as the kindest, sweetest, most non-threatening person I've ever known. I've never seen him do anything mean on purpose." This friend also discounts the effect of drugs. "Everybody says it was drugs, but even at Brian's peak, he never did function well on a social level. As far as I'm concerned, the only difference between Brian in 1965 and Brian in 1985 is that he's not having hits. Otherwise, he's just the same.

"Remember, Brian was never a normal guy. You never know when he's being serious or putting you on. But I do know that when Brian comes into a room, if there's a piano he can sit at, not to play but just so he can put his hands on the keyboard, he'll be relaxed." And when he makes music, "he can still play those magic chords . . . Part of his therapy is to be out onstage with the Beach Boys to see the end result of writing music. He can't just be locked away in a room writing songs. He has to have a purpose to write. Seeing the music connecting with an audience is great for his self-worth, but not all the time."

What lies ahead for Brian? "If he's 'cured,' a lot of people will be out of work. So for certain people, it's better to hold him back enough so that they control him." And yet, as this friend admits, "Who knows? Maybe without the total control, Brian would be a lunatic."

Nobody really knows the right thing to do. One former employee of the group recalls that the first time he worked with Brian, he was reminded of hyperactive children who suffer from taking too many food additives like monosodium glutamate. Another friend of Brian's postulates that Brian's impatience and seemingly short attention span are the result of an organic hyperactivity, and why, this friend believes, "Brian liked to take stimulants, a recommended treatment for hyperactivity. They helped him to concentrate." Dr. Landy told the *L.A. Times* that doctors, in the past, prescribed tranquilizers for Brian to calm him down. "The problem with most medication," Landy noted, "is that it really helps the people around the patient and not the patient." One friend of Brian's thinks that these powerful pharmaceuticals may have caused more serious damage than cocaine and LSD ever did.

A psychologist who has been a fan and longtime observer of Brian's public and private behavior terms Brian "passive-aggressive. He won't confront people with his real feelings, so that when he finally explodes, it seems like he's out of control." As one friend of Brian explains, "Brian responds to being yelled at . . . being told what to do. I don't know much about Landy's methods, but I think he's really turned Brian around. And at bottom, I don't think Landy's really malicious; actually, he's kind of pathetic. But he's on Brian's side, and it's good that Brian has somebody to fight for him because he won't fight for himself.

"However, I also know you can't hire somebody else to do your 'dirty work' for you. Landy seems to have control over Brian which isn't necessarily in the best interests of the Beach Boys. Ironically, it's Landy who holds the Beach Boys' career in his hands. And they're the ones who brought him back into the picture. My grandmother used to have a saying. 'The wheel turns.' And now, it's the Beach Boys' turn. Brian doesn't have any plan in his head. It's just karmically time for them to suffer. Brian is so powerful, and you can't mess with that power without getting burned."

In public, Brian's eyes often seem to say, "nobody's home," but in private, Brian's eyes often betray hurt, disappointment, and sadness.

The public Brian, says one close observer, "has put up a wall against life. He doesn't let in emotion, and while it may have begun as a cat-and-mouse game, it's no game anymore. Brian puts a lot of energy into keeping this wall intact," a problem that Brian's then collaborator David Sandler examined in the early 1970s in his hopefully titled song 'Walls Come Tumblin' Down.'

Living behind a wall for so long, it seemed to me that Brian had basically given up, quit on life, decided that the satisfaction he got from putting his heart on the line isn't worth the pain that goes with it. In essence, Brian just hasn't wanted to do it, and all the cajolery and threats and orders from headquarters are no match for the power he has—the self-control that holds back his magic in a grand petulance.

Steve Desper explains that, to this day, there is a basic pressure that holds Brian back. "Brian wasn't allowed to record songs; he was expected to write hits. He couldn't just write for pleasure to explore his talent or to devise new ways of expressing himself. There was always commercial pressure for another hit."

Desper thinks "Brian wanted to be a producer; he felt at home doing that. But when he gave production of the Beach Boys over to them, he didn't have anything to produce anymore." By 1970, as Steve Desper remembers, "Brian was looking for people to produce. But he just didn't know how to go about it. He even tried to produce the housekeeper; he did fairly well with [the then Beach Boys manager] Jack Rieley."

Desper: "Brian would be good at films. Ever since *Pet Sounds*, he tried to create music through the senses. We'd be in the studio, and he'd say to me, 'I want this to sound like the taste of a chocolate milkshake after you've been running.' Or, 'I want this to sound like the way trees smell after it rains.' That's what he would be visualizing as he was playing.

"Somebody should get him a low-budget film, even a UCLA student film. But whatever he does, it's gotta be good, not like the stuff he's done lately. He knows better; he knows it's no good. And yet, he needs the right to fail, to grow. It was always, 'Don't make a mistake.' Or 'How could you make a mistake?' Brian's got to be given the time and the courtesy to redevelop his confidence."

In the 1960s, Brian's success didn't come solely from his jazz-influenced chord changes and spiritual melodies. It was his novel arrangements, masterful use of harmonics, plaintive voice, total understanding of how music fits together, and the ability to use the studio and the studio musicians as one complete instrument that made Brian's organ-based sounds the ultimate in religious rock 'n' roll. Brian's hit songs were elaborate sketches, and it was on the records that he painted with his most vivid colors.

If Brian in 1985 only writes songs, if he doesn't bring sustained focus to the record-making process, and if he doesn't arrange the Beach Boys' voices, then the group's records will always feel vaguely incomplete because we are used to such fulfilling work from Brian. If the music is his sole source of gratification, what will reactivate his interest in the satisfying self-expression he once got from making records? Maybe Brian would respect a collaborator like Van Dyke Parks who would have enough sensitivity to Brian and the process that "it" will happen again. Maybe the damage to Brian makes it unlikely that his skills will ever jell again.

One musician close to the Beach Boys observes that "creative people are like volcanoes, and Brian had his big eruption back in the mid-1960s. Afterwards, when people try to figure out what happened and why it's not happening anymore, they look for things to blame it on. And then they wonder when or if there will ever be another eruption like that. There are just times when the flow is stronger for creative people, and maybe Brian's time will come again."

To add to the problem, "when you're too famous, you get caught in a trap and lose the creative flow. Music is a stream of consciousness that comes through him. But Brian's surrounded by the pressure of paying the bills and that blocks the flow. The guy's so sensitive." Because "Brian is not a go-getter, he needs somebody to give him a project, something to write for. I've suggested to the Beach Boys' management that they do just that, but so far, nothing's happened.

"For creators like Brian Wilson and Stevie Wonder, they are so sensitive both to the musical vibe and to criticism that they really don't understand nor can they take it when they are knocked, be it by the media, the record company, the public, their group, whomever."

This successful arranger/producer expresses his awe of what Brian can do: "There's no question that Brian's one of the heavyweight writers who taps into the universal music . . . but he doesn't have the pulse of the world anymore." This person also thinks that a film would be a good vehicle for Brian.

Many think that even if Brian wanted to, he is incapable of producing music worthy of the legend, that his attention span has become so short that a project like *Pet Sounds* is impossible.

Says one friend of Brian's, "What looks like poor concentration is Brian constantly recreating. It's hard to explain exactly what I mean, but Brian has the art of recreation down. To him, his music always exists in the 'now,' and that's what gives it the quality of timelessness. But Brian's music isn't nostalgia any more than Beethoven's is. When you hear his records, you don't think of the good times in your past. Brian's songs actually *change* your mood. That's what separates him from most other contemporary popular composers.

"Don't forget, Brian originally created his music to make himself feel better, so you can just imagine how unhappy he was to make such powerful sounds. I don't care what anybody else says or thinks about Brian. I know that Brian is a real guru, an enlightened spiritual being who was plopped down in the wrong place. Then again, most gurus don't really reach their heights until they're old men, so we can look forward to that with Brian."

After the Inaugural Gala telecast, this friend of Brian's was visibly brightened by Mr. Wilson's performance and appearance. "He sounded great and with all that hair, slimmed down so tall and fit and trim, he was the only one of the group who looked like he could ever even have been a Beach Boy. On top of everything else that makes Mike jealous of Brian, as funny as it sounds, it's Brian's hair. That and the fact that Brian is truly spiritual."

This person then proceeded to provide me with the most lucid explanation as to why Brian's behavior is so unpredictable: "Brian doesn't always intend to do what he says he's going to do, but he always says exactly what he feels. Because that's what Brian does. He *feels*. So he couldn't possibly do what he says he's going to do because when it comes time to do it, he's feeling something different. If the Beach Boys would only do what Brian says when he says it, everything would be fine. But nobody listens, really listens to him.

"It is Brian's ability to put his feelings into music that has made him so successful as an artist, and at the same time, his living according to his feelings has made his life a mess because he's the only one who's like that. It's made it difficult for anybody who counts on Brian for their wealth or their emotional health, because there's no way of knowing where he'll be tomorrow. But if you love him as I do, unconditionally and in spite of what might be perceived as 'character flaws,' he'll never let you down. Brian has always been right there for me. And he's there for everybody else, too. Just listen to the music."

As you've probably noticed, almost all of the statements in this section (as well as many quotes throughout the book) are not attributed to the person who made the observation. It seems that if my "sources" want to see Brian and deal with the Beach Boys, they have to be careful not to publicly disapprove of those who control Brian's life. Those powers-that-be are apparently very sensitive to public dissection. Despite that limitation, I think their comments are worth including because they come out of years of close, personal experience and can help us to understand this important artist better.

In another sense, all of this analysis is unnecessary. There has always been one arena in which Brian has never been misunderstood, where, in Steve Desper's words, "Brian is opened up, naked to the wind, baring his inner self."

That place? The recording studio.

THE LEGACY

During the past eight years, I've had the privilege to enjoy hours of unreleased Beach Boys' music, ranging from Brian's demos to completed productions, from alternative versions to backing tracks. These tapes, combined with the already released recordings, provide an intimate story of Brian Wilson's life and are the accumulated evidence of his immense talent.

Twenty-five years ago, Brian Wilson created a remarkable musical instrument that was called the Beach Boys, and he played it with a unique virtuosity. At his peak, Brian displayed absolute and unparalleled command of the recording process. As Van Dyke Parks recalls, "Brian literally saturated the tape with music. And given the technology of the times . . . that Brian was operating under a Phil 'Spectre' . . . what he did was way beyond what anybody else, to this day, has done in the studio."

Even without another note from Brian, his place in musical history is secure. However, it's the possibility of new music from Brian that we long for. Direct, emotional communication from the master is our dream, and in the near future, we may get our wish fulfilled.

As Brian gears up to share himself through his music again, the creator inside must be apprehensive as to how he'll be received. If we keep Brian's past achievements in perspective and if Brian's new work is the best he can do, we won't be disappointed. And when he finally overcomes the intimidation of trying to recapture the fun feeling of the hitmaking years and makes a record that is completely his own, then Brian's career may finally move into the long-delayed future.

Great philosophers have expressed the belief that there are no sadder words than "what might have been." I still long for a time when Brian's "California Rhapsody" is no longer one of the greatest "what ifs?" in musical history.

Brian's creative life is the stuff of legends, and, undoubtedly, his story will one day be the basis for a movie on the level of *Amadeus*. Great parallels can be drawn between the creative conflicts portrayed in that film and those experienced by Brian. However, unlike Mozart, Brian's artistry may receive proper recognition during his lifetime. Maybe Brian's future works will make all this speculation and myth-making unnecessary, but probably only the passage of time will bring Brian his due.

If my Grandpa Kroll were alive, he would read my endless theorizing and make me president of his "Woulda, Shoulda, Coulda" club. In this story, I prefer to end with words from his wife. As my ninety-two-year-old Grandma Kroll always says, "Where there's life, there's hope." For Brian Wilson, there is a universe filled with people who pray that, in Brian's own words, someday he'll find his world.

David Leaf
Los Angeles, 1985

THE BEACH BOYS AND THE CALIFORNIA MYTH

2022 Update

AUTHOR'S NOTE TO THE 2022 EDITION

I started work on this update last November by reading *The Beach Boys and the California Myth* for the first time in over twenty years.

I was twenty-five years old when I wrote the first edition, a naive, idealistic kid; I knew virtually nothing about the reality of the music business, hadn't yet seen first-hand how difficult it was to "make it" in the world of music, let alone sustain a career. I knew very little about songwriting, and I didn't know what it took to be a successful artist, the kind of pressures that were brought to bear by the demand for more and more hit records. I hadn't seen the impact of "fame and fortune." Beyond that, I really didn't understand much about life.

It was a book I began as a devoted fan. As I wrote in the 1978 edition, "This is what I found when I came to California in search of the Beach Boys." My intention was to tell Brian's story as best I could so that I, and the readers, could better comprehend what had taken place. But I had another goal too. I truly believed that if I "explained" Brian Wilson to the world, all would be fixed. How innocent or hopeful, or even crazy, was that?

The first edition was based on a half-dozen very obsessive years of fandom, research, and personal observation. I scoured radio documentaries, TV shows, magazine articles, and even press releases to find revealing quotes from previous interviews Brian and the group had done. I was a wide-eyed guest at their fifteenth-anniversary party on New Year's Eve, 1976 at the L.A. Forum. I was invited as "press" to the "April Fool's Day" launch party at Brother Studio in spring 1977 for *The Beach Boys Love You* album.

More crucially, there were dozens of one-on-one interviews. In 1977 and 1978, I was able to hear about key events from those who had actually been there, lived *through* them, had perspective on what they'd experienced. That's why I believe one everlasting value of the book is that it's part "living history," especially significant as so many of the people I interviewed are no longer with us.

As you've read, I spoke extensively with people associated with Brian during various eras of his life and the group's career. Each had so much to contribute. When I met Bruce Johnston, it was five years after he'd left the Beach Boys, and he hadn't yet rejoined the group. As he told me at the time, "I feel like I'm the Albert Speer of the Beach Boys in that I'm technically innocent of any of the bizarre elements of the band." His "insider" observations remain keen and essential.

The book was written so long ago that all three Wilson brothers were alive. I got to talk with Audree, their proud mother, about her boys. In *The Myth*, I wish I had written even more about Mrs. Wilson's role in this epic tale. When we spoke, she was always candid. As she said about her sons, "Their relationship has been very off and on. At times, they've been very close . . . they care very much about each other." In my mind, I can hear Brian on a 1970s radio documentary telling the story about his mother and the idea of "Vibrations." Why didn't I use that story? I don't remember.

During the writing of the book, I did get to know Brian and Dennis a bit. I had several conversations with Dennis and did one marathon interview with him that lasted until past dawn. When I sang backup vocals on 'He's a Bum,' a new song of his, our first line was "He's a dog without a bone."

The comments and quotes in the book, made by close friends and associates of Brian and the Beach Boys—sometimes anonymous or even off the record—came from these countless hours of conversation. What I gleaned from those interviews mixed together with direct quotes from Brian were central to the narrative. I asked those who I thought knew or understood Brian best to help me sort it all out. For months, file folders filled with little bits of paper, each one a quote, covered the living room floor of my apartment in West L.A. I synthesized this mountain of information into what you've just read. I was trying to get to "the truth"; I was also trying to write a book that a fan like me would want to read.

The events of Brian Wilson's life make for an oft-times controversial story. Even the creation of the music raises lots of questions. "Who exactly did what?" Many of these questions remain unanswerable.

However, what I can't do now is rewrite my own history. I have to live with it. *You* get to judge whether *The Myth* is a fair accounting of the story I set out to tell, one focused on the artistic journey of Brian Wilson. As a journalist, as a biographer, now as his friend, that certainly was and still is my purpose, my intention.

Reading the original book in 2021 was almost an out-of-body experience. Emotionally exhausting, too. In particular, I found the chapters from the 1985 update to be the work of an author still trying to find "the answer." That's especially true of "Retrospective, 1985," "Shades of Grey" and "The Legacy." Those sections are, to me, very intense; I can feel myself struggling to figure out what was "right" and "wrong." Toward the end of the 1985 update, instead of reaching definitive conclusions, I presented the observations and insights of those I considered to be Brian's friends, offering their analysis of the current situation.

When the book came out in 1985, it was early in "The Landy Years, Part Two." Brian's friends were expressing concern about Landy, as well as thoughts on what could and should happen. Now, I realize we were all doing our best to explain the inexplicable. It's just what we thought and felt and believed at the time.

In re-reading it all, I can see now, with the benefit of maturity and hindsight, that it was written with a sense of both hope and sadness. There's also a bit of "mea culpa" in the 1985 update. What is true today is that the adolescent passion that drove me when I first wrote the book is now, I believe, a more sophisticated dedication to the subject. Informed by life and a lifetime of experience. That means that for this new edition, I can look back with empathy, with a perspective born of age and experience.

I see there are not only two sides to the story but sometimes three or four or ten. Perhaps more significantly, I realize my opinions, despite what I might have thought at the time, are just that . . . mine. It's why I named a chapter "Shades of Grey."

There's no question there are countless unknowns in this tale. Unfortunately, neither Dennis nor Carl wrote a memoir. So much of the story is still locked behind Brian's eyes. There are the private memories and thoughts of such central figures as Brian's first wife, Marilyn, and her sister Diane.

Brian and Marilyn were so young when they married. Marilyn was only sixteen. Clearly, at that age, you are still evolving, growing up. What was it like, suddenly, being not just part of the Beach Boys world but at the center of it with your husband as "the head Beach Boy"?

Marilyn had to quickly adapt to the life of an artist. Then, she could only helplessly watch as Brian slowly pulled backed from and ultimately abandoned his role with the group. With the births of their two daughters, Carnie and Wendy, Marilyn had to assume the major weight of the responsibilities of parenthood. All before she was twenty-five. That was the age when I wrote *The Myth*. Now, looking back, I can only imagine how difficult it was for her to ride those waves of change.

Was *The Myth* too melodramatic, judgmental and self-righteous? That's for others to decide. But it was written with the hope that, as I state in the last paragraph of the first edition, "Brian must be respected as a human being. Then he must be freed as an artist."

Who was *I* to demand this? Was I even right?

When I wrote *The Myth*, what I didn't understand was that I came from a completely different world than the Beach Boys. When my friends and I talk about politics, I sort of joke, "I was born in New York City, grew up in the suburbs and lived in Santa Monica for nearly forty years. So I've never lived in America." But it's true. What used to be sneeringly called "flyover" country *is* America.

When I moved to Los Angeles, I was stunned to see the sprawling ordinariness of so much of it. Now, nearly a half-century later, I understand that much of the South Bay, where Hawthorne is located, is working class. Many of the homes still standing there were built for those who had *earned* the G.I. Bill. Constructed for those who *served the country* during World War II and the Korean War.

During the Great Depression, the Wilson/Love clan worked hard to build successful businesses that could support their families. My father and mother both went to college. I grew up expecting to go to college; I got to choose my career.

For the Wilson brothers and Mike Love, the good fortune of becoming the Beach Boys was virtually impossible; given how quickly it happened, it was almost like winning the lottery. When 'Surfin'' hit, Mike was twenty, had already assumed adult responsibilities; but the Wilson brothers, especially Dennis and Carl, were just high school kids. While Brian could guide them musically . . . and the DNA of their beautiful harmony was filled with the most intense brotherly love . . . there was nothing in their world that could have prepared them for the music business, for the hard work ahead or the perils of stardom. Barry Gibb told me long ago that the biggest challenge the Bee Gees faced was "surviving 'first fame.'"

In *The Myth*, I was looking back at what had happened. But what did it *feel* like for the Beach Boys when the first big checks arrived, to live in the middle of that emotional maelstrom, when they fired their father, when Brian quit touring, when they returned from the road and heard new songs like 'I Just Wasn't Made for These Times'? How did they feel when the rock press in England was praising Brian for his genius and wondering if they were Brian Wilson's puppets . . . when they saw how Brian had changed, heard the *SMiLE* songs and felt that Brian might be moving in his own direction? It all had to be frightening, unnerving, scary.

In 1966, Brian felt as if he was locked in a creative battle with the Beatles. In 1966, the Beach Boys were focused on playing a great concert. The conflict between an artist in the recording studio following his muse and a group on the road facing an audience was one I didn't understand or fully address.

Perhaps, most significantly, in terms of the creative journey I wrote about, the 1960s Beach Boys albums I owned had inaccurate songwriting credits; they were finally corrected after Mike Love won a lawsuit in 1994. That's why in *The Myth*, I didn't always properly acknowledge his contributions on so many of the group's songs. It was often Mike's lyrical hooks that to this day have everybody, including me, singing along in our cars and at the concerts.

(L-R) Brian and Mike at work.
Credit: Michael Ochs Archives/Getty

So, to be clear, especially in the early days, Mike Love was the songwriting partner with whom Brian had the most success. His rhymes, swiftly constructed, perfectly fitted the idea of what the Beach Boys' image was: sun, sand, surf, cars and girls. 'The Warmth of the Sun' remains one of their all-time best songs together. Mr. Love should get credit where credit is due.

That said, while Brian may have written only some (or not even any) of the lyrics to a song, in a sense, many of the Beach Boys' best albums, especially the 1965–1966 trio of *The Beach Boys Today!*, *Summer Days (and Summer Nights!!)* and *Pet Sounds*, were filled with the work of a new kind of popular art form: *emotional* songwriting.

And despite what's been said and written in the past, by me and by others, I think there's no question that Mike Love knew how great the *music* was on *Pet Sounds* and *SMiLE*. But as the frontman at the concerts, as the group's primary lead singer, perhaps he was unsure as to whether these new songs were right for Beach Boys fans. He might have wondered, "Do the songs fit our image?" "How can we play them live?" If that's the case, from a business point of view, his concern was and is understandable.

Unlike Dylan, post-1964 Lennon and McCartney or Joni Mitchell, Brian didn't always write alone. But whether it was with Mike Love, Tony Asher or Van Dyke Parks, Brian wanted and sometimes needed somebody to help him lyrically express what he was thinking and feeling.

And because *feel* is what matters most in Brian's best compositions, he could write great songs with almost anybody, including his father ('Break Away'). That's true from his earliest 1960s collaborators (Bob Norberg on 'The Surfer Moon' and Gary Usher on 'In My Room') to today.

He wrote hits with Jan Berry, only two songs (but both classics) with Russ Titelman, and rarely but beautifully with brother Carl. Other songwriting partners through the years have included Al Jardine, David Sandler, Jeff Lynne, Andy Paley, Joe Thomas, Scott Bennett, and the poet Stephen J. Kalinich. One of my favorite twenty-first-century songs of Brian's, the rarely performed 'Walking Down the Path of Life,' was written by Brian with our mutual friend Jerry Weiss, who turned out to be a very capable wordsmith.

In many of the songs written with others, the musical *idea* of the song would typically come from Brian (like 'Surf City' or the symphonic opening of 'California Girls'). Roger Christian and Van Dyke Parks were two notable exceptions. As Roger told me, Brian wrote music to his poems. Van Dyke's lyrics came out of ideas he and Brian discussed; then, he drew from his own impressionistic feelings as Brian created the melodies. The results were often magical, from 'Don't Worry Baby' to 'Heroes and Villains.' And so many more.

Brian could also write beautifully alone, as was evident right from the start with 'Surfer Girl.' There are so many other solo songwriting classics to point to: 'Busy Doin' Nothin',' 'This Whole World' and ''Til I Die' . . . much of the *Love You* record and his '88 solo album and some of his subsequent cuts like 'Cry.' The point of this pontificating is that Brian Wilson's work, regardless of his numerous collaborators' contributions, was primarily that of a rock auteur.

And that artist was and is my focus.

I probably should have written more about how important Carl Wilson was to Brian's studio work. That Carl (and Dennis too) understood and felt the spiritual nature of what Brian was creating. Also, I took it as a "given" that the reader knew how remarkable a voice Carl had, that his vocals both in the studio and in concert were not just incredible but miraculous. For me, his voice was the reason that Beach Boys concerts were always filled with magical musical moments.

I should have made it crystal clear that, on tour, it was Carl who kept the band true to the spirit of their greatest music. And that after Brian withdrew from full-time producing duties, Carl took the responsibility, became the essential Wilson in making the post-*Pet Sounds* albums up through the mid-1970s as good as they could be.

In addition to all of that, as Fred Vail, a longtime friend of the Wilsons who began promoting their first headlining concerts in 1963, recently observed, "Carl was the Beach Boys' musical leader onstage and the group's peacekeeper on- and offstage. He was the group's most compassionate member and the most unchanged."

I mentioned Dennis Wilson's songwriting, but I could have been more effusive. Dennis wrote terrific songs. He was the group's second-best composer. And, like Brian, he had the instinctive ability to express his deepest feelings in music. And I might have made more of the fact that from the very beginning to today, Alan Jardine's voice has remained strong, an essential element in the Beach Boys harmony blend. A talented lead singer too. As is his son Matt.

In the 1978 edition of *The Myth*, I wrote: "Mike's role in the Beach Boys' success cannot be underestimated. It was he who sang the lead vocal on most of the up-tempo hits the group is best remembered for . . . the group's longevity and popularity as a live act are due largely to Mike Love." Today, that's even more true. During the past quarter century, nobody has worked harder than Mike to keep the Beach Boys alive.

But back in 1978, I wasn't writing a book about the touring Beach Boys. I'm still not.

★   ★   ★   ★

For most of my Brian Wilson journey, my late wife, Eva Easton Leaf, was by my side. Brian had brought us together in 1977, and in the subsequent thirty years, nothing was more important to us than Brian's well-being. When she got sick in 2008, our focus changed. It became about her health. My parents had moved from New York to Santa Monica to be closer to us; they lived a mile away. In between the beginning of Eva's illness and her death in 2016, I lost both of my parents. I was consumed with loss.

It wasn't until I began working on this update in 2021 that I was once again able to fully immerse myself in the world of Brian Wilson. As part of that "deep dive," I finally sat down and read both Brian's and Mike Love's valuable 2016 memoirs. I learned so much from both of them.

THE AFTERMATH

Unlike the update to *The Myth* you're about to read, virtually everything artistically significant in the Beach Boys story happened before I moved to Los Angeles.

But much of what I wrote in 1985 about what might or should happen regarding Brian is valid today. Within two years of the publication of the second edition of *The Myth*, what had been speculated upon in the book played out. Brian embarked on what has become an award-winning, honor-filled solo career. Landy was permanently banished. Most triumphantly, the "what ifs?" of *SMiLE* have been answered as best as can be.

In the 1985 edition of the book, I wrote a "Requiem" for Dennis. Sadly, Carl Wilson's heavenly voice was stilled; he died in 1998.

Since *The Myth* went out of print, as it became something of a collector's item, I was often asked why I didn't update it, republish it. One primary reason was that, even as I was concentrating on my own career, it also seemed like every year for at least twenty years, there was one Brian or Beach Boys-related project I was working on. I felt I was kind of updating the book in real time.

THE TITLE, THE AUTHOR: CLARIFICATIONS

What did confuse some in 1978, and I think it's a fair criticism, is that while the book is primarily about Brian, *The Beach Boys and the California Myth* had the Beach Boys name in the title, their picture on the front cover. The title of this edition more accurately reflects my scope of interest, while illustrating the evolving and sometimes conflicted nature of my relationship to the subject.

An example of what I mean: in 1986, I was the co-writer of the Beach Boys' twenty-fifth-anniversary television special. In 1988, I was hired by Warner Brothers Records to write the press kit for Brian Wilson's first solo album.

In 1990, I wrote the liner notes for the original CD reissues of the group's legendary 1960s Capitol Records catalogue, then the chapters on the Beach Boys and the Beatles for Capitol Records' fiftieth-anniversary book. In 2004, I wrote the liner notes for *Brian Wilson Presents SMiLE*.

I was a producer and wrote the books for two Beach Boys box sets: 1993's best-selling *Good Vibrations: Thirty Years of the Beach Boys* and 1997's acclaimed, Grammy-nominated *The Pet Sounds Sessions*. Capitol Records presented me with a platinum award for *Pet Sounds* as well as a gold record for my work on the *Good Vibrations* box. Nonesuch Records would similarly award me for my contributions to *Brian Wilson Presents SMiLE*.

I received *Q* magazine awards in 1990 and 1993 for my work on the Beach Boys reissues and Grammy nominations for *The Pet Sounds Sessions* and my film, *Beautiful Dreamer: Brian Wilson and the Story of SMiLE*.

I've also written, produced, directed, consulted on and been interviewed for numerous Brian Wilson film and television projects including the Don Was documentary *I Just Wasn't Made for These Times* and Morgan Neville's *A Beach Boy's Tale*. When I was interviewed on camera for Morgan's film, I remarked, "Brian's turned the other cheek so many times he's gotten whiplash." I thought I was quoting somebody else. Turned out it was my line.

Since the last edition of *The Myth* came out, I've had a lot to say about Brian Wilson, publicly and privately. During the 1990s and into the early 2000s, I worked closely with Brian and Melinda Wilson, acting as a volunteer part-time personal manager, consultant and publicist. I was "Cheerleader-in-Chief." With Brian, I would help ghostwrite letters or speeches. Even magazine articles. Or as legendary L.A. music historian and author Harvey Kubernik put it, I was "a benign and loveable Minister of Propaganda."

Today, what I did would be called "branding."

I write all of this for several reasons. One, my love for writing and talking about the subject remains strong. And two, my friendship with Brian Wilson has created epic moments: at the top of my list, the 2001 *All-Star Tribute to Brian Wilson*, the world premiere in London of *Brian Wilson Presents SMiLE*, my 2004 *Beautiful Dreamer* film, and the *Brian Wilson Presents SMiLE* album which became landmarks for him . . . and for me.

Today, over twenty years into the twenty-first century, the Beach Boys are universally recognized as one of the most important and successful groups in rock history. And Brian Wilson has indeed taken his place as one of the greatest and most influential artists of his generation. And of all time. All of this has taken a lot of hard work and dedication. That, as we can see looking back, is the nature of a career. Any career.

I trust it's clear that I love the music that Brian and the Beach Boys created, that I love to share my passion for their harmonies, their melodies, their records. It was always about how the music made me *feel*. Selfishly, I wanted more music from them that would give me that same feeling.

As you read in the 1985 update to *The Myth*, with the exception of some still unreleased Brian Wilson music and *Pacific Ocean Blue*, Dennis Wilson's terrific solo album, fans like me were often disappointed by the group's new albums. I now have no expectations.

As the sun sets on the Beach Boys' recording career, their body of work is more than enough. Grammy Award-winning producers Alan Boyd, Mark Linett and their team have made sure that the group's twenty-first-century archival releases brilliantly document the group's most significant work, including *SMiLE* and the *Sunflower/Surf's Up* era.

THE UPDATE

In the course of writing *The Myth*, some of the people I interviewed became friends. Others, people in the music and television industries, became friends *because* they agreed with the book's point of view. In both cases, these friends are people I would often work with again and again.

In the new chapters, I'll focus primarily on behind-the-scenes stories of the highlights and sometimes heartbreaking moments along the way. My public and private position in all of this isn't easy to define. I went from fan to biographer to crusader to friend to collaborator and once again, here in 2022, to author. Or something like that. The lines have frequently been blurred. Often, I have played two or three roles at the same time.

The new chapters are based primarily on my personal experiences as Brian's friend as well as on observations, thoughts and ideas garnered from working with him since 1985.

To help me sort it all out, I've asked my closest friends who were also part of this trip (including the aforementioned Ray Lawlor and Jerry Weiss) to make sure my recollections jibe with reality, that my memories haven't been conflated. Since 1995, Ray's probably spent more time in a recording studio with Brian than just about anybody else except Darian Sahanaja. Since 2000, Jerry has probably spent more time on the road with Brian than anybody other than longtime band members. I long ago passed the baton of "stall dog" to Jerry. His work allowed him to travel with Brian on tour, which he's done, off and on, for over twenty years. Now retired, he was most recently on tour with Brian in the fall of 2021. I've also talked with other friends and colleagues and used their recollections to "season" my experiences, to enhance our understanding of what happened at key moments.

Now, let's go back in time and find out what happened to Brian (and me) after the second edition of *The Beach Boys and the California Myth* was published in 1985.

CHAPTER 16

'TIL I DIE: THE BATTLE
FOR BRIAN WILSON

FROM THE MOMENT OF HIS RETURN IN LATE 1982 TO HIS DEPARTURE IN 1992, the Landy Years were marked by tumult and accomplishment, strange and scary days and, sometimes, truly wonderful music. There were investigations. Behind-the-scenes intrigue. Landy's unusual and controversial therapy meant one thing: his control over Brian was iron clad.

I witnessed and was privy to just some of the chaos Landy caused. To be honest, I got opportunities to work on certain projects because of Landy's approval and/or insistence. But all of us did our work, to almost quote the Beach Boys song 'Marcella,' with "one eye over our shoulder." There was always tension. Watching and waiting for some explosion. Because it almost always came, the hissing snake turning into an overbearing monster.

To contextualize what I experienced, a few overarching observations: very simply, Brian might have died forty years ago if Landy (or somebody like him) hadn't been hired. Yet there's no way to calculate the damage done to Brian by the medication administered by Landy.

Considering what had happened in 1976, why was Landy brought back in? As Carl Wilson (circa 1996) said to Brian's friend and collaborator, Andy Paley, "When the prayer went up, we couldn't be too picky about who might answer it."

The choices the Beach Boys and Brian's family made turned the 1980s into unbelievably complex and stressful years for everybody who loved Brian. And most of all, for Brian himself.

I think of the Landy Years as "The Battle for Brian Wilson."

★   ★   ★   ★

From the time I arrived in L.A. in the fall of 1975 to the release of the second edition of *The Myth* in 1985, I was "a struggling writer." There was no straightforward road map you could get at the Auto Club on how to become successful in television or film or publishing or music. It wasn't like going to medical school or law school in pursuit of professions with a prescribed path.

I had many goals: to write for a sitcom, screenplays, perhaps even a novel. I had worked in news and sports in New York, but in L.A., I bounced from one TV production job to another. Some were incredible, like working on a Frank Sinatra special, *Sinatra and Friends*; others were less rewarding, like *The Battle of the Network Stars*.

In 1976, I had a short stint in the mailroom at Casablanca Records; I sold occasional freelance articles and wrote a regular column for *BAM* (*Bay Area Music*) magazine. In late 1980, I was briefly on the air for ESPN, reporting on the Lakers. For a year, I was the Director of Development for Caesars Palace Productions and produced my first documentary, a half-hour film on the 1981 Caesars Palace Grand Prix.

I met the Los Angeles Dodgers Hall of Fame announcer Vin Scully through my boss at Caesars; I was honored when Mr. Scully asked me to write for him when he hosted the annual Retinitis Pigmentosa charity dinner. That began a twenty-year association with the organization, important to me as both my grandmother and mother suffered from the eye disease. I wrote a novella (unfinished, unpublished), feature scripts (unproduced) and sitcom scripts (unsold).

On the strength of pre-publication galleys of *The Myth*, thanks to RSO's Jay Levy, I was hired in the summer of 1978 to write the Bee Gees authorized autobiography; that marked the beginning of a friendship with Barry Gibb and his family band that continues to this day. Videotaped interviews I did with the brothers Gibb were central to the acclaimed 2020 HBO Bee Gees documentary. Because of my Bee Gees connection, Brian, a gigantic Bee Gees fan, would have a magical, albeit brief, encounter with Barry. More in the next chapter.

The Myth and the Bee Gees biography were followed by an authorized bio on KISS (yes, *that* KISS); for a labyrinth of reasons, it remained on the shelf. *KISS: Behind the Mask* was finally published in 2003. Each step of the way, I learned more about writing, how to tell a story and "The Business."

Because of my books and my nerd knowledge of pop music history, I got hired as a researcher on *Solid Gold*, a very successful syndicated music TV series in the 1980s. Occasionally, I would be sent with a video crew to interview a rock star like Ozzy Osbourne, but overall, it wasn't a demanding job. Meaning I had a lot of free time at Paramount Studios in Hollywood where the show was videotaped; it was in my office there that I wrote the update for the 1985 edition of *The Myth* that was simply titled, *The Beach Boys*.

A year before the book's release, I remember Brian playing me some new songs, including 'There's So Many,' that were very impressive. Pure Brian Wilson. As he would later tell me, "My songwriting cycles are natural. When I get ready to go into a songwriting period, I feel that if I go to the piano and sit there long enough, something's gonna happen, my hands are gonna be lifted up by God and plopped down on the keys. It's that automatic."

But songwriting and survival are two very different things. Behind the scenes, during the early 1980s, my soon-to-be wife, Eva Easton, and a few others in our circle saw Brian from time to time. Even when he would play us a new and breathtakingly beautiful song, we had genuine concern. He was rapidly sliding downhill. By the time Landy was again hired, this time by the Beach Boys, Brian's life was indeed in jeopardy.

It quickly became clear that despite the slimmer and trimmer Brian the public soon saw, there was trouble in paradise. In the 1985 update of *The Myth*, I had written and wondered about what might happen going forward. Would Landy stay out of Brian's creative process? The answer, we all soon found out, was "No."

In 1986, Brian began working again with one of his first collaborators, Gary Usher; they had most notably written '409,' 'The Lonely Sea' and 'In My Room.' Whether Gary's ideas for what would make Brian sound "commercial" in the mid-1980s were right, the old friends had reunited, were writing and recording.

However, I heard more than once from a worried Gary that Landy was not just a "buttinsky"; Gary's concerns, expressed to me, were more about Landy's control of Brian. (Gary's diaries of their year together were made available to a State of California investigation of Landy, made public in a June 1988 *L.A. Times* article about Brian and Landy called "Bad Vibrations," and became the basis of *The Wilson Project*, Stephen J. McParland's explosive book.)

In the 1985 edition of *The Myth*, my comments about Dr. Landy were circumspect. That's because, in advance of publication, it had been politely "suggested" by a representative of Landy's that I should be very careful. That there might be legal action taken against me.

The truth, as we now know, is that Landy would constantly interfere in Brian's work. As the boss, Landy would be credited as "Executive Producer" on Brian's first solo album as well as co-writer on five songs. Whether it was writing lyrics for Brian or determining who had access to him, Landy was in charge. Day or night, Brian did what he was told, followed Landy's "program."

Landy had a team of people watching and videotaping Brian's every move and reporting back regularly. If you wanted to work with Brian, if you wanted Brian to sing on your record or be on your television special, if you wanted to have dinner with him, Landy was the door that could open or shut those possibilities. It seemed like Brian was in Landy's "cult of one."

I don't recall the exact moment I became aware that Landy was overstepping his role as therapist, but once I knew, I had to act with extreme caution. There was my work on Beach Boys/Brian projects. There was my career. And then the inevitable moment that brought me into contact with those investigating Landy for California's State Board of Medical Quality Assurance. On top of balancing all that was something else more important to me that I needed to keep separate: my friendship with Brian.

For the time being, as if he were running a music-business KGB, Dr. Landy regarded me as an "asset," a writer on Brian's side. Landy played a role in my being in Hawaii for the Beach Boys twenty-fifth-anniversary TV special; he got a "Special Consultant" credit on the program. That show was a big deal for me. It was for ABC, one of the three major TV networks, produced by the award-winning producer/director Marty Pasetta. The same guy who directed the Oscars and the Grammys. It was my first Writers Guild job! My first trip to Hawaii!! And on a Beach Boys special!!!

My actual input into the content of the show wasn't major. Writing for television isn't exactly like writing a poem. TV productions are typically a group effort with lots of people throwing out ideas. Some of mine became part of the show. Some of my words are in the script; I suggested several booking ideas.

One highlight that really stands out: the introduction of and performance by Ray Charles of 'Sail on Sailor.' There were other great moments:
the Everly Brothers' version of 'Don't Worry Baby.' A reunion with Glen
Campbell. And, with Brian on piano, I was thrilled when Three Dog
Night, and especially Danny Hutton, finally got to sing 'Darlin'.' Carl
performed my favorite of his solo songs, 'Heaven,' and the all-cast finale
of the program featured a brand-new Wilson–Usher–Tom Kelly song, 'The
Spirit of Rock and Roll.' Brian sang lead.

The name of the program, *The Beach Boys: 25 Years Together*, felt a little
sad. It was as if it was describing a marriage where the parents had remained
married "for the kids." In this case, "the kids" were the dozens of hits that
audiences loved hearing the group perform.

What nobody knew at that moment was that a divorce was in the
offing; Dr. Landy was about to take Brian "solo." Brian did play live and
appear on TV (such as their *Endless Summer* TV series) with the group
off and on into the mid-1990s. But as best as I can tell, other than 1996's
Stars and Stripes, Brian wouldn't really be a full-time Beach Boy again
until their successful fiftieth anniversary tour and album in 2012.

Regardless of his motives, perhaps nothing in Brian's life or the story
of the Beach Boys was more significant than the decision Landy made
for Brian's next album to be under Brian's name. That it wouldn't be a
Beach Boys record. This was a major split. It wasn't the first time. After
all, in 1966, Brian had dipped his toe in the water when 'Caroline, No'
was released as a solo single. But he was at the top of his game back then.

What would happen in 1987 and 1988 when Brian actually wrote and
recorded an album with Dr. Landy involved? So many questions, with not
always happy answers. But, looking back now, I believe that in regard to
his career, this was the one good thing Landy did for Brian.

The first time I saw what a Brian Wilson solo career might look like
was on *The National Academy of Songwriters Salute to the American Songwriter.*
I wrote and co-produced that show for three years, 1986–1988, and every
year, more than a dozen songwriters would perform hit songs they had
written. Sometimes, as with Carole King or Randy Newman, the stars of
the show were singer/songwriters. More often—as with Leiber and Stoller,
Livingston and Evans or Sammy Fain—they were songwriting legends.
Jimmy Webb (who I'd met when I interviewed him circa 1977 for *The
Myth*) did an incredible set. Thom Bell and Lamont Dozier both lit up

the stage. As did so many others such as Tom Kelly and Billy Steinberg, who were in the midst of a run of big hits for Madonna, Cyndi Lauper, et al.

It was on these shows that I really began to appreciate and understand songwriters (leading to my UCLA course "Songwriters on Songwriting"), and it was on the 1986 show that Brian appeared, by *himself*. (Google: Brian Wilson Live '86.)

Brian can be an incredibly intimidating presence. People are in awe of him, afraid to say the wrong thing. I was backstage, quietly encouraging him; his set included not just a couple of classics, fascinating stories and versions of 'Surfer Girl' and 'California Girls,' but a new song as well. To show the audience he was still writing. When Brian introduced 'Let's Go to Heaven in My Car' at the show, he added "which is a good title." Which got a great response from the audience. And I can still see his face when he played the instrumental bridge. Was it a sincere smile or was it because somebody was coaching him?

I ask that because throughout the Landy Years, Brian was constantly being told what to do, what to say. Sometimes even with cue cards. For a meeting, he might have to learn "a script" from Landy.

Although it was a Wilson–Usher song that was performed that night, I don't think Gary Usher was invited to the show. Gary, witness to how Landy was manipulating Brian, was talking to the State of California about what he had experienced and observed. My conversations with Gary during this time are what turned me into a Brian Wilson secret agent. That role would last until 1992, when Brian and Landy were permanently separated and the psychodrama was over.

In the meantime, in my work for the group or for Brian, I had to compartmentalize, put aside the allegations and speak with Dr. Landy in a reasonable manner. That's because nobody could talk with Brian, personally or professionally, without Landy's approval.

At this point, Landy was at the height of his powers, at least with Brian. And despite what Usher would tell the state amid an ongoing investigation (there was a Patient X who had accused Landy of sexual assault), Landy was still in charge.

I have to mention a seemingly inconsequential moment in Beach Boys history, because of what it portended. Tom Wszalek, a dear old friend's husband, worked for Mattel. Like the Beach Boys, the toy company was founded in Hawthorne. He asked me to put him in touch with Beach Boys management. The result? A single was recorded that was included in the package with the "California Barbie" doll.

Three million dolls were sold, sort of making it the Beach Boys' biggest single ever. Barbie was, in the words of the song, 'Living Doll,' indeed a "California dream." I got a pseudo-gold record award for it. Songwriting credits on 'Living Doll' foreshadowed what was to come: it was written by Wilson/Landy/Morgan. Alexandra Morgan was Dr. Landy's constant companion.

In January 1987, when Brian inducted the songwriting team of Jerry Leiber and Mike Stoller into the Rock and Roll Hall of Fame, he sang an a cappella version of one of their classics, "On Broadway." The often-blasé industry audience was impressed. Within minutes, the wheels were set in motion. Seymour Stein, the President of Sire Records, was there and determined to make an impression on Brian, he called Andy Paley in London for advice. Seymour later told me: "Andy fed me a bunch of lines, what songs to tell Brian I liked, not my obvious favorites like 'God Only Knows' but real obscure ones . . . like 'Solar System.'"

Andy Paley, a staff producer at Sire, was at Trident Studios in Soho, working on the *Dick Tracy* soundtrack, producing a demo with Harry Connick Jr. Paley: "I was back at my hotel; it was like three in the morning. I got this call from Seymour. He was at the Hall of Fame dinner at the Waldorf in New York. So it's five hours earlier.

"I was well known to my friends in and out of the business as a Beach Boys freak. In the early 1970s, when the Beach Boys touring band was at their very best, my brother Jonathan and I would follow them from city to city. We got to know Carl, Dennis, Blondie and Ricky very well.

"And once, around 1974, when we were in L.A., Carl and Ricky took us to meet Brian. It was very strange. He was living in this weird little building behind his Bellagio mansion. It was a mess, like a sloppy college dorm room, but it didn't have windows. He had a record player, and the Crystals' 45 of 'Da Doo Ron Ron' was on it. Brian didn't have a 45-rpm adapter, but the single was carefully, perfectly centered."

Everybody involved remembers the night of the 1987 Rock and Roll Hall of Fame dinner vividly, albeit a bit differently. That same evening, another member of the audience, Warner Brothers President Lenny Waronker, allowed a long dormant fantasy to be reactivated. Lenny told me: "Brian's speech was so wonderfully sweet. I remember thinking, 'My God, maybe there can be more stuff like he used to do, maybe he should do a record. It was clear that Brian was on the way back; this wasn't the Brian Wilson of the 'Brian's Back' hype of 1976."

Lenny said nothing to anybody about his reverie, just sat back and fondly recalled the long-ago time "when I was just starting out as a producer, and Brian was working with my good friend Van Dyke Parks. I loved the things they were working on, like 'Heroes and Villains' and 'Cabinessence.' I had never forgotten how great that music was . . . I was thinking how wonderful it would be if Brian could do a record, and he could do a bunch of things like 'Cool, Cool Water'. . . a new age record with Brian Wilson."

Flying back to L.A. from the Hall of Fame dinner, Lenny, in the darkened cabin, looked out the window and then toward the aisle, where he was startled to see Brian Wilson sitting across from him, headphones in place, playing his portable Casio. Lenny smiled to himself and turned away, not wanting to interrupt Brian.

"When I got back to L.A.," Lenny continues, "Seymour called me and said, in passing, that he was thinking of signing Brian. I said, 'Great! That's a brilliant idea. As a matter of fact, I've been thinking about the same thing.' And I told Seymour what I thought, about how I wanted to make a record filled with 'Cool, Cool Water' type of tracks. And Seymour said, 'Why don't we do half songs and half what you [meaning Lenny] call 'arts and crafts'?" (Sire was a "sister" label to Warner Brothers Records.)

Leaving London, and after a brief "pit stop" in Boston at his Beacon Hill residence, Andy came to L.A., where he picks up the story: "I was so excited to actually go to Brian Wilson's house. To talk with Brian Wilson. To have anything to do with Brian Wilson was a gigantic thrill for me." The tale of this record would soon become convoluted, but, as Andy explains, it began simply. "Seymour and I went out to his Malibu house. Landy was trying to be charming; the various people who worked for him were hanging around, videotaping everything. All of that was ridiculous. I knew Brian's history. And I knew what was going on with 'the shrink.' It just got down to the fact that Brian was interested in playing music for us; as he played, Brian might be saying, 'This isn't finished.' There were [some] songs I knew because I had all the bootlegs, although I didn't know Brian well enough to say so."

In 1988, Seymour told me that after listening to Brian's stockpile of songs, he quickly realized Brian had plenty of solid material. "I had a vision of making an album that would be to the music world what [the Academy Award-winning film] *The Miracle Worker* had been to the screen."

What Andy heard, knowing Brian's musical history so well, was a mixed bag. "The music was cool, the melodies, some of the chord changes." Andy is such an intense student of Brian's body of work that he is confident he knows Brian's lyrics: "I can hear a very natural Brian Wilson lyric; I'm pretty good at spotting those. And I am a big fan of Brian's lyrics; I really am. He's told me some of the ones he's very proud of, like 'My four-speed, dual-quad, posi-traction 409.' He singled that line out once at a rehearsal; he wanted us to know that he came up with that line, not Gary Usher."

The lyrics to the songs Brian played that day, Andy notes, "were kind of awkward, just kind of plodding. They were bringing the songs down rather than lifting them up. And it was pretty evident from the start that Landy was writing these things with Brian. Maybe Alexandra too. There's no getting around that."

Andy also recalls Landy trying to show that he knew how to deal with a record company president like Seymour. None of that mattered. Without the quality of songs Seymour and Andy heard that day and Andy's confidence and determination to handle this difficult set of circumstances, it's unlikely there would have been a deal. Andy, a staff producer at Sire, moved to L.A. to supervise the project.

Lenny: "That was the beginning. Seymour, of course, moves much quicker than I do. He picked up the ball and made the deal." That was the easiest part of the project. The making of the album would be stressful beyond belief. Andy: "I knew it was going to be *nuts*. I didn't know *how nuts*. You know as well as me, David, how bad it was. It was really bad. As far as Landy and everyone around him constantly putting in their two cents. For that entire solo record, there were an awful lot of cooks."

In 2018, Seymour Stein admitted to *Endless Summer Quarterly* (*ESQ*) editor David Beard, "I knew what I was getting into and had heard stories . . . It was about ten times worse than I expected . . . I thought Brian was a lovely person . . . still do. He's a gentle soul." But working with Landy, as Seymour describes it, was "horrible. He was trying to put words into Brian's head in order to get co-writing credits."

The issues surrounding Landy's songwriting were only one problem. Perhaps a bigger issue was the constant surveillance. Landy's assistants, the so-called "Surf Nazis," videotaped everything. Everybody on Landy's staff wore a beeper so Landy could get an instant report of what was going on. Back in 1976, Landy didn't have total control. As Andy puts it, "This was his second opportunity, and he wasn't going to blow it this time."

Andy's first day in the studio in 1987 was to work with Brian on two songs, one of which was 'Let's Go to Heaven in My Car.' Andy: "I played piano and drums and sang on both of 'em. Brian did tons of vocals and stuff on synthesizers. And Dick Dale was there too. Gary Usher was producing. Brian and Gary were definitely checking me out. Trying to see what I was capable of. Very soon after that, work began on the Sire album. And I'm not exaggerating; it was a really crazy process. Everything had to go through Landy. I was under his microscope; I was also trying to do a good job for Warner Brothers. It was really weird. I would report back to Lenny and Seymour and play them anything I had. I was the ultimate double agent.

"Landy would leave screaming [answering machine] messages for me. One time, Brian and I were driving to Orange County to see the Righteous Brothers, and I was playing this bootleg tape in the car, 'Celebrities at Their Worst.' And when the famous Buddy Rich rant came on, Brian said, 'He sounds just like Landy.' He was right.

"The most important thing was that Brian and I hit it off right away. How well we hit it off was really encouraging to me. His sense of humor came through even in these ridiculous circumstances. That, under those conditions, we were able to start writing songs and make a record was a real accomplishment. I felt great about that, and I know Brian did too."

That Andy and Brian loved and knew many of the same songs helped them connect. Andy: "He's a fan of songwriting in general, has been since he was a little kid." From the Gershwins, the Great American Songbook–era tunesmiths, to the Brill Building writers, to Motown icons like Smokey Robinson, Brian, as Andy points out, "always respected great songwriting. And I think it rubbed off on him. Obviously, he's got an incredible gift for melody and an amazing ear for harmony. But he also enjoys the whole craft of songwriting; he likes the process of writing songs. When it's done right, it's fun. It's really fun! Brian's worked with really good lyricists. Landy was a pretty bad lyricist."

Andy was like a life preserver, and throughout it all, amid this terribly stressful situation, he worked tirelessly. Explaining what he brought to the project, Andy reveals, "I knew he was not the guy from 1966, but there was enough of that guy inside of 1980s Brian Wilson that if you kick-started him or jump-started him or if you knew which buttons to push, you could get some great stuff out of him. That's what I was good at . . . I'm a big fan of his chord progressions and his melodies, and I think that's what he's going to be remembered for.

"The thing about Landy is that he did not hover around the studio that much. He would be on his cell phone, driving around Malibu and Beverly Hills in his Maserati. And he'd check in from time to time. He'd have the guys that worked for him watching us. Because they didn't understand what was going on, we were able to write without interference.

"I remember one time Brian was stuck for lyrics because he didn't like the lyrics that Landy or somebody had written for 'Melt Away,' which is a beautiful song. I'm just sitting there watching him and he's playing it over and over again, and finally he goes: 'I feel just like an island / Until I see you smilin'.' I think this was an example of his being a great lyricist. I'll never forget that. I witnessed him doing that . . . rhyming 'island' with 'smilin'.' Things like that didn't happen all the time, but I loved that moment."

Andy recalls other memorable musical moments: "Brian playing the bass line for 'Baby Let Your Hair Grow Long.' Very cool, syncopated bass line. Played on a fuzz bass. It sounds so funny when you hear it on its own. But put it together with everything else, it became really groovy, beautiful. And how about 'the planets are spinning around' on 'There's So Many'? Just gorgeous. Hearing that was definitely a highlight." For everybody.

The depth of their mutual musical knowledge became part of the album in ways that wouldn't be obvious. Andy: "On 'Walkin' the Line,' we talked about the Bobby Vee record 'Walkin' With My Angel,' and we actually wanted to get that same kind of footstep sound. One of the girls had some pretty noisy boots on, so we recorded her walking on the hard wood floor in the vocal booth."

Getting great lead vocals from Brian could be a challenge. Andy: "It's only natural that his voice matured. I don't expect him to sing like he did on 'Blue Christmas' or 'Surfer Moon'; it's not that I don't care what his voice sounds like, but I dig his stuff so much that just hearing the guy who wrote these great songs perform them is a treat! When you're however old he is and been through as much as he has, abused his voice with cigarettes and cocaine, it's just ridiculous that people expect him to sound like a choirboy twenty or thirty or forty years later. It's really tough."

However, Brian was still capable of so much vocally. As he told me back in '88, "the backgrounds were pretty good, but the leads, I had to keep doing them over. I was having trouble with my voice, but I found a great voice coach who helped me out a little bit. You know, I wasn't singing much. My voice is basically a falsetto kind of voice, and when I try to sing in legitimate voice, I become self-critical of my voice. A lot of people said, 'Brian, great vocals.' But I'm essentially a falsetto singer."

A few of the lead vocals on the album weren't what "old school" fans wanted from a singer who once had an effortless three-octave range. I wondered if, in certain places, Brian, in his passive-aggressive way, was almost sabotaging the record. It was something he hinted at in conversation.

The production of the album could be, to put it mildly, a torturous time. Sire and Warner Brothers needed help. Early in his career, in 1965, Russ Titelman had collaborated with Brian on a pair of terrific songs, co-writing the brilliant, *Pet Sounds*-esque 'Guess I'm Dumb' that Glen Campbell recorded. By 1988, Russ was a Grammy Award-winning producer. As a producer, the tracks he worked on with Brian—including 'Love and Mercy,' 'Melt Away' and 'There's So Many'—are among the best on the record. In 2018, Russ told *ESQ Quarterly*, "Those songs are directly from Brian's brain and his heart . . . like [Paul McCartney's] 'She's Leaving Home,' they're heartbreakingly beautiful melodies and soundscapes."

Brian told me that 'Love and Mercy' and 'Melt Away' are "probably the most philosophical songs on the album." And the planets line, from 'There's So Many,' was, according to Brian, "a subtle inference that astrology affects our lives . . . probably the most spiritual part of the whole album. It just had a vibration to it, you know? It was like, 'Whew.' I didn't know where it was coming from. I listened to it, and I felt 'What!?'"

From what Russ Titelman would explain to me for the "making of the album" story I wrote, Brian's singing was amazing to watch. Russ described a burst of creative energy. "We did about four or five days of great work. In that first week, we finished 'There's So Many,' added a bridge and did some great vocal stuff on 'Love and Mercy' . . . a tremendous amount of work in a few days. It was so exciting. Brian was 'on it.' Once he would get going, it was amazing . . . I'd say, 'Let's do the background vocals.' And he'd say, 'Give me eight tracks.' And he'd go out into the studio, and in twenty minutes, he would have all the backgrounds done. It was like the old days when you'd finish a whole record in one day."

In putting Russ's work in perspective, Lenny Waronker believes that "Russ did a real good job of helping Brian realize the beauty of his music. Brian hasn't done this in a long time, and he needed help with the technology. And where it needed some small fixing, Russ was able to show Brian how to do it in a simple way.

Lenny is enthusiastic when he recalls "what Russ said to me early on. I got a call one night from the studio. Russ was so excited. He just kept repeating. 'There's nothing to do here. It's all Brian. All I have to do is help him in a few areas, but it's his thing.' Russ sounded so thrilled, telling me that watching Brian work was like magic, a producer's dream."

When Lenny heard the results of all the hard work, "the idea that Brian was able to do this after so much time away was really shocking, beyond what anybody could expect. Brian hadn't been actively involved in the studio in many years, and he really just needed to get back in shape. By the end of the record, he was moving so quickly, like somebody on an exercise program who's progressing at a really rapid pace." In 1988, Lenny marveled, "The whole record-making thing came back to him. In some ways, he's similar to Prince in that he moves quickly."

To me, the most important piece Brian and Andy worked on together was 'Rio Grande,' a SMiLE-like song/musical suite that Lenny Waronker pushed Brian to do. In regard to 'Rio Grande,' Brian explained that "Lenny wanted me to get a little bit into that kind of SMiLE bag, and I did . . . It wasn't directly influenced by SMiLE, just the vibe of it, the basic feeling . . . That was a labor of love, and that's probably the best thing on the whole album. It's taken the longest to do, and we tried to pull it together so that it makes sense. So that people can hear it and it will flow naturally from one thing to another. Real hard to do at first . . . Andy did a little more with lyrics than I did, but I did a little more music. The two were a perfect marriage."

In 1988, Brian picked the "Take Me Home" section as his favorite part of 'Rio Grande,' explaining that the character in the song "has so many obstacles that he just wants to go home . . . run away from that stuff and go back to his home, wherever that might be [like] in the sky. That's symbolism right? God cannot be conceived of, so therefore we give him a literal meaning, and he's in the sky so that people can understand what is being said."

Andy recalls that track with great joy. "There are a couple of little things on 'Rio Grande' . . . parts of it I'd show him and he'd get off on . . . He's a great collaborator in that way. Traditional 'Brill Building' work ethic."

Brian's work ethic was excellent. What made the album such a contentious project was Dr. Landy's endless interference. Russ Titelman ultimately banned Landy from coming into the studio. As Russ told *ESQ*, "We need to be able to work unobstructed. Brian needs to be able to do what he wants." Still, Landy would continue to monitor what was going on through the "Surf Nazis." Russ: "And then [Landy would] call in and say, 'I don't want you working on 'Love and Mercy.' I want you working on this other song.'" As Russ described it, "My brain would just start to explode . . . Lenny knew how to talk to Landy, to stop him." Lenny Waronker would often have to play "bad cop" in the studio to get Dr. Landy to back off. Russ explained, "Lenny protected the work."

Andy survived the craziness because working on music with Brian was the ultimate reward. One of his favorite stories, though, is about a very rare day off. Andy: "Landy had me on a beeper. I didn't work for him, but he thought I did. I was either going to Brian's house every day or into the studio every day. I was deeply involved in this thing. I was living close to Warner Brothers Records. It was a crazy-long round-trip drive to Malibu every day from Burbank, but it was worth it. Because I was working with Brian Wilson. I had to keep telling myself that.

"And yet, I didn't really have to keep telling myself that because there were plenty of high points, plenty of really good collaboration. But I was beat. This friend of mine from Boston came to visit me. He said, 'You look exhausted. You've got circles under your eyes.' I said, 'Look, man, look at this situation! This crazy, psychotic, fake shrink has me on a beeper. His office calls me a hundred times a day. And I'm actually working with someone who is, to me, one of the greatest songwriters ever!'

"My friend said, 'We're going to put this beeper here in your bureau. I'm going to take you out to play eighteen holes of golf. It's Monday; the course will be empty.' And we did. I really did relax, and I had a great time. And, of course, when I got back there were like thirty-five messages on the answering machine. Messages from Landy like: 'Where the fuck are you? I've been trying to reach you for an hour and a half. You better call me right away. You're missing a golden opportunity!'"

It's something of a shaggy dog story, but the reason Landy was especially crazed that day was that, as Andy explains, "he and Brian had run into Bob Dylan at the Malibu Emergency Room. Brian was there for his monthly check-up and Dylan to get some stitches on his left hand. Brian suggested that I could come over and join them at the house in Malibu and play guitar because Dylan had a bandage on his hand and couldn't play."

Dylan did sing on a version of 'The Spirit of Rock and Roll,' but Andy's favorite part of the story happened the next day. "When I show up, Brian says, 'You'll never guess who was here yesterday. Folk music's Bob Dylan.' Just to hear him say that made all of Landy's yelling worth it."

Andy explains that he "couldn't have gone through all these things with Brian had he not been one of the funniest people I've ever known! And he knows how funny he is! I'm serious when I tell you that humor is equally important to him as music. Working with him, one on one, is a blast! He's hilarious!"

One Paley story is an example of how aware Brian was of his circumstances. Andy: "We did some sessions at the Sound Castle, a little studio in Silverlake near the old fire station on Hyperion. There was a basketball hoop outside, in the parking lot; we would shoot hoops once in a while. Brian missed a shot, and the ball went over the fence onto Hyperion. And it started rolling down the street." As Brian started to go for the ball, he said to Andy, "You realize, right now I could get out of this whole Landy program. I could just split. I could go grab that ball and make my escape right now. You think I should do it?" Andy said, "Brian, whatever you feel like."

In a sense, Andy was trapped in the program too. So when Eva and I met Andy, the two of them, real rock 'n' rollers from upstate New York, bonded instantly. Brother and sister. The three of us connected over our love for Brian and our concern for his well-being.

Andy now had friends of Brian's outside the project with whom he could share the madness. And for the first time, we had a musician/song-writer on our "team." Someone who was doing his best every day to keep Brian sane in an insane world.

Sometime in the fall of 1987, I was invited to the studio by Dr. Landy to hear the "work in progress." With Brian watching, Landy played me a half-dozen or more unfinished recordings, candidates for the solo album. During the writing of the first edition of *The Myth*, I was around when Brian made the still unreleased *Adult Child* album and the cult favorite *Love You* LP. But I had never really "lived through" the making of a Brian Wilson album; now, in this "work in progress," I could hear how promising the work was but also how important arrangement and production are. Given what I heard, I'm not sure I was even convinced at that point there was even going to be an album.

The world at large, of course, knew nothing of this. For Beach Boys and Brian Wilson fans—even Brian's friends—almost all of this was happening out of sight. But in 1988, everybody heard this remarkable bit of news: a Brian Wilson solo album would be out that year on Sire Records. If we hadn't met Andy, the news of the solo album would have had Eva and me just cheering from the sidelines. That is, until another bit of serendipity plunged me inside the madness.

In February 1988, I had begun working as a staff writer on the situation comedy *The New Leave It to Beaver*. Two weeks after we started work on the scripts for the new season, the Writers Guild went on strike. That meant that other than a few hours each day on the picket line, I was available.

In 1977, when I had published the first issue of my *Pet Sounds* fanzine, it was Bob Merlis, the head of Warner Brothers Records' publicity depart-ment, who had bought 1,000 copies of it, triggering the events that led to my book contract to write *The Myth*. Now, a decade later, Merlis was still Warners' head of publicity, and he hired me to put together a press kit for the forthcoming Brian Wilson solo album. The record was due for a late spring/early summer release.

As I began to work on a Brian, as opposed to a Beach Boys, promo-tional biography, I realized I had to reintroduce Brian to the music world, to contextualize his work and properly credit him for his role in the group. And, given the nature of the new album, also focus on his more artistic endeavors like *Pet Sounds* and *SMiLE*. I doubt Merlis or I expected I would write what was probably the longest press kit in history; it was so extensive that instead of it being in a folder, it had to be distributed in a three-ring binder. It included a bio, a wide-ranging interview with Brian, a "making of the album" story that included quotes from all the key producers and executives, and a track-by-track discussion with Brian of the album. Plus, two pictures: a typical black and white publicity shot and a color photo too.

Essentially, in this and the EPK (Electronic Press Kit) Warner asked me to edit, we were rebranding Brian Wilson, the genius behind the Beach Boys, now making his first solo album. I also had to write it in such a way that it would pass the Landy "approval gauntlet."

This is where it began to get really tricky. We all felt the pressure not to piss off Landy. That was part of the job. The press kit had a lot of incredible material in it, especially the interviews with Brian. The bio I wrote was truly how I saw his story. But the section on "the making of the album," well, that had a lot of public relations bullshit about Landy's role. Or what we might more appropriately call half-truths. Landy was acting like a madman but a madman completely controlling Brian.

I found a way to write it that we could all live with, and by "all," that included two major record company presidents, Seymour and Lenny, and the primary co-producers, Russ and Andy. I had to write it the way I did, or Landy would have tossed it all in the trash. In this chapter, I'm just giving you a sense of those nightmarish days. My work on the press kit is why in the late winter and spring of 1988, I was at Warner Brothers Records almost every day, and sometimes, in the afternoon or at night, hanging around the studio (usually Ground Control in Santa Monica) with Andy and Brian.

As the work dragged on, the album was becoming one of the most expensive records of the decade. Maybe ever. It cost close to a million dollars. Besides Andy Paley and Russ Titelman, Brian was recording with other co-writers and co-producers: Jeff Lynne and Lindsey Buckingham. And Lenny Waronker was in the studio too. But as Lenny couldn't be in there every day, he wanted to know as much as possible about what was going on. This is when I really began to learn about how the record business worked. Lenny and I started to get together regularly. At first, we met at least once a week for an hour, eventually closer to once a day. What did we talk about?

Lenny's goal: the album had to be worthy of the name Brian Wilson. As Lenny said to me, given that it was over twenty years since *Pet Sounds*, the new album had to answer the question "Is it worth the wait?"

The challenge? Dr. Landy was endlessly interfering.

The great surprise? With Lenny's encouragement, Brian and Andy had delivered the goods with 'Rio Grande.' This was the kind of *SMiLE*-like art piece that got the usually soft-spoken Waronker genuinely enthusiastic and excited.

Lenny told me this in 1988: "Brian really is a serious artist, very complex, very special. Working with him, I found him as a person to be considerate, kind, always sweet. As a collaborator, he's incredibly kind and generous. He has a way of taking an idea, no matter whose it is, and bending it in such a way that it works. And he doesn't even want to take the credit, that's how generous he is. What's really exciting is I sense that a lot of music is about to come out of him like an oil well that's about to blow. And I really think that this record shows he's doing something special, something that's missing in today's music, a unique pattern of colors, sounds that only Brian can make." Lenny truly felt that, and because we all believed that the music was so strong, so beautiful, we were publicly putting as much positive spin on the experience as possible.

In the midst of all of this, the Beach Boys were inducted into the Rock and Roll Hall of Fame in January 1988. To contextualize the moment, it was the year of the bittersweet Beatles induction; John Lennon had been murdered in 1980, and Paul didn't attend the ceremony.

Elton John introduced the Beach Boys. Brian spoke first. Wearing reading glasses, he recited a heartfelt speech about music being "God's voice," about music helping and healing. He said he wanted to write "joyful music." Brother Carl took to the microphone for a brief but moving speech about their late brother Dennis. So far, so good. Then, the roof sort of fell in. Mike spoke, sometimes to applause. He introduced Muhammad Ali. He talked about the planet. Sometimes what he said seemed to surprise, almost stun, the crowd.

Later in the evening, when Bob Dylan took to the stage, he thanked Mike for not mentioning him. Mike's was a headline-grabbing speech. At the time, and now, looking at it through the lens of history, it turned out to be not a great moment for the group. Google it and watch. You'll see what I mean.

Back in L.A., the months went by. Brian might be told to say "Dr. Landy's lyrics will prevail." Songs were rewritten and lead vocals re-recorded. My meetings with Lenny Waronker became more frequent. I was once asked if Brian needed somebody like his father to act as a kind of palace guard, to take care of everything except the music so he could focus solely on the music. The answer is "Yes," but the problem was Brian no longer had the ability to stand up to a loud, abusive figure. That made Brian something of an "easy mark" for Landy. Playing amateur psychologist for a moment, it's obvious that Landy understood the weakest aspect of Brian's nature. From his childhood on, Brian didn't like being yelled at; he would do anything to avoid that.

In the earliest days of the Beach Boys' career, the group and Brian needed Murry to keep "the suits" away. But Murry created his own static, which is why the Beach Boys eventually fired him. But the damage Murry had done to Brian made it more likely for him to be victimized by Landy. Landy was cunning, knew how to create and dominate an irrational atmosphere. He not only took more control of Brian than anybody in Brian's life had, before or since, but was also administering drugs in such a way as to keep Brian under his thumb.

To create at the highest level, the recording studio needs to be a sanctuary, almost a fortress that keeps out reality. Landy and his minions never stopped intruding. But the industry's love and appreciation for what Brian had created in the 1960s and what he had brought to this new record were so strong that they were willing to put up with anything—even including trying to reason with someone so unreasonable—to get the record made. The conversations about how to "stop" Landy were endless. He had the power to grind it all to a halt. With the finish line of the record finally in sight, compromises were reached.

As for my work on the press kit, the formal interviews I did with Brian for the album were the first extended ones I had ever done with him "on the record." Interviewing Brian is always an unusual experience because it doesn't seem like he says a lot. I recall, after our first conversation, driving home from Malibu depressed, feeling like it was a failure, a disaster. Then, when I listened to and transcribed the tape, I realized that he had given me "gold." He can express so much in just a few words.

Under "normal" circumstances, this would have all been the thrill of a lifetime. But Landy's seeming control over every aspect of Brian's life—diet, exercise, socializing and, more frightening, from what we were hearing, prescription drugs—was total. Making it a terrifying time. For the moment, all of those issues were set aside; I don't say that with pride. But everybody's primary goal was making this first solo album as good as possible and one that would sell a lot of copies.

Despite all of the palace intrigue, I think it's easily Brian's best solo album. The sheer quantity of quality songs: 'Love and Mercy,' 'Melt Away,' 'There's So Many,' 'Baby Let Your Hair Grow Long' (a kind of *Pet Sounds* sequel), 'One for the Boys' (his a cappella tribute to the Beach Boys). The autobiographical reveal of 'Walkin' the Line.' The cool groove of 'Night Time.' The sixties vibe of 'Meet Me in My Dreams Tonight.' 'Little Children,' and its sweet nod to his girls, Carnie and Wendy. The pure Beach Boys/ ELO fun of 'Let It Shine,' the easiest track to listen to because of Brian's smoothest vocals. And topping it all off, there was the exciting and successful return to modular experimentation with 'Rio Grande.'

The Warners publicity and marketing machinery was gearing up to "sell" the record. But in June 1988, a month before the album hit the stores, the *L.A. Times* published a major article on the Brian/Landy relationship. It's a "must read." (Google: Bad Vibrations + *L.A. Times*.) One quote from "Bad Vibrations": Russ Titelman called Landy's lyrics "'third-rate greeting card romantic drivel,' and says he finessed keeping them out of songs as much as he could . . . 'It was always an anti-creative atmosphere when he was involved,' Titelman said of Landy. 'A lot of shouting and irrational and argumentative behavior.'"

The craziness was now out in the open. For fans, for outsiders, for critics, a reasonable question might be: "What the hell is going on?" So when the album came out, there was excitement *and* concern.

The July 1988 release of the album included a significant publicity blitz. You can Google "Brian Wilson + 1988" and see him on David Letterman. On another show, he performed 'Night Time' on TV wearing a most unfortunate leather outfit. You can hear a lengthy interview he did with the gentle Deirdre O'Donoghue on L.A. public radio. You'll find it on Google as a "lost Brian Wilson interview" or "Bent By Nature extra: Brian Wilson – KCRW."

One question everybody had for Brian was, "Why are you making a solo album now?" For the press kit, Brian told me, "It's the right time, a good time to make a record. The music has got to surface eventually. I think we're all afraid of what's inside of us and all our memories. That stuff got in the way, but you become more at peace with yourself. You have a handle on all the bad things that happened to you in your life. You say to yourself, 'There's no way to get over this,' but somehow, you do anyway. I'm driven by my ego and my love for music. You gotta get it out. To me, the highest thing in the world is to make music." Perhaps all of the talk and my gigantic press kit were unnecessary. In one sentence of our marathon interview, Brian summed it up: "Love is the theme of my whole album."

The album itself got mostly great reviews. Here are a few highlights, what the industry calls "pull quotes":

"11 new songs that retain the pure, appealing harmonies and heart-tugging vulnerability of his best Beach Boys songs . . . a deft ability to bend modern studio technology . . . to his own poignant themes."
Timothy White, *New York Times Magazine*

"A remarkable work that recalls the exhilarating sweep of the Beach Boys' most endearing hits . . . an album with moments of both wonderful innocence and poignancy . . . the most dramatic return to artistic excellence since John Fogerty."
Robert Hilburn, *L.A. Times*

"A stunning reminder of what pop's been missing all these years. It is also the best Beach Boys long-player since 1970's *Sunflower*, although Wilson is the only Beach Boy on it. The songs are full of sunshine and choirboy harmonies and sing-along hooks . . . the eerie similarity in tune and texture of *Brian Wilson* and *Pet Sounds* . . . suggests the newly liberated Wilson has merely picked up where he left off two decades ago."
David Fricke, *Rolling Stone* (it was a four-star review)

"Not only the comeback of the year . . . a strong case for the argument that genius isn't a perishable commodity."
Paul Grein, *L.A. Times* (four check marks)

"A stunning display of mastery over the textures of rock 'n' roll."
Geoffrey Himes, *Washington Post*

"A timeless, placeless masterpiece . . . angelic in its fundamentalism"

John Wilde, *Melody Maker*

"Call it a miracle."

David Hinckley, *New York Daily News*

"Sparkling first solo album . . . begs comparison to *Pet Sounds* . . . one of the year's happiest, most essential releases."

Billboard

"As if Brian never went away."

Andy Gill, *Q* (four stars)

Unfortunately, the record wasn't a major chart success. The singles didn't become hits. In retrospect, perhaps the vibe of Landy around Brian just sent the message, "Stay away. Something weird is going on." Possibly, it was just not "commercial." Whatever that means. And maybe radio programmers felt there was only room for one new Beach Boys song on the airwaves that summer. That record, 'Kokomo,' went to #1, the biggest-selling chart hit of the group's career. Brian, to his everlasting regret, wasn't on it.

★   ★   ★   ★

I had been able to work on Brian's first solo album because of the Writers Guild strike, but one moment during the walkout brought me back to Universal Studios, where we filmed *The New Leave It to Beaver*. Before the strike, we had "cleverly" named the character of a teacher in one episode "Mr. Hawthorne," after the Beach Boys' birthplace. And Brian was going to play the part.

Brian Levant, the man responsible for the rebirth of *Beaver* and the showrunner of the series, was directing that day. He got the best performance he could from Brian. Afterwards, if I remember correctly, he said that working with Brian was like directing a child actor. That's how he got what he needed. A funny moment in a very tense time. (Google: Brian Wilson + Mr. Hawthorne.)

★   ★   ★   ★

The build-up to Brian's first album had been enormous, the work on it intense and too often unhappy. With the positive publicity in the rear-view mirror and sales of about 300,000 copies not quite what everybody had hoped for, especially given the cost of it, there was disappointment. And very little desire from the industry to deal with Landy again. The follow-up album was never released but bootlegged as *Sweet Insanity*.

The Writers Guild strike ended in August, so by late summer of 1988, I was back in the writers' room, coming up with smart-ass lines for our *Beaver* characters. I even wrote a short song and co-wrote another that ended up on the show, earning me membership in the songwriters' performing rights organization, ASCAP.

What came next was what surely had to be very good news. On April 1, 1989, the *L.A. Times* reported: "Eugene Landy, the flamboyant psychotherapist who guided singer Brian Wilson's comeback but was criticized for allegedly exerting too much control over his patient, has lost his license to practice psychology in California for at least two years." There's much more; you can read innumerable stories about this on the web. But for those of us who had been working toward—praying for—this day, it quickly became an enormous let-down. We thought that as Landy would no longer be able to legally practice psychology, that would be the end of his ties to Brian. We were so wrong.

Without a license, Landy and Brian became business partners. We were dumbstruck. Their company, Brains and Genius, wasn't illegal, per se, but it was certainly immoral, especially given the control, pharmaceutical and otherwise, Landy still exerted over Brian. It would be nearly three years before Landy would be "gone for good."

As was dramatized in the 2014 biographical feature film, *Love and Mercy*, Melinda Ledbetter had met Brian when he came into the Martin Cadillac showroom in West L.A. Landy thought it would be a good therapeutic experience for Brian to buy a car. Brian did buy a "Caddy," and he and Melinda started dating. As with everything in Brian's life, Eugene Landy had to have total control, and so when Dr. Landy thought it was no longer a good idea, the dating stopped. Not long after that is when my wife and I met Melinda. She, Eva and I quickly became good friends.

Somehow, word of this got back to Landy. A month after meeting Melinda, I was at Yamashiro, a Japanese restaurant in the Hollywood Hills; it was a record release party for Van Dyke Parks's new album, *Tokyo Rose*.

Waiting for a moment when I was standing alone, Dr. Landy sauntered over. In his quietly menacing way he whispered, "Well, I hear we're a Melinda Ledbetter fan now." Message delivered, he slithered away.

Still, he knew that, in my work, I would write glowingly about Brian. So, with his recommendation/insistence, I was hired by Capitol Records to craft the liner notes for what came to be called the "twofers." This was the long-awaited release of the Beach Boys' entire 1960s catalogue on CD: everything from their first album, *Surfin' Safari*, to the long out-of-print minor classics like *Friends* and *20/20*. Even *Stack-o-Tracks* made it to CD, but, for some reason, not their Christmas record.

The highlight of that experience for me included an interview with Paul McCartney for the *Pet Sounds* album, which was to be released on CD by itself. Through the years, I'd read in interviews that Paul loved Brian's music and *Pet Sounds*. Now, just before taking the stage, on the other end of the phone from Tokyo, there he was, my lifelong musical hero. Telling me how much Brian, 'God Only Knows' and *Pet Sounds* meant to him. His admiration for the album knew no bounds.

Paul told me, "It was *Pet Sounds* that blew me out of the water . . . I love the album so much. I've just bought my kids each a copy of it for their education in life—I figure no one is educated musically 'til they've heard that album." Paul confessed, "I've often played *Pet Sounds* and cried." As to its influence on the Beatles, he explained that "I played it to John so much that it would be difficult for him to escape the influence." Paul described it as "a total, classic record that is unbeatable in many ways." In conclusion, Paul noted, "I'm still a big fan. I figure, with what you're gonna write here, he'll know that. Just let Brian know that I love him, and that I still think he's gonna do great things. Tell him good luck, stay healthy for me and think good, positive thoughts."

It was a thrilling half-hour of conversation, and almost the entire interview was included as in insert in the 1990 *Pet Sounds* CD and the now out-of-print *The Pet Sounds Sessions* box set.

In my "regular" career in television, I was hired by George Paige Associates to write/co-produce a music series. I suggested we call it *The Spirit of Rock and Roll*. I thought Brian's song fitted the idea of the show, which presented a series of pop and rock legends singing their biggest hits. New York DJ Bruce Morrow, aka "Cousin Brucie," was our host. Guests included Jerry Lee Lewis, Frankie Valli of the Four Seasons, Neil

Sedaka, Felix Cavaliere of the Rascals, Martha Reeves, Gary Puckett, Peter Noone ("Herman" of Herman's Hermits), and Dion DiMucci. And Brian.

I remember meeting Dion backstage. I was a fan, but I'd never spoken to him before. Dion, I learned instantly, has a very droll wit. Very New York streetwise. (That meeting would inspire me to make a film on Dion, *Born to Cry*, in post-production at this moment.) Having observed the arrival of Brian with Dr. Landy, Dion said something like, "I remember when I was starting out in the business, there were managers. Then [referring to Yoko Ono] there were wife-managers. Now [referring to Dr. Landy] we've got the doctor-manager." He said it in a way that we all laughed, but it wasn't funny.

The six-episodes, filmed in Orem, Utah at the Osmond Brothers Studios, were filled with great music. But because of Landy's control, I wasn't able to spend a meaningful private moment with Brian. The series itself ran into financial problems and was never broadcast in the U.S.A.

Brian appeared healthy during the Landy Years. But the credible and incredibly frightening stories we heard of him being drugged by Dr. Landy were extremely disturbing. We had counted on the state's investigation to end the relationship. Now, Dr. Landy and Brian were partners. Here's how concerned and helpless we felt, how crazed and desperate we were.

One day, Ray Lawlor was visiting us at home in Santa Monica. Eva came up with the idea of kidnapping Brian from Landy during his daily run and hiding him at Ray's Long Island beach house. She said, "Landy would never look there." We were laughing at the absurdity of it. Ray said to Eva, "How the hell are we going to move him 3,000 miles? Someone is going to realize he's not out jogging." Eva, who was both fearless and half Italian, replied: "Don't worry. I got this." Nothing came of that or other similar conversations.

For a music-based magazine piece or a book about Brian, I was usually contacted by a reporter or author. But the most important and meaningful story I ever consulted on was Diane Sawyer's exposé on Dr. Landy for the highly rated ABC-TV program, *Primetime Live*. Ostensibly, the intended focus of the ABC story was Brian's first autobiography, *Wouldn't It Be Nice: My Own Story* which was being released by HarperCollins. Back then, as *Primetime Live* producer Shelley Ross explained in a recent conversation, "We would do lots of in-depth book promotions."

In the pre-streaming, pre-internet era, in the competitive world of network television, the network magazine programs battled for big stories. Ross: "I was working for a long time to get the [Brian] autobiography [exclusively] for *Primetime Live*. And I had a couple of sources, including, I can say now because he went on camera, [attorney] John Mason."

Ms. Ross had a much bigger story in mind than the book itself: Dr. Landy. "I was working on an investigation into Brian Wilson's 'care,' and I use that term loosely, for almost a year." From what she had learned, the release of the autobiography was another "financial opportunity for Landy; I was tipped off to that." Shelley had met John Mason during the notorious Menendez Brothers case which they covered on the ABC program. "We weren't friends, but John Mason always thought I treated the [Menendez] story fairly. When I contacted him about Brian, at first, he hesitated to go on camera. Then he decided that it [meaning Landy's control] was so bad that he had to speak up. And he trusted me."

In the 1988 *L.A. Times* article on Landy and Wilson, Mason, identified as Brian's lawyer in the story, had defended Landy. But two years later, he felt differently.

Shelley Ross: "I had done quite a bit [of research]. I think I had already convinced Landy to participate. I know I was calling everybody, but I was actually keeping certain calls until later because I didn't want to tip Landy's hand."

Exactly how I got involved is lost to the mists of time. Shelley: "I think you wrote me a note. Or left a message identifying yourself as 'Beach Throat.' I'm pretty sure I didn't know your name in the beginning. And I just thought, 'Well, this person has a real great sense of humor.' As we got to know each other, as I got to know and trust you, I realized you were telling me things I didn't know. Filling in as you do, and *only* you can do, the nuance of everything. The texture. The fabric. So, while you may not have created the story, you created the tapestry of truth. You filled out the picture.

"Once I had Landy on tape, a lot of people were willing to go on camera. But you really prepared me for interviews with everybody else. In terms of the story, I had the whole forest. With your knowledge, I could identify on which trees to focus. I felt like I knew the entire story and certainly that entire story wasn't going to be in [Brian's] biography.

The questions you raised . . . there were details that you knew, I think, for things we could ask Landy in the interview."

For those of us who wanted to see Landy gone, the story was a big deal. It was broadcast on October 10, 1991. You can see it on the web. Within six months, a restraining order was issued to keep Landy away from Brian. And while he violated it once, on Brian's fiftieth birthday, finally, blessedly, Landy was in the past.

Here is an excerpt from the section of the Wikipedia entry on the last days of Landy: "Peter Reum, a therapist who met Wilson while attending a Beach Boys fan convention in 1990, was alarmed by Wilson's demeanor and speculated that he may be suffering from tardive dyskinesia, a neurological condition brought on by prolonged usage of antipsychotic medication. Reum phoned biographer David Leaf who then reported Reum's observations to Carl Wilson."

There were so many moments like that, times when concerned fans and karma seemed to come into play. One significant one was this: Brian had done an interview at KROQ radio and a VHS tape was left behind. An employee who found it contacted Wayne Johnson at Rockaway Records. The KROQ person knew Wayne was a big Brian/Beach Boys fan. Wayne gave me the tape, and our friend Lauri Klobas carefully screened it. She found a few seconds of footage in which it seemed obvious that Landy was asking Brian what drugs he wanted or needed.

That was just one piece in a long chain of evidence. There's lots more at Wikipedia and in Peter Carlin's excellent Brian Wilson biography, *Catch A Wave*. What happened during Landy's time in Brian's life and their ultimate separation could easily be a very unhappy book all by itself. It would become a big part of 2014's excellent *Love and Mercy* film. In 1992, the end of the Wilson-Landy partnership was cause for celebration.

Landy's leaving changed the landscape of Brian's life and legacy in ways that led to surprising, unpredictable triumphs, remarkable career moments and the ups and downs of life itself. There would be all sorts of reunions in the years ahead. Melinda Ledbetter and Brian would begin to date again and eventually marry. Van Dyke Parks and Brian would record *Orange Crate Art* and ultimately complete *SMiLE*. Tony Asher and Brian would resume their songwriting partnership and one of their songs would be recorded by Carnie and Wendy Wilson.

What mattered most was that Landy was out of Brian's life. Forever.

And everything about being Brian's friend was about to become a lot easier.

Long after this battle was over, Brian would describe it by saying, "I served time for nine years." Finally, his prison sentence was over. Brian could now do whatever he wanted. The question was, what *did* he want to do?

CHAPTER 17

MELT AWAY: BRIAN WILSON'S PERSONAL RENAISSANCE BEGINS

WITH THE DEPARTURE OF LANDY, THE HAPPIEST, MOST INTENSE AND significant years of my friendship with Brian began. For the next fifteen years, I would be intimately involved in much that happened in his career and his life. Some of it, as his friend, is too private to share.

But for a while, in the 1990s, I did everything I could to help Brian. At his request, working closely with Melinda, I acted as a personal manager, handling requests for his participation in all sorts of projects. I introduced him to Lee Phillips, who became his attorney. Before the Lippin Group was engaged to handle his publicity, I was also something of a quasi-publicist, getting comments from him for articles and interviews. To maintain our friendship, even as I took on these duties, I was never on his payroll.

In my memory, before I began work on this update, the journey back from Landy's "imprisonment" to a truly meaningful career for Brian took place in baby steps. When I started looking through my files, the amount of activity as well as the extent of my involvement was overwhelming. Countless emails and correspondence and project files jolted me to recall some of the tales you'll read throughout this chapter.

There was so much correspondence to everybody involved in his career, including lengthy memos to at least four record company presidents. I would often accompany Brian to an important event, like McCartney at the House of Blues, Springsteen at Dodger Stadium or Elton John's sixtieth birthday concert in 2007, which coincided with his sixtieth show at Madison Square Garden.

If somebody was interviewing Brian, they might ask for advice. I always began by saying, "Don't ask him a 'yes' or 'no' question. Ask him about how something felt." If somebody was making a documentary about Brian, they typically engaged me as a consultant or interviewed me for the film. Or both. I worked with *Mojo* magazine on an interview with Brian when 'Good Vibrations' was voted their number-one single of all time.

If Brian didn't give a journalist a satisfactory interview, I might be asked to fill in a few blanks. And if I didn't like the tenor of an article about Brian, I might even write a letter to the editor. Sometimes, if Brian wanted to get a message to somebody important in his personal life, I would help him compose a letter he wanted or needed to send. In writing them, I never told Brian what to say or what to do. We just talked it out.

More importantly, from my point of view at least, was that we just spent time together. Without Landy or his goons eavesdropping. Without any ticking clock. In *The Myth*, I had told others how I thought Brian should be treated. Now, the shoe was on the other foot, and it was my turn to do as I had said. It was time-consuming and sometimes difficult and occasionally exhausting or even exasperating, but mostly it was fun. Brian loves to laugh, and we shared a lot of laughs. Once, he gave me two souvenir trophies, one for "World's Greatest Writer" and one for "World's Greatest Comic."

Now that Brian had been freed from Landy, he would often call to go out to dinner or go swimming at the Santa Monica "Y". Our friend Jerry Weiss laughingly recalls Brian and me coming back to my Santa Monica apartment with swimming-goggle marks around our eyes. We would just hang out. I remember that he and I could go to Morton's for a steak dinner, and even with salad and dessert, be finished in less than forty-five minutes. And not feel rushed.

Several Thanksgivings, Eva and I were welcomed to the Wilson home. There were two years, when my parents were in Santa Monica, that they were invited too. I have what strikes me as a funny memory of my older brother and Brian, sitting next to each other, comparing which medications they took for their mental disorders. Brian came to my father's seventy-fifth birthday party at the Bel-Air Bay Club. As Brian walked in, a friend of my father's, with his back to the entrance, was talking about being president of Capitol Records. It was fascinating to watch Brian accidentally overhear that, snap to attention and shift instantly into "professional Brian Wilson." Until I told him the guy was a joker.

It was a wonderful time. All my worlds had come together. And somehow, given my own burgeoning career, I was always available when Brian called. I had believed that if Brian was treated with respect, great things would happen. And slowly but surely, they did, making the 1990s the beginning of something of a Brian Wilson "Renaissance" and setting the stage for what was to come in the new millennium.

★   ★   ★   ★

The Brian Wilson Wikipedia entry is filled with a treasure trove of dates and details. There's also a Wikipedia page for every project in his career. Same with the Beach Boys. So I'm mostly writing here about the parts of Brian's story that intersected with mine, events that were significant and relevant to the unfolding story of the artist. In the 1990s, there were a lot of those.

One of the biggest was when Brian and Melinda began seeing each other again. We became a foursome, with Eva and me eating lots of dinners with them. It was like going out with two teenagers. Usually, we were at a steakhouse, often at an old-school Santa Monica restaurant called Bob Burns. Eva almost always insisted that we pay. She knew that for his entire adult life, people had expected Brian to pick up the check. He loved being treated. Not as much as he loved eating, but he got a kick out of somebody else slapping down their credit card.

Musically, as Andy Paley remembers, "Brian called me on the day the restraining order was served to Landy and the conservancy case was over and he said, 'Andy, what are you doing? Can you come over right now and write with me? I'm free! I can do whatever I want now!' And I did drive right over. And we worked on something!" Off and on, "Brian would come over to my house in Los Feliz whenever he felt inspired. There were periods when that would go on for a week or two, here and there. It started soon after Landy was gone but it would happen in spurts over a period of years. That's when we did a whole bunch of writing. I recorded most of it on a boombox, but we'd go to real studios once in a while."

Capitol Records was pleased with my liner notes for the Beach Boys CD catalogue, and in 1992, they again hired me, this time to write the Beach Boys and Beatles chapters for their fiftieth-anniversary book. As I'd just written the liner notes for the reissues, this was a new challenge for me: finding a way to tell the Beach Boys story in a different and meaningful way.

I began: "Spring, 1962. In Hawthorne, California, an obscure, working-class town just about a dozen miles 'with the top down' from the Capitol Tower, lived a nineteen-year-old Adult Child who was poised on the cusp of immortality. One day soon, he would create a body of work so commercially and artistically valuable that, with his family, he would simultaneously solidify rock's importance in the marketplace, confirm its validity as an art form and challenge and overturn the conventions that governed artists in the music business. That boy, drawing on a creative well as deep as the nearby Pacific, would, between 1962 and 1968, embellish, embrace and conceive musical innovations that would forever change both the creative record-making process and the record company/artist relationship."

One other favorite line of mine from the piece: "Brian's best compositions were hook-filled melodies seemingly plucked from the heavens." And the chapter in Capitol's book ended with a reference to the 1990 "twofer" CDs: "This made the music available to a new generation of fans, so they could hear for themselves why composers like Randy Newman consider Brian Wilson's work with the Beach Boys the most important pop music of our time."

And that was just the latest version of my journalistic dance that continues to this day: giving Brian Wilson proper credit while fairly balancing what he did (compose, arrange, produce, sing) with the contributions of the other Beach Boys, arguably the greatest vocal group in rock history.

In 1993, Capitol again hired me, this time to compile and produce (with Andy Paley and engineer Mark Linett) the first Beach Boys box set, *Good Vibrations: Thirty Years of the Beach Boys*. The technical work was done by Linett, who has worked on almost every Beach Boys reissue since then.

There were many drafts of track lists. Looking back, I know we left off at least one key Carl Wilson song, 'Feel Flows.' But we were thrilled to include several significant unreleased songs by Dennis and Brian from the "*Sunflower* era," presaging the brilliant 2021 Beach Boys box set, *Feel Flows*.

In putting the collection together, I was focused on two goals: give fans their money's worth and include music from the *SMiLE* sessions. The first would happen, with Capitol agreeing to my idea to include a fifth bonus disc full of all sorts of demos, vocal sessions, outtakes, live versions, et al. Material that had never been commercially available. The bigger challenge was *SMiLE*.

Following my instincts and trusting his, I sat down with Brian to go over the suggested track listing Andy and I had come up with for the box. Brian had a few ideas which were easily incorporated. Then, I gingerly brought up the subject of *SMiLE*. I told Brian, "If we look at this list, between the released versions of 'Good Vibrations' and 'Heroes and Villains,' there's a giant hole." I explained that, "as this is a career retrospective, we should include some of the never-before-released songs from the *SMiLE* sessions. That it wouldn't be seen as *SMiLE* being finished but just part of the Beach Boys' career."

Brian thought about it for a moment, and then said, "OK," and asked which songs I thought we should include. Having heard bootlegged *SMiLE* material, I had a sense of which pieces were closest to being finished. I suggested what were, to me, key recordings from the era. My list purposely didn't include 'Fire,' the recording of which had become something of a flash point in him shelving *SMiLE*.

Brian agreed to the additions; I was relieved and excited. When we submitted the track listing to Capitol, they were blown away by how much *SMiLE* sessions music the box had; they knew it would be invaluable in the promotion of the collection. I think close to forty percent of the box was "never-before-released" material. That helped make it a giant success, and it earned a gold record.

More importantly to me, the *SMiLE* conversation with Brian had started, with a positive result. The music had been released, and the world, or at least Brian's world, hadn't come to an end. What I learned from the process was that if you respected that this music was *Brian's* creation, that if you presented a reasonable case for doing something, he would respond reasonably. It was the beginning of a very fruitful and productive time for us.

In the booklet for the box, Brian wrote about the production team who had put it together: "David Leaf, an old friend, also put a great deal of effort into this project. His knowledge of my and the Beach Boys' history is incredible, and he put it to good use here, so that the songs seem to tell a story as the years go by. He also had to write his thoughts in a very limited space, and he did a great job."

For the box, just a year after writing my essay for the Capitol fiftieth-anniversary book, I was again telling the Beach Boys story. I had to begin with a different approach. This time, I wrote: "An American family making music just because they loved the way it made 'em feel . . . it all began so simply so long ago."

Toward the end of this version of the story, I quoted one of Brian's oldest friends: "Brian Wilson is a healer. He always told me that his musical message is love, and he truly believes that all we need is love . . . he wants us to love each other. That may seem simplistic, but you can't argue with a man whose music has brought so much joy and love to everybody who opens their heart and listens."

Then, I wrote, "As the primary creator of the music on this set, it seemed appropriate that Brian have the last word about what his music does for him, and by extension, us. Brian: 'It takes away fear. It adds strength. It's life supporting.'" And finally, a lyric from *Pet Sounds*. "Listen to my heart . . . beat. Listen. Listen. Listen."

The dream that had driven me in 1971 appeared fulfilled. I had moved to California, written a book about Brian, become his friend, and he trusted me enough to let us include *SMiLE* music on the *Good Vibrations* box. For the moment—I thought perhaps forever—this was as good as it would get. I was wrong, but there would be some fascinating trips and bumps in the road before we could eternally *SMiLE*.

In 1992, Van Dyke Parks had begun work on a new album, and he approached Brian to sing on what would be the title track. I think Van Dyke felt there was a lot of unfinished business between the two of them. At first, Brian agreed to sing on the title song. At that initial vocal session, as Peter Carlin reported in *Catch A Wave*, Brian asked Van Dyke, "Wait a minute. What am I even doing here?" Parks's snappy reply: "You're here because I can't stand the sound of my own voice!" Brian couldn't disagree. "Well, that makes sense! OK, take one."

I was thrilled to hear that he and Van Dyke were working together again. The result? A beautiful album called *Orange Crate Art*, filled with stunning Wilson vocals, vocal arrangements and trademark harmonies, all in service to a premier collection of Van Dyke Parks's songs. To this day, I believe it is one of the best things Brian has done in the past half-century. If a question in the 1990s was, "Can Brian still sing?," this record answered the question with a rousing "Yes." So impressive was the record that I was involved in trying to put together a Brian Wilson/Van Dyke Parks tour to promote it. Unfortunately, it didn't get off the ground.

The studio reunion of Brian and Van Dyke, the two old friends and collaborators, was happening at almost the same time the first Brian Wilson feature documentary was being made: the Don Was film, *I Just Wasn't Made for These Times*. For that project, I got two different single-card, on-screen credits, "Creative Consultant" and "Historian," and I was interviewed by Don.

The film was the first biographical documentary on Brian and, in many ways, the most fascinating. The highly stylized piece includes a remarkable cast of stars, but, more significantly, in his scenes with Melinda and by himself, Brian is talkative and revelatory. All of Brian's immediate family—Audree, Carl, Carnie, and Wendy—are seen on-screen in often painfully candid interviews. Brian's daughters express their anger and sadness at what it was like to grow up with a father who was not paternal; his ex-wife Marilyn speaks with an honest pain about her time with Brian, and the challenges he faced with the Beach Boys and with being married.

The intragroup struggles aren't ignored. Brian explains the tug of war simply: "I wanted to do my kind of music, and they wanted to do their kind of music."

Carl talks about the *Pet Sounds* prayer sessions and Mike's issues with Van Dyke Parks's lyrics for *SMiLE*. Carl admits that Mike felt "the lyrics were not relatable. To him, they were artistic, airy fairy, too abstract. Personally, I loved them."

There are many highlights of the film, including terrific commentary from Danny Hutton, David Crosby and Graham Nash, Tom Petty, distinguished musicologist Daniel Harrison, Hal Blaine, and Brian's favorite engineer Chuck Britz, who says that, as far as he was concerned, Brian was the Beach Boys.

The two musical moments in the film that stand out for me as timeless are Brian and Van Dyke Parks's duet on 'Orange Crate Art' and Brian, Carl and Audree's version of 'In My Room.' It's not a long film, but it says a lot. And probably for the very first time, we get genuine glimpses of the real Brian Wilson. Brian is as articulate as you'll see him in just about any interview or documentary. It's on YouTube. Watch it.

My personal favorite moment of the production of the film came on the day I arrived on the set, and Don was talking with Lindsey Buckingham, the brilliant artist/producer. Don introduced me, saying, "I don't think you know him, Lindsey, but this is David Leaf." When Lindsey heard my name, his response stunned me. Something like: "Oh my God, David. When we were making *Tusk* [Fleetwood Mac's experimental, two-album set], I had your book in the studio. And I kept re-reading the chapters about *SMiLE*." And that's how, as he explained, he got through the sessions without compromising his vision.

What he was saying was clear. At least to me. He wanted to make sure that nobody threw him off track. To follow his instincts, his creative inspiration. It was OK that this new album was going to be different than the previous two Fleetwood Mac multimillion sellers. What he said was unbelievable validation for me. I was truly taken aback. I was a big fan of Lindsey's work, so I was genuinely thrilled that my book had a big impact on such a successful artist. It meant a lot to me. Then and now. In the press release for his documentary, Don Was said:

> In the fall of 1989, I was working with a band who turned me on to the bootlegged recordings of Brian Wilson's legendary, aborted SMILE sessions. Like a musical burning bush, these tapes awakened me to a higher consciousness in record making. I was amazed that one, single human could dream up this unprecedented and radically advanced approach to rock 'n' roll.
>
> I was really stunned when I met him several months later. Far from the catatonic drug burn-out the tabloids loved to depict, the guy I got to know was lucid and happening . . . How could a talent so great be so misunderstood and underappreciated?

For Don, the purpose of the documentary was to attempt "to explain to the non-musician precisely why the phrase 'Brian Wilson is a genius' has appeared on the lips of three generations of musicians like holy gospel."

SMiLE had inspired another project! Like most documentaries, the film was backwards-looking. Telling us what had already happened and what it meant. What made this film different was that Don's approach made it artistically and historically successful. We knew why Brian was a genius. But, at that point, we were still a small cadre of true believers. I was pleased to see a movie that put Brian in the spotlight. Singing some of his classics. I felt that anything that spread the gospel of Brian was positive.

What, I wondered, would be the next big Brian Wilson thing?

Fate or kismet or serendipity—whatever you want to call it—was about to knock on Brian's door. Or at least play music that connected with his one good ear and his heart, a major moment that reverberates to this day: Brian heard the musicians who would become essential members of his touring and studio band.

In 1994, Paul Rock, among many things a big California music fan, had produced a tribute to the Byrds and was now planning one to honor Brian. His Wild Honey Foundation concerts were charity events, so everybody participated happily. In a recent conversation, Paul reminded me, "You were responsible for arranging for Brian to bring his band [which included Andy Paley, Andy's brother Jonathan, voice artist and musician Billy West, and the Cars' Hall of Fame guitarist Elliot Easton] to the Morgan-Wixson Theatre in Santa Monica on November 3rd, 1994."

Paul recalls that during the show, when he was "backstage, Brian, for the first time, heard the Wondermints [Darian Sahanaja and Nick Walusko's terrific 'progressive pop' group] performing and was deeply impressed, thus laying the groundwork for their eventual inclusion in the touring band that would come together in the next few years." Paul Rock also remembered that a few months later, "you arranged for us to come to Brian's house to record the Everly Brothers' 'Dream' with Danny Hutton—probably one of my biggest thrills!"

One of *my* biggest thrills and honors as a friend of Brian's came next. On February 6, 1995, Brian and Melinda were married at the stunning Wayfarers Chapel on Palos Verdes Peninsula. Melinda's sister Marsha (R.I.P.) was her maid of honor; Brian's brother Carl was best man. Eva and I were both in the wedding party: she as a bridesmaid, me as an usher. I seem to remember escorting Mike Love and his wife, Jacqui, to their seats. But maybe we just nodded hello.

Before the vows were taken, I was standing "backstage" with my fellow ushers, Danny Hutton and Andy Paley. And Carl. What improbable circumstances had brought us together? We were nervous, so to lighten the mood, I made a dumb joke; Carl smiled tolerantly. The "I dos" were strong and firm. It was a very blissful day for all of us who had wondered if Brian, in the words of his song, 'Still I Dream of It,' would find his world. He and Melinda had found their world together.

Brian and Melinda have just taken their vows. A very happy day.
Credit: BriMel Archives

Just before the wedding, I came up with the idea for a bachelor party I thought would be perfect for Brian; I called it "Brian's Bachelor Bowling Bash at Bayshore." I reserved five lanes at the Bay Shore Lanes in Santa Monica. It was a few blocks from the Santa Monica Pier. Just across the street from the Santa Monica Civic Auditorium, where *The T.A.M.I. Show* had been filmed, a great Beach Boys triumph in 1964.

The invited guest list spanned Brian's entire life. One team was "Carl's Clan," featuring his sons Jonah and Justyn and Carl Wilson's former brother-in-law and longtime Beach Boys sideman Billy Hinsche (R.I.P.). "Paley's Ponies" featured Andy, Andy's brother Jonathan and Elliot Easton. Danny Hutton was on Brian's team. Beach Boys manager Jerry Schilling was there, as was Melinda's nephew Lenny. So was Luis Ramos, husband of Brian and Melinda's close friend Gloria. Me too.

There were others invited, and I don't remember the exact guest list or who won. I had hoped for a bigger turnout, kind of a Beach Boys reunion. But it didn't matter. We had pure, old-fashioned fun. Following the bowling party, one of Brian's friends insisted on a more traditional bachelor party, and we all drove to a Hollywood strip club. After a few uncomfortable minutes, Brian asked me to drive him home.

Not long after that time, maybe it was doing promotion for *Orange Crate Art* or the Don Was project, I was hovering off-camera as Brian was being interviewed. Asked why he had become so active, he told a reporter one of the most important things I'd ever hear him say. His answer was but four words, but to me, they spoke volumes. Brian said, "I have emotional security." Without it, he wouldn't or couldn't work. Without "emotional security," he might just hibernate, eat and drink too much and get terribly overweight. With it, he was delighted to make music.

At that point in time, because Brian didn't have a formal manager, I was still helping out. Because he didn't seem overly ambitious, Melinda, now Mrs. Wilson, faced the biggest challenge: trying to figure out what was best for Brian's career. She was his "emotional security." There was so much to do.

The success of the 1993 *Good Vibrations* box had set my mind reeling with ideas for how to create more box sets. I thought of myself as a surrogate for the fans. What did *we* want? I talked with Brian about it, and together, we came up with a five-year plan that would start in 1996. Each collection, like 1993's *Good Vibrations* box, would be pegged to a thirty-year anniversary.

In the fall of 1995, Brian and I went to the Capitol Tower and had a very positive meeting with the head of the catalogue division. He loved our ideas. First up, for May 1996, would be what I called *The Pet Sounds Sessions*. For the fall of 1996, a 'Good Vibrations' sessions two-CD collection. For the spring of 1997, a *SMiLE Sessions* box. And more. But as these were Beach Boys projects, the group and its management had to approve. So we waited. And waited. And watched the months go by. To get it released in May of 1996, we needed to get to work. But the "green light" wasn't quickly forthcoming.

If I recall correctly, the Beach Boys said yes to the box set in January 1996, so finally, in late January 1996, Capitol told me and engineer Mark Linett to get to work. Everything had to be finished by the first week of March. It was an insane sprint, but I resolved to talk with everybody alive who had a key role in the production of the record. Every day, I spent a dozen hours on the phone, with the receiver cradled in my ear. I typed their words as they spoke. There was no time for transcribing. I did this so much that I ended up with a giant crick in my neck.

I soon realized that I would need two books, one on the history of the album and a separate book that would include all of these fascinating interviews. Capitol agreed.

My ideas for what *The Pet Sounds Sessions* should and could be made perfect archival, historical and creative sense to me. It was, I believed, what a fan would want to hear: the original album in mono and stereo, backing tracks without vocals, the vocals without tracks. Outtakes from recording sessions. Lots of sessions. These ideas weren't, to use the cliché, "brain surgery." I was a fan. I knew lots of fans/friends to talk to about this, and we were all excited. I'd discussed it all with Brian, and while he may have been surprised that people were so interested, he was excited too. After all, *Pet Sounds* was *his* greatest creation.

Unfortunately, by mid-March, there were issues facing the project. In part, I think, it came down to what I'd written. I was told the box was "too pro-Brian." Even the cover credit, "Produced by Brian Wilson," seemed to cause controversy.

I asked everybody who would listen what I'd done wrong. I pleaded my case: "Except for 'Sloop John B,' Brian composed every song on this record. He arranged and produced every instrumental track. He arranged the vocals. Of four of the thirteen cuts on *Pet Sounds*, there are two instrumentals and two on which Brian sings lead without background vocals. 'God Only Knows' features Carl on lead and only Brian and Bruce on backgrounds. That means that on five of the thirteen songs, there are no 'Beach Boys' group vocals at all." I continued, "On *Pet Sounds*, Brian is the primary lead singer." How, I wondered, was it possible to give Brian too much credit on that record?

Nobody at the label would disagree with me, but it didn't matter. According to my files, *Billboard* had scheduled a special tribute to *Pet Sounds* and *Rolling Stone* was ready to commission a major article. I recall that *Saturday Night*

Live mentioned it, as did the *L.A. Times*, *USA Today* and other media outlets. George Martin and Paul McCartney were eager to hear it.

I was now experiencing first-hand the complications of family and business that I had written about in *The Myth*. Google: "Still No Vibrations + *Washington Post*" to read more. Or the Wikipedia entry on *Pet Sounds*.

The positive side of working on *The Pet Sounds Sessions* box set is that it had taken me ever more deeply into Brian's creative life. It was during this time that I first interviewed George Martin about the album and its influence on the Beatles. Shortly afterwards, he was knighted. There was no connection between those two events. However, the relationship I established with Sir George on that occasion would bring more magic into Wilson World. (And my work, too, beginning with a wonderful interview Sir George did with me for my 2000 Bee Gees documentary, *This Is Where I Come In*.)

The *Pet Sounds* project had also triggered a brand-new creative endeavor; it would start perfectly and end in something of, what was to me, a car crash. Tony Asher had been interviewed for *I Just Wasn't Made for These Times* and, in interviewing him for *The Pet Sounds Sessions*, I had triggered a lot of old and positive memories of working with Brian. I must have mentioned it to Brian because he wanted to see Tony, to try and write with him again. I think it happened pretty simply. Brian asked me to call Tony, and before we knew it, they were back at the Wilson piano writing songs. It was magical. Terrific songs. 'Everything I Need.' 'This Isn't Love.' The latter would make it to record as an instrumental on a 1997 Windham Hill album, *Songs Without Words*, and the Wilson/Asher version on Brian's 2000 *Live at the Roxy* CD.

Around the same time that Brian and Tony had reunited, Brian's daughters, Carnie and Wendy, expressed interest in working with their dad. They'd had a great time singing 'Do It Again' together in the Don Was movie. In my mind, a light bulb went off. Brian and Tony would write what would be the sequel to *Pet Sounds*. And Brian's "girls" (their successful group Wilson Phillips had recently broken up) would join him on an album called *The Wilsons* that he would write, arrange and produce. As *Pet Sounds* had been, this would be a family affair. Was this just my delusion?

At the first instrumental tracking session, it was clear that Brian's skills were intact. Like the old days working with the so-called, legendary "Wrecking Crew," he took sixteen players into the studio and cut a great backing track for 'Everything I Need.' In three hours. Ray Lawlor was there, and after the session was over, he asked Hal Blaine, "How close is this to 1966?" Answer: "Eighty-five percent." Ray asked, "What's the fifteen percent that's missing?" Hal replied, "Ego." Back in '66, Brian had written a song titled 'Hang On to Your Ego.' Clearly, Brian hadn't been successful. But eighty-five percent of Brian Wilson was still incredible. It was exciting beyond belief.

I never found out exactly what happened, or I've blocked out the memory, but after a few sessions—after a lot of father/daughter love—something went amiss. There would indeed be an album called *The Wilsons*. But other than 'Everything I Need,' Brian wasn't meaningfully involved with the writing or production of the album. I was beyond disheartened, but it was hard to know how Brian felt. Perhaps there had been so many such disappointments in the past thirty years that he could shrug his shoulders and move on. As Ray notes, when something like this happens, "Brian loses interest and it's over." To me, though, his poker face was etched with the pain of a lifetime of hurts, large and small. The reunion with Tony was sweet, but brief. In part, I felt like this was my fault. I had encouraged him to take command of his work, and then he had lost control. I now understood viscerally why he didn't want to fight anybody.

In 1996, Brian and Melinda adopted the first of five children; they asked Eva and me to be Daria Rose's godparents. We joyously accepted, and to this day, even during the COVID-19 pandemic, Daria and I text and Zoom and talk. The professional and personal continued to intertwine in wonderful ways.

As to *The Pet Sounds Sessions*, the box was finally released in 1997. I don't recall the exact circumstances but, as far as I could tell, not one word I had written was changed. It was a good lesson in what it meant to be on Brian's side in the Beach Boys world. Regardless, it was a big success, earning rave reviews and my first Grammy nomination, for "Best Historical Recording." Because Brian was singled out in the reviews and was named in the title as the producer of it, the Beach Boys' reaction was reportedly less than positive. I was mystified; he had produced all of the original sessions. All we'd done was organize and edit. Nonetheless, even its success seemed to create some grumbling within the group.

At the Grammys, I remember sitting next to Brian, and when our category was announced and the legendary engineer/producer Phil Ramone said, "And the winner is," Brian started to stand up. He assumed we were going to win. We didn't. But a few years later, Phil would become central to a major career moment for Brian.

Despite the triumph of *The Pet Sounds Sessions*, the plans Brian and I had presented to Capitol for a series of boxes and collections were, unfortunately, shelved. *The Pet Sounds Sessions* was the last time I would formally work on a Beach Boys project.

Nineteen ninety-seven did include another genuine highlight: Brian inducted the Bee Gees into the Rock and Roll Hall of Fame. Brian, who never likes to give speeches, needed a little encouragement/convincing to do this. I was the right man for this job. Our foursome—Brian, Melinda, Eva and I—went to Cleveland for the big event. Bonnie Oviatt, a smart, sweet, music-loving woman who worked with the Hall of Fame, was by our side as we worked on making this happen.

The night before the induction, we were all in the hotel room when Brian and Barry Gibb met. Big fans of each other's work, both were shy in the presence of greatness. Barry's nervous laughter put Brian at ease. It was like watching creative twins who had been separated at birth. The oldest brother and primary creative force in each family band. In the hotel room, Barry worked with Brian on 'Too Much Heaven,' the song Mr. Wilson would be singing in salute to the Bee Gees.

When I was researching my Bee Gees authorized biography, I was in the studio the night Barry had cut the lead vocal for that beautiful song. In a darkened control room, other than the engineers, I was the only person there. Watching as Barry sang, his hands holding the headphones, his body swaying to the rhythm. I sat in awe. Looking through the glass, I'd never experienced anything like it. Was this song as great as I thought? Yes, it was. And still is. And I was at the United Nations in January 1979 for a concert when they performed it and donated the song to UNICEF.

That 1997 night in Cleveland, with Brian and Barry together, was another full-circle moment for me. You can see the Bee Gees induction on YouTube, and in the speech I helped write, Brian pointed out that the Bee Gees matter because "there's nothing more important than spiritual love in music." I couldn't find Brian's performance of 'Too

Much Heaven' on the web. What I remember is that on the bridge, when Brian hit the high note on the phrase "you're my life," we could hear David Crosby, at the next table, react: "Oh my God." A very loud exclamation from one of rock's greatest harmony singers. That's how we all felt.

In 1996, during the making of the Beach Boys' country duets album, *Stars and Stripes* (I love Willie Nelson's 'The Warmth of the Sun'), Brian and Melinda had become friendly with that record's producer Joe Thomas and Joe's wife, Chris. A deal was made for Joe to work with Brian on a solo LP. The Wilsons bought a second house outside Chicago near the Thomas's home in St. Charles, Illinois, where Brian spent much of the next year making the album. The very strong record is filled with great singing and background vocals from Brian and a number of terrific new Brian Wilson tunes; my favorite is probably 'Cry.' (You can watch a documentary on *Imagination* on the web.)

I remember when Melinda told Eva and me about this; she said, "I can't believe now that great things are happening, you guys won't be there." There was nothing we could do about it; we both had jobs in L.A. We did visit them in St. Charles a couple of times; it was so much fun to spend time with baby Daria. Coincidentally, Mark Nadler, one of my best friends from college, lived in the same town, and we were able to catch up and realize we were still "on the same page."

Back in L.A., my documentary and television careers were both briskly moving forward, but I was often the person people called if they wanted to get in touch with Mr. Wilson. That led to one of my all-time favorite Brian Wilson days, when Sir George Martin came to Brian's house for a taping of his multipart series, *The Rhythm of Life*.

The session was set for March 13, 1997, and in advance of it, I sent a three-page memo to the producer outlining the day and, at the end, I offered a few suggestions: "Having interviewed Brian on numerous occasions and talked to him about the nature of music many times, there is no question that he has fascinating things to say about the *spirituality* of music. He strongly believes that music brings love to people. And given that a part of your series is about what music does for the people who make it and the people who hear it, these promise to be fruitful areas for discussion.

371

"Obviously," I continued, "he can talk about his music. That's a given. But I've found that he can be most profound when he talks about what takes place when he hears music. If you want, I can tell you who many of his favorites are, but in previous interviews, I've seen him enthusiastically talk about and play songs by George Gershwin (in particular, *Rhapsody in Blue*), the Beatles, the Bee Gees, and the Four Freshmen. You don't need to limit yourself to those artists, but they're almost guaranteed to evoke a strong response. (Other favorites include Elton John, Paul Simon and Stevie Wonder.) Let me know if I can provide any more information in this area."

This was typical of my involvement in projects like this and being present on the day of the taping was the reward. As was also typical of that era, Eva was with me when we drove to the Wilson home. When Sir George arrived, the four of us were in the foyer. Brian greeted him, holding two of the Wilsons' Maltese puppies. After the first "hellos," George asked the names of the dogs. Brian held up the dog in his right hand and said, "This is Paul." Holding up the other in his left, he said, "This is Ringo." Taken a bit aback, George, with a hint of a grin, inquired, "Where's John?" Eva said, "He's dead." That was the kind of *Goon Show* irreverent humor that had endeared Sir George to the Beatles. He stifled his laugh.

Now, it was time to work. The camera crew set up in Brian's music room, and I was off to the side of the camera, watching as George interviewed Brian. Knowing how much Brian loved the Beatles records, I was puzzled, wondering why he was not being more forthcoming. Then, George asked Brian a question by demonstrating something on the piano. And I saw the light bulb go on, and from that moment forward, Brian was engaged, talkative.

What had happened? In my analysis, Brian had entered the record industry in an era when the credit "producer" often meant not much more than scheduling a recording session and saying, "Take 1." It didn't necessarily mean you were a musician. So, when George asked Brian a question about a chord change, Brian realized, "Oh, George understands music, so I can talk with him on that level."

After the taping session at the house, the crew, Brian and George went to Mark Linett's home studio, where Sir George had the chance to remix 'God Only Knows.' As you can see (Google: Brian Wilson + George

372

Martin dissect the Beach Boys), Brian was more than enthusiastic and complimentary when he heard Sir George's mix.

There are so many things that happen in the everyday life of an artist, so many demands on his or her time. For over twenty years, Jean Sievers, first as publicist and now as co-manager (working solo after the passing of her partner, the very kind Ronnie Lippin), has been the person who has to decide what's important enough for Brian's attention.

But before Ronnie and Jean became Brian's managers, as his solo career was still taking shape, we were all figuring it out on the fly. One person who was a big help was Lauri Klobas. I don't remember the exact day she started as Melinda's assistant, organizing the home office, handling all sorts of requests, but one story she shared showed Brian's kind and gentle side.

From Lauri's diary: "Kerry was eleven and small for her age. But her size and years were far outweighed by her determination. She had contacted Brian Wilson, requesting an interview. 'I've been a fan of the Beach Boys as long as I can remember,' she had stated in a pencil-written letter done carefully in her very best hand.

"When I called to follow up on the request, I found out it was part of a project from a school north of Los Angeles. A sixth-grade teacher had developed Kids, Incorporated, a media outlet that used radio and TV as jumping-off topics to educate children. When one called Kids, Incorporated, children answered the telephones in a very professional manner. Kerry was a 'go-getter,' her teacher told me. She had even contacted and interviewed actor Christopher Reeve. Interviews conducted were edited by the boys and girls into a radio show which was broadcast on the local Fresno outlet of National Public Radio."

The request was granted, and on a sunny spring day in 1996, Kerry, a classmate, an NPR sound recordist, her parents and teacher arrived at the Wilson home. Only Kerry, her teacher and the sound man were allowed in the room.

Again, from Lauri's diary: "Brian sat stiffly in his big, overstuffed armchair in the formal living room, clutching a pillow in front of his stomach as he often did when anxious. The mic had been set up on the arm of Brian's chair. And Kerry sat very, very straight on a hassock in front of him. She had a sheaf of papers in hand containing her questions.

"Her hand trembled as she faced the great man. The papers wavered, the only outward sign of her anxiety. Brian's eyes were focused on the papers. He leaned forward. 'Are you nervous?' he whispered to the girl. Kerry looked up and nodded. Brian suddenly relaxed and smiled. 'It's OK,' he soothed. 'So am I.' With that, he settled back in the chair and the interview proceeded." Like a tuning fork, Brian's sensitivity had saved the day.

Artists like Brian are inundated with fan mail and dealing with it was part of Lauri's job. Lauri helped Brian write a letter to an elementary school class. Here's an excerpt: "I just got the incredible letters your class wrote, and I can't tell you how much it means to me that they like my music so much . . . Remember, music is a spiritual force in our world, so 'add some music to your day.'"

Lauri's spirit was a positive presence in all of our lives and in the Wilson organization. And she is missed. Rest in peace.

In 2021, a question was posted on Brian's website. He was asked, "If you could be any other person, who would it be?" His answer? Paul McCartney.

In the 1960s and 1970s, Brian and Paul had met on a few occasions. In 1966, as Paul told me, they'd met at publicist Derek Taylor's office. Paul: "I remember Brian bringing it ['Good Vibrations'] around to me when I visited Derek Taylor's house in L.A. . . . It's funny, you don't always remember the most interesting things—you remember silly little things, I always find . . . The *main* thing I remember about the meeting was—well, one, hearing 'Good Vibrations,' which was a great track, and I was really pleased to get an opportunity to hear it early . . . but the thing was, Brian was wearing sunglasses, and he sort of asked me if I minded him wearing sunglasses . . . I said, 'Man, it's your life, you know—I don't mind. Whatever you do is fine.' It was kind of cute of him, you know?"

In 1967, Paul had dropped by a session for 'Vegetables' during the *SMiLE* era. Stories from that day are wildly inconsistent. Brian remembers that Paul played 'She's Leaving Home' at the piano for him and Marilyn. What stood out from that visit, as Paul explained to me, were "crazy things. They had *millions* of echoes; Brian was telling me about all the echo facilities—about a hundred possible echoes on the little patch board . . . and I remember the switches were the kind of switches you see nowadays, impossible little ones, you had to have midget fingers to operate them—Brian was telling me about that. I remember all the guys at the control desk, and just chatting about that. I think I'd just finished *Pepper*, and they were onto, probably, 'Heroes and Villains.' It was good to see him. It wasn't this sort of huge social event, it was really just touching base, saying hello."

In June 1976, when Paul was on his first American tour, *Wings over America*, he was coincidentally in L.A. for Brian's birthday. He and his wife Linda came to the party, which was filmed for a 1976 NBC-TV special, *It's OK*.

When asked in interviews what they thought of each other, Paul and Brian always had the highest praise for each other's music. In 1990, in the course of scheduling the interview I did with Paul for the *Pet Sounds* CD, I became good friends with Bill Porricelli, a senior executive at MPL, Paul McCartney's company. He is an enormous Brian Wilson fan and our goal became, whenever possible, to get these two legends into the same room. The ultimate objective, finally realized in 2003, was that they would make a record together. But there were a lot of steps along the way.

In September of 1999, Paul was hosting a listening party for his latest album, *Run Devil Run*, at West Hollywood's House of Blues. Mr. Porricelli made sure Brian and I were on the guest list and would see Paul at the post-listening party event, in the V.I.P. area. After hearing the album, as we were walking upstairs to the reception. Brian wondered if Phil Spector would be there. I reminded him not to mention Phil in front of Paul. He knew what I meant. From Paul's point of view, Spector had irreparably damaged the *Let It Be* album, especially 'The Long and Winding Road.'

The wait seemed interminable to Brian, who isn't the most patient person. He spoke again about Phil Spector, and I had no choice but to be forceful. I did it by reminding him that what Spector had done had really hurt Paul's feelings. Feelings are what Brian relates to best. I didn't hear Spector's name the rest of the night. After we spent some time at the fruit and vegetable buffet, I was a bit concerned when it looked like Brian's eyes rolled back. Was he ready to sleep?

And then, *finally*, Paul walked in, a beverage in his right hand. At first, he greeted a familiar face. And then, looking to his left, he saw Brian. Who waited expectantly. Paul's slightly creased face broke into a grin as wide as the Mersey. "There he is," he exclaimed, setting down his drink and throwing his arms wide. "Give us a hug," he said. The years melted away, and it was 1966. Paul gave Brian a really warm, love-filled embrace. It was just what Brian needed. It's quite possible that he not only needed to feel that love, but needed to feel it from *Paul*, perhaps the only person on the planet who really knows what it means to be Brian Wilson.

First, off to the side, they had a private conversation. I overheard Paul say, "You get over it, but you never get over it." Paul was probably sharing his feelings about grief, as the year before, he had lost Linda McCartney, his beloved wife of nearly thirty years. Brian's brother Carl had passed away in 1998 too. Brian introduced me to Paul, and I could feel Paul eyeing me. It was like he was doing an instantaneous computer brain scan. In his life and career, Paul learned to quickly size up people. He had to. And for a moment, he seemed to wonder, "Hmmm, is he the new Landy?" I reminded Paul of the interview we'd done about *Pet Sounds* and that helped.

The conversation quickly turned to music. Brian said, "I'm having a hard time getting a song going." He mentioned a song title. I said, "What do you mean? That's a finished song." Paul said, "Well, he is a perfectionist." As soon as Paul's undivided attention began to waver and others moved into conversational range, Brian was ready to go. He said to Paul, "I'm gonna go downstairs and have my dinner."

Later on, at one of our regular spots, the West Hollywood Hamburger Hamlet, Brian mentioned that "the same way *Rubber Soul* inspired *Pet Sounds*, *Run Devil Run* will inspire 'How Could We Still Be Dancing,'" an upbeat song that wouldn't see the light of day until five years hence.

But back to Paul. There was more, much more to come. In June 2000, Paul rekindled their long-distance friendship when, with an emotional speech, he inducted Brian into the Songwriters Hall of Fame, in his remarks calling Brian "one of your great American geniuses." A memorable and jubilant night. You can see that on YouTube.

In June 2001, Paul saw Brian in concert for the first time. He entered the Greek Theatre in Los Angeles, just moments after Brian had dedicated 'God Only Knows' to him. As the crowd roared to its feet, Brian spotted his old friend, and, after the bridge, quickly altered the lyric to "God only knows what I'd be without Paul."

In June 2002, Brian and Paul finally sang together when they appeared onstage for the very first time at Buckingham Palace at the Queen's Jubilee. Brian joined Paul and an all-star group to sing 'All You Need Is Love.'

Two nights later, Paul and his then-fiancée Heather came to see Brian and his band in Brighton. That night, the deal was sealed for their first concert together. So, finally, at last, the bass-playing Geminis joined forces at a landmine benefit in L.A., with Paul coming onstage to sing 'God Only Knows' and Brian taking the lead on 'Let It Be.' You can and should listen to it on the web.

A few days after that event, writing with the poet/lyricist Stephen J. Kalinich, Brian composed a new song about how he felt about Paul. And on September 25, 2003, Paul came to Ocean Way studio in Hollywood, the birthplace of such records as *Pet Sounds*, and sang and played on the recording of 'A Friend Like You.' It's on Brian's 2004 album, *Gettin' in Over My Head*. Sir Paul would figure in Brian's world several times before that. More in Chapters 19 and 20.

Another favorite Brian/Paul moment for me would be when Brian sang a spectacular version of Paul's "Wanderlust" on a McCartney tribute album. I love Paul's recording of it, but hearing Brian add his harmonies to his friend's song was a highlight.

There's no question that theirs is an illustrious mutual admiration and inspiration society. Brian has said many times that *Rubber Soul* was the record that made him want to do better, and *Pet Sounds* was the result. After *Revolver*, Brian followed up with 'Good Vibrations,' which just blew everybody away. And the question was, "What was Brian Wilson going to do next?" In 2004, we would get the answer. And Paul would be there, cheering him on.

I can't end this section without one last note. The two men were born only two days apart: Paul on June 18, 1942, Brian on June 20, 1942. Nothing was funnier than seeing Sir Paul's reaction when the ever-so-slightly younger musician referred to Paul as "Old Man Pablo." I don't think anybody else could get away with that.

The death of Carl Wilson in February of 1998 meant that there were now no Wilson brothers onstage at Beach Boys concerts. Without Carl's angelic voice, the concerts took on a very different tenor. In honor of his brother, Brian would headline Carl Wilson Foundation benefit concerts in 2002 and 2003 at UCLA's Royce Hall; I had a big hand in producing those shows. (Much to my surprise and delight, I would ultimately be back on campus as a professor at the UCLA Herb Alpert School of Music.)

Perhaps the best/sweetest/funniest moment of those benefits was in

2002 when Eric Clapton was the special guest. Brian's band really wanted Eric to play his classic, 'Layla,' but neither they nor I as producer of the event could really ask. When an artist plays a charity show, they get to choose which songs to perform. Hopeful that Eric would want to play it, they learned the song as faithfully as they had every one of Brian's. At rehearsal, with the band's coaxing—I think it was falsetto king and band leader Jeffrey Foskett who gave him the final push—Brian, in a friendly, irresistible plea, said, "Eric, play 'Layla' for me." Eric was a bit taken aback by the request, and said, "Does the band know it?" The answer was in the affirmative, and they launched into a spectacular version of the song. Eric was impressed; that night's audience was thrilled.

The Beach Boys weren't part of the Carl Wilson Foundation shows. I don't recall why, but it was during a time when there was apparently ill will between the surviving members of the group; the year before, Brian hadn't been part of all of the festivities when the Beach Boys were honored with a "Lifetime Achievement Award" at the Grammys in 2001. In 2012, after having proved all he needed to on his own, he rejoined the group for a Grammy tribute, a new album and a very successful and well-received Beach Boys fiftieth-anniversary tour.

That was all in the unforeseeable future. And it couldn't have happened if, in the meantime, Brian didn't do the unexpected. He was about to embark on the most unpredictable adventure of his career.

Brian was going on tour. As a solo artist.

CHAPTER 18

BRIAN HITS THE ROAD!?

WHILE BRIAN WAS WORKING ON THE *IMAGINATION* ALBUM, HE AND MELINDA spent a lot of time at their St. Charles home in 1997/1998. With my career in television keeping me busy and really beginning to take off, we didn't see them quite as often. So when it was announced that Brian was going to go on tour to promote *Imagination*, the news was a surprise to us. Eva and I had the same reaction: "That's a bad idea. Sure glad it isn't ours." We were wrong. Very wrong. A moment to reflect upon how wrong we were.

Going on tour would turn out to be probably the best thing that happened for Brian in the past quarter-century. But before the tour began, surprisingly, suddenly, out of nowhere, the four of us were together again. In February of 1999, Brian called from Chicago and said, "I need you guys here. I can't do this without you." And just like that, *we* were headed out on tour too.

We flew to Chicago. Hung out for the last few days of rehearsals. I guess for Brian, we were part of the "emotional security" blanket he needed. Chicago winters, however, aren't exactly California summers. It was freezing outside and a bit chilly in the rehearsal room too. The band—made up of terrific Chicago musicians and the Wondermints—was busy learning the songs. About thirty of 'em. Beach Boys hits and classics and new ones as well. There was a genuine nervousness. It was tense. Could Brian pull this off?

The tour began with a bang of a blizzard. Fortunately, for Brian, Melinda and Eva, I was our tour driver in a big SUV. Having grown up in the northeast, I knew how to navigate the interstate in winter weather. The band wasn't as lucky. The heater on their tour bus broke down. It was literally freezing on the bus. Let's put a positive spin on it. Call it a bonding experience.

379

Worries about whether touring was a good idea vanished during the first show. And it happened very quickly. Because there had been so much uncertainty surrounding this four-show tour, a concert program hadn't been printed. Later, I wrote an essay for the tour program that would be used for the rest of the year:

Ann Arbor, Michigan. Monday, March 8. The forecast of a late-winter blizzard had brought us here a day early and given us plenty of time to sit around the hotel and nervously anticipate tomorrow's opening night of the tour—the first ever Brian Wilson solo tour. Yeah, we'd just witnessed a great weekend of final rehearsals, but nobody really knew what to expect. We were all pretty jumpy except for Brian, who was as calm as a summer breeze.

Just before dinner, an old friend from New York arrived; he'd only been waiting about thirty years to see a Brian Wilson solo concert. After dinner, Ray [Lawlor] and I headed out into the storm (it too had arrived just as predicted) to find an open grocery store (milk for baby Daria).

Unsure of where to go, we accidentally turned up the street where the concert theater was. And as we turned the corner, rising up like an apparition in some episode of *The Twilight Zone*, there it was on the marquee: *An Evening with Brian Wilson*. Even though we were in Ann Arbor for the show, we still looked at each other in disbelief. Was it real?

We both know our Beach Boys history pretty well. And as far as we could tell, the last time Brian had made history in Michigan was thirty-three years earlier, in 1966. Brian had flown in to supervise the group's first live performance of his latest production . . . a "little" number called 'Good Vibrations.' In the context of that event, how was this show going to live up to a momentous occasion like that?

Well, very simply. It did.

Backstage, an hour before show time, all was bustling around Brian. He sat quietly . . . contemplating, meditating. The band and he had a brief prayer; then Chicago radio personality Steve Dahl went out to welcome the audience.

Dramatically, the lights went down and everybody began pacing restlessly behind the screen, listening as Alan Boyd's remarkable [biographical] film played. The audience applauded, laughed and cheered in all the right places. Clearly, they were ready for Brian. For me, the crowd's reaction to the film brought a sense of relief and release. It was all starting to seem overwhelming. Like the feeling you might get at your child's graduation ceremony. Or wedding. Pride mixed with nervous anticipation of what was going to happen next.

And finally, it was time. As the final moments of the film played, the band members took their places. And then, Brian went out and showed all the doubters that he could do it. And the son-of-a-gun made it look easy, as if he'd been headlining concerts his whole life.

What were the highlights? I know there must have been quite a few, because the Ann Arbor crowd gave Brian and his terrific band more than a dozen standing ovations. I lost count. Was it fifteen or sixteen?

For me, the real highlight was seeing my friend share himself with 2,000 strangers. To see him be "Brian Wilson" onstage, for ninety minutes, was such an unexpected treat. The way he sang, bending old notes in new ways, revealing a sexy rock 'n' roll growl one moment, a tender, heartfelt sound the next. The way he spoke to the crowd and, in his uniquely spontaneous manner, got us clapping. And how he applauded the audience after each song, making everybody part of the show. It was both sincere and something I've never seen anybody else do.

Finally, the sweetness that I've been privileged to see in private, that I've been "preaching" about —that we've all heard in his music for thirty-seven years—was beginning to flower in public. And it was, in the words of the title of Brian's old song, 'Wonderful.'

The other thing that came out of this first show was the sense that Brian's music had become truly classical. The concert showed how timeless his compositions are. And how even though these musicians were not part of the original recordings, when they performed his songs with care and integrity and feeling, infusing them with energy and intensity and modernity in a way that the artist's original intentions remained intact, it gave the songs a real presence. They sounded as if they were written just that morning. Or 200 years ago. The power of love indeed.

We had left Los Angeles on March 5 with enough anxiety to fuel our 767, and by the time we returned on March 15, we had seen nothing less than a rebirth. Yeah, I know "Brian Is Back" blah, blah, blah. Nobody is more sick of that claim than I am. But this time, it was true. Because during that first leg of the tour, what we witnessed was no less than an artist reclaiming his legacy.

I was sorry when the curtain came down on closing night. Because each concert had been a special celebration. Like how he taught the audience to do a "quarter note" clap. Or in Milwaukee, the way he did his first solo encore, a segue from *Rhapsody in Blue* into 'On Wisconsin.' Or in Minneapolis, when, at the last minute, he added a verse and chorus of 'Love and Mercy' to the show. Each night was different. But in one sense, each show evoked the same feeling. The two hours flew by. It was like a visitation.

That's what I meant about how wrong we were, how a seemingly "bad" idea can lead to great things happening. The thought of Brian touring, let alone during winter in the Great Lakes states, made no sense. Ironically, by the end of the tour, Brian had gotten stronger every night and reached a new level of confidence, while the band members were frozen from the bus rides, fighting colds, a couple as "sick as dogs". Back to L.A., back to my production company and the freelance writer's life.

We had a great time on a June mini-tour of the northeast, as Brian got better and better. My East Coast friends, who had heard me talking about Brian for decades, came out to see it with their own eyes. It was a very happy week, and that tour also planted the seeds for what would happen soon.

Now, there was no question that Brian liked playing with his crack band, loved hearing how beautifully they recreated his classic songs, loved telling his "cigarette lighter" joke. Meanwhile, when I had time in between projects, I did what I could to help, like going to Japan for what turned out to be an unforgettable week, one of the more rewarding experiences of my Brian Wilson journey.

It was just before I began work as a producer on a "once-in-a-lifetime" Millennium program. It was to be a worldwide twenty-four-hour broadcast, the day the twenty-first century began, and would take me to Turkey, South Africa, the south of France and multiple times to London. This July trip to Japan would be a good warm-up for the upcoming months of international travel. Brian's tour included one show in Osaka and three in Tokyo, and in both cities, the venues were magnificent, what one might expect if you were on tour with Pavarotti. The concerts were all SRO, the sound perfect and the audiences respectful and enthusiastic.

There was one issue. Joe Thomas, who had produced the *Imagination* album with Brian that was being promoted on this tour, who had helped put the touring band together and been onstage for the American concerts, was still back home. Joe said he was afraid to fly; he kept promising to get on a plane. Awaiting Joe's arrival, as Darian Sahanaja recalls, "We were all walking on eggshells. Then, the tour manager Paul Natkin asked me if I was ready to step up, to move my keyboards to the front line, because Joe wasn't coming." Darian was ready. He'd been preparing for this moment for his entire life. And he's been there ever since.

The only uncomfortable moment on the tour was just before the soundcheck for the Osaka concert. Ray and I were there with the band. Brian said something like, "What should we do without Joe?" There was a moment of silence. Then, I stepped in. "Brian, it's not fair to ask the band. You're in charge. What do you want to do?" Brian said, "On with the show."

The concerts were all terrific, but it was the day off that led to a life highlight, an event that proved the cliché that music really is an international language. We'd flown into Osaka for the first show of the tour, then taken a remarkable train ride to Tokyo. Before the first Tokyo concert, Brian, Melinda and I took a day trip to Kyoto, the ancient and holy city. She hired a private guide to show us around. At the last stop of our tour, a legendary shrine with a beautiful garden, Brian and Melinda went into the gift shop to buy presents for their two little girls, Daria and Delanie.

I waited outside with our guide, and when I asked him, "Do you know who he is?," the answer was "No." I explained that Brian was the man who had written the Beach Boys' music, arranged their harmonies, produced their most popular records. Our guide was immediately overcome. Entranced. He loved that music. I instantly invited him and his wife to a concert in Tokyo. Could he take a day off to come? I gave him my contact information. One of the great pleasures for me of being on tour was helping real fans connect with Brian. Frequently, I would give them backstage passes to meet Brian. But this was different.

When he called to say that he and his wife could come, I asked the promoter for tickets. Unlike the U.S. concerts, I was stunned to learn that there were no seats available. Except for the royal box. Well, then, the royal box it would be. Before the show, I met our guide and his wife; they were so excited to be there. And beyond thrilled as to where they were sitting. After the concert, I escorted them backstage. There was much bowing and smiles. They had brought gifts for all of us.

Our tour guide, in his limited English, said to Brian, "Your music makes my heart soar." I don't know if there's ever been a better description.

Right after they left, Brian and I walked back to his dressing room, talking about what a wonderful moment this was, *the* reason to tour . . . the pure joy his music brought his fans and the love that came back to him in return. Both of us reveled in the feeling that he'd really touched somebody deeply.

Brian and his band were getting rave reviews everywhere; our concern that had greeted the first tour announcement had long since evaporated. Invitations for Brian were now coming for all sorts of events, none cooler than Neil Young's Bridge School benefit. Because it was on a weekend in October, we were able to go, and it was so rewarding to see Brian mingle with his peers, such as Pete and Roger from the Who.

Bridge School concerts were all acoustic, and Brian and his band had rehearsed songs that could work without electric instruments. That meant no organ, no theremin and no 'Good Vibrations.' During Brian's set, I watched from the side of the stage in the most surreal setting I could have envisioned; I stood in the wings, stage left, between Pete Townshend and Neil Young. Pete, one of the greatest and most ambitious composers of his generation, stared as if he was seeing a ghost. Maybe he was thinking of Keith Moon, who was the biggest Beach Boys fan in the Who.

Neil Young had been a Brian Wilson fan forever; in 1973, he used 'Let's Go Away for Awhile' in his first film, *Journey Through the Past*. Now, in the present, as the producer of the event, he watched with more than just curiosity. As the show unfolded, Brian felt the prepared set wasn't quite working, and after a song, off mic, he turned to the band and called for 'Good Vibrations.' They shook their heads. They hadn't rehearsed an acoustic version of it. After the next song, the same thing happened. Neil

Young asked me, "What's going on?" I explained what Brian wanted and what the band was saying "No" to.

Then Brian showed what happens when he chooses to be "Brian Wilson." *On* mic, so the audience could hear, he said, "You want some 'Good Vibrations'?" Tens of thousands of fans roared. As the band began an unrehearsed, acoustic version of 'Good Vibrations,' Neil turned to me with a big smile and said, "I love it. He's still out there." 'Good Vibrations' received a gigantic ovation.

Of course, not every moment was momentous. At some point during his second year of touring, somebody came up with the very clever idea to use a piece of the Barenaked Ladies song 'Brian Wilson' and segue into "Til I Die.' In 1971, when I first heard "Til I Die,' it gave me faith that Brian could still make meaningful music. Now, amazingly, he was going to perform it *live*. As it may be the saddest song he's ever written, one day, to try and lighten things up after a rehearsal of "Til I Die,' I said to Brian, only slightly altering the lyric, "I'm that Leaf on a windy day." He just shook his head.

The concerts had been so well received that, in 2000, Jean Sievers thought it would be a great idea to do a live album. And it was. The venue of choice would be the intimate Roxy Theatre on Sunset in West Hollywood. The club has played host to an incredible roster of musical legends: Joni Mitchell, Neil Young, Bruce Springsteen, Bob Marley, Prince et al. as well as the original stage production of the Rocky Horror Picture Show. I'd actually once slept overnight on the sidewalk outside the Roxy to get Springsteen tickets, and if you listen to the radio broadcast of that show, it's me yelling for 'Candy's Room.' Anyway, when these shows were first announced, the mere *thought* of Brian Wilson at the Roxy boggled the mind.

Though only a few miles long, when Brian had cruised the Sunset Strip in the 1960s and 1970s, it was the center of the West Coast music world. He might be on his way to his favorite recording studio (Western at 6000 Sunset), Capitol Records (just north of Sunset on Vine), the Beach Boys' corporate offices (in Hollywood, just north of Sunset on Ivar), the Radiant Radish, his health food emporium (south of Sunset on San Vicente), a favorite masseuse (heading south on La Cienaga) or perhaps his preferred record store, Wallichs Music City at Sunset and Vine. Or in

1988, Tower Records, where he'd done an in-store event for his first solo album.

In 1962, with the Beach Boys, Brian had played at Pandora's Box, a tiny club set on an island at the intersection of Sunset and Crescent Heights. It was where, according to the legend, he met Marilyn Rovell, his first wife. A few years later, that club was the flash point for the 1966 "Riot on Sunset Strip," which was the subject of the Buffalo Springfield song, 'For What It's Worth.' The poster for the 1967 movie about the curfew riot inspired Mark London's terrific 2000 Roxy poster. In 1970, Brian had played a couple of sets with "the boys" at their "comeback" shows at the nearby Whisky. But that was pretty much it.

By the mid-1990s, I think the only times Brian was on the Sunset Strip was on the way to Hamburger Hamlet, a favorite steak restaurant like Arnie Morton's, or to buy CDs at Tower. He hadn't spent much time on the Strip in decades. But he sure made his musical return memorable. When these shows were announced, tickets sold out with the speed of an email blast. The chance to see Brian in a club was one that had everybody calling, and the demand (only five hundred could get in each night) was such that a week of shows wouldn't have been enough.

Who was lucky enough to be there? There was family (including daughter Wendy, nephews Jonah and Patrick, mother-in-law Rose and, of course, Melinda). Eva and I were there. Ray flew out from New York and Jerry and Lois came in from Philly as that threesome always did for major Brian moments. The audience was filled with great old friends (David Anderle, Carol Kaye and Rich Sloan), a superstar (Bette Midler), a long litany of rockers (Jackie DeShannon, Nancy Sinatra, Elliot Easton, Jon Bon Jovi and Heartbreakers Mike Campbell and Benmont Tench), punk legend Patti Smith (who in 1977 gave *Love You* a glowing review), Peter Buck (from R.E.M.), opening act Grant Lee Phillips and L.A. studio whiz Jon Brion.

There were industry figures as wide-ranging as Russ Regan (who is credited with naming them "The Beach Boys"), Don Was, and American Records founder and record producer Rick Rubin. Legendary producer/ impresario/Roxy owner Lou Adler cheered Brian on from the lighting booth.

All watched in awe.

Amid the sprinkling of famous and familiar faces and industry insiders, the place was essentially filled with extremely enthusiastic (read: very loud) and ecstatic *fans*. One serious fan and a friend said to me after the two shows, "When Carl died, I thought that was it. I never dreamed that the best Beach Boys concerts I would ever see would be those Brian would give." Nobody did. Even the blasé "seen-it-all" waitresses danced in the aisles. A security guard in his early twenties was heard to gasp, "I can't believe Brian Wilson is playing here."

As for the highlights of the show, well, for me, the musical "goose-bump raisers" were the new coda Brian added to 'Good Vibrations,' which had its debut that weekend, and his lead vocals on 'Please Let Me Wonder' and 'Love and Mercy.' In between songs, Brian was as relaxed and casual as I've ever seen him onstage, chatting with the crowd, waving, clapping and telling jokes; his introductions to 'Add Some Music' and 'Be My Baby' and the *Pet Sounds* instrumentals were wonderfully sweet.

Brian also played two songs that hadn't yet been recorded, the spiritual 'The First Time' and 'This Isn't Love,' the Wilson/Asher tune (which, going back to my *The New Leave It to Beaver* days, became the "love theme" of director Brian Levant's *The Flintstones in Viva Rock Vegas*).

And if all that incredible music and emotion wasn't enough, after the Saturday night show, Capitol Records finally presented Brian with a platinum sales award for *Pet Sounds*. A big smile from the big man, a truly memorable moment in a weekend full of them. You can hear the show on CD. It sounds terrific. But, and I hate to say it, "You really had to be there."

There was one other important person in the audience that night at the Roxy. He wasn't famous, but his presence was about to change the course of Brian's career in a most important way. He had come from New York to see for himself. He was a fan, still is, but he had another reason to be there. His name is Brian Diamond.

CHAPTER 19

THE TRIBUTE
AND THE QUEEN

TO UNDERSTAND WHY BRIAN DIAMOND WAS AT THE ROXY, WE NEED TO GO back to 1995. Even further.

Long before Brian had begun touring, my friend Chip Rachlin and I were discussing a Brian Wilson tribute. Chip's bona fides in the music industry include having worked for the truly legendary Bill Graham at the Fillmore East. The concert business may have been Chip's destiny. The first shows he presented were in high school in New Jersey.

Back in 1971, he was something of a twenty-one-year-old rookie in the big-time concert promotion business, but he was such a big Beach Boys fan that he and a couple of friends rolled the dice and promoted the group's first and what would become a legendary concert at New York's Carnegie Hall. The show was a turning point for the Beach Boys; they had been playing a lot of college gyms. It would also lead to Chip becoming, from 1971 to 1978, the group's agent. So he was a big part of what was the unprecedented 1970s Beach Boys comeback. Chip also managed Carl Wilson during Carl's solo break from the Beach Boys. As I write this, his personal and professional relationship with the Wilson family and the band has spanned over a half-century.

I'd long dreamed of some sort of night at the symphony filled with Brian Wilson music. I had no practical idea of how to make it happen. Neither Chip nor I remember exactly when we started talking about a tribute show other than it was in the mid-1990s. At the time, it didn't even include Brian being anywhere but in the audience. The idea of him having a great band, of him taking the stage, was at that time, to put it mildly, unlikely.

In our conversations, the tribute had a number of permutations. By 1999, the one that made the most sense was a superstar tribute and a full performance of *Pet Sounds*. We would bring together all the rock stars who loved Brian in one place on one night. Easier said than done.

I had worked on a few tributes as a writer and segment producer in the 1990s. An Elvis event in Memphis in 1994 wasn't a big success. That same year, *Carnegie Hall Salutes the Jazz Masters: Verve Records at 50* (with Herbie Hancock and Vanessa Williams as hosts) was a memorable night. Writing for *The Billboard Music Awards* show and being backstage at *Solid Gold* for five years, I'd seen some of the problems—budget, network and ego issues—that face and could potentially derail a production. *Any* production. Even when I was starting out as a production assistant on *Sinatra and Friends*, I had witnessed several eye-opening moments of behind-the-scenes drama.

The goal in a tribute is to have as many "once-in-a-lifetime" moments as possible. But until you are the producer, you don't really know how hard it is to make it actually happen, from idea to the network sale to budgeting to casting to taping to post-production to the broadcast. A million steps in between.

And this time, I was writer/producer, so together with Chip Rachlin and Brian Diamond, we were in the eye of the hurricane. Now, I didn't have to guess what it would take. Almost every waking hour was consumed with details. But, again, I've gotten ahead of the story.

In looking to find a financing partner for this project, Chip contacted Eddie Micone, a lifelong friend from high school. Two teens from Summit, New Jersey who'd gone into the music business. In the 1990s, Eddie was Executive Vice President of Radio City Entertainment in New York. He oversaw shows at Madison Square Garden and Radio City Music Hall. Brian Diamond worked for Eddie as Senior Vice President of Original Programming and Production for Radio City Entertainment.

In the fall of 1999, Chip brought the project to them; they both loved our idea and agreed to join forces. But despite our assurances, Eddie and Brian needed to know we weren't just two fans blowing smoke. Was Brian Wilson's band as great as we said? Was Brian really capable of taking the stage? That's what brought Brian Diamond from New York to the Roxy show. In a recent conversation, Brian reflected on the night at the Roxy: "I just remember thinking. This is great in a little club. How awesome would this be on the Radio City stage with any number of musicians that we could get? Which, of course, was a major hurdle."

However, before the "booking" process could begin, we needed a broadcast partner. Again, Brian Diamond: "I'd just worked with Sandy Shapiro [Executive Producer at TNT, the U.S. cable network] on a Johnny Cash tribute, and I took it to her." Sandy was immediately interested. In the words of Chip Rachlin, "We just needed to deliver two whales." In show business parlance, that meant two superstar guests. Chip also "delivered" on another front. His colleague, Michael Lopez, put in $700,000 for the home video rights, another critical element in our assembling the financing.

Our conception of the show was to include a start-to-finish performance of *Pet Sounds*. We figured that would be a unique part of the night. But then, in 2000, Brian did what nobody had ever thought possible: he took *Pet Sounds* on the road. Those shows were beyond remarkable. His band, determined to be as great as the music, played the entire album with the depth of feeling with which Brian had infused every single note.

In the 2000 *Pet Sounds* tour program I wrote: "What makes tonight's concert so special is that since the original *Pet Sounds* recordings were made in 1966, neither Brian nor the Beach Boys has ever performed the album in its entirety . . . In fact, if the question had been asked as to when such an event might take place, the answer would have been 'God Only Knows.' And yet here we are, only a year after his very first solo tour, and Brian and his dedicated band are 'on the road again' making musical history.

"It's really no exaggeration to say that seeing *Pet Sounds* played live (as it was once at an L.A. tribute concert several years ago) would be the rock world's equivalent of going to a concert hall back in the twenties, where, if you were really lucky, you might have seen *Rhapsody in Blue* performed with its composer, George Gershwin, at the piano. Given the album's place in the pop pantheon, that's not an overblown comparison."

The 2000 *Pet Sounds* tour was incredible; everybody thought, "Is this really happening?" After Brian played the Hollywood Bowl, there was another big turn in the story. I got a call the next day from Melinda. She'd just heard from Rob Reiner, who was so excited and enthusiastic about what he'd seen at the Bowl that he wanted to talk about making a film on

Brian's life. Melinda said to me, "You have to get involved." So I happily met with Rob.

But what did this *Pet Sounds* tour mean to the tribute? Our now "not so original" idea to have *Pet Sounds* performed as the composer had originally intended wasn't quite as hot. Still, we decided that it was such a significant part of a tribute to him that it should stay as a part of our live event. (To this day, the entire tribute performance of *Pet Sounds* has never been seen, except by those at the show.)

At any rate, Chip, Brian and I worked with talent booker Ali Gifford to get not just "two whales" but an entire lineup of great performers. Although the first few confirmations came relatively easily, getting artists to come to these shows is a long, strung-out, difficult, and seemingly impossible process. I remember Elton John agreeing almost immediately. I went over to his table at the annual Grammy MusiCares dinner, said hello and discussed with him and his manager what song Elton would do. Telling him we were going to present a full performance of *Pet Sounds*, an album I knew he worshipped, I suggested 'I Just Wasn't Made for These Times.' Elton's manager very politely replied, hinting that Elton "should have something a little more well known." I was still hoping Paul McCartney was going to come and sing 'God Only Knows,' so I chose 'Wouldn't It Be Nice.' Elton was pleased, and before I left, he smiled and said, "Don't worry, I'll be 'easy-peasy' on this one." He knew his reputation, and it was his way of letting me know that paying homage to Brian was so important to him that, in the phrase Quincy Jones used for the "We Are the World" sessions, E.J. would check his ego at the door.

Our next big booking was Heart's Ann and Nancy Wilson (no relation).

Because of the Beatles/Beach Boys connection, I felt it was important that a key Beatle person be on the stage. Talking about it with Bill Porricelli, my friend at Paul McCartney's MPL office, Paul expressed his concern that his presence might overshadow the night. Very gracious. And very disappointing. I had another idea. I wrote to Sir George Martin and asked him to come as a presenter. By this time, we'd worked together three times: on his documentary, and I'd interviewed him for *The Pet Sounds Sessions* and our Bee Gees documentary.

After a few days, I mentioned to Eva that I was surprised and frustrated not to have heard back. She said, "Did you tell him that all expenses would be included? First class?" I hadn't. I immediately wrote to Sir George again. Early the next morning, around 4 a.m., we were awakened by the fax machine in my office. It was in the second bedroom of our apartment. I woke up, got out of bed, and said, "I wonder who's sending a fax at this hour?" It was from London. Where it was noon. It was from Sir George. The phrase that has stayed in my memory all these years is that "Wild lorries couldn't keep me away." His presence—and what he said that night—was one of the most important and exciting parts of the tribute.

But after Elton, getting the second "whale" we needed to satisfy the network had come to a halt. We were getting nervous. In the wake of a round of legal issues, here are excerpts from a funny/serious email Chip Rachlin sent to Brian Diamond and me in November 2000:

> I am not a religious man by nature. Besides, it's a little late to rewrite history. But as we approach an anniversary of our first dedicating ourselves to this project, I want to take a second to reflect. I vowed a long time ago never to be a victim of an STD or lawyers. Now I'd like the chance to catch something, but that's another story.
>
> We must triumph and produce. Produce a great spectacle. A musical extravaganza that will make millions of people happy for a fleeting moment . . . Remember, no contract has ever made the top of the Billboard Charts. No lawyer's video has ever been enshrined on *TRL* [*Total Request Live*].
>
> We must band together to fight the morally bankrupt and bring culture to the masses. Amen, brother.
>
> Chip "I never met a knish I didn't like" Rachlin

It should be noted that Chip's message was written 'round midnight.

Chip and I had been talking about Phil Ramone, the mega-Grammy-winning producer, being involved in the show. At some point, we decided to make him a partner in the production and musical director. That was the smartest thing we did. Without Phil, the show might have collapsed. With him, it took wing. And throughout, he was an absolute delight to work with. He made everybody feel comfortable. The art of production.

Relatively quickly, Phil was able to get both Paul Simon and Billy Joel to say "Yes." More than that, Phil's presence gave great comfort to everybody else we had asked. They now knew they would sound great, and the "Maybes" we'd been hearing became "Yes. Yes. Yes." David Crosby, Carly Simon, et al. And while there would still be more "wild tales" on the "talent" side of the production, the show now existed. For real. With a budget of over $3 million, Radio City as the venue and the music of Brian Wilson and the Beach Boys as our repertoire. We were on our way.

In retrospect, and at the time too, perhaps the best and most unexpected addition to the talent roster was Vince Gill. In Brian Diamond's office at 2 Penn Plaza (the office building towering above Madison Square Garden), there was a big white board. On it, Brian recalls, "We had written down all the songs that we wanted in the show and what songs Mr. Wilson wanted. And it was changing based on who was playing which song. We would meet there regularly."

While there had to be some hits, I had created a list of songs that I believed would showcase the more legendary songs. At the top of the list was 'Surf's Up.' Essential to include, but the question was, "Who could sing it?" Ali Gifford, our talent executive, said, "Let me pray on that." A few days later, she suggested the country artist Vince Gill. I think she said, "Trust me. He can pull it off." Brian Diamond recalls her saying, "You won't regret this." We didn't. To say the least.

Part of any great project is pulling together as a team, and so we relied on Ali's judgment. And I remember on rehearsal day at Radio City, I was standing next to Vince Gill's manager as he sang both 'The Warmth of the Sun' solo and then 'Surf's Up,' with David Crosby and Jimmy Webb. (You can and should find both on YouTube.)

I was more than blown away by the beauty of what I heard. And told Vince's manager, who smiled as he said, "As good of a singer as he is, he's a better guitar player. And as good of a guitar player as he is, he's a better golfer." From my days on the links and as a sportswriter, I quickly answered, "Then he must be a scratch [meaning no handicap] golfer." His manager nodded. "He is."

The week before the event, at the off-site band rehearsals, particular attention had to be paid to songs Brian's band had never done live before, especially 'Heroes and Villains' and 'Surf's Up.' These were the two most complex SMiLE songs in our rundown; the Beach Boys had performed them beautifully in their phenomenal concerts in the early 1970s, but

Brian's band had never played them. The story of how 'Heroes and Villains' ended up on the show is worth telling.

But first, a step back. In the fall of 2000, it was thrilling to tell Brian there was going to be a tribute to him. That people like Elton John and Sir George Martin would be there. A shy smile creased his face. A look of disbelief flashed in his eyes for a second. "Me?" he seemed to be asking, "There's going to be a tribute to me? Are you serious?"

What he eventually said publicly was, like his music, a bullseye shot straight from the heart. "This is amazing. I'm really touched. I am so honored that these artists are going out of their way to be there for me. I believe it's going to be one of the greatest nights of my life." What I wrote in the concert program was, "For his part in the event, Brian is promising some real surprises, including several songs he's never performed live."

I could only write that because of what happened near the end of 2000, three months before the tribute. We were at band member Scott Bennett's home for a Christmas party. In one room, there was a piano; Brian and Eva were sitting on the piano bench, their backs to the keys. Brian asked Eva what she wanted for Christmas. Without hesitation she said, "Play 'Heroes and Villains' for me." He said, "OK," turned around and played it. As if it was 1966. Brian's band members, hearing the song, came rushing in from the other room. And watched in disbelief. When he was done, Eva or I then said, "You've gotta play it at the tribute." Brian again said, "OK." Brian's band, thrilled to hear him play it solo at the piano, now had to learn it.

The rehearsals in New York were filled with unforgettable "Brian" moments. After the Boys Choir of Harlem had finished singing 'Our Prayer,' Brian was so moved that he got up and ran over to them and proudly said, "You know I wrote that." As Jerry Weiss recalls, "The choir was dumbstruck. Brian was nearly in tears. Filled with delight and rapture. Mesmerized at hearing it performed live. Maybe the first time he'd heard it since it was originally recorded during the SMiLE sessions."

Brian Diamond has another favorite memory: "During rehearsal, Brian's band is running through songs. No vocals. Brian was lying down on a couch near the far wall. He looked like he was asleep. But then the song ends, and they're about to start talking about what they need to do. And he shot up like somebody lit a fire under his butt. He goes, 'I don't know who it was, but you were sharp. It was supposed to be C minor and you were C major.' It was like, 'Wow, even in his sleep he's still hearing what's going on.'"

When rehearsals moved to the stage at Radio City, I remember asking David Crosby to introduce 'The Warmth of the Sun,' and before he could say no, I said, "Let me explain why." Knowing how much he loved the Kennedys, having heard that he'd written the CSN classic 'Long Time Gone' the night of the assassination of Senator Robert F. Kennedy, I knew he would relate. He read the script I'd written and said yes, although there was one name he didn't want to say. I insisted he include it, and he did. At the show, I recall he almost whispered those words, *sotto voce*. We fixed it in the mix.

Billy Joel's concern at rehearsal was that the show was on a school night for his daughter. I seem to remember Eva, who was bold as brass, saying something to him like, "Dedicate the song to her," and Billy looking at her as if to say, "Who the hell are you to tell me that?"

One of the most unexpected moments at rehearsal was when Paul Simon ran through 'Surfer Girl' for the first time. It was literally jaw-dropping. His interpretation of the song was spectacular, honoring the original but offering a beautiful variation on the theme. Just stunning. A real artist, in the truest meaning of that word, paying tribute to another artist. (Google it.) After Paul Simon had finished, Eva tapped me on the shoulder and motioned for me to follow her. As is my nature, I wondered what was wrong. We walked to the back of the orchestra. She hugged me and said, "You did it."

During the course of pre-production, so much happened every day. There were all sorts of contractual, financial and legal issues that the lawyers dealt with. One worth mentioning, however, is the support we got from the network. As Brian Diamond points out, "We [meaning Radio City Entertainment] were splitting the budget with TNT. And Sandy at TNT said, 'Listen, I want to make the show great, and I want to get really good people, and if it costs more money just tell me what it is. Don't be shy.' The entire cost of the production ended up being in the neighborhood of $3.5 million, and even when we went over budget, TNT didn't blink." This was important because costs were mounting. As an example, one artist's travel, hotel and incidental expenses ended up being over $100,000.

What was exciting to me, for all of us, was watching the creative side of the show come together. With Phil Ramone's brilliant ear, artists were unexpectedly being matched with songs, new trios were being created, like David Crosby, Jimmy Webb and Carly Simon for 'In My Room.' Simon, notorious for her stage fright, was not just willing to get past it to be there. She *insisted* on it. Her attorney told me she wondered why she hadn't been invited. That's an example of how much Brian Wilson's music meant to her. We were pleased to add her to the lineup.

Same with the aptly named singer/songwriter Matthew Sweet. He overcame his fear of flying to come to New York. Darius Rucker, Hootie and the Blowfish's lead singer, flew back and forth to South Carolina to be with a child who was ill. He came to New York for rehearsal, went home, then back for the show. The twosome performed a memorable duet on 'Sail on Sailor.'

To make it a family affair, a reunited Wilson Phillips brought Carnie and Wendy, Brian's two oldest daughters, to the stage for a rousing 'You're So Good to Me.' Singer/songwriter Michael Penn and his partner, the very cool Aimee Mann, collaborated on a *Pet Sounds* classic. In addition to singing on 'Good Vibrations,' the Boys Choir of Harlem added their soulful presence to the opening 'Our Prayer' and the closing 'Love and Mercy,' two bookended highlights. The four Wilson children—Carnie, Wendy, and the very tiny Daria and Delanie—brought flowers out to Brian after the final song.

There almost wasn't a false note. TNT, as networks do, wanted us to include at least one contemporary "pop" star. Tisha Fein, who was consulting on the show, told us she could get Ricky Martin, but we'd have to take another act from the same record label. Those are the kinds of compromises that happen every minute in television. We made it work.

There were so many artists we wanted, artists who wanted to be there, who couldn't make it. In producing the video packages that would be part of the show, I made sure we included a video clip of Paul McCartney inducting Brian into the Songwriters Hall of Fame in 2000. That way, Paul was "in the room."

So many cool ideas didn't happen. Brian Diamond: "We had talked about the possibility of, during 'Good Vibrations,' Elton being on the massive Radio City pipe organ, and the curtains revealing him for that section of the song." I don't remember if the idea was more than a pipe dream. Chip Rachlin recalls that we considered assembling a section of famous backup singers that would have included Gerry Beckley (of America) and Lindsey Buckingham. That didn't happen because it wasn't necessary. Brian's band handled the background vocals flawlessly.

"On the surface, our choice for host," Brian Diamond notes, "seemed most unlikely, but Chazz Palminteri turned out to be perfect for the New York crowd. And the sight of him joining in on the jam at the end, towering over Elton John, Billy Joel and Paul Simon, made them look like a street corner doo-wop quartet crooning 'Barbara Ann.'" The sight of Elton and Billy dancing together was one for the ages too.

Recording the voiceovers for the pre-recorded historical segments created an interesting sequence of meetings. As Brian Diamond recalls, "Cameron Crowe came in first, did his piece, and on his way out, there was Sir George Martin. I'd worked with Sir George once before, but still, when you get to shake 'God's hand' more than once, it's pretty cool. He was so nice. When Cameron came out, he was blown away to see Sir George. Then Sir George went in, and Dennis Hopper showed up. And I was sitting with Dennis, and I said, 'It'll be a minute. George Martin's in there.' And now Dennis Hopper, a man who was in his mid-sixties, basically reverted to a sixteen-year-old kid. When George came out, Dennis took his hand and said, 'The Beatles meant so much to me.' It wasn't the first time George had heard that, but he was very pleasant, so very sweet."

I wrote the scripts for Chazz, all our presenters, the video package narrations, and segment hosts, and they were all a pleasure to work with, although Dennis Hopper made an interesting edit the night of the show. A very smart and instinctive choice. After the video retrospective played on screen in Radio City, rather than continuing to read what I'd written, he just went for the gold. "Ladies and gentlemen, Brian Wilson."

One of the funnier moments of the night was when Brian and Elton duetted on 'Wouldn't It Be Nice.' I had asked Elton to take Brian by the arm after the song and walk offstage together. I expressed my concern that this was a different kind of experience for Brian. Elton understood. Said he would handle it. Well, when the duet was over, Elton turned around, but Brian had already bolted offstage. When Elton came into the wings, we had a laugh about it.

Writing the script was, for me, a personal dream. I could express everything I ever wanted to say about Brian in one place for millions to hear. Perhaps the funniest and potentially most personally embarrassing moment came from one of the narrations I'd written for the videotape packages. We were with ace audio mixer Sue Pelino when I realized that Dennis Hopper had read the year of Brian's birth as 1943. I, the so-called expert on the subject, had gotten it wrong. Dennis had read "1943" because it was what I had written. I turned pale. Sue turned to Brian Diamond and me and pointed at the audio booth and said, "One of you get in there." If you listen carefully to that moment in the show, you might recognize me saying "1942."

When I was seven years old, our family had seen the movie *North by Northwest* at Radio City Music Hall. It was amazing to watch Cary Grant clinging to Mount Rushmore on the huge screen. And now, forty-two years later, I had written and produced a show in that legendary venue, an event with a remarkable parade of musical icons, all there on March 29, 2001 to pay tribute to Brian Wilson.

One moment that really stood out for Brian was what Sir George Martin said: "Nobody made a bigger impact on the Beatles than Brian . . . a living genius of popular music." Check out his entire speech by Googling George Martin + Brian Wilson tribute. Brian was in disbelief when he heard what George said. "The producer of the Beatles said that about me—it was hard to even imagine. I was so honored."

Another lesson learned: regardless of people telling Brian how much he had influenced the Beatles, to him that was just talk. But he couldn't deny what had taken place in front of him.

To this day, when I watch the video and Dennis Hopper says, "Ladies and gentlemen, Brian Wilson," and the entire audience at Radio City Music Hall rises at once . . . well, I still get goose bumps and tear up.

It's over twenty years since we produced the All-Star Tribute. I feel enormous pride that we made it happen. It's one of the greatest achievements of my career, and, for Brian, one of the most significant events of his solo years. Even over two decades since it happened, it doesn't seem possible. Brian Diamond: "It was one of the hardest things I ever worked on because of all the moving parts."

After the show was over and we'd finished editing it, with great work by Wyatt Smith, we were breathing normally for the first time in six months. Relieved. All of my necessary and unnecessary anxiety was now gone. To that point, it was the most difficult production of my entire career, but well worth it for everyone involved. Brian was thrilled. Genuinely moved.

The ultimate impact of the show on *SMiLE*—the performance of three *SMiLE* songs at the Tribute—was an extra bonus, unexpected and beyond belief.

The *All-Star Tribute to Brian Wilson* aired on TNT on July 4. One unforeseen by-product of the special was that, in the summer of 2001, Brian toured with Paul Simon.

Then, soon afterwards, America found itself in the midst of genuine horror. Our world was turned upside down. 9-11. In the wake of the terrorist attacks, I was chosen, thanks to David Wild, to be one of the writers on an all-network telethon, "A Tribute to Heroes." Another remarkable experience. There were unbelievably meaningful "close encounters" with George Clooney and others.

But nothing was more exciting than being right there with Muhammad Ali, who had always been a personal hero. Ali had long been suffering from Parkinson's syndrome, so we were unsure of what he could do live on camera. We needn't have worried. He looked at the script page I handed him, nodded and then went out, stood with Will Smith, and without a script, rose to the occasion in heroic style. Talk about being a champion.

In terms of my life and career, it felt like I had reached another mountaintop.

L-R: Jimmy Webb, Phil Ramone, Brian and David Leaf.
Credit: Robin Siegel

399

In the wake of the Radio City Tribute, Phil Ramone and I went to work producing a television series, *The Score*, featuring directors and the film composers with whom they worked. During pre-production on that series, conversations began regarding Phil producing the next Brian Wilson solo album. I was really excited by the prospect of this. I prepared a long list of unreleased songs for his consideration. There were so many tunes in the Brian Wilson "vault" that I thought worthy of his ear, perhaps worthy of release. Some were almost finished. Some were demos. Some were just fragments that needed development.

What was needed was a producer who knew how to work with legendary songwriters, and given Ramone's credits (Paul Simon, Billy Joel et al.), I knew that Phil would treat Brian as a great artist. In my files, I found one list which included 'City Blues,' 'Where Is She,' 'I Searched the World,' 'Rainbow Eyes,' and one melody I personally considered (and still do) a spirited masterpiece: 'Saturday Morning in the City.' There were many more, including a few still unreleased ones from the *Adult Child* and Wilson–Paley sessions. Lots of lists were made, tapes listened to, conversations and meetings had. Talks with Brian's team got quite serious, but the record didn't happen.

Phil, however, was about to bring Brian Wilson to the biggest stage in England. In January 2002, the year after the Radio City tribute, Brian took *Pet Sounds Live* to the U.K.; he played an extended engagement at the Royal Festival Hall in London. For British music fans, this was a major moment. After all, the U.K.'s *Sunday Times* had once declared *Pet Sounds* "The number one album of all time." And Elton John had said, "A landmark album. To say I was enthralled would be an understatement. I have never heard such magical sounds. It undoubtedly changed the way that I, and countless others, approached recording. It is a timeless and amazing recording of incredible genius and beauty."

Recreating that magic live? No pressure on Brian and his band—they rose to the challenge every night, always to standing ovations. The incredible band on that tour deserves a moment in the sun: the Wondermints (Darian, Nick, Probyn Gregory and Mike D'Amico), Andy Paley and the Brian/Beach Boys stalwart Jeffrey Foskett, as well as the Chicago players (Jim Hines, Bob Lizik, Paul (Von) Mertens, Scott Bennett and Taylor Mills). Versatile multi-instrumentalists, almost everybody played and sang too.

While we were in London, one of the quietest yet most eventful meetings I've ever had took place. Mr. Ramone asked if I could meet with him and somebody who worked with the royal family. The three of us got together in a private spot in the Marriott County Hall, where Brian and his entourage were staying. The morning coffee and tea conversation was very proper, very polite and very straightforward. In June, there would be a concert celebrating the Queen's Golden Jubilee, marking the fifty years since Queen Elizabeth II's ascension to the throne. "Would Brian want to play the concert to be held at Buckingham Palace?" I didn't see why not. On first blush, this Yank really didn't understand the magnitude of the invitation. I politely said, "I'll ask him." And that's how in June 2002, Brian, Melinda, Eva and I—and Daria and Delanie—found ourselves on a plane to London.

Rehearsal day was filled with insanely memorable moments. First, we arrived at Buckingham Palace to go through a very thorough security check. After 9-11, it was extremely tight. Then, we had a fascinating ride by cart on a concrete path to the backstage area. As we rode, taking in every "once-in-a-lifetime" sight, the guide informed us that we shouldn't stray from the pathway as there were snipers in the trees. Whoa. We were also told not to address the Queen. The latter wasn't quite as frightening.

Backstage, we waited patiently for Brian's rehearsal, but just as he was brought onstage, his escort pointed to the roof of Buckingham Palace and asked, "Is that a fire?" Sure enough, there was smoke rising from the roof. We were instantly evacuated. There was genuine fear that this was a terrorist attack.

Despite having been told to never veer off the path, hundreds of us now walked away as briskly as possible, with no concern as to whether we were on the grass. Within a minute or two, we were all at the far end of the palace grounds, near the tennis court, wondering what was happening. We all stood or sat on the immaculately groomed lawn, waiting for our "marching orders." Only one person had a seat: Brian Wilson. He had asked his "palace escort" to get him a chair. Brian knows who he is, what he wants and just how to get it.

Anyway, Eva and I were sitting on the grass alongside him when he suddenly said to us, "I want to sing with Paul." He meant McCartney. Who was topping the bill. Momentarily surprised, I quickly said, "Well, there's Sir George. Let's go talk with him."

Sir George Martin and Phil Ramone were the musical directors for the event. The three of us walked over to Sir George, who greeted us. Brian didn't hesitate. He said, "I want to sing on 'All You Need Is Love' with Paul." Rod Stewart and Joe Cocker were already set to sing on the song with Paul. George asked, "What part do you want to sing?" Without missing a beat, Brian said, "John's part." George gulped, a bit surprised. Of course, that's what Brian wanted. An example of how Brian saw himself, the kind of rock royalty in which he belonged.

After a while, it was determined that the fire in the palace was from an electrical short. Everybody breathed a sigh of relief. Given that the *SMiLE*-era 'Fire' sessions had derailed Brian back in the day, I was relieved that this 'Fire' wasn't going to spook him. Heading back to the stage, I found myself in conversation with Sir George. Walking alone, with a Knight of the British Empire at Buckingham Palace. I wish I had a "selfie" of that.

Brian's rehearsal went smoothly, but we couldn't leave until after Brian's rehearsal with Sir Paul McCartney. Not exactly a burden. We were so excited to sit up front in the vast area of empty seats. The only people watching were Brian's band, Eva and me.

Finally, Paul took the stage, and he directed Brian to sit at his "magic" keyboard. It's the rainbow-colored one from which he usually sings 'Hello, Goodbye.' *Nobody* sat there. Yet another indication of Paul's love and high regard for Brian.

We watched, waiting for the rehearsal to start. However, there was some sort of technical glitch; Paul was standing about fifteen feet behind Brian with his back to him as he consulted with the tech crew, Phil Ramone and Sir George. Brian, as per usual, was extremely impatient. After about ten minutes, he leaned into his mic and said, "C'mon. Let's go." Used to commanding his stage, Paul wheeled around. He looked quite surprised. When he saw it was Brian, he didn't say anything. Finally, all was fixed, and the rehearsal began. As Cocker and Stewart hadn't come for the run-through, Brian had a clear musical path. He sang his part on 'All You Need Is Love' with gusto.

The last song of Sir Paul's set was 'Hey Jude.' As usual, when he got to the second half of the song, he directed the "crowd" to join in with him, "All the fellas sing," and Brian's band and I joined him for the "na, na, nas." Then he said, "Now the ladies." While Taylor was in Brian's band, Eva and I were sitting much closer to the stage. Eva was the only woman Paul could see, and he sang directly to her. Talk about a moment you dream of. After singing her part, when Paul returned to the climax of the song, Eva leaned over to me and whispered, "Take me now. It'll never get any better."

Concert day was exciting in a different way. We sat in the crowd, with very good seats, as some ten thousand watched this remarkable all-star show in person. Thousands more were viewing it on big screens set up outside the palace and millions tuned in on television. During the concert, Brian's performance was solid, and he looked terrific in the handsome blue bespoke suit that Melinda had tailored for him. Unfortunately, during "All You Need Is Love," Cocker and Stewart were there, front and center, and with the stage filled, Brian stood at the keyboard in the background, looking a bit lost.

At the end of the show, as the entire cast joined in together, Queen Elizabeth II came out of the wings to center stage. As she passed by, Brian couldn't resist. As Darian Sahanaja tells it, Brian almost shoved Ozzy Osbourne out of the way to get the Queen's attention. "Hi Queen." Brian waved to her too.

That's Brian Wilson. The rules just don't apply.

Two weeks later, Brian turned sixty and Melinda threw a big surprise party for him at The Grill in the Beverly Glen shopping center, just steps away from Brian's favorite breakfast spot, the Glen Deli. The guest list was the story of his life: family members included Brian's older daughters, Carnie and Wendy, and the younger girls, Daria and Delanie. Mother-in-law Rose. Gloria Ramos and her husband Luis. Brian's managers, Jean Sievers and Ronnie Lippin. Eva and me. Jerry, Lois and Ray flew in from back east. As did Michael DeMartin, Brian's website designer.

His lifelong friends from the music business were there: Fred Vail, Danny Hutton, Van Dyke Parks, Tony Asher, Carole Kaye, Don Randi, Steve Desper, Nancy Sinatra, Billy Hinsche and his sister Annie (Carl's ex). Brian's old *SMiLE*-era partner David Anderle had a mile-wide smile. Brian's band was there. Andy Paley too. Stephen Kalinich, longtime L.A. scenemakers Rodney Bingenheimer and author Harvey Kubernik and graphic designer Mark London, Wayne Johnson from Rockaway Records, Neil Warnock (Brian's international concert promoter), Mark Linett, and filmmakers Alan

Boyd and John Anderson. High school pal Rich Sloan was busy taking pictures. More friends. Lots of spouses.

When Brian arrived, he was not only surprised but a bit unnerved. He made a beeline for the buffet, gulping down a few pieces of shrimp cocktail to calm himself down.

Jeffrey Foskett, the beautiful falsetto singer and guitar player in Brian's band, was the master of ceremonies. There were so many heartfelt speeches: Carnie, Wendy, words of love from wordsmiths Tony Asher and Van Dyke Parks. Danny Hutton. Melinda almost had the last word. But Lance Freed, Brian's longtime publisher, followed her, as did her cousin Steve and mother Rose Ledbetter.

My speech, atypically for me, was short: "There are people who have known Brian longer than me who are here. Who are related by blood. By marriage. But I'm pretty sure that nobody has written more words about him than I have. I'll be short. No books tonight. I just want to say this. Brian brought us all together. For a very good reason. To help spread love to the world. He inspires us. He gives us everything we need. And all I can say is 'Thank you.' . . . Nothing has given us more pleasure or more meaning than being able to be part of your life. God bless you."

Brian topped off the formal festivities by thanking everybody and saying, "There's a love vibe tonight."

Ray's favorite memory from the party was that Brian kept running over to where Van Dyke and Danny were sitting to tell them how well 'Heroes and Villains' was going over in concert. After getting over the initial surprise and nervousness, Brian was really moved by it all. It was a wonderful occasion. Harvey Kubernik remembers what David Anderle said to him that night. "This is what I imagined Brother Records was supposed to be."

During these years, all was good in my life. And my career was filled with music and success and even awards and rewards. With Brian, there had been a long litany of "dream come true" events. As 2003 began, Brian Wilson had indeed reclaimed his legacy. What was left?

Melinda Wilson had an idea. A brilliant idea. She brought it to the two people who could make it happen: her husband and Neil Warnock, the international concert promoter. Neil had made the Royal Festival Hall in

London something of a home for Brian when the U.K. *Pet Sounds* tour was launched there in 2002.

For decades, Brian had been constantly asked, "When are you going to finish *SMiLE*?" The idea of sorting through all of those tapes, of recapturing "the creative moment," of facing the biggest disappointment of his career, had elicited different responses. Sometimes, it was stony silence. Sometimes, he would say, "It's inappropriate music." At least once, he compared finishing *SMiLE* to "raising the *Titanic*."

But Melinda didn't bring any baggage to *SMiLE*. She had seen how well the *SMiLE* music on 1993's *Good Vibrations* box had been received. 'Our Prayer,' 'Surf's Up' and 'Heroes and Villains' were major moments in the 2001 Radio City Tribute. And after that, on tour, 'Heroes and Villains' had become a highlight of Brian's concerts. In 2002, he and the band added other *SMiLE* songs to the concert repertoire.

L-R: Brian, Carl, Mike, Al and Dennis in London, November 1964. Forty years later, London's Royal Festival Hall would become the home of what many regard as Brian's most significant concert, the world premiere of *Brian Wilson Presents SMiLE*. In 2007, *Rolling Stone* would include it in their list of '50 Greatest Concerts of the Last 50 Years'.
Credit: Michael Ochs Archives/Getty

What made Melinda's concept viable was that it didn't address finishing the record. And, for Brian, that made it an electrifying possibility. The pressure to organize and finish the original *SMiLE* sessions might have just been too much. And so, a stunning announcement was made, one that would change the course of music history. Brian's life and his career. Mine too. Nearly two decades later, it still feels unbelievable. But it did happen. Of that we're all sure.

Brian was in London in May of 2003 to accept the Ivor Novello Award when this flashed across the wire. The announcement said simply that *Brian Wilson Presents SMiLE* would be unveiled to the world on February 20, 2004 at the Royal Festival Hall. At these shows, Brian Wilson was going to present the music of *SMiLE*. In its entirety. He wasn't going to finish it on record, but in a live, concert presentation.

Nevertheless, it still seemed like the challenge of a lifetime. Nearly forty years since he had abandoned the project in 1967, over thirty years since it had become my "grand obsession," over ten years since some of the *SMiLE* sessions had been released on the *Good Vibrations* box set, it seemed that *SMiLE* was actually about to come to life. In the most unexpected way. In concert?

We didn't know what that announcement meant, other than that Eva and I *knew* we would be in London to see it with our own eyes.

CHAPTER 20

BEAUTIFUL DREAMS AND
BEAUTIFUL DREAMER

IN THE EARLY 1990S, BECAUSE OF MY WORK AS A SEGMENT PRODUCER ON Disney's *Salute to the American Teacher*, making short films about great educators, I was hired to write a documentary called *Be My Guest: The Making of Beauty and the Beast*. It was a behind-the-scenes look at the Disney animated film.

Around that same time, I also wrote and co-produced a three-part documentary on the legendary comedy team of Dean Martin and Jerry Lewis. And thanks to Ron Furmanek, an old friend from my Beatles collecting days, I was hired to write and produce my first *music* documentary, *You Can't Do That: The Making of A Hard Day's Night*.

Unexpectedly, I was making documentaries. I found that I loved interviewing people, talking with them about their work and then shaping a film that would present an important story for the viewing audience.

Throughout the 1990s, I continued to direct short films on various television specials, most memorably, about Travis Roy for a Christopher Reeve tribute (Google: Travis Roy + Christopher Reeve), and all sorts of music-related programs. I was learning how to use words and pictures to tell a story. Additionally, with my producing partner at the time, John Scheinfeld, I began writing/producing/directing what would be a long stream of pop culture retrospectives: the Marx Brothers, Peter Sellers, Frank Sinatra, Nat "King" Cole, Rosemary Clooney, Dean Martin, Jonathan Winters, Buddy Holly, and many more.

But there wasn't yet a feature-length music documentary on my résumé. That changed when the Bee Gees and their manager, Carol Peters, entrusted me to tell the group's story. In 2000, *This Is Where I Came In* aired on

A&E's *Biography* series, and in the process of making it, I knew—and more importantly, the industry knew—I could craft a narrative about important artists that could hold an audience for two hours.

After the earth-shattering announcement about *SMiLE* in 2003, given my passion for the subject, I didn't immediately think, "I should make a film about *Brian Wilson Presents SMiLE*." It actually didn't even cross my mind. Brian was my friend. We were excited and nervous for him. And, of course, we wondered what *Brian Wilson Presents SMiLE* would be.

In 1993, Brian and I had gone over a possible track listing for *SMiLE*. Working at the kitchen table of his home with a pile of 3×5 index cards, the name of each song on a card, Brian and I tried to create a *SMiLE* song sequence. Nothing came of it. Beginning in the late 1990s, I began trying to create a symphonic version of *SMiLE*, but I wasn't able to attract interest. In my files are an endless series of proposals.

Flash forward to a warm summer day in 2003. Brian and I were walking up the 3rd Street Promenade in Santa Monica. We'd just been to the movies and were heading back to my apartment. All was right in our world. Then Brian turned to me, and, as he would do from time to time, dropped a bombshell.

Two sentences that would change my life and his. Out of nowhere, Brian said, "I can't do *SMiLE* without you. I need you there." He made it clear he wanted me by his side every step of the way. I was stunned. Four years earlier, he had made a similar "request" before his first tour. I thought about the amount of time and the kind of commitment he was asking for. I said, "Brian, the only way I can be there every day is if I make a documentary about it." He liked the idea.

Within the week, I was in the upstairs den of the Wilson home, outlining the story as I saw it. Melinda asked, "What do you think the fans will think of this?" My response was blunt, but not really. "I don't care what the fans think. They're a tiny percentage of the audience. We're trying to get to everybody else who's never even heard of *SMiLE*."

Of course, I cared what fans would think about it. But we fans tend to watch and listen from a different perspective. My point was that I believed that this was such an important story that even if you didn't like the Beach Boys or didn't know what *SMiLE* was, this story should resonate.

I felt it in my bones. Because it was a story about survival and determination and artistic dreams delayed and fulfilled. About the most famous unfinished album in rock history. And, we all hoped, a story with a happy ending. Since Brian had shelved *SMiLE*, those had been rare in Brian's creative world.

Back in 1966, Van Dyke's lyrics were an extremely important part of *SMiLE*. The ambition of the music was such that it demanded lyrics that could stand up to repeated listening. And I think that part of the triumph of the *SMiLE* songs is that he accomplished just that. We can listen to 'Surf's Up' and 'Wonderful' and 'Cabinessence' and 'Heroes and Villains' hundreds of times and never tire of the lyrics. That's a big part of what makes *SMiLE* special.

Brian instinctively chose Van Dyke, because he knew that Van Dyke would make a major contribution to the record. And now, thirty-seven years later, they would have to recreate the vibe of that 1966 "moment," somehow complete the unfinished masterpiece, so that *Brian Wilson Presents SMiLE* could really happen. Brian, Van Dyke and Darian Sahanaja went to work structuring the piece. My main contribution to this, as Darian recalls, was opening my archives, which included the original handwritten lyrics to 'Do You Like Worms.' I'd gotten them years earlier from *SMiLE* artist Frank Holmes. (Those lyrics became a key story point in my *Beautiful Dreamer* film.)

Meanwhile, I started to look for financing for the documentary. This would be a different and difficult challenge. It would require somebody who cared about Brian Wilson to "get" what I wanted to do. I had become friendly with Richard Waltzer, a successful producer and a former HBO executive. He had contacted me because he had the idea to produce a jukebox musical of the Beach Boys music; when we met, it was clear he was a gigantic fan. As Richard reminded me in 2021: "Like you, I had set out to write a book about Brian Wilson, and I interviewed many of the people who we subsequently interviewed thirty years later for the film."

The jukebox musical didn't happen, but when I told him about the idea of making a documentary on *SMiLE*, I didn't have to explain what *SMiLE* was. I asked for his help in setting it up. He was good friends with Joan Boorstein, a key programming executive at Showtime. Richard: "At the meeting with Joan, she said, 'It sounds great.' We told her what the budget was, and we were pretty much a 'go.'"

The Showtime license fee alone wasn't going to be enough to make the film, but I was confident that with a home video advance and international sales, we would be OK. My partners at LSL Productions were less sure, especially as, Richard Waltzer recalls, a business affairs executive at Showtime wasn't writing checks very quickly. Or at all. I remember a meeting, probably in December of 2003, just before shooting was to begin. John Scheinfeld, one of the producers on the project, hesitantly closed the door to my Studio City office; he and our exec in charge of production expressed their concern. My response was a bit hot-headed but true: "I'll make it here or I'll make it somewhere else. But I'm going to make it."

We began shooting the first day of vocal rehearsals in January 2004. The world premiere of *Brian Wilson Presents SMiLE* was less than two months away, so the fact that the first two days were epically terrible was beyond disheartening. Brian's band was ready from day one, but Brian was extremely disengaged, disinterested, and distressed.

As you can see in *Beautiful Dreamer: Brian Wilson and the Story of SMiLE*, on the second day of rehearsal, Brian was terrified enough to drive himself to the emergency room at St. John's/Santa Monica Hospital. The hospital called to tell us Brian was there, and Melinda and I immediately drove to the ER. Eva rushed over from her nearby office. After Brian was released, we headed back to the car. Walking east on Santa Monica Boulevard, Brian and I were about ten or fifteen feet ahead of Melinda and Eva. We couldn't hear what they were talking about, and they couldn't hear our conversation either.

For forty years, first as the "head honcho" of the Beach Boys and then in his solo career, nothing could happen without Brian. Since 1968, when he would work—or not—there was often a certain withholding if he was displeased with the circumstances. For years, Carl Wilson had been the one to make sure the records shone. By 1976, Brian was no longer a perfectionist; unlike in the past, "good enough" had become good enough. And now, in 2004, Carl was gone. It was up to Brian.

At the first tracking session Brian produced for *The Wilsons* record, Hal Blaine had said the missing ingredient in Brian was "ego." To be a great artist, you need many things, such as ego, ambition, energy, and control of your art. Along the way, Brian's talent remained intact but it seemed he no longer had what it took to completely shoulder all the other aspects of the creative process, to stand his artistic ground and stay the course for an entire project. From time to time, when the music would be bursting out of him, he would write a great song, cut a great track, sing amazing vocals. But to do it for an entire album? Since his 1988 solo record, he hadn't evidenced the emotional stamina that would be required.

Finishing *SMiLE* for the fast-approaching world premiere was clearly weighing heavily upon him. Did he have what it took to produce a masterwork? Brian knew that *Brian Wilson Presents SMiLE* would require him to step up. He would have to demonstrate the kind of artistic integrity, work ethic and quarterbacking that he hadn't brought to bear on a full-length project since he'd abandoned *SMiLE* in 1967.

And maybe that's why he had shied away from *SMiLE* for so many years. Because it meant so much to him—and he knew what it was going to take to finish it—he didn't want to desecrate the original creation.

To walk out of a rehearsal and drive yourself to the emergency room is clearly a cry for help. He was scared. And I wanted him to know that as much as we were excited about the prospect of *SMiLE* being presented live, it was up to him. I don't know if anybody had ever given him that kind of choice before.

All of that was in my head. But I was his friend first. After we had walked a block in silence, I said to Brian, "Your health is more important than anything. If finishing *SMiLE* is going to make you sick, then let's forget about it. You don't have to do this."

Brian looked at me with a steely determination I'd never seen. Forcefully, he said, "No. I have to do it." For the moment at least, that relieved the pressure. The admission that this was a "no turning back" crossroads seemed to give him a certain confidence. The four of us went out to a nice dinner.

Work resumed the next day, with a somewhat more positive and optimistic flow. Brian started to become part of the process. Progress was slow, but as he heard his brilliant singers bring his harmonies to life, *he* began to come to life. By the end of vocal rehearsals, he was actively participating, perhaps even enjoying singing his songs and hearing his original harmony arrangements.

A dozen years after they had heard *SMiLE* tapes at my apartment, Darian Sahanaja and Nick Walusko were now deconstructing every single instrumental part for the band to learn. Darian: "I went through all the guitar parts with Nick and he helped identify exact chords, fingerings, and in most cases, specific guitars used."

So when all the players came together to rehearse the whole piece in a bare-bones hall out in the San Fernando Valley, it was clear that this would work musically. Brian's devoted band had successfully embraced the challenge. Hearing these songs come alive was beyond exciting. There were so many wonderful moments during this time. Carole Kaye spent an afternoon there to show her support. Van Dyke stopped by too, encouraging everybody.

One of my favorite rehearsal days had to do with 'Good Vibrations.' I had become good friends with Tony Asher, and at some point, he gave me the original lyrics he had written for that song during the *Pet Sounds* sessions. One day, I printed them out and brought them to rehearsal. I walked over to Brian at his keyboard. Told him what I was holding. He snatched them out of my hands faster than a cat burglar. Read them. And almost instantly, he made them part of *Brian Wilson Presents SMiLE*.

In my head, I had structured the documentary like a narrative feature film, as a three-act drama. After an opening tease, the first two acts would include Brian's origin story, the early years of the Beach Boys' career, the artistic adventures of *Pet Sounds*, 'Good Vibrations' and the *SMiLE* sessions, Brian's withdrawal from the music world and his return to the studio and touring. I had to cram sixty years into about sixty minutes.

But I couldn't write the third act because it was unfolding in real time. All I could do was show up with a crew at rehearsals, watch what happened and record it, *cinéma vérité*-style. And hope we would have a rousing and upbeat climax for the film in London. Back at my production office, we were busily researching photographs and archival footage that could be used in the still-untitled film. Outlining the story. Figuring out who to interview.

When we began taping those interviews, I talked with those who were involved in and around during the original *SMiLE* sessions: musicians, observers, family. As we hadn't yet determined the visual look of the film, those were shot "green screen" so we could digitally insert behind them whatever image was appropriate to that point in the story.

During the course of the next few weeks, in addition to taping the rehearsals (well over fifty hours of footage of which are compressed into the third act of *Beautiful Dreamer*), I had another idea. Perhaps I was overconfident. The shooting of the band rehearsals had been going very well.

But this one particular shoot was almost a complete disaster. I tried to do a "pre-London" interview with Brian. We set up at one of his favorite studios. We had what was, for a documentary, a big crew, including a jib camera. This was going to be a key interview for the film. Or so I assumed.

I wanted to elicit Brian's thoughts on everything that had happened in the past, everything that was taking place in 2004, have him talk about the upcoming world premiere. With this enormous challenge looming, I wanted to know how Brian felt. Did he have any specific fears? How did he think it would go over with the crowd? Did he think, in a word he had used in the past, that it was now "appropriate" to finish *SMiLE*?

I had a lot of questions. Brian answered none of them. The conversation went nowhere. I only asked a few before it was clear that he just did not want to talk or discuss *SMiLE*. Period. And it didn't matter how gently I phrased it; he didn't give us anything usable. This was about to become a "budget buster" of a day. Our solution? Have Brian play music.

From making documentaries, I knew we could use instrumental versions of songs as "B" roll, to underscore and illustrate key moments of his career. So we quickly reset and spent the rest of the session with him at the piano. I was able to persuade Brian to play a few of the most important songs he'd written and one piece of music that had inspired him, *Rhapsody in Blue*. I knew I wanted to use *Rhapsody* in the film. We did get great footage that day. Phew.

But, as a filmmaker, as a storyteller, as a producer, it made me more than a little apprehensive. I needed Brian to tell *his* story. Was he going to "withhold" throughout the entire production? There would be no more formal interviewing with Brian until after the London premiere. Every now and again, at the end of band rehearsals, I would have my main cameraman and director of photography (the terrific and dedicated Jim Mathers) stand next to me while I asked Brian a question. We got a usable sound bite or two that way.

The London shoot was actually a double production. At the same time my documentary crew and I got to the Festival Hall to cover the world premiere of *SMiLE*, we were also setting up, with a completely different production team, to tape the concert.

I was planning to use pieces of it in the documentary, so we hired real music concert pros to get that footage. I also knew that this was an historic event. There needed to be a complete record of Brian's first performance of *SMiLE* for posterity.

While director Maurice Linnane and his crew were busy setting up, I was working with my "behind-the-scenes" team, capturing all sorts of moments that you can see in the film and on the DVD (and as with the rehearsals in L.A., dozens of hours that are still in the vaults).

For many of us in attendance in London, it was a "holy grail" night. We had believed in Brian, believed that he could do it. That with enough support, he could come back from the depths and triumph again.

Outside of the Festival Hall, Richard Waltzer and a camera crew were interviewing fans. Richard: "I talked to all the people that had congregated from around the world, literally, to hear *SMiLE*." The montage of these devotees in the documentary helped create the excitement that was building and became one of my favorite scenes. Disciples had gathered—from Tokyo, Cape Town, from all over Europe, the U.S.A. and the U.K. We were the "true believers," and there was an almost evangelical nature to what had brought us all together for this moment.

The day of the concert was when I actually *felt* I became a director. I'd previously gotten the credit quite a few times on various projects. My visual approach tended to be minimalist. But now, for the first time in my career, I was really "seeing" the film in my head. It happened just hours before the concert. Backstage, near the stairway to the stage, I was telling the *cinéma-vérité* cameramen where I wanted them to stand. I told one to be high up, near the last row of the Festival Hall, for a shot that would show Brian as almost a little dot on a tiny stage. I wanted another camera at the back of the stage to get a reverse shot, looking toward the audience to capture what I was certain would be a gigantic ovation when he came onstage.

Most important was the third camera. I wanted one camera to follow Brian up the stairs to the stage. I described it like this, "You know the movie *Dead Man Walking*? I think Brian is going to be slowly plodding up those stairs as if he's heading to the electric chair. This is probably the bravest and scariest moment of his musical life. We should feel the hesitancy, the fear, the dread."

I realized that, even though the footage hadn't been shot, I had already "edited" the scene. Yet, as I gave the crew this direction, we still didn't know if Brian was even going to walk up those steps. It infused everything with real tension. We now waited for release.

February 20, 2004. The performance of *Brian Wilson Presents SMiLE* would be after the intermission. The first half of the concert went off smoothly, to great response. But the ardent audience was on edge, hungry for the main course. At the intermission, while everybody wanted to pretend that nothing unusual was about to take place, there was no way to deny that the moment of reckoning was nearing. Inside the venue, the nervous anticipation was mostly excitement and disbelief. Approaching a crescendo. For longtime fans, a mystery was about to be "solved." What was *Brian Wilson Presents SMiLE* actually going to be?

Backstage, it was tense, almost completely dead silent. Quiet. Nerve-wracking. Brian sat, mostly by himself, thinking, meditating. Worrying? You can see in *Beautiful Dreamer* the intense look. What was he thinking? Nobody knew. And while we could all encourage him, tell him how great *SMiLE* was, how the audience would love it, how we loved him . . . he was the one who had to face the music.

Finally, it was time. Intermission was over. With all of my cameras in place—for both the documentary and the concert production—I watched him start up the stairs to the stage. For a second, tentatively, then confidently towards his fate. I dashed to my seat. Eva and I had waited for this moment forever,

It was astonishing. *Brian Wilson Presents SMiLE* was everything we could have wanted and more. Throughout the performance, the audience was ecstatic. The rapt attention to the music bordered on the religious. After each of the first two movements, the applause was thunderous. And at the end, the standing ovation went on and on, the longest one I ever saw Brian get. It was so long that Brian seemed a bit embarrassed. Like, "OK, enough already." He even leaned into his microphone and said, "Hold it. Hold it."

The audience would not stop. And in *Beautiful Dreamer*, you can see Brian bow his head, step back, take a deep sigh and acknowledge the approval. He took it all in. At that moment, I believe he finally accepted that his *SMiLE* music had been welcomed into the world.

Adorably, he called Van Dyke Parks to the stage to share the moment. And there they were, the giant Wilson and his diminutive partner. Like Yogi Bear and Boo-Boo. They took a charming bow, had a grand and gratifying emotional moment together.

As you can also see in *Beautiful Dreamer*, during the seemingly endless standing ovation at the end of the concert, Sir George Martin and Sir Paul McCartney are standing and applauding. They were *SMiLE* believers too.

From where Eva and I sat at the concert, Sir George was in the row in front of us, just to our left. Sir Paul was in front of him, just to his left.

During the ovation, we saw George look at Paul. It seemed like he was wondering what was going through Paul's creative mind. What was he thinking? Of course, Paul was thrilled, Paul loves Brian. You can see him raising his arms, cheering wildly at Brian's triumphant moment. He would even come backstage afterwards to congratulate all the musicians. But, because *SMiLE* was so adventurous, did Sir George sense something more? (Note: Sir Paul and Sir George attended the fourth night of the world premiere series of concerts.)

The applause continued. Brian let it wash over him. And then, Eva and I individually saw something that startled us both. It was as if ghosts were flying out of Brian's head and toward the rafters. We looked at each other and said, "Did you see that?" Was it a dual delusion? No. To us, it was affirmation that Brian had indeed conquered his demons. Brian would later confirm that he felt that way too.

Perhaps nobody was more excited/relieved than Brian, except, perhaps, for Van Dyke Parks. He, more than anybody else but Brian, had long given up hope that this day would ever arrive. He had been hurt so much by the end of *SMiLE* that he never even dared to believe or imagine *SMiLE* would ever see the light of day. He was, as we all were, both thankful and beyond overjoyed.

It had begun with Brian and Van Dyke's idea: an American musical travelogue, starting at Plymouth Rock and ending in Hawaii. And now, finally, thirty-seven years later, Brian and Van Dyke and Brian's band of beautiful souls had shared it with the world.

You can watch *Beautiful Dreamer: Brian Wilson and the Story of SMiLE* to see how this all happened. Or read the Wikipedia page of *Brian Wilson Presents SMiLE* and get endless detail of how the music was created and emerged from the psychodrama and all came together.

But, finally, thankfully, that was all now in the past. There was overwhelming bliss in the hall and backstage. Afterwards, we rode the backstage elevator down to the stage door, down from the incredible high we were all riding an hour after the ecstatic standing ovation that had greeted the world premiere of *Brian Wilson Presents SMiLE*. Brian summed up how we were all feeling. As always, it didn't take him but a few words. He smiled and said, "Our *SMiLE* dream has come true."

★　　★　　★　　★

The rest of the London engagement was a series of nightly triumphs. For those of us who had long dreamed of this moment, the living full-time members of "The Team" who had made the journey—Debbie, Eva, Ray, Jerry and Lois, and our Stateside compadre Peter Reum, many other U.S. and U.K. friends like Mike Grant who were "team adjacent," SMiLE historian Domenic Priore, dozens of longtime fans and friends—we were all elated too. For we SMiLE fanatics, it was as if we had gone to the mountaintop and received the sacred scrolls. Our faith had been rewarded. Our hero had lived up to our hero worship.

During the week in London, we kept shooting, including an interview with Brian and Van Dyke together at the Festival Hall, excerpts of which would become bonus features on the DVD. All too soon, it was back to L.A. to get to work on screening the footage and shooting more interviews. One personal favorite moment came after the interview with Tom Nolan. I told him that it was his Rolling Stone article in 1971 that had set me on the SMiLE path to what I'd done with Brian. He was misty-eyed to hear the impact his work had on me. Van Dyke Parks's first wife, Durrie, teared up during our interview. In 1967, she had experienced first-hand the emotional wreckage that the death of SMiLE had caused.

In terms of editing the still-unnamed film, the easiest way to start was to cut together the footage of the concert. I now was certain it would be the climax of the film, and while I didn't know how much of the actual show we would use, I knew I wanted to start the editing process there. It took only four days to assemble a rough cut.

As this process unfolded, my creative confidant on the project was the terrific writer/director Rob Reiner. When we had met in 2000, we had hit it off. Rob wanted me to be a big part of his team in making a Brian feature, an executive producer on the film, consult with him every step of the way. During the next few years, I had come to understand how smart Rob was, how a great director looks at a story and tries to bring it to life on screen. It wasn't easy. It wasn't automatic. It didn't matter how many successful movies you had already made. Each project presented new challenges. By 2004, after years of trying, although Rob was still eager to bring the project to life, he hadn't yet put "the package" together.

I took the rough cut of the Brian Wilson Presents SMiLE concert to his office. I wanted to get the benefit of his filmmaker's eye. He loved it. And he said something like, "All this time, we should have been approaching the story as a documentary."

For almost a decade, I had been talking with David Bither, the President of Nonesuch, a classical label distributed through Warners. He was a big fan of the work Brian and Van Dyke had done. He too believed in the importance of *SMiLE*. And now that *Brian Wilson Presents SMiLE* existed, his label would become the home for the studio version of the music. When Brian and his band went in to cut the album, our cameras were there to record it. Some of that footage made it into the movie, too.

There were more interviews to do. Again, the key ones would be with Brian. And this time, without the looming pressure of London, he was as talkative as I needed him to be. It's when, much to my surprise, he played and sang the first lines of the Stephen Foster song, 'Beautiful Dreamer.' Then, with a childlike sweetness, he said, "Beautiful Dreamer Wake. B.D.W. Brian Douglas Wilson. That's me!" The movie finally had a title. And an opening scene.

This time, the studio interview went perfectly. Brian is always most comfortable talking at the piano. We had two cameras, giving us different angles on him. In the extensive interview, Brian played boogie-woogie music and talked about his dad, the Beach Boys, the Beatles, and most significantly, for the story of the film at least, answered the question, "Why, back in 1967, had he stopped working on *SMiLE*?"

I was taken aback by the conviction with which he answered my question, almost with exasperation at having been asked so many times. The way he said it to me that day felt like, "If I tell you, will you [and the world] stop asking me?"

Here's what Brian said: "I'll tell you from my heart. In 1967, the reasons why I didn't finish *SMiLE* were that Mike didn't like it. I thought it was too experimental. I thought the 'Fire' tape was too scary. I felt that people wouldn't understand where my head was at at that time. Those are the reasons."

It was a crucial moment in the story of *SMiLE*. And for the film, too.

Clearly, Brian's loyalty to his band was paramount. He threw himself on the sword of *SMiLE* to save the group. He put the Beach Boys above his artistic aspirations. Would it have been different if everybody encouraged him to push the boundaries? What if somebody had said, "Put *SMiLE*

out as a solo album; then we can make the next Beach Boys record"?
Would it have changed the course of history? Or was it too late? Was
Brian already "broken?" We'll never really know.

Anybody who makes movies will tell you that it's in the editing room
that a film either succeeds or fails. I asked Peter Lynch, who had never
edited a feature, if he wanted to cut it. Pete had impressed me with the
work he'd done on shorter pieces for our company. As a film school
student, he clearly understood artistry. I had great confidence in his taste
and sensitivity. And like me, he was a workaholic. It might have seemed
like a risky choice, but it wasn't. It was probably the best decision I made
during the entire production of *Beautiful Dreamer*.

That said, the editing didn't go easily. Richard Waltzer was there every
step of the way, when we shot the interviews and in the editing suite
while we were trying to "find" the movie, and he watched me struggle.
In editing, our methodology was to start by making what's called a "radio
cut," stringing out all the interview sound bites as if it were an audio
documentary. That "radio cut" is always longer than the final film, but the
first *Beautiful Dreamer* radio cut was absurdly long. I was trying to include
every great moment we had on tape in the film. There were too many.

In terms of the story, "Act Three" was going to take place in 2003/2004:
the announcement of *Brian Wilson Presents SMiLE*, the rehearsals and the
world premiere would be the climax of the film. As Peter Lynch remembers, our first radio cut of the third act was almost two hours. It needed
to be more like thirty minutes. I was lost inside the story. At the suggestion of Pete and John Scheinfeld, my other producing partner on this
project, I stepped away for a bit. And when I came back, I was ready to
chop away. Whole sections of the rehearsals had to come out.

At the same time Nonesuch Records was preparing to release *Brian
Wilson Presents SMiLE*, we were racing to finish the film for the near-
simultaneous fall premiere on Showtime. One day, we thought we were
ready. I've said, mostly to myself, that each of my films has an audience
of one, that there's one person who *has* to love it or I've failed. With the
Bee Gees documentary, *This Is Where I Came In*, it was Barry Gibb. With
The U.S. vs. John Lennon, it was Yoko Ono. With my Dion film, it's Dion.
With *The Night James Brown Saved Boston*, I had a much larger constitu-
ency: Black America.

With *Beautiful Dreamer: Brian Wilson and the Story of SMiLE*, it was Brian. I nervously invited him to the editing suite to see it. That day, when he arrived, I couldn't sit next to him as he watched. Instead, I sat behind him and peered uneasily over his shoulder. About twenty minutes into the screening, Brian, the master of "Vibrations," turned around and patted me on my right knee. "Relax," he said. "It's fine." And when it was over, Brian jumped up and said, "I love it. Can I bring Van Dyke tomorrow to see it?" Brian wasted no words. I was beyond relieved. That was probably my personal peak day on the project.

There were many more memorable moments to come. We had a celebratory wrap party for the entire production team, screenings and a Q&A session at the Grammy Museum. Brian and I appeared on *Charlie Rose*; you can see the entire episode on my website, www.leafprod.com. We got a Grammy nomination for best long-form video.

For Brian, there had been the world premiere of *Brian Wilson Presents SMiLE* in London, the big success of the record—it sold nearly a million— the *SMiLE* tours, and his first Grammy Award for "Best Instrumental Recording." It all would inspire him to write a new rock opera.

But personally, as a fan, as a biographer and Brian's friend, nearly thirty-three years after I had first made it my mission to hear *SMiLE*, it had finally come to life. I had heard it. And Brian's *SMiLE* was every bit as

The author and Brian arrive at NBC Studios in Burbank to promote
Brian Wilson Presents SMiLE, fall 2004. Credit: Mark London

great—actually, even greater—than I could ever have dreamed. How often in life does something not just meet but exceed expectations? Maybe never?

That I was there, that I played a significant role in it, was as rewarding a feeling as I've ever had. In 1971, I had begun this Quixote-like quest to hear *SMiLE* completed. With *Beautiful Dreamer*, I had now told the story for all the world to see. The cherry on top was the completion and release of the record and movie to positive response and reviews.

But this long journey was not just mine; it was a metaphor for all of us. As Brian had said, "*Our SMiLE* dream has come true." It happened, as Eva said, because our faith in Brian was almost like Tinker Bell in *Peter Pan*. Proof that if you "think wonderful thoughts," believe in something strongly enough, it can come back to life. It can fly.

Yes, there would be more great music to come, more meaningful events too, but for a moment, I could just take a deep breath and *SMiLE*.

CHAPTER 21

THAT LUCKY OLD SUN

IRONICALLY, *BRIAN WILSON PRESENTS* SM*i*LE WAS PROBABLY THE EASIEST studio album of new material to record in his solo career. All of the music had been so well rehearsed for the live concerts that it was "just" a matter of getting it down on tape and mixing it, although mixing is never a straightforward process.

During a break from *SMiLE*, *Gettin' In Over My Head* was finished and released. It's a very good album. It has some of my favorite Brian Wilson solo compositions on it, including 'Rainbow Eyes' and especially the chorus of 'Don't Let Her Know She's an Angel.' The duets with Elton John and Paul McCartney are to be treasured. I was very glad to hear long-lost songs like 'City Blues' and 'Saturday Morning in the City' finally make it to record. There's a new collaboration with Van Dyke Parks. But somehow, in the wake of the first U.K. *SMiLE* tour and in advance of the *Brian Wilson Presents SMiLE* album, it seemed, if it's possible, to be both pre- and anti-climactic. Or maybe I was just too busy editing and polishing *Beautiful Dreamer*, preparing for its premiere.

In the late summer and fall of 2004, we did a lot of promotional work to set up the release of the *Brian Wilson Presents SMiLE* album and *Beautiful Dreamer* documentary, which would have its U.S. debut on Showtime in October 2004. Brian himself was back on the road with *SMiLE*, including SRO concerts in prestigious venues like Carnegie Hall, L.A.'s Disney Concert Hall and the Sydney Opera House.

Since 1976, whenever devoted fans had talked about a new Beach Boys or Brian Wilson record, the conversation had always included the qualifier. "I like the songs on the new record, but I don't like Brian's lead vocals." Or "I like the songs and the vocals, but I don't like the production." Or "I like that song, but there are better ones that aren't on the record."

Brian Wilson Presents SMiLE was an absolute masterpiece. The celebration that had begun in London in February 2004 continued into 2005. I think giving his version of *SMiLE* to the world helped Brian in a way that made 2004/2005 a sunny time for all who cared. Both the record and the documentary positively and enormously raised his profile in the industry.

All of the "branding" work was paying off because Brian's greatest twentieth-century music had been brought back to life, "live" on tour in the twenty-first century. Brian was finally being properly recognized as the creative genius behind the Beach Boys' most successful and significant records. The concerts were indeed worthy of his name.

In February of 2005, the National Academy of Recording Arts and Sciences, the people who put on the Grammy Awards, honored Brian as their "Person of the Year" with the annual MusiCares tribute. Four years after our Radio City event, another all-star group of artists came together: the show included the Red Hot Chili Peppers, the Backstreet Boys, the Barenaked Ladies, Michael McDonald, John Legend and living legends like Darlene Love, Billy Preston, Earth, Wind and Fire and Jeff Beck. Perhaps most movingly, Neil Young dedicated his version of 'In My Room' to Brian and his deceased brothers, Dennis and Carl.

On his 2005 European tour, what stands out in memory, besides the music, is when Ray Lawlor, Eva and I were at the Vatican with the Wilsons. We wanted to be with Brian when he saw *The Last Judgment* as well as Michelangelo's beautiful, timeless ceiling and the Renaissance frescos. Getting into the Sistine Chapel, as Ray recalls, was a bit of an Abbott and Costello routine. "You and Eva got separated, way ahead of me, Brian and Melinda. You called me on my cell, 'Where are you?' I said, 'Down by the dead popes.' We were in the catacombs. And when I looked up, Brian was standing, head bowed, in front of the tomb of John Paul II, who had died earlier that year." Finally, the five of us were reunited and entered Cappella Sistina together; Brian was moved in a way we hadn't seen him before. Humbled, perhaps. Great art does that to great artists. But, as Ray remembers, "We didn't stay long. Brian took it all in very quickly. Then, it was time to eat."

Brian's concert in Rome, while musically terrific, was seen by one of the smallest, albeit enthusiastic, audiences he ever played for. According to our friend Jacopo Benci (artist, musician, educator, and our Rome tour guide), ticket prices were just too high.

A historical Wilson/Beach Boys event during that era was the unveiling of a monument at the site of the Wilson family home in Hawthorne, California. The house had been knocked down to make way for a new L.A. freeway, and a group had banded together to mark the spot with a monument. Fans and friends and associates of the group contributed to the cost of it. Eva and I bought four bricks and across them had inscribed, "The sound born here changed the world. Forever . . . "

Our usual entourage attended the event. Brian was the only living Wilson brother, so he was front and center and the focus of much of the day. Carl's sons' band, In Bloom, played. Al Jardine spoke. Some were notable by their absence.

As 2006 began, Brian devoted his attention to a serious new piece of work, while I was focused on a new feature documentary (more on that later). It would be a film about an artist who was one of Brian's favorite vocalists of all time. I remember sometime in the 1990s, Brian was asked by a magazine to make a list of who he thought were the best singers, had the ten best voices. He rattled off a list that included Rosemary Clooney, Dion and John Lennon. When I asked him about Paul, he shook his head. "Paul is versatile." It was a sideways compliment and an insight into how Brian regarded his Gemini twin.

In 2007, when the John F. Kennedy Center for the Performing Arts announced the selection of who would receive the Kennedy Center Honors that year, Brian's name was right there, alongside comedic actor and writer Steve Martin, "Supreme" singer Diana Ross and Academy Award-winning director Martin Scorsese.

Before we all left for D.C., there was a party in Brian's honor. Family and friends feted him. I was the master of ceremonies. I probably spoke a bit too much. Then, we headed east. Just a few blocks from my college dorm—the place where I'd first been inspired by Brian's music, the place where the seed had been planted for my next film—we watched and applauded at the Kennedy Center as Brian received one of the nation's highest artistic awards. Another pinnacle in Mr. Wilson's career.

An idea had been percolating for a while, and finally, in the early 1990s, I had written a short treatment called "The Secret War Against John Lennon," the story of the U.S. government's determination to deny him a visa because of his anti-war activities. It had been inspired by my love of the Beatles and my college years at George Washington University. I was in D.C. during the anti-war movement, during Nixon's criminal presidency. My dorm was five blocks from the White House, and we were on the receiving end of government suppression of free speech. Troops surrounding the campus. Tear gas. Club-wielding riot police.

In 2000, after the Bee Gees film was finished, Steve Sterling (then with Eaglevision, our home video partner) said he'd enjoyed working with me. Did I have another project in mind? I told him about the Lennon idea, and he introduced me to Peter Shukat, the Lennon estate attorney. It took years for the project to develop, but after a long series of meetings and phone calls, I soon found myself working closely with another lawyer from the firm, Jonas Herbsman, who dealt with Yoko Ono on a day-to-day basis. The decisive day for me would be when I met Yoko at her apartment in the Dakota.

March 2005. It was a cold, rainy winter morning. When I got out of the cab, on the southeast corner of Central Park West at 72nd Street, I held an umbrella and stood at the corner, looking at the imposing building. I felt a bit like *The Exorcist* in the movie poster, just before he enters the house. I was looking at the exterior of the fictional home for *Rosemary's Baby*.

More to the point, this was the horrific, real-life location of John's murder. As I stood there, in the rain, all I could think of was that I had to walk across the spot where John had been killed by a madman. To meet one of the reportedly most intimidating, and if truth be told, most disliked women in rock history. Maybe the most unjustly hated woman in the Western world.

I knew that if I went into the building with all that in my head, the meeting would be a disaster. So, I told myself a different story, spinning a new yarn. "Wait a second. You're going there to meet with John's widow to tell her a story of a movie you want to make in which she is one of the heroes. And you like meeting famous people too." With that, I felt calm (what a friend of mine later described as "JewBu"—Jewish Buddhism), crossed Central Park West, entered the building, went upstairs, and was greeted by one of the most familiar faces on the planet. At the door, she smiled and asked me to take off my shoes. She led me to the kitchen, which would be the site of all our meetings. On the way, we walked past John's white 'Imagine' piano.

Seated across from her at the kitchen table, I told her the story I wanted to tell and how I wanted to begin the film. She immediately responded. She liked my idea for the opening title sequence (unfortunately, never realized). She felt it was analogous to book burning in Nazi Germany. We spoke for well over an hour, and by the time I left, I had her approval. With that, we were able to find financing with partners Lionsgate and VH1, and from that moment on, my days (and often nights) were filled with work on *The U.S. vs. John Lennon*. Years later, a top Lionsgate executive told me that it was just about the easiest "green light" of his career. As he put it, "A John Lennon film from the guy who did *Beautiful Dreamer*? Yes."

So in 2005/2006, while I was happy to be crazy busy with my next documentary, I wasn't around as Brian and his bandmate Scott Bennett collaborated on a new piece, written a bit in the style of *SMiLE*. Brian, inspired by an old standard, titled it *That Lucky Old Sun*. One day, I was working away in my Studio City production office when he called to tell me all about his new project.

He explained there would be spoken-word pieces that would connect the songs. And he asked me to write that narration. Through the years, Brian had often asked me to write lyrics and I always said "No." Lyricists in his life came and went. I was a friend. But to me, this seemed different. This was similar to what I did in *my* work. At least that's what I told myself. We talked about it for a while. He didn't know how many pieces of narration he would need. I also suggested they call it *That Lucky Old Son*. I thought the irony was clever. He didn't.

Very quickly, I wrote and sent him a first draft. And I waited for him to call back. When he finally did, I could instantly sense something was amiss. Brian always clears his throat when he isn't sure how to say something. "[Clears throat.] Uh, David. [Clears throat again.]" Finally, he blurted it out: "Van Dyke's going to write the narration for *That Lucky Old Sun*." I said, "That's great." He was so relieved. He thought I would be upset or hurt. I was not only glad to hear he and Van Dyke were working together again, but it took me out of the line of fire, too. In researching this update, I found the narration I'd written in my files. Is it any good? Let's just say that Mr. Parks's narration works just fine.

Eva and I went to London for the world premiere of *That Lucky Old Sun*, again at the Festival Hall, in September 2007. Playing a forty-plus-minute song cycle that had never been heard before? That was very brave. And it was very good. As it came to an end, the entire audience rose to its feet. For decades, we had believed that if Brian would finish *SMiLE*, if he got that albatross off his neck, he would be freed to make great *new* music that would resonate. That night, we were proven right.

As Darian Sahanaja recently described it, "I thought, songwriting-wise, like *Beach Boys Love You*, they were very personal and genuine and honest Brian Wilson songs. It felt pure. It was the first time working with him where I felt the songs were really sincere and really coming directly from him, from his soul. I think that was the most significant thing about that collection of music."

Not too long after our *That Lucky Old Sun* false start, Brian and I did complete a collaboration. He called and said, "I want to cut 'Mr. Tambourine Man.'" He asked me to print out the lyrics to all the verses and meet him at a small studio. When I got there, he had already recorded a backing track. Unexpectedly, he told me that he wanted to sing it as a duet. He directed me to sing the lead, told me which verses to sing. "Then, I'll add my part." I sang it once. "Double it," he said. I sang it again. "OK. We're done." I'd been "tricked" by the master. He had no intention of singing on it. For some reason, he wanted to produce me singing Dylan's classic. He handed me a CD of the finished recording. That was and is quite a gift.

Brian's and the Beach Boys' music was showing up everywhere. In 2007, the Tate Museum in St. Ives had an avant-garde art exhibition called *If Everybody Had an Ocean*, inspired by the group's recordings from 1962–1967. Brian was inspiring artists. And he frequently returned the favor.

Since the end of the Landy regime, Brian has often been a guest vocalist on other people's records. Most recently, his work in 2018 on Janelle Monáe's 'Dirty Computer' shows the everlasting elasticity of his harmonic magic. For me, the one that stands out as a personal favorite was when he sang on Linda Ronstadt's version of Jimmy Webb's magnificent 'Adios.' Brian loves Jimmy's work. And vice versa. Google it and listen to Linda's recording of 'Adios,' then read on as she describes watching Brian work in this excerpt from *Simple Dreams,* her autobiographical memoir.

In the studio, under Brian's direction, we recorded his harmony parts for 'Adios' with five separate tracks of unison singing on each of the three parts, fifteen vocal tracks in all. He didn't seem concerned if some of the tracks veered slightly out of tune but took advantage of the slight 'chorused' effect it created when he came back into the control room to mix the harmony tracks into the creamy vocal smoothness instantly recognizable as the Beach Boys.

Brian was making up the harmonies as he went along, but sometimes, when he was having difficulty figuring out a complicated section, he would scold himself and say that he needed to work for a time at the piano. However, when he sat down at the piano, he never played any part of 'Adios,' but instead would play a boogie-woogie song, very loud in a different key. After a few minutes of this he would go back to the microphone and sing the parts perfectly, without a trace of hesitation.

That kind of vocal genius would be in evidence in 2010, when Brian recorded an entire album of Gershwin songs, including his favorite part of *Rhapsody in Blue*, a piece of music he'd heard in childhood that became something of a life theme. The tenderness he brings to songs like 'Someone to Watch Over Me' is touching. His rendition of 'Summertime' is surprising, and he brings rock 'n' roll fun to other songs, like 'I Got Rhythm' and 'You Can't Take That Away From Me.' He even got to collaborate with Mr. Gershwin by finishing two incomplete Gershwin songs. In the past thirty years, there's been something about singing songs by *his* favorite songwriters that often seems to put Brian at ease and brings out the best in his singing and arranging.

In 2011, he took on the classic Disney songbook, finally recording one of his all-time favorites, 'When You Wish Upon a Star' and a slew of others, including Elton John and Tim Rice's Oscar-winning hit, 'Can You Feel the Love Tonight.'

The year the Gershwin record came out is when I began teaching at UCLA. I named my first course "Docs That Rock, Docs That Matter." Every year, in the last class of the quarter, I screen *Beautiful Dreamer: Brian Wilson and the Story of SMiLE* and tell my students a little bit about my SMiLE dream. My goal is for them to understand that they can achieve their dream, whatever it might be.

In 'Beautiful Boy,' a song on his 1980 album, *Double Fantasy*, John

Lennon sang: "Life is what happens to you while you're busy making other plans."

My wife, Eva, had gotten sick in 2008, and in 2016, after her passing, I was in a deep depression. Without Eva, I had lost my moral compass. My bearings. My ambition. And perhaps, of most significance to this book, the person who had teamed up with me back in 1977 and had been the spirit guide through all the work I'd done with and about Brian. She had always been right there; we were partners. Together, we had helped Brian navigate the minefield that was his life and career.

I'm not sure exactly what triggered the idea, but sometime in 2017/2018, it came to me. The way to honor what Brian had meant to both of us, and what Eva meant to Brian, would be to endow a scholarship. I named it "The Brian Wilson Scholarship for Composing, Arranging and Producing Popular Music." At the UCLA website, it says that the scholarship was established "in honor of his friend Brian Wilson and in memory of his late wife, Eva Easton Leaf. David and Eva shared a decades-long friendship with Brian—who helped to introduce them—and had a special love for his music and his artistry."

On October 20, 2019, in the last pre-COVID gathering of the Brian Wilson tribe, we held a special event in Schoenberg Hall at the UCLA Herb Alpert School of Music. The irony of celebrating Brian, an artist beloved for his soaring melodies and harmonies, in a hall named after a man who was known for "atonality" wasn't lost on the musicologists there that day. I chose to ignore that and focus on the fact that Schoenberg Hall was just across from where I taught my courses—on the Beatles, on songwriting, on music documentary—in Jan Popper Theater (now Lani Hall).

In the audience of nearly five hundred were students, family, friends and those who had generously contributed to the scholarship fund. Among the V.I.P. guests were my fiancée, Vicki, and my future mother-in-law. Brian and Melinda's five children, Brian's manager, Jean Sievers, and Brian's dear friend, Gloria Ramos. Many, many others who were important to Brian, important to me.

I introduced the audience to David Ghesser, the student I had selected as the initial recipient: "In my opinion, there is no more appropriate student for the first Brian Wilson scholarship." When I first met David in my songwriting class, he reminded me a bit of Brian. Shy. Reserved. Then, when he sat down at the grand piano and started to play, it was instantly clear that David was a gifted composer of classic pop melodies. Check out his work at davidghesser.com.

I reminded the UCLA-savvy audience of what was probably Brian's first time on campus. In 1963/1964, on UCLA's famous Janss Steps, the Beach Boys had posed for the picture that's on the 'I Get Around/Don't Worry Baby' picture sleeve.

There were two major highlights that day. First, we showed, on a big screen, something that had never been seen before: the entire world premiere concert of *Brian Wilson Presents SMiLE* from London in 2004. Even as low-resolution video with an unmixed audio track, it played incredibly well. The audience loved it. Brian too.

And then, I welcomed to the stage Brian and one of his key band members, Probyn Gregory. Of course, Brian received a heartfelt standing ovation. But he wasn't really in the mood to talk much that day. Fortunately, Probyn was there to share his insights about *SMiLE* and Brian. It was a gratifying day, but a slightly bittersweet one too. Brian was in pain from back surgery. But the discomfort didn't stop him from touring. Neither

Brian on his birthday in 2018 with his and Melinda's kids. Clockwise from upper left: Dylan, Daria, Delanie, Dakota and Dash.
Credit: David Leaf

that nor the pandemic could keep him entirely off the road. Nor from going to the studio.

As 2021 ended, Brian's latest album, *At My Piano*, surprised fans with its understated approach. It finds Mr. Wilson revisiting some of his most famous and beautiful melodies, handpicked by the composer himself. In the truest sense of the word, it's a solo record. It features Brian playing piano-only versions of more than a dozen of his classic compositions. And despite the internet chatter, Darian Sahanaja confirms that "Brian did all the playing (every part, every overdub)."

In my opinion, Darian is one of the biggest reasons that all of Brian's tours, starting in 1999, were always true to the music and, regardless of Brian's mood on any particular night, were triumphant celebrations of Mr. Wilson and his art.

For 2000, Darian, his Wondermints partner Nick Walusko, and everybody in Brian's band had superbly studied and recreated the original arrangements of *Pet Sounds*, making sure the live performances were a highlight of our musical lives. His work with Brian and Van Dyke on SMiLE was vital. And for the live premiere of *SMiLE*, Darian was in front, literally Brian's right-hand man on stage right, helping give Brian the confidence to face this ultimate challenge. Without Darian's devoted and dedicated musical brilliance, so many such spectacular musical moments might never have happened.

How did he end up as such an important part of Brian's world? Well, in one sense, it was Darian's talent combined with *his* quarter-century obsession with *SMiLE* that made it all work. And it started with a book. *This* book.

Something I didn't find out for many years, something I hinted at in the introduction to this edition of *The Myth,* is Darian Sahanaja's story about what my book means to him. As Darian told me in November 2021, "When I was fifteen, I heard and loved 'Wouldn't It Be Nice.' I got *Pet Sounds*. On 8-Track! But I have to admit I wasn't feelin' it. Where were all the fun, sunshine sounds of girls and cars? Then, I bought *The Beach Boys and the California Myth*, and that's when I realized that this Brian Wilson guy was pulling off what the Beatles were doing but without the help of outside producers and arrangers. What kind of person is capable of that?"

Darian continues: "I needed to know, and the book helped me to understand. With that I was able to go back and listen to *Pet Sounds* with a whole new appreciation . . . one of creative growth while overcoming self-doubt that really resonated with me. And, of course, it was also how I was first introduced to the great lost masterpiece that was *SMiLE*. And that would become the real 'California myth.'

"About a dozen years later, I met you, and you invited me and Nick to your place in Santa Monica to listen to some of the unreleased *SMiLE* music. A lot of which we had never heard before. Of course, it blew our minds and helped to place a few puzzle pieces into proper musical context."

At Paul Rock's 1994 Brian Wilson tribute, the Wondermints were one of the bands playing. As Darian remembers, "Apparently Brian was so knocked out by what he was hearing that he said, 'If I had the Wondermints back in 1967, I would've taken *SMiLE* on the road.'" Talk about prescient.

Darian: "For the next several years, Brian would come out to see us play clubs and asked us to be his musical accompaniment for radio interviews. And then in 1998 we got a call about the possibility of us backing him up on some shows to promote his then-new album *Imagination*. We weren't a shoo-in as there was talk of using the mostly Chicago-based session musicians who worked on the album. But," as Darian recounts, "Brian said, 'I want some of my guys' and his guys were *us*, on the West Coast. So, thanks to Melinda, you and Eva and Rodney Bingenheimer championing us for the job, we did end up making the cut."

From what I saw in those early, incredibly exciting touring years, 1999-2007, Darian, Nick, Probyn (and Mike D'Amico too) were responsible for the authenticity and the heart of the live shows. Jeffrey Foskett's voice was beautiful and essential. Having played with the Beach Boys, Jeff's bearing, his guitar playing and especially his singing were almost like having Brian's brother Carl onstage. Taylor Mills and Nelson Bragg each added to the soundscape, and the Chicago contingent (Bob, Paul, Scott and Jim) was terrific, all very talented and dedicated players. Great guys, too.

But I think it was the Wondermints—gifted musicians who were also superfans—who were determined, from the very beginning, that everybody treat Brian's songs with the reverence they deserved. There wouldn't be any "dumbed down" arrangements. Truth is, it wasn't a "hard sell." And working together, they all learned and played the music with complete integrity and sonic fidelity. They became a *band* . . . a band that brought new life to the hits, the deep cuts and Brian's most sophisticated and complex compositions from *Pet Sounds* and *SMiLE*. Throughout, Darian, as musical director, was leading the way.

Darian returns the ultimate compliment. "Whenever I see that you've worked on something I can always trust that it will be in the best interest of the visionary. It was from reading your book that I would come to recognize the virtues of being an auteur, and from that point on all my favorite films, artwork and music have been made by auteurs."

Darian had a dream: to make memorable music. He and Nick did it as the Wondermints. And that led them to becoming key members of the band that helped one of the greatest artists ever successfully reach for the stars. We all miss Nick, but what he and Darian did still fills me with wonder.

So, in a way, that brings the book full circle. Like dropping a stone in the middle of a pond, the ripples are beyond our control. When he was fifteen, Darian read about *SMiLE* in *The Beach Boys and the California Myth*. As Darian told me, "That book changed my life." A decade later, I played him *SMiLE* outtakes. A decade after that, he was helping Brian and Van Dyke Parks finish *SMiLE*. In its own way, my book, which I had conceived to help finish *SMiLE*, actually did.

And now, as Darian approaches sixty, he's still by Brian's side—a brilliant musician, the musical friend that Mr. Wilson needs, whether onstage, backstage or in the studio.

As I approach seventy, I've revisited my first book for what will probably be the last time. Darian, myself—and millions all over the globe—all brought together by the music and sounds that came from the head and heart of Brian Wilson.

Looking back, how can we do anything but *SMiLE*?

AN EPILOGUE: WITH LOVE AND MERCY

FROM AN INTERVIEW I DID WITH BRIAN IN 1988: "I WAS IN MY PIANO ROOM playing [the Bacharach–David standard] 'What the World Needs Now Is Love.' And I just went into my own song . . . worked very hard to get out what's in my heart . . . it's a perfect message from me to people."

> I was sittin' in a crummy movie with my hands on my chin
> Oh the violence that occurs seems like we never win.

Those words are the first verse of Brian's 1988 classic 'Love and Mercy'; it's the song which has been the final encore of his concerts for over twenty years.

Again, Brian: "We accomplished what we set out to do, which is to bring some spiritual love to people. We wanted people to be covered with love because there's no guarantee of somebody waking up in the morning with any love . . . Mercy would be a deeper word than love. I would think *love* is a gentle thing and *mercy* would be a more desperately needed thing in life . . . a little break here and there for somebody who's having trouble . . . 'Love and Mercy' is probably the most spiritual song I've ever written."

And so, *finally*, we are at the beginning of the end.

Brian's musical prayer, for the audience and to himself, is "Love and mercy that's what you need tonight / Love and mercy tonight." The last line of the last song of his concerts, it is the exact opposite of the upbeat 'Fun, Fun, Fun,' that concludes the typical Beach Boys show. Perhaps that best explains the difference between Brian and the group he co-founded so very long ago.

In January 2022, on an episode of *Jeopardy*, the most popular American TV quiz show, the answer to a question in the category "Music Biopics" was "Love and Mercy: This Genius of the Beach Boys." If you were the first to buzz in and ask, "Who is Brian Wilson?" you won $1,600.

It's clearly now a cliché to say "Brian Wilson is a genius" in the same way it's almost a cliché to write that, over sixty years after their birth, the Beach Boys are not just an American band but *the* American band. Their musical and personal stories almost perfectly reflect the country's recent history, from the Wilson/Love clan's mid-western roots, western migration, their ambition and reinvention, unbelievable commercial and creative successes, terrible crises, and personal tragedies. Through it all, the Beach Boys have left their mark.

If you want a *Dragnet*-style, "Joe Friday-esque" straightforward telling of "just the facts, ma'am" of everything they've done, everything that's happened to them, that's obviously not this book. There are the official websites, countless Wikipedia pages, and endless fan sites and discussion groups devoted to Brian and the Beach Boys, where just about every aspect of their career is continuously dissected and debated. I expect this new edition of *The Myth* will become part of the conversation as there are those who like my work and those who feel I'm too "pro-Brian."

However, this book was not written to be the complete tale of Brian or the group. There are dozens of Beach Boys and Brian Wilson books out there, each with a distinct focus, each adding insight and layers of incredibly dense information. One relatively new place to revel in the discovery and rediscovery of the music is the Giggens YouTube show, a terrific Brian/Beach Boys video podcast. There are others you might find more to your taste, some more academic, some more performance-based.

But obtaining a deeper understanding or any sort of consensus is harder to find. For that reason, my favorite book on the subject might be Tom Smucker's *Why the Beach Boys Matter*. That title is the reason I've done what I've done. Because the music Brian and the Beach Boys created does matter.

In going back down the rabbit hole to write this update, what I discovered is that in both Brian's and the Beach Boys' story, there is so much new information. We learn more every day. And there is so much we still don't know, will never know.

For example, there's Brian's long-ago friendship with Linda Ronstadt. I knew she'd recorded a magnificent cover of the *Pet Sounds* classic 'Don't Talk (Put Your Head on My Shoulder).' And in her book and the Don Was documentary on Brian, Linda had made it clear how strongly she regarded Brian as a musician and marveled at how he worked in the studio when he recorded the background vocals for 'Adios.'

But I never knew until I read this excerpt from her 2013 memoir, *Simple Dreams*, that in the 1970s, Linda Ronstadt was one of Brian's "Guardian Angels."

I had known Brian Wilson briefly in my Troubadour days, when he was separated for a time from his first wife. He was always sweet and friendly and never pressed any romantic agenda. Several times I discovered him at my back door, studying a little pile of coins he held in his hand, which he said was ten or fifteen cents shy of the price for a bottle of grape juice. He said it was important for him to drink grape juice in order to solve some health problem that was troubling him. I would provide the remaining ten or fifteen cents, and we would climb into his huge convertible with the top always down, the back stuffed with a sizable accumulation of Brian's dirty laundry. As a bachelor, he seemed to have difficulty coping with domestic arrangements, so I would suggest a trip to the Laundromat, where we would fill an entire row of machines. (I had a lot of quarters.) Afterwards we would sit in my living room, drink the grape juice, and listen to my small collection of Phil Spector records. Brian really liked Phil Spector.

To me, that's just a stunning reminiscence, almost like an archaeological find. It also raises lots of questions about Brian's life. Long ago, a very wise "music man," A&R great Lenny Waronker, cautioned me that one of the keys to working successfully in the music business is to "consider the art, not the artist." Meaning that just because somebody makes music you love doesn't mean you're going to admire or even like them as a person.

In the day-to-day work of the industry, and in the long run of music history, that makes sense. Because it's only the art that survives. But in my life, in my friendship with the artist named Brian Wilson, in this book, I've disregarded Lenny's wisdom. I'm focusing on the artist. My goal in the update is to provide an even deeper understanding of Brian to you. And for me, too.

That's why in this epilogue, I've included a number of stories like Linda Ronstadt's, those that didn't have a natural home in the new chapters of this edition of the book as they took place in the 1970s, after *The Myth* was originally completed and published. I've included a few of them here as examples of the 'Love and Mercy' Brian has experienced, important because they shine additional strands of light on the truth of his life.

In a 2021 *Rolling Stone* interview, Robert Redford said: "Truths can be elusive . . . just follow your instincts and keep searching for the truth." And that's what I do. The "truth" in this story, any story, is hard to define, even for those who were there. Writing biographies can be tricky. There are many different ways to tell this or any story. So while the Beach Boys are in the title of the book, the first line of *The Myth* is "This is the story of Brian Wilson." That's the path I chose to take.

With a nod to Pete Townshend, this update is my personal 'Amazing Journey.' No longer on the outside looking in, here in 2022, I'm on the inside, concentrating on *my* memories, what I experienced, and how it changed *my* life.

Here's one of those nights that begs credulity, a story that might answer the question, "When did I go from being a biographer to a friend?" It could have been a fall evening in 1978.

I was at my Saltair Avenue apartment in West L.A. with Peter Reum, the legendary collector (and counselor) who was instrumental in helping put together the imagery for the original edition of this book. For his help, as recompense, I promised him that he could have all the "one of a kind" pieces I had gathered during my research. When the book was finally at the printer, he flew out from his Colorado home to get everything. It was to be a quick, uneventful trip: come to L.A. in the afternoon, leave the next morning with a small suitcase filled with rarities, a big addition to what was probably, outside of the Beach Boys world, the premier Beach Boys record and memorabilia collection.

We had just gotten back from dinner at a favorite (and now sadly gone) nearby restaurant, La Barbera's on Wilshire Boulevard. There were a couple of leftover pizza slices I put in the almost bare refrigerator. As the evening wore on, in talking about how brief this trip was, Peter mentioned that he had never come to L.A. without running into Harvey Kubernik and Rodney Bingenheimer.

Rodney was and still is a popular DJ, for almost forty years the host of *Rodney on the ROQ* at KROQ-FM. Harvey's a successful author now; back then, he was the L.A. correspondent for England's *Melody Maker*. He and I had met when we were sleeping outside the box office of the Santa Monica Civic Auditorium to get tickets to see Bruce Springsteen. During the course of that 1976 Labor Day weekend campout, we had talked a lot about Brian and the Beach Boys.

Around 1 a.m., Peter and I were startled by a knock on the door. Who could be visiting at that hour? There stood the two people we'd just spoken about minutes earlier . . . Harvey and Rodney. And with them? Brian Wilson! Harvey said something like, "We didn't really know where to take him, so we brought him here."

In a 2021 conversation, here's how Harvey remembered that night: "I was living in West Hollywood around the corner from Rodney. He always had demos and acetates of a lot of U.K. music; I'd go over there a couple of times a week to listen. One night on Sunset near Curson, I parked my car and noticed a man in a bathrobe in the middle of Sunset Boulevard, dodging cars. I was concerned. There is no stop light at Curson. I called upon my former quarterbacking skills; I was like Fran Tarkenton that night. I scrambled to grab him from horn-honking vehicles and walked him to the pavement. If I wasn't on Sunset at that very moment, there very well could have been a bloody scene of splattered remains.

"As we staggered to a nearby 7-Eleven store, I realized it was Brian. He mumbled something about Wallichs Music City. [His favorite record store had recently closed.] He was definitely high. I tried to talk some sense into him. When I said, 'Are you OK?,' he slurred, 'Yeah. I took too many reds.' I told him Rodney lived down the street. Brian's response: 'Does he have any mono albums?' I walked him over to Rodney's apartment. Rodney and I were both a little freaked out. All Brian kept saying was that he wanted Rodney to keep spinning 'Be My Baby' by the Ronettes. Twelve times in a row.

"I thought we should first go to 7-Eleven to get some coffee for Brian. Brian wanted something to eat. I wanted to call the paramedics. I have a partial degree in health and did some work earlier in the seventies with

DEFY, Drug Education for Youth. Keep the person engaged. Perhaps it wasn't an emergency situation, but we were very concerned. Brian didn't have a phone number to call for help. [He had recently separated from his first wife, Marilyn.] I asked Brian if he had insurance. He didn't even have a wallet with him. Dazed and confused. But he was breathing OK, not even sweating. We decided to drive him over to your place with a sort of understanding that you would monitor him or take him to a hospital. You were always the adult in the room.

"Brian fell asleep in the car. In the back of my mind, I thought this was kind of serious, but you could take Brian to UCLA as a 'walk-in.' You knew hospitals better than we did because of your sick brother. We were scared. Brian has always had the constitution of a horse. But this was our friend. [After we dropped him off,] we both assumed you took Brian to the UCLA hospital."

That's Harvey's memory. What happened next was much less dramatic. After Harvey and Rodney left, Brian asked if I had anything to eat. I heated up the two slices of pizza in my toaster oven, he wolfed them down and went to sleep on my couch. Peter and I sat there, quiet and stunned. Speechless. We had just spent the last year working on *The Myth*. In our conversations, we had shared concern for Brian's well-being, and now we were witness to the life he was actually living. Not exactly what you read about in *Rolling Stone*.

Anyway, a few hours later, around 3 a.m., Brian woke up and asked me to take him home. We got in the car, and I asked him where his home was. He was silent. I headed down the California Incline to the Pacific Coast Highway, towards where his house was in Pacific Palisades. I knew where to go because a few weeks earlier, I had driven there with our mutual friend (not yet my girlfriend), Eva Easton. She had taken some new towels and sheets to the rental house he was living in after he moved out of his Bel-Air home.

I kept asking Brian for directions. He said nothing until I was on Sunset, perhaps a quarter of a mile away. Then, he started giving directions, that the house was coming up on the north side of the street. We stopped. He jumped out of my orange Volvo. Dashed to the front door. Peter and I waited out front until he was safely inside.

Until Harvey told me his side of the story in November 2021, he never knew what had happened after "the drop-off."

There are lots of stories like that. And as many stories of mine as I've added to the book in the updated chapters, there are perhaps fifty times as many untold tales. Probably more. I chose the ones that I thought were most relevant to my friendship with Brian and his artistic life. And most carefully, only included ones that I felt didn't cross the line, didn't betray confidences. I hope I've succeeded in that.

Back in 1977/1978, not "betraying Brian" was important to everybody I met and interviewed when I researched and wrote *The Myth*.

The first "insider" I really got to know was a young woman named Debbie Keil. She had begun working at the Beach Boys office in 1969, cleaning up the fan club "mess." A lot of unopened mail had piled up. The job turned out to be her entry into the inner sanctum.

In 1977, when I met her, I decided that her perspective on Brian, the Beach Boys and Wilson family dynamics was important, a valuable addition to the original edition of *The Myth*. Debbie and I spoke a lot; she wanted to help me understand what was going on in Brian's world without saying anything that would harm their relationship. That's one reason she's not quoted "on the record." Debbie never tried to shape the narrative. I felt her observations were insightful, very different from what I'd been reading. I included them to help me, and the reader, get "inside" Brian's head. There are several "anonymous" sources like that in *The Myth*. I can reveal now that she was one of them; when a quote was attributed to "a friend of Brian's," it was often Debbie's.

Now, forty years later, Debbie Keil Leavitt has a few things to say about Brian, the Beach Boys, the original edition of *The Myth* and everything that's happened since then. Debbie: "I knew the first time I met Melinda that Brian had the right person who could help him get his independence from Landy and get the right medical treatment—essentially saving his life. It only took a brief conversation with her; I knew almost immediately that she really loved Brian. I think if you love someone whole-heartedly, you recognize the others who share that. I was really happy that she was going to join you, Eva and Ray in loving and supporting Brian, not only in his career, but his entire life."

Debbie's understanding of the complexities of Brian's life were hard won, but they began very simply. Remembering the first time she met Brian circa 1970 at the Beach Boys' Ivar Street office: "We started talking about music." Unlike the way he was portrayed in the media, Debbie notes, "This was not that deeply troubled, unhappy person. I don't know how to exactly describe it, but he really just appreciated meeting someone who loved his music. He said, 'What's your favorite album that we put out? I mean, aside from *Pet Sounds*.' And I said *Friends* and he goes, 'Yes!' He was just thrilled that somebody looked at it the same way he did. He was just sort of brimming with 'I love music, and it's nice that this person gets the music that I make.'"

She told Brian about John Sebastian's first solo album, *John B. Sebastian*. "He said he hadn't heard it, didn't have it, and I said, 'Well, if you want to hear it, I've got it at home.' He came over to my place [on Beachwood Drive in Beachwood Canyon]; I had a roommate and my place shared the stairwell with [Wilson family friend and Beach Boys promoter] Fred Vail. Our doors were always open. We were always going back and forth between the apartments. This wasn't a place for a 'rendezvous' with a girl.

"Brian loved the [Sebastian] album. Just a normal guy, a sweet guy. I guess what happened when he went home [as he told me later] was that he told Marilyn where he'd been. And she got really angry, and he said, 'Marilyn, Debbie and I knew each other before we ever met,' meaning that he and I had instantly connected, felt that we had known each other for who knows how many lifetimes. I don't know how that stuff works, but it did feel that way.

"But Marilyn got really furious. And so, whenever she came to the Beach Boys office, they would hide me in the room that used to be the sauna. It's where they kept all the records and acetates. They'd stick me in there, and I would be reading the titles of all the [unreleased] songs. Anyway, they would close the door until she left, and then let me come back out to work. It was pretty funny."

Debbie really loved the Beach Boys. Dennis in particular appreciated the work she did. "He told everybody, 'She does so much for us.' He said to me, 'The way your face lights up whenever you can do something for us, that means a lot.'"

Debbie worked for the group for about a year, then left for more "grown-up" jobs, eventually becoming the office and administrative manager, supervising a staff of ten, at the ultra-exclusive Bel-Air Bay Club perched on a cliff above the Pacific Ocean in Los Angeles. During the 1970s, Debbie was a friend to Brian during very difficult times, including before and after Landy, Part One and before Landy, Part Two. Debbie: "I think there's no question that however depressed he was, he wanted to live. He just didn't want the constant demands. If Murry Wilson is your father and you're a musical genius, I think you'd become truly adept at passive-aggressive language and actions.

"But he loved to use the word 'will.' He has a very strong will to survive. I never thought he wanted to die; he just didn't like the way his life was and didn't know what to do about it. To him, there seemed to be no good way to handle all the people he was expected to support. They had an idea of what he needed to do to support them. Basically, I think he wanted to be a creative person, do his best work and make money the way he always had, by being innovative."

We began our December 2021 conversation by discussing her feelings about the brothers. "I guess I favored Dennis, because he always fought for Brian, what Brian wanted to do. He would fiercely defend Brian. Carl, to me, was a little distant, but I saw how intense the familial relationship was and, really, how proud Brian was of them as brothers and what they could do vocally. But also, there was a spiritual connection between Brian and Carl."

That spirituality might have been best expressed musically in Carl's vocal on 'God Only Knows.' While Brian had originally recorded a terrific lead, Brian decided that Carl, who had done very few lead vocals up until then, was right for the record. Carl's magnificent singing on that song and 'Good Vibrations'—both in the studio and in concert—became, for me at least, major highlights of the group's body of work, the high points of their shows. They made the idea of Beach Boys music being a kind of white gospel rock 'n' roll real.

In the original edition of *The Myth*, Brian's astrological chart is on page 104. It was done by Debbie. As an astrologer, Debbie had explained to Brian that his and Carl's charts "had all these oppositions. What one had, the other didn't," and when they were in the same space, "it was like the energy would come together."

Debbie: "I think Brian always saw that as really special. His face would light up when you mentioned Carl, especially after I told him about the oppositions. Brian isn't an astrologer, but he sure knows and thinks about it. There was a time when I didn't see him for ten years, and when I saw him, he was talking about the oppositions in this chart with Carl, and I said, 'Well, Carl was your angel voice.' And his face just lit up and he goes,

'Yes. Yes!' It was very sweet and very touching. I didn't know Carl that well, but I would say there was definitely a competition between them. Their mother, Audree, was very comfortable with Carl, and Brian was always a handful."

As to cousin Mike, "Every time I would see Mike I was with Brian, and he was just wonderfully gracious and charming, a perfect host, generous and welcoming. And he also wanted Brian to do a record, obviously. We went into a studio one time; that was part of the deal. I'm not going to say that he had Brian come up to visit him in Santa Barbara just to record a record with them, but . . . "

When Debbie and Brian were alone, and Mike's name came up, "Brian basically just said that Mike sort of wasn't open to the new stuff . . . to Brian, it seemed like it might be a personal thing. Like Mike just might be too competitive. I think he was tired of fighting with Mike over creative issues, but Brian wasn't telling me anything surprising. He was just referencing things that were common knowledge among serious Beach Boys fans at that time."

An example of the competitive nature of all of them was a night in the early 1980s when, as Brian's divorce was almost final, Debbie was "at Brian's home on Sunset, and Carl was staying over. Carl had his first solo album with him, and he wanted Brian to hear it. He brought it into the bedroom, handed Brian the album. Brian was using this little portable stereo that belonged to Carnie when she was a child, this thing where small speakers lift off. That's what he was left with as listening equipment after the separation.

"Brian put the record on, and I remember it got to the third song. And that's when I saw this huge paw, Brian's giant hand, and it was kind of like dark shadows just arching over and slamming on top of the turntable so hard that everything just stopped. Not like you heard the needle skipping across or anything else. Just 'bam.' And then dead silence.

"And Carl said, 'Well, I guess you've heard enough,' and in this nervous little boy way, he scampered off. I thought it was funny. It wasn't funny to Brian."

To me, the reason it might not have been amusing to Brian is that, beginning in 1977, Dennis, Carl and Mike all did solo projects outside the Beach Boys, but Brian's work was always for a Beach Boys album. For example, in 1977, Brian said in an interview that he wanted to call the next record *Brian Loves You*. "You know, like *Jesus Loves You*." The album was released as *The Beach Boys Love You*.

As to her time with Brian, Debbie says, "A lot of what happened in that house was just incredibly funny. One night, I got there, and he was pretty drunk; none of his assistants were there. After I arrived, he walked into the bedroom. I was out in the living room. And I heard this crash. And he said, 'Somebody broke my mirror. I'm going to call the cops.' He was the only one in that room; it was obviously him. And I thought he was faking it, because he often did things like that just to see how you would react. Not that time.

"About five minutes later, the police showed up at the door. And I opened the door and the officer says, 'Is this *that* Brian Wilson?' I sighed and said, 'Yeah.' They said, 'Well, just keep him inside; then we don't have to arrest him for public drunkenness,' and I said, 'OK.' About an hour later. Another knock on the door and it's the same police officers with another police officer; he said he just wanted to come by because he's a big fan of Brian's. That was kind of how things happened around Brian a lot."

Brian celebrates his birthday in 2016. Credit: Jerry Weiss

As Debbie recalls, they did laugh a lot together. "One thing he said to me long ago, 'You know, Debbie, no matter how bad things get, there's always something to eat.'"

Brian had what Debbie refers to as an "intuitive instinct" about people. "I remember the first time he met my mother. She and my dad [Harold and Gerry Keil] were in the living room of our apartment on Montana Avenue [where Debbie lived with Eva]. When Brian walked into the living room, he just made a beeline for my mother, sat down next to her, put his arms around her neck and his head on her shoulder. And my mother just started patting him, and [afterwards] she said, 'I wasn't sure what I was supposed to do; it seemed natural just to do that.' He instinctively felt and recognized how sweet she was and that she would always accept and love him."

As to my work, Debbie explains that "I love your book. It was painful to read when I was living it. I can't wait to read the new edition. But back in 1978, it was the first, and maybe only time, that the truth has really been told. You really got into the challenges he faced, not just inside the studio and within the group but also how hard it was to be Brian Wilson, the artist, and also be Brian Wilson, the benefactor. There were a lot of reasons I never took nor asked for money from Brian. I wanted there to be at least one person who wasn't there for the money and/or reflected glory.

"The 'drainers,' as I called them, never let up. It just became all too much for him, and I was a safe harbor to escape to. Brian knew that regardless of what he did or didn't do, I would love him . . . I was sort of 'the other woman,' but not really. Because with Brian, there was nothing traditional."

Debbie has many stories, some wonderful, some hilarious, some very sad. But they all end the same way. With Brian, always childlike, always getting his way. And, eventually, it became too much.

"The weasels," as Debbie refers to the hangers-on, "were concerned about one thing: keeping their job. Their so-called 'love' for Brian was for his checkbook. I remember around 1980, you, Eva and I were very concerned; he seemed to be sliding downhill. I asked you to recommend doctors, and you got the names of some reputable UCLA psychiatrists. And I gave them to a cousin who was on Brian's payroll. But 'the weasel' told me to 'butt out.' That their attorney would recommend a doctor."

The circumstances exhausted Debbie. She explains, "I always felt that to survive as 'the girlfriend,' I would ultimately have to be Murry for him every so often. He seemed to always be looking for something to rebel against and withhold from. I didn't have it in me. So, toward the end of 1981, when I could no longer deal with it all, I asked you to take care of Brian. And you did. (Laughing.) I didn't know you would end up devoting most of your life to it. So, thank you for looking after the man I loved. Without you, Eva, Ray, and, of course, Melinda . . . all the great things we've experienced with Brian wouldn't have happened.

"He deserves all the respect and kindness that Melinda and everybody have shown him in the past thirty years. Without all of you, he probably would have died a long time ago. But because of everybody who really loves him, Brian has come out of the darkness and back to his music."

Their relationship ended over forty years ago, but Debbie offers another perspective that might give context to all of our connections to Brian. Debbie: "One thing that people are confused about is Brian's pursuit of spirituality. He has really traditional values—going to church, having the prayer circle before the shows. His fascination with angels. His music reflects the beautiful harmonies from our Western spiritual practices."

Brian: "I was really freaked out on astronomy when I was a kid." In 1977, in his song 'Solar System,' Brian asked "What do the planets mean?" In 1988, in "There's So Many," the multi-part harmony on the lyric "The planets are spinning around" was one of the highlights of Brian's first solo album.
Credit: BriMel Archives

"At the same time, he's been very curious about all forms of spirituality—his knowledge of astrology/astronomy is only a part of what he's explored. I gave Brian all six volumes of *The Life and Teachings of the Masters of the Far East.* [The songwriter] Tandyn Almer was stunned that Brian was reading them. When I didn't act surprised, he said, 'Brian never reads!'

"Brian has, as we all do, I guess, a direct connection with a central energy source, the universe, or something . . . and what it can hold. Brian had a particularly intense connection. I think that's probably still the way he views that [energy], although he does do the traditional thing. He knows the power of the word 'God.'"

That shouldn't come as a surprise. After all, when Brian was asked what *SMiLE* was going to be, he described it as "a teenage symphony to God."

Or, as U2's Bono explained it, "The genius of his music is the joy that's in it. I know that Brian believes in angels. I do too. But you only have to listen to the string arrangement on 'God Only Knows' for fact and proof of angels."

Debbie: "Other than sharing it powerfully through his music, ultimately Brian's very private about his spirituality. He's well aware of a universal source of power for good and the power of his own name when he connects with that power. That's something he's truly serious about. All of our connections—you, me, Eva, Ray, Melinda, the good guys who connected—all of us are there to support Brian. Being human, we did the best we could with that astounding power of his that allowed him to reach millions and terrified him . . . and probably us . . . at times. As Ray has often said, 'He knows he's Brian Wilson.'"

Continuing, Debbie notes, "I know that's a lot to take in, to accept, but for anyone to grasp who we are and why we did what we did, that's an important context. Especially for some of the stranger happenings. I don't think most people, including me, know exactly what the source is, this 'powerful love.' I think that's the best way I can put it. We didn't know where it came from, but we could share. We could see it when he was creating his musical miracles that actually healed people."

In talking about *Pet Sounds*, Brian once said, "I wanted people to hear what I felt inside my soul. 'Cause I knew there was so much. I wanted to share it with people." With the help of a heavenly harmonic choir, aka the Beach Boys, and empathetic musicians, the music was how he could express it.

Debbie: "I think a lot of people just didn't recognize what it took to be him. The other stuff, the stories and all, are just entertaining. He is funny. He was making me laugh all the time . . . But being Brian Wilson is a very special gift and a challenge, at this point in time an almost overwhelming challenge, I think."

In 1977, Debbie was the first person (and, for this edition of the book, the last) to give me a peek inside the mind of Brian. But I was still an outsider when I wrote *The Myth*. Brian, as you've read in the stories from Linda Ronstadt and the night at my apartment with Peter Reum, Harvey and Rodney, was always showing up in unexpected places.

I didn't know it when I wrote the first edition of *The Myth*, but all these misadventures must have been common in Brian's life. The "truth" may be that other than his years with Landy and before he married Melinda, there was probably nothing all that exceptional about any of these days or nights. Fortunately, Brian had guardian angels, like Linda Ronstadt and Harvey Kubernik and Debbie Keil, all around town. And I believe standing alone at the top of the list is his friend Danny Hutton.

When I wrote the first edition of this book, I wasn't able to interview everybody who played a role in the story I was trying to tell, everybody who I thought was important to Brian. The most reluctant potential interviewee was Danny Hutton, one of the founders and lead singers of Three Dog Night. Danny was one of the lucky few who had been in the studio watching Brian's sessions in 1966/1967. In the 1970s, when Brian needed to hang out, to escape, to hide out, Danny's house was where he often went. I had heard that Danny was Brian's best friend; naturally, I wanted to talk with him. But I couldn't get a message to him. Or Danny was ignoring my entreaties.

But with the help of Harvey Kubernik, I sort of gently "shanghaied" Danny one night at a restaurant. Harvey recalls calling me "from a phone booth outside Casa Escobar," a restaurant not far from where I lived in West L.A. He told me Danny was sitting alone, in a booth. I jumped in the car, drove there, walked inside, walked past Danny and then turned around and said his name, pretending to know him. Having been a rock star for a decade, Danny had met thousands of people, so he was cordial. But, completely protective of his friendship with Brian, he didn't do an interview. That said, he has always been helpful in my understanding of the story.

In the chapter in *The Myth* entitled "Beached," I had briefly written about Danny Hutton's group, Redwood, who Brian had signed to Brother Records. Many years later, Chuck Negron, one of the lead singers of the band, published a memoir with a story that spoke volumes to me. In *Three Dog Nightmare*, Chuck described working with Brian—"as eccentric as Brian could be, he was always a nice person"—and a scene from 1967 that I found to be disturbing.

Chuck wrote: "Brian had written two songs especially for us to record, 'Time to Get Alone' and 'Darlin'.' We worked on the numbers with him for several months, and he thought we were the hottest voices he had heard in years." Continuing the story, Chuck remembers that when the Beach Boys showed up at the studio, they were upset that their creative leader was working with another group.

As Danny Hutton recently explained, it was "understandable from their point of view. You come off the road and hear that your leader is giving away a hit." Danny explains: "We were his boutique group; his creative outlet. Mike was the business guy. Brian, intimidated, backed down."

If I had known about this in 1978, it would have definitely found a place in the *SMiLE*-era chapters. To me, reading the tea leaves *now*, perhaps that became the moment when Brian could no longer "hang onto his ego." He had already abandoned *SMiLE*. But he hadn't stopped writing and recording brilliant music, like 'Can't Wait Too Long.' Nor had he lost the ambition to make great records. He had cut two terrific tracks for Redwood. (You can hear Redwood's version of 'Time to Get Alone' as a bonus track on a Three Dog Night compilation for which I wrote liner notes. 'Darlin'' was a rewrite of a 1964 song Brian and Mike had written for a single Brian produced for Sharon Marie.)

When I read Chuck Negron's description about how the session with Redwood was shut down after the arrival of several of the Beach Boys, I felt like I could see Brian's shoulders sag. It wasn't said aloud, but Brian might have thought, "The Beach Boys won't support my vision, and they won't let me work with another group. I'm done." That's just my interpretation.

However it played out that night, 'Darlin'' soon became a Beach Boys hit single, and the fact is every Beach Boys album for the next six years had brilliant Brian solo songs, secret classics like 'Busy Doin' Nothing,' 'Passing By,' 'Diamond Head' and 'I Went to Sleep.' There would be the ineffably beautiful "'Til I Die.' 'Let the Wind Blow,' a Brian and Mike collaboration on *Wild Honey* is one of those hidden gems. The *20/20* album featured a magnificent Carl Wilson lead and Beach Boys vocal arrangement on 'Time to Get Alone.' 'Break Away,' one of my favorites, credited to Brian and Reggie Dunbar, who shockingly turned out to be Murry Wilson. There were the rockers, 'Marcella' and 'Sail on Sailor.' Brian couldn't turn off the music. Mini-masterpieces like 'This Whole World' still came through. It and many of the songs Brian wrote alone in this era had brilliant lyrics.

But it seems, to me at least, that the episode with Redwood helped snuff out what remained of his grander ambitions, his competitive spirit.

The almost-instant karma? Redwood left Brother, changed their name to Three Dog Night and became the most successful vocal group of the next half-dozen years. Brian and the Beach Boys would not share in that success.

In the 1970s, Danny's home was often a sanctuary for Brian, and their friendship was strong. In *Beautiful Dreamer: Brian Wilson and the Story of SMiLE*, Danny talks about how Brian was calling him every night, "sometimes four or five times" in the same night, just before leaving for London and the world premiere of *Brian Wilson Presents SMiLE*. Brian needed the kind of reassurance that only a friend who had been in the studio during the *SMiLE* era could offer.

That's why I wanted to interview him for *The Myth*. Danny was there, in the booth during the *SMiLE* sessions, and he could provide the observations of a musician *and* a friend.

In *I Just Wasn't Made for These Times*, Danny tells a wonderfully funny story of Brian, Alice Cooper and Iggy Pop. But much more importantly than that anecdote, he also describes Brian with insight and power that comes from knowing somebody for over a half-century. His description of the Brian he knew in the mid-1960s is priceless as it helps us understand Brian "the producer." Danny described one string session: "I'd see him work with the L.A. Philharmonic, the string players, [they] would play it perfectly. Eight times. [And Brian would go] 'No, no, no, no, no.' And he'd go out there [into the studio] and say, 'You've gotta slide. It's gotta cry. It's not sad enough.' And this guy was hitting all the notes perfectly. Then [Brian] would push him to one more place. That the guy hadn't thought that way. The [musician] was thinking about notes. Time.

[Brian pushed] him past that." Brian wanted *feeling* in the recording, and nothing would stop him from getting it.

What was it like to be around Brian back in the day? Again, Danny: "I saw some very talented musical people who kind of stepped back when he came around. He was awesome. Intimidating. Scary. [Smiling.] And a little bizarre. So innocent and bizarre and truthful that he frightened people who were into the bullshit schmooze [of the business]." Danny explains that the way people looked at Brian had to do with chart position. For a half-dozen years, Brian produced a seemingly endless stream of hits. Then, having lost the insatiable need to have another hit record, he stepped back. Danny: "In the business, he wasn't as hot. Very simple fact. You're allowed to be crazy or different in the business if you're hot. Then you're eccentric. Well, as soon as you're not hot, then you're kind of nuts."

To Danny, however, Brian was always the same person . . . his friend.

In 2019, of everybody who generously contributed to it, Danny Hutton made by far the biggest donation to the Brian Wilson Scholarship at UCLA. A real friend, to this day. And that's the truth.

MYTHS AND LEGENDS

I moved to Southern California in 1975. I wanted to go to 'Surf City.' My *California Myth* was baby boomer, very white and, in retrospect, a childish, teenage fantasy. "Two girls for every boy."

It didn't rain once the first year I was in Los Angeles. Actually, it was closer to sixteen months before there was a storm. I learned a new word: drought. The ocean was right there; you could get your feet wet. But you couldn't drink it. And drought remains a component of the California myth because parts of Southern California are a semi-arid desert. A remarkable fact considering that, from 1910 to 1950, Los Angeles was ranked as the most productive agricultural county in the nation.

After a few years in L.A., when friends back home in New York would ask me about life in California, I described it as "future world." By that, I meant that what I observed was that something would become popular here. Then, it would be picked up and disseminated by the New York-based national media, which would spread it across America. But it happened first in Cali. From health foods to the Reagan Revolution to self-help training right up to the tech revolution.

When I wrote the first edition of *The Myth*, I sold the book in part by promising to write about California. But, for me, the "California Myth" section was an add-on. The publisher wanted it; I thought it was a catchy title.

The book should have been called *Brian Wilson of the Beach Boys.* That was the book I wrote. As to the California myth, for the most part, I had blinders on, an East Coast bias. And in writing about a myth, I didn't study the real history of California—not the Gold Rush nor the farm belt, the giant Redwoods or all of the "movements" that began in California, from the John Birch Society to the est training. I knew nothing of the

452

north–south rivalry in the state. Not a word in *The Myth* about Silicon Valley, even though a favorite cousin was already a computer genius there in the mid-1970s.

My version of the California myth didn't include the music pouring out of San Francisco and Oakland, the barrio of East L.A. or any other corner of the state. I barely touched upon surf culture or "surf music." Except for Brian Wilson's, there's not a sentence about any of the experimental music born here. Truth is, in terms of California's homegrown music, I was more enthralled by the music of Disneyland's Main Street Electrical Parade than Frank Zappa's *Freak Out!* Simply, I love hook-filled melody and harmony.

Through the years, I've seen and learned about the adult reality of California. Like much of America, it's pretty great if you are white and have a college degree. But California, like America's past—and present— is filled with just as many horrors against humanity as anywhere else in the country.

For me, as an outsider, California was the movie and TV business. Actually, the fantasy factories were just a very small part of the story. In 1978, I didn't write about the state's history: the Chinese Exclusion Act or a 1913 law that banned "aliens" from owning land. That mostly meant Japanese immigrants and their descendants, who were born American citizens. And until I made a film about it—2019's *To Tell the Truth*—I knew virtually nothing of the internment of Japanese American citizens during World War II.

I didn't grasp that California's economic wealth came from oil, real estate, and the immense agriculture industry, family farms and the bigger factory farms, built on the backs of migrant workers. I didn't know about oil spills, about redlining and real-estate covenants that would keep white neighborhoods white. I was ignorant as to how freeways were often routed through poorer (read: black or brown) sections of town, destroying communities. I hadn't heard of Bruce's Beach (Google it).

I didn't know that, after World War II, research, development and manufacturing for "the Military–Industrial Complex" that President Eisenhower warned about became such a big part of California's economy. Same with the aerospace industry. And as the American motor companies lost market share, it was picked up by Japanese car companies with their American headquarters in Southern California.

I was a transplanted New Yorker, but soon found out the state of my birth was number two. The population of California, the most populous state in the nation, exceeds the total population of over twenty states *combined*. The economy of California is bigger than most countries in the world, ranked recently at number five, just behind India and ahead of Germany. That's not a myth.

I didn't know that California was responsible for a gigantic percentage of America's food, growing over half the country's fruits, vegetables and nuts. From legendary activist Cesar Chavez, I did know a little about the plight of the farm workers, but it wasn't in the front of my mind, even as I drove north to Oxnard to buy the most delicious, just-handpicked strawberries.

But all one had to do was pay attention. Born in Manhattan, where ghettos and public housing and upper-class buildings are almost side by side, I wasn't blind. My grammar school, where we had school busing, was in between "the projects" for the poor and middle- and upper-middle-class neighborhoods. By the time I saw Spike Lee's *Do the Right Thing*, heard Public Enemy's "Fight the Power," and N.W.A. released *Straight Outta Compton*, I understood quite a lot more.

However, I'm not Joan Didion. I didn't write of dislocation and Santa Ana winds. Or earthquakes. When I wrote *The Myth*, I hadn't experienced a big one yet, and even if I had, the chaos I concentrated on was what was going on in the life of one particular genius.

The California Myth I wrote about was melodic, created by a small group of very talented musicians. People who created sounds that they sent out into the world. And one particular person, the primary focus of a significant portion of my life, was and is the artist (not that I knew that word when I was eleven) who gave birth to the song 'Surf City.'

My myth came from my naive suburban "Wonder Bread" experience. The reality of being here since 1975 has educated me. Ironically, now, after living in Southern California for nearly a half-century, after working in television and in the music business, after writing endlessly about Brian Wilson and the Beach Boys, I've come to realize that the original title of this book actually was almost right.

There *was* and is a California myth. Millions of people live that dream, not too far from the ocean. And there are millions more all over the world to whom it remains an unattainable fantasy, who come as tourists to visit, to go to school. And maybe to stay.

In recent years, my myth ultimately became my reality. I'm a UCLA professor. My fiancée grew up in a town near Hawthorne, the Beach Boys' birthplace. So, at last, I got my California girl. I've come as close to *The Myth* as I can. You can too. Through the music. Which is where it all began.

Yet perhaps the biggest irony of all is that the music itself has nothing to do with California. It's an accident of birth, where Mr. Wilson was born. The melodies, Brian's gospel, are heaven-sent.

Regardless, I not only wasn't in California for Brian and the Beach Boys' triumphs in the 1960s, I wasn't even aware of most of them. I was just a kid in New York who was much more interested in baseball and the Beatles. But since moving west, I've often been by Brian's side, here in L.A., in New York, in London, for many of his triumphant moments and greatest artistic achievements.

Back in 1971, over a half-century ago, when I first read about the Beach Boys, my self-described mission was to promote Brian's art and "save" him. It led me down a never-ending road, to shine a light on a man who, most improbably, was going to become my friend. I would be an usher at his second wedding. Godfather to the first daughter of his second marriage. And for years and years, the primary chronicler of his remarkable comeback.

In 1978, when I wrote *The Beach Boys and the California Myth*, I had no idea it would become, as a critic once described it, "the indispensable bible for Beach Boys fanatics." If it's a "bible," then the original edition of *The Myth* is filled with the testimonies of many of Brian's "disciples." The book belongs to them as much as me: "The Book of Audree Wilson." "The Book of Rich Sloan." "The Book of Fred Vail." "The Book of Gary Usher." "The Book of Roger Christian." "The Book of Hal Blaine." "The Book of Tony Asher." "The Book of David Anderle." "The Book of Van Dyke Parks." "The Book of Derek Taylor." "The Book of Bruce Johnston." And many others.

I was, more than anything, the grateful scribe who recorded their stories, their memories, their perspective, all for *The Myth*. For the 1985 edition, add "The Book of Steve Desper." In this edition, while there are significant contributions from friends and colleagues, it's mainly "The Book of David Leaf."

Yet, as my relationship with Brian became closer, there was much I couldn't write about. But it could inform my work and make it even deeper. It reached a personal peak in 2004 with *Beautiful Dreamer: Brian Wilson and the Story of SMiLE*.

I had once thought, "by doing something important, it would make *me* important." Now, looking back, it feels as if I did just that. In a 2007 article, *Rolling Stone* magazine called the world premiere of *Brian Wilson Presents SMiLE* in London one of "The 50 Greatest Concerts of the Last 50 Years."

Through the decades, I've met most of those who've written extensively about Brian and the Beach Boys. The late Timothy White—one of the best rock music essayists ever—and I became good friends and colleagues many years ago. As Editor-in-Chief of *Billboard* magazine, he's the reason I got hired on *The Billboard Music Awards*, the reason I got to work with George Harrison. His authoritative biography on Brian and the Beach Boys was thoroughly researched. He always supported and applauded the work I did with Brian.

Long ago, in his Beach Boys biography, author Steven Gaines surprised me by calling me "The Beach Boys Rabbi." That wasn't exactly a job I wanted. But I now understand what he meant. And I also now see how everything in my story is tied together. Like columnated dominoes falling one after another, as if they were destined to tumble in exactly that way.

A similarly unlikely path brought me to UCLA. In 1977, it was the place where I printed my *Pet Sounds* fanzine. In 2010, I began teaching there. As Dr. Robert Fink, Associate Dean and Chairman of the Music Industry program at UCLA explains, "David has a formal appointment as an Adjunct Professor of Musicology, largely based on [his] groundbreaking historical and critical work on the Beach Boys ... *The Pet Sounds Sessions* sets that masterful album in context ... Brian Wilson as a creator comes alive, as he does in Leaf's writing about the band."

Possibly up next for me at UCLA is a course on this subject. A few years ago, Dr. Fink suggested that once my Beatles course had been launched, I might teach a course about Brian and the Beach Boys. Sometimes, I can still be a class clown. I said I would if I could call it "Bad Vibrations." He shook his head. I said, "OK. How about 'Good and Bad Vibrations'?" He smiled and told me I would be calling it 'Good Vibrations.'

As to *The Myth*? Well, exactly the same as you, I still am as close as we can come to it. Through the music. Which is where it all began. And still lives. Lots of amazing moments. Lots of good vibrations.

FINAL THOUGHTS

As I write this, Brian is approaching eighty. He was twenty-nine when I first became obsessed. I was nineteen. This book is imbedded in my soul. The fact that *The Myth* has not been available except at collectors' prices has been frustrating for decades. At last, I've returned to it, to further illuminate the life and work of Brian Wilson.

I hope it has. To me, and for many of my friends and his fans, it's a personal touchstone. It's how we first connected. And regardless of what I write, the Beach Boys and their music will live forever.

The good news is that I don't have to proselytize anymore. The students in my UCLA courses come to class without any bias; they both love the music of the Beach Boys and know Brian Wilson's place in music history.

There is so much we've learned since I wrote the original book. From the Redwood scene in *Three Dog Nightmare*. From countless interviews and books and documentaries. From Brian and Mike's 2016 essential if very different memoirs.

Some of what was once hidden behind closed doors has been revealed. There's an audio tape from 1965 known as "Help Me, Murry" on which you hear a belligerent—and drunk?—Murry Wilson at the 'Help Me, Rhonda' recording session berating his sons. You also hear a strong and focused Brian trying to calm his dad down.

You can read on the web what's been called a "poison pen" letter written by Murry to the group in 1965—after he was fired—in which he threatens retribution. It was probably never sent.

Had I seen or heard these in 1978, I almost certainly would have included them in *The Myth*. But I'm not including details of those Murry documents because this update is about what happened long after Murry passed away. Now, it's just tangible "evidence" as to what drove the Wilson boys to success and what also helped drive them a bit crazy.

I prefer to think about the ethereal sounds created in the face of sadness, melancholy, even terror. How Brian wished upon a star and wrote 'Surfer Girl.' How, obsessively in love with 'Be My Baby,' he came up with the cosmically beautiful 'Don't Worry Baby.' How he could turn his love of 'This Whole World' into a gorgeous melody. Or channel his feeling as insignificant as a grain of sand into ''Til I Die.'

Brian himself said, modestly, "I'm not a genius. I'm ingenious." I beg to differ. There's so much originality and creativity in his work that I won't accept his diffidence. Besides, if Sir George Martin and Sir Paul McCartney and Sir Elton John and Sir Barry Gibb think he's a genius, who am I to argue? I can't analyze his work, but I know how the melodies, the chord changes, the pure vocal sounds, instrumental arrangement magic, production invention and wizardry inspire me, make me feel. And that can only be described by one word: genius.

Brian Wilson has long since proven that he's worthy of that word. He is indeed, a "Beautiful Dreamer." From his music, we know how Brian feels. But when it comes to understanding this "Life of Brian," it's often hard to know what he thinks.

Lost in all of the publicity and success, and the journey from Hawthorne to the Rock and Roll Hall of Fame, is Brian, the human being. As he told me many years ago, "I'm a much more creative person than the legend. Somebody with many more personal ideas floating around in his head than any person that considers me a legend would be able to conceive of." Wow.

Since *The Myth* was first published, quite a few films have been made that include revealing interviews with Brian. Today, when everybody has a cell phone video camera, it's not unusual to see video from the studio. In 1966, not so much. Google: Good Vibrations + Lost Studio Footage. This is a piece of genuine musical history. It's Brian and the Beach Boys in the studio, at work on 'Good Vibrations.' When one sees four minutes like this, all of the troubles and controversies "melt away," to quote the title of one of Brian's best solo songs.

In all of this, separating the myth from the reality from "the truth," well, it's almost impossible. As much as I can, I've focused on Brian and the music and how it motivated me to write this book. And through the years, I would come to understand that Brian's music always expresses the powerful emotions of its creator. And that feeling would come across, wherever you lived. Even, as I learned in Japan, if you didn't speak or understand very much English.

For Brian, composing his music was not an intellectual pursuit. It has always been an emotional one. He can put it beautifully, poetically, when he feels like it. As he said in the Don Was documentary, "Once in a blue moon, your soul will come out to play." In fact, in an interview he gave circa 1965/1966, he talked about going to the piano and playing what he called "feels." Of that, he is a genuine master.

There have been many triumphs for us to celebrate since 1992. Our small team, including Debbie, Eva, Ray, Jerry, Lois, and a few others. Melinda, of course. Gloria Ramos. His musical colleagues. Friends and fans all over the country. In the U.K. Around the world. A critical mass of millions more. And myself. We had asked Brian to make our dreams come true. And he did.

THE BEACH BOYS TODAY

For many years, I was considered to be an "expert" on Brian Wilson and the Beach Boys. I was constantly being asked, "Why did they do this?" Or "Why didn't they do that?" The questions were smart, but I finally grew weary of trying to "explain" the Beach Boys' history. After all, without any of my mythologizing, they've survived over sixty years, and the music is indeed for the ages.

Besides, it's all in the past. Nothing can be changed. The wrong turns can't be righted. What I realize now, looking back, is that what happened is typical of most groups, most artists, most family bands too. Perhaps the Beach Boys were just the best, or maybe the worst, at it.

Nothing can be done about the fact that since the first edition of *The Myth*, the Beach Boys haven't recorded any albums at the level of their 1963–1973 output. Or anything as brilliantly eccentric as *Love You*. But with those albums, from *Surfin' U.S.A.* to *Holland*, one can make a pretty strong argument that, other than the Beatles, they are the best and most important group in popular music history. And perhaps, musically at least, they were and still are as influential as the Fab Four.

Brian Wilson, of course, is the main reason for all of this, and his place in the firmament is secure. To recognize that, he should be inducted two more times into the Rock and Roll Hall of Fame, as a solo artist and as a producer, joining a very select few who have been honored more than once. He's earned that. Of course, I'm partial. Always will be. But the case is strong.

In the "Welcome" to this edition of the book, we read what his peers, an endless litany of great musicians, had to say. Since embarking upon his solo career in 1988, Brian has made a number of memorable albums, won acclaim for his incredible tours—*Pet Sounds, Brian Wilson Presents SMiLE, That Lucky Old Sun* and more—been inducted into the Songwriters Hall of Fame, been feted by multiple tributes including a Grammy salute and the Kennedy Center Honors.

Nowadays, Brian's not a man of many words. He used to talk endlessly, but Brian doesn't say a lot, as you can see in *Long Promised Road*, the new, intimate documentary that was released in the fall of 2021.

But he can say the most amazing things in the shortest sentences. Once, over twenty years ago, he walked into my home office, took it all in and said, "It's amazing how big things can come from such small spaces."

Brian has participated in all sorts of projects, perhaps none that tells the story better than the BBC's all-star 'God Only Knows' video. It's one of the greatest honors any songwriter has ever received. There have been lots of excellent "cover" versions of Brian's songs, but nothing compares to this one, filled with generations of artists including Sir Elton John, Stevie Wonder and Brian May. Check it out: Google BBC Music + God Only Knows.

With all of these great achievements in the rearview mirror, as I turn seventy and Brian eighty, it seems like the right time to celebrate what Brian has done and what I've shared with him. To look back with pride and wonder and mark these personal and musical milestones. But understanding all that's happened? Well, definitively "explaining" Brian Wilson can be something of a fool's errand.

I asked Jerry Weiss, who has had so many great moments with Brian, to provide a few final meaningful memories; he laughed at the impossibility of the task. Then, he began telling me of the random nature of what Brian might say at the most unexpected times—that, to Jerry, was "an example of Brian's great intellect. One day, we were on the tour bus sitting opposite each other at a table . . . Brian looking towards the rear of the bus and I'm facing the front. Brian said, 'I'm looking into the past and you are looking into the future at the same time we are in the present . . . isn't that amazing?'"

During a sound check, Jerry says "He was trying to get the band pumped up and to pay attention. He said, 'Come on guys. If you wanna be crazy, you can't be lazy.' We all cracked up, but he was serious. There was work to do." Jerry picks out just one of the many "Brian" moments. "On a trip to London, the flight attendant said, 'Good morning, Mr. Wilson. For breakfast, we have a full English breakfast or pancakes with blueberry compote or an omelette with crispy bacon and potatoes.' Brian said, 'I'll have everything, thank you.'

"Much more revealing," Jerry describes "a memorable moment that reflects Brian's deep compassion, what could happen in the middle of our daily tour routine. Every day, to get some exercise, we would go for long walks. One day, we were walking outside a venue in Texas. Brian saw a homeless man lying on the ground. He walked over and handed him $25 and said, 'This is for you buddy. But promise me you won't buy any booze with it.' The grateful man promised, saying, 'Bless your soul, sir.' Brian told him, 'I know what it's like being on the street.'"

Perhaps most simply and beautifully, Jerry remembers a very sweet sentence Brian uttered one day, after a shower. Brian said, "I give thanks for every day of life."

All of their time together has led Jerry to one overarching observation. "Brian is the most spiritual and caring person I have ever met. He's an incredibly deep and complex thinker who also enjoys and covets the simplest of pleasures. That paradox can be understandably intimidating for many who meet him. He loves loving. He loves to feel love and loves to give love. On tour, where I spent the most time with him, he lets the music speak for itself. And it always does."

As a person, Brian is filled with as much complexity as his music. He is completely aware of everybody and everything around him. Even when his eyes are closed. You see, he's brilliant at playing possum. His sensitivity is staggering. And, as his primary focus has always been on music, his insensitivity to others can be too.

"From what I've seen in the studio," Ray Lawlor explains, "he makes very complicated music in a most uncomplicated way. His genius is making it look so easy. He hears things, and if it's not working, he immediately changes on the fly. Fixes it. But nobody else thought of it." As Ray notes, when things go awry, Brian's amazing at "calling audibles." For those of you who aren't American football fans, that means when Brian sees an obstacle, he can instantly and brilliantly change direction.

He has always expressed what he thought and felt through music. But can any of us imagine the strength it takes just to *be* Brian Wilson? He is the ultimate survivor. As Ray Lawlor says, "His music is a shaft of light cutting through terrible darkness."

In interviews, in his evocative 2016 autobiography *I Am Brian Wilson*, Brian has often talked about hearing voices in his head. The voices in his head sometimes say, "We're gonna kill you." Imagine what that's like. And then try to imagine the strength he drew upon to overcome those demons to create the most harmoniously beautiful music of his time. What kind of courage does that take?

Like Brian's intimate music and memoir, I hope my friends, colleagues and I have shed some welcome light. I've had the privilege of being Brian's friend for forty years, over half of my adult life.

Yet, even with all I've personally experienced with Brian, certainly more than any other biographer, I don't present this as the final word on the subject either. This is just my version of my story with Brian. If I didn't cover something that matters to you—and this book is not historically comprehensive—you can ask me about it at my website, leafprod.com.

The years since I first met Brian have flown by. In 2018, Brian invited me to his birthday party. He and Melinda's five kids were all there, and it was a lovely moment, with Brian at the keyboard. Coincidentally, the night before, I'd had my first date with Vicki, a woman who lived directly across the street from the surgery rehab center where Brian's festivities took place. Before the year was over, she and I were engaged.

During the pandemic years of 2020 and 2021, there have been no big birthday celebrations. When I began work on this, I told Melinda and Brian's manager Jean Sievers that I wanted this edition of *The Myth* to be something of a gift for Brian's eightieth birthday. In 2022, at his birthday party, even if we're all still wearing masks, I look forward to singing "Happy Birthday." And giving him a big hug.

It's forty-five years since I began writing *The Myth*, and you may have noticed that bringing it to an end isn't easy for me. To echo the title of the book, I thought of finishing with a lyric from Brian's own song. I could sing "God only knows what I'd be without you." Seemed a little obvious.

His music celebrates the joy of life. Do I quote one of his happiest songs? Or one of his saddest? No, I'll just say, this is "My Life with Brian." As I remember it. Thank you again, Brian, for letting me be a part of your world.

As to the music he has shared with "This Whole World," in what I think was a most remarkable 1988 interview he did for his first solo album, Brian offered the philosophy that guides his creative soul. "People are being loved under the guise of a record, but something much higher inspired the record. A record is an apparent level of sound and experience. But it's intangible in itself in that it's art. And art is intangible. Art is not a finite thing; it's an infinite thing."

In explaining how he sees the purpose of making music, Brian continued: "We wanted somebody somewhere to understand what we'd gone through, and at the same time they could say, 'Well, I did too. And I can vouch that I went through the same thing. I feel very close to that song.' You know, that's the same old story for years now—people say, 'I love that song.' What they're really saying is, 'That song makes me feel spiritual.' You know, that's all it is. It takes away fear. It adds strength. It's life-supporting."

Perhaps these were the kind of profound things Brian and David Anderle discussed years ago during the *SMiLE* era. It certainly helps us all understand what kind of deep thinker Brian is. Given the depth of feeling in his music, it shouldn't be a surprise.

Sometimes, though, he just says it very clearly. In a 1988 interview I did with him for the press kit for his first solo album, Brian explained his *raison d'être*. "I make music that will make people happy, 'cause that's what makes me happy. It does. It really does. It is the high point of my life. To me, the highest thing in the world is to make music."

Brian once told me, "The spirituality of my music is explained by the fact that if you don't take it upon yourself to create something, no one will. Some of my songs are very spiritual, like 'The Warmth of the Sun' from the early Beach Boys days. And 'Love and Mercy' . . . Maybe love and spirituality are about the same. How can you really differentiate love and spirituality?"

For Brian, there isn't a difference. Brian believes that "Music is God's voice."

And that may be all we need to know.

ACKNOWLEDGMENTS

1978 EDITION

I am greatly indebted to the close friends of Brian Wilson who have helped me begin to understand his complex life, so that I could tell fact from public relations.

In 1976, Brian said, "interviews are for publicity." Because of statements like that, Brian's friends' assistance has been invaluable. Besides those who must remain nameless, I want to especially thank four people who have spent countless hours recalling their experiences with Brian and the Beach Boys. They are: Rich Sloan, Fred Vail, David Anderle, and Bruce Johnston.

I also want to thank everybody who patiently and generously shared their time, memories, and insights with me. Also, particular thanks to all who loaned me photographs from their personal collections and helped me tell this story both in words and pictures.

Special thanks to . . .

Holly Graham, for her friendship, support, patience, and editorial perspective, which made her contribution incalculable and vital to the integrity of the book. Robbie Leff, for his friendship, help, and the hours of endless talk about Brian and the Beach Boys. Jon Goodchild for his patience, design skills, and support of me and this project. Bruce Johnston and Michele Myer for the use of their personal collections. Richard Bernacchi for his advice and support. The Leaf family for their support in my travails and travels. And to Ricky Leaf.

Earl Leaf, Jules Siegel, Paul Williams, Tom Nolan, and David Felton for their efforts, the most important part of the creation of the Brian Wilson legend. Their writings provided me with my first insight and appreciation of Brian. Peter Reum, for the generous sharing of his extensive photographic and memorabilia collection, for his collector's knowledge, interest in this book and its accuracy, and for sharing the obsession. Michael Patterson, Dwight Whikehart, Angela Jones, Liz Jones, Stephen Neill, Derek A. Bill, and Toni Lorenz for their research assistance. Ray Lawlor, Ed

ACKNOWLEDGMENTS

Mandlebaum, Duke Janukowicz, and Dave Morano for their devotion to Brian, support of this book, and research assistance.

Jeannie Sakol and Stephanie Bennett for their guidance, help, encouragement, the opportunity and artistic freedom they gave me in telling this story, and for their belief in its importance. And to Grosset & Dunlap for their support.

Thank you to . . .

David Rensin, Richard Cromelin, Lou Irwin, Timothy White, David Herman, Ken Barnes, the BBC, Neal Gabler, Steven Gaines, Ben Edmonds, Tom Smucker, Alan Betrock, Gene Sculatti, and many other writers and broadcasters for their groundwork in interviewing Brian and the Beach Boys' family and reportage on the subject. Their efforts were essential in piecing this puzzle together.

Capitol Records, Warner Brothers Records, Brother Records and to the Beach Boys' organization for their generous help. Rogers and Cowan for setting up the interviews. All the photographers and artists whose contributions are so valued.

Pete Fornatale for playing the music.

The following people, who in some way contributed to this project: Ellen Vogt, Greg Biggs, Skip Brittenham, Henry Fetter, John Branca, Dean Torrence, Tricia Roach, Karen Handman, Chris Kable, Ed Roach, Jan Bridge, Ron Furmanek, Peter Kanze, Scott Bergstein, Bill Johnson, Rodney Bingenheimer, Harvey Kubernik, Lester Cohen, Jeff Gold, Ray D'Ariano, Barry Bernstein, Alice, LuCindi Templeton, Sally Rose, Roger Young, Jim Bickhart, Arlene Colbert, Steven Peeples, Ray Taylor Jr., Stephen Peters, Marty Taber, Brian Gari, Don Spears, Tim Blixt, Michael Ochs, Steve Resnik, Suzie Shaw, Jack and Billie Schwartz, Janice Tweedy, Jan Holdenfield, Warren Seabury, the Pitaliks, Rhino, the Hatcheteers, David Poleno, Richard Hart, Steve Watsky, Ted Krever, Bob Jenkins, Gareth Pawlowski, Teri Brown, Bill Kamer, Don Malcolm, Janice Lent-Koop, Jasper Dailey, Lanny Aldrich, Guy Trebay, Mr. Glidden, and Robert Clancy.

Brian and the Beach Boys, for all the joy their music has given me.

The original edition of the book included the dedication *To Bob, with love and hope.*

1985 EDITION

In retracing many of my steps from the first book, a number of people have been most helpful and have even led me down completely new paths, for which I'm very grateful.

First, I must thank Peter Reum, Ray Lawlor and Ed Mandlebaum who for years have supported my effort to get this book back in print and for their continuing friendship.

For their public support, a special thank you to Joel Selvin, Harvey Kubernik, Jeff Tamarkin, Colin Larkin, David Morrison, Ralph Newman, Robert Lloyd, Pete Fornatale, and Dave Marsh.

For their contributions to this edition, special thanks go to Michael Patterson, Stephen Neill, Steve Desper, Daryl Dragon, Neal McCabe, Jim Gray, Ben Edmonds, Chris Kable, Susan Gambol, Patti Davis, Wednesday, Toni Lorenz, Gary Stewart, Robert Lloyd, Greg Biggs, Dave Zimmer, Cary Darling, Domenic Priore, Marty Taber (we miss FOTBB), Michael Ochs, Roy Gudge, Don Cunningham, Andrew Doe, Les Chan, Dave M. (R.I.P. Duke), Ron Furmanek, David Schwartz, Brad Rosenberger, Brad Elliot, Ray D'Ariano, Ken Barnes, Wayne Johnson, Jeffrey Peisch, Scott Shannon, Greg Fields and the "Solid Gold" Party Boys, Michael Wolf, Mike Kastner, Bob Sullivan, Patti Searle, Winnie Kerr, Richard Stevens, Pat Rizzo, Holly Jones, Steve Baum, Alan Bergman, Gigi Stevens, Henry Root, Dr. Susan Reynolds, Alice, David Nemeth, Tricia Burlingham, Jeff Gold, Robbie Leff, Doris, Breck, Impact, and Herbie J.

Also, thank you to Jerry Lazar and Robert Hilburn for their recent articles on the Brian Wilson/Dr. Landy relationship. And to Steven Gaines, John Milward, Ilene Churna and all those whose interest in my book in 1984 provided much of the impetus behind this new material being written in 1985.

A special thank you to Lanny and Jeannie for trying again, and a very sincere thank you to Geoffrey Himes for allowing me to quote extensively from his *Musician* magazine articles about the Beach Boys. His interview with Carl Wilson is, to my knowledge, the best one with Carl that's ever been done.

Love and thanks to my wife for her boundless enthusiasm, faith and support of my work, my family for their endless encouragement, the

ACKNOWLEDGMENTS

"Big Six" and family, Rita T. for her courage, Joe T. for his stories, Pam M. for wanting everybody to do "the right thing," Sigmund and the whole gang (and Hank & Giz, too), and, of course, to the very special men and women who, in their love for Brian, continue to tell me the truth.

And most of all, thank you to Brian, who always inspires me like nobody else can.

2022 EDITION

This edition of *The Myth* was created with the help of trusted friends and those whose passion for Brian Wilson and his work has never waned.

A special "thank you" to everybody who spoke with me for this edition, making sure I remembered everything as accurately as possible, and who shared their personal memories. You know who you are.

A big tip of the hat to so many people in the music industry who have been there for Brian (and me) through the past thirty-five years: Mo Ostin, Lenny Waronker, Seymour Stein, Russ Titelman, Andy Paley, David Bither, Eddie Micone, Brian Diamond, Chip Rachlin, Phil Ramone, and John Eastman.

Thank you to Brian's band for welcoming me into their world, to the entire production teams for *An All-Star Tribute to Brian Wilson* and *Beautiful Dreamer: Brian Wilson and the Story of SMiLE*. To Bob Merlis for tapping me twice with his magic wand. To Sujata Murthy for her support of my work on so many Beach Boys re-issue projects.

For adding their words to mine, a special "thank you" to Sir Paul McCartney, Sir Barry Gibb, and Jimmy Webb, who has shared his wisdom with me since we first met at Campo de Encino. To Lee Eastman, Dick Ashby and Laura Savini for making it happen. Special thanks to John Boylan and Linda Ronstadt for their kindness.

To Sir Elton, who is always there for Brian.

To Danny Hutton, Brian's great friend, who knows the truth. And who introduced Elton to Brian all those years ago.

To Kevin Gershan for everything he does and John Clemens for keeping me electronically enabled. To Robert for pushing for this update and to Richard, who was there when it all started.

Thank you to Harvey Kubernik for remembering everything and to Peter Carlin, Jason Fine, Elliot Easton, Van Dyke Parks and Darian Sahanaja for their friendship and kind commentary about me and *The Myth*.

Thank you to the "legal eagles," especially my dear friend Harold Brook for his savvy advice. And to Jeff Burkett for looking out for me.

Thank you to David Barraclough, Imogen Gordon Clark, and their team at Omnibus Press. A special thanks to Seán Costello for his yeoman editorial work . . . a gentleman and a real pleasure to work with.

To Dr. Robert Fink, who has given me a new home at UCLA.

Thanks to my editorial crew: Robbie Leff, who always makes sure I write something that makes sense and is worth reading, and to Celina Nishioka for her smart copy-editing.

Thank you to "The Team": Ray Lawlor, Jerry Weiss and Lois Weiss . . . to Debbie Keil Leavitt for again sharing her unique insight into the saga and shedding her anonymity, and to my late wife, Eva Easton Leaf. We all did this together.

And finally, a special "thank you" to people who are so very dear to me:

The amazing Vicki. Thank you for your tireless work helping to shape the new material, for being the voice of editorial reason and the guardian angel of the project. Very simply, without your inspiration, this new edition wouldn't have happened. I love you.

Jean Sievers, who makes everything happen.

Gloria Ramos, who is our unsung hero.

Melinda Wilson, who is the reason so many great things have happened in Brian's life and career since 1992.

And finally, to Brian, who trusts me with his story and whose music has touched my heart forever.

Brian and David Leaf at the author's 70th birthday party, April 2022. Photo by Gloria.